WOMEN AND MEN AS FRIENDS

RELATIONSHIPS ACROSS THE LIFE SPAN IN THE 21st CENTURY

LEA's Series on Personal Relationships
Steve Duck, Series Editor

Bennett • Time and Intimacy: A New Science of Personal Relationships

Christopher • To Dance the Dance: A Symbolic Interactional Exploration of Premarital Sexuality

Honeycutt/Cantrill • Cognition, Communication, and Romantic Relationships

Miller/Alberts/Hecht/Trost/Krizek • Adolescent Relationships and Drug Use

Monsour • Women and Men as Friends: Relationships Across the Life Span in the 21st Century

WOMEN AND MEN AS FRIENDS

RELATIONSHIPS ACROSS THE LIFE SPAN IN THE 21st CENTURY

Michael Monsour
University of Colorado at Denver

2002

LAWRENCE ERLBAUM ASSOCIATES, PUBLISHERS
Mahwah, New Jersey   London

#4663422

Lawrence Erlbaum Associates, Inc., Publishers
10 Industrial Avenue
Mahwah, NJ 07430

Cover design by Kathryn Houghtaling Lacey

Library of Congress Cataloging-in-Publication Data

Monsour, Michael.
Women and men as friends : relationships across the life span in the 21st
   century / Michael Monsour.
        p.   cm. (LEA's series on personal relationships)
      Includes bibliographical references and index.
ISBN 0-8058-3566-0 (cloth : alk. paper)
 ISBN 0-8058-3567-9 (pbk. : alk. paper)
1. Man-woman relationships. 2. Friendship. I. Title. II. Series.

HQ801 .M72 2002
302.3'4—dc21

                                                    2001033000
                                                    CIP

Books published by Lawrence Erlbaum Associates are printed on acid-free paper, and their bindings are chosen for strength and durability.

Printed in the United States of America
10 9 8 7 6 5 4 3 2

I dedicate this book to Wanda Gregory Monsour,
my mother, who died April 16, 1999.
She was, and will always be, my friend.

Contents

Series Editor's Foreword

This series from Lawrence Erlbaum Associates (LEA) is intended to review the progress in the academic work on relationships in respect of a broad array of issues and is intended to do so in an accessible manner that also illustrates its practical value. The LEA series includes books intended to pass on the accumulated scholarship to the next generation of students and to those who deal with relationship issues in the broader world beyond the academy. Thus, the series comprises not only monographs and other academic resources exemplifying the multi-disciplinary nature of this area, but also will include textbooks suitable for use in the growing numbers of courses on relationships in the future. The series has the goal of providing a comprehensive and current survey of theory and research in personal relationship through the careful analysis of the problems encountered and solved in research. At the same time it also considers the systematic application of that work in a practical context. These resources not only are intended to be comprehensive assessments of progress on particular "hot" and relevant topics, but also will be significant influences on the future directions and development of the study of personal relationships. Although each volume is focused and centered, authors all attempt to place the respective topics in the broader context of other research on relationships and within a range of wider disciplinary traditions. The series already offers incisive and forward-looking reviews and also demonstrates the broader theoretical implications of relationships for the range of disciplines from which the research originates. Present and future volumes include original studies, reviews of relevant theory and research, and new theories oriented toward the understanding of personal relationships both in themselves and within the context of broader theories of family process, social psychology, and communication.

Reflecting the diverse composition of personal relationship study, readers in numerous disciplines—social psychology, communication, sociology, family studies, developmental psychology, clinical psychology, personality, counseling, women's studies, gerontology, and others—will find valuable and insightful perspectives in the series.

Apart from the academic scholars who research the dynamics and processes of relationships, there are many other people whose work takes them up against the operation of relationships in the real world. For such people as nurses, the police, teachers, therapists, lawyers, drug and alcohol counselors, marital counselors, and those who take care of the elderly, a number of issues routinely arise concerning the ways in which relationships affect the people whom they serve. Examples are the role of loneliness in illness and the ways to circumvent it, the complex impact of family and peer relationships on a drug-dependent's attempts to give up the drug, the role of playground unpopularity on a child's learning, the issues involved in dealing with the relational side of chronic illness, the management of conflict in marriage, the establishment of good rapport between physicians and seriously ill patients, the support of the bereaved, and the correction of violent styles of behavior in dating or marriage. Each of these is a problem that may confront some of the above professionals as part of their daily concerns and each demonstrates the far-reaching influences of relationship processes on much else in life that is presently theorized independently of relationship considerations.

The present volume is a case in point because it clearly shows the social importance, in the 21st Century, of the growing number of cross-sex friendships (i.e., nonromantic relationships between people of different sexes). The author reviews a tremendous number of different types of research across the life cycle and so has something to offer early developmentalists all the way through to gerontologists. As well as illustrating the nature of these overly suspected relationships in modern society, Michael Monsour makes a compelling case for the relevance of understanding relationships between the sexes from the cradle to the grave and offers an important scholarly counterweight to other books that attempt to draw misleadingly thick communicative boundaries between men and women. By giving considerable weight to these relationships instead of regarding them as aberrations—a fate they have suffered in other writings and in the popular imagination—Monsour is able to show the important role that such interactions have in such matters as self-esteem and the ways in which individuals come to see themselves in relating to other people. The book also illuminates and pierces some of the more peculiar myths that surround cross-sex friendships as they are experienced in a network of others (other friends, parents, children, neighbors) and also how they appear in the context of personal development across the life span, as interests, goals, and emotions are experienced in different ways.

This book offers all of us a new way to conceptualize the connections between such friendships, self-concept development and broader social processes (even including gender and the organization of occupational segregation right through to the ways in which mass media influence our convictions about friendship itself). It will be obvious that the book has a great deal to say not only to scholars (whether they be from communication, social or developmental psychology, or sociology) but also to practitioners who face some of the issues arising from miscommunication between the sexes, such as therapists, counselors, and the police.

—Steve Duck
University of Iowa

Preface

Relationships between women and men took center stage in the theater of public attention during the last decade of the 20th century. The public's fascination with male–female relationships was largely due to books such as Deborah Tannen's *You Just Don't Understand* (1990) and John Gray's *Men are From Mars, Women are From Venus* (1992). Those books popularized the notion that women and men are fundamentally dissimilar and that they come from different cultures—indeed, even different planets. As is often the case with books highlighting male–female relationships, the books by Tannen and Gray focus on relationships between women and men who are romantically involved or work together and give little attention to *friendships* that women and men form with one another.

The importance of same-sex friendship to individuals in American society is well established and accepted by academic, professional, and lay communities (Adams & Allan, 1998). Unfortunately, cross-sex friendships (i.e., nonromantic friendships between males and females), have been marginalized and relegated to second-class relational citizenship in the world of scholarly and trade publications and in the lives of many individuals (but see Werking, 1997a). Despite the documented advantages and increasing relevance of cross-sex friendships (Monsour, 1997), those friendships have been under-studied, under-appreciated, and under-utilized by academicians, lay persons, and professionals (Werking, 1997a).

Cross-sex friendships offer significant and unique benefits in every stage of the life cycle (Monsour, 1997). Furthermore, conditions in society have highlighted the importance of cross-sex friendships, increased their likelihood, and strengthened the need for further exploration of these neglected relationships. With the arrival of AIDS in the last 15 years of the 20th century, the large number of teenage pregnancies (Leaper & Anderson, 1997), the increasing proportion of women in the workplace (Gini, 1998), the expanding popularity of computer-mediated friendships (Parks & Floyd, 1996), and the 10 million older adults who live alone (Harvard Health Letter, May, 1999), understanding and encouraging cross-sex friendships has increased in importance. As I intend to show in this book, cross-sex friendships are becoming more commonplace throughout the life cycle and should no longer be considered relational anomalies, aberrations, or functionally identical to same-sex friendships. Encouraging cross-sex friendships from an early age has the practical potential of reducing instances of sexual harassment in the workplace, lessening the number of cases of sexually transmitted diseases, and providing a buffer against loneliness in every stage of the life span.

This book is about the friendships of women and men of all ages and how those friendships influence their self-concepts. In chapter 1, I introduce the three basic themes of the book. Considerable attention is devoted to each theme because they are revisited in every chapter. At the end of the first chapter I offer a definition of cross-sex friendships and a rationale for taking a life-cycle approach in my analysis of those relationships.

Chapters 2 through 6 each focus on different stages of the life cycle: early childhood (ages 18 months to 6 years, chap. 2); middle and late childhood (ages 7 to 11, chap. 3); adolescence (ages 12 to 17, chap. 4), young and middle adulthood (ages 18 to 34 and 35 to 64; chap. 5); and old age (ages 65 and over, chap. 6). In each chapter the same three themes are documented and applied to the corresponding stage of life. First, cross-sex friendships enrich an individual's social network in generic and unique ways. Second, social and structural barriers interfere with the formation and maintenance of cross-sex friendships. The first two themes are linked to the third and final theme which also serves as the book's central theoretical premise (i.e., cross-sex friendships affect and are affected by an individual's ongoing social construction of self throughout the life cycle).

In chapters 2 through 6 I also address special topics of developmental relevance to cross-sex friendships and self-concept construction. Those topics are incorporated under one or more of the three themes of the book. As individuals go through life they experience predictable developmental changes resulting from equally predictable developmental processes. Developmental changes refer to cognitive, emotional, sexual, physical, biological, and social changes. Some of those changes are relevant to both cross-sex friendship and self-concept formation. For example, individuals in middle childhood engage in gender segregation (primarily a social and cognitive change), adolescents go through puberty (encompassing physical, biological, cognitive and sexual changes), and the elderly become less mobile (primarily a physical change). Those developmental changes impact self-concepts and cross-sex friendships that, in turn, reciprocally influence the developmental changes and processes individuals are experiencing.

In the final chapter I present summarizing and integrating observations about the three themes of the book as they relate to cross-sex friendships across the life cycle. I also propose a rudimentary, heuristic conceptual model of the interconnections between self-schemas, gender schemas, and schemas representing same-sex and cross-sex friendships. The model is designed to illustrate how those four schemas co-occur and co-mingle throughout the life cycle, with the most important area of overlap being between self-schemas and cross-sex friendship schemas. A second model depicts how the schemas of two cross-sex friends overlap in ways that produce a cognitively, emotionally, and communicatively shared view of their friendship.

The literature on cross-sex friendships across the life span is sparse and fragmented (Monsour, 1997). However, it is also highly suggestive of the developmental significance of cross-sex friendships and their increased likelihood as we move further into the 21st century. The commentary offered in this book proposes new ways of understanding the connections between cross-sex friendships, self-concepts, and broader social processes such as gender and occupational segregation, crowd and clique formation, and mass media influences on the conduct of friendships. Because of the small size of the cross-sex friendship literature, some of the arguments made in this book are extrapolated from other literatures that are directly and indirectly relevant to male–female friendships throughout the life cycle.

Although this book is primarily aimed at friendship scholars in a variety of disciplines (e.g., communication, developmental psychology, gerontology, and sociology), I believe (and hope) it should be of interest to anyone curious about how cross-sex friendships influence our lives and our self-concepts. Similarly, the book should be useful to professionals and practitioners who confront some of the problems that directly and indirectly arise from having or not having friends of the other sex, such as loneliness throughout the life cycle, sexual harassment at work, peer-rejection at school, and even sexually transmitted diseases.

One final comment before you begin. Because I have taken a life-cycle and developmental approach in my analysis of cross-sex friendships, each chapter of the book representing a stage of life is inextricably linked to every other chapter. Therefore, to get the "full picture" you should read the entire book. However, knowing from personal experience that students and scholars often read only those chapters that are directly relevant to their concerns, I have tried to be sensitive to those needs and make each chapter stand on its own merits.

ACKNOWLEDGMENTS

There are a number of individuals I would like to thank for their direct and indirect contributions to this work. First, the various staff and editors at LEA worked patiently, professionally, amicably, and tirelessly on the manuscript. On a personal level, I owe a debt of gratitude to my wife (Margaret) and three children (Mikey, Hannah, and Lily) who had to share their husband and father with "the book" for 3 years. I hope their sacrifice was not too great. I also thank my friends, female and male, old and new, casual and close, for the friendships that served as the inspiration for many of the ideas in this book. Also important to note is that two of my older sisters, Michele and Susan, felt sorry for their younger brother and helped me compile the author index. My father, although not contributing directly to the content of the book, made the writing of the book possible through his never-ending support of my efforts throughout my life. My mother-in-law, Tillie NeJame, offered perhaps the most consistent level of encouragement for a book that she can't wait to purchase (I hope she isn't disappointed, and of course, she gets a complimentary copy). She was (and is) not only a surrogate mother, but a cross-sex friend in every sense of the word. All of my family was supportive in more ways than they will ever know. I thank them all.

On a professional and personal level, I thank Bob Brady who served as my advisor while working on my master's degree at the University of Arkansas. Bob was the first to get me excited about the scientific study of personal relationships and their tremendously important impact on our lives. Additionally, my former advisors at the University of Illinois at Champaign, Dean Hewes and Sally Planalp, instilled in me an appreciation, understanding, and fascination with cognitive processes and their inextricable link to interpersonal communication. I believe their influence will be obvious throughout the book. On a strictly personal note, Bob, Sally, and Dean did much more than give me professional guidance and inspiration—they extended their hand in friendship, which I deeply appreciated. I want to extend special thanks to Steve Duck who, like he has done with dozens of other aspiring scholars, served as a constant source of support, guidance, and mentoring since I left the University of Illinois in 1988. He, along with Paul Wright and Kathy Werking, read the original version of the book and helped to make it into a more accurate and insightful rendering of the cross-sex friendship literature. I also offer my thanks to Don O'Meara, Bill Rawlins, Kathy Werking, and Paul Wright whose exemplary and pioneering work in the field of male–female friendships served as a standard of excellence that I have tried to emulate. Finally, I say thanks to my friend and colleague, Steve Corman, who listened to me ramble on endlessly about my book every weekend for 3 years.

1

Cross-Sex Friendships and the Social Construction of Self Across the Life Span

Cross-sex friendship is a relationship ripe for study.

—Kathy Werking (1997a, p.166)

Cross-sex friendships (i.e., nonromantic relationships between persons of different sexes) occupy an unusual place in the relational fabric of society. Because they lack the prominence and notoriety of same-sex friendships, romantic relationships, and family ties, they have had to struggle for recognition in the scholarly and lay communities. The majority of friendship scholars have either ignored or given little attention to cross-sex friendships. As a result, the cross-sex friendship literature is young, fragmented, meager, and fundamentally atheoretical (Monsour, 1997). Mirroring the lack of scholarly attention, many individuals for various reasons in different stages of life do not have friends of the other sex. The reasons for having and not having cross-sex friendships are explored throughout this book.

The relative lack of attention given to cross-sex friendships by scholars and lay persons is unfortunate. Changes occurring in society suggest that structural opportunities for cross-sex friendship formation are increasing and will continue to do so as we move further into the 21st century. Two of those changes include the increased presence of women in the workplace (Gini, 1998), and the growing use of the internet for friendship formation (Adams, 1998; Parks & Floyd, 1996). Those changes and others described in this book will make cross-sex friendships far more prevalent in the next 20 years than they have been in the last 20.

The marginalization of cross-sex friendships by the scholarly community and the avoidance of those friendships by many lay persons throughout the life cycle is unfortunate for another reason. As I intend to document throughout this book, cross-sex friendships enrich the social networks of children, teenagers, adults, and senior citizens in generic and unique ways. Those friendships also have a significant impact on how individuals in all stages of life view themselves and members of the other sex. Indeed, as suggested by the title of this chapter, cross-sex friendships play an important role in the social construction of self across the life span.

The current chapter previews the organizational format followed throughout the book and is divided into three major sections. In the first section I introduce the three central themes of the book in order to lay the groundwork for subsequent presentation of the themes in the remaining six chapters. In the second and third sections I provide an explanation for my adoption of a life-cycle perspective on cross-sex friendships and offer my definition of those relationships.

THREE THEMES OF THE BOOK

Three interrelated themes are developed in each chapter and applied to the corresponding stage of life. The first theme is that cross-sex friendships enrich the social networks of participating members. The second theme is that structural and social barriers interfere with the formation of cross-sex friendships throughout the life span. My third theme is also the central theoretical premise of the book (i.e., cross-sex friendships affect and are affected by an individual's perpetual social construction of self throughout the life cycle). Each of these themes are now briefly explained.

Cross-Sex Friendships and the Enrichment of Social Networks

Enrichment of social networks through the formation and maintenance of cross-sex friendships occurs in two primary ways. First, because cross-sex friendships possess many of the same characteristics as same-sex friendships (Werking, 1997a; Wright, 1989), cross-sex friendships are able to provide many of the same benefits supplied by their same-sex counterparts. The benefits of cross-sex friendships that mirror those of same-sex friendship are referred to throughout the book as *generic* benefits. Cross-sex friendships also enrich social networks by providing *unique* benefits that are difficult or impossible to obtain in same-sex friendships.

Generic Benefits of Cross-sex Friendships.   Generic benefits of cross-sex friendship are benefits that are provided to a similar extent (sometimes more, sometimes less) by same-sex friendships. Although generic benefits furnished by cross-sex friends may vary from one stage of life to the next, several of them are available throughout the life cycle. Two of those benefits are the provision of social support and protection against loneliness.

Social support can come from almost anyone in an individual's social network (e.g., family, friends, neighbors, and coworkers). Friends provide one another with various forms of social support (Rawlins, 1992). Social support can involve very concrete things such as helping a friend move into an apartment or helping him or her install a new computer program. Social support is also manifested in more abstract ways, such as providing emotional support to a friend in a time of crisis or just enjoying each other's company. Scholars have been unable to arrive at a consensus on the exact meaning of social support because of its multifaceted nature (Crohan & Antonucci, 1989; Sarason, Sarason, & Gurung, 1997). Nevertheless, I have adopted the definition of social support presented by Crohan and Antonucci because it seems sensible and similar to other conceptualizations found in the literature (e.g., Fleming & Baum, 1986; Hansson & Carpenter, 1994). They define social support as "interactional transactions that include one or more of the following key elements: affect, aid, and affirmation" (p. 131, 1989). Affective transactions involve expressions of emotional support, liking, admiration, respect, or love. The provision of aid refers to more concrete transactions such as giving information and practical assistance. Finally, affirmation is expressed when a partner agrees with the appropriateness of some action or attitude of the other. The three elements of social support often overlap. For example, if one friend discloses something very personal about herself and the other friend reacts in a positive fashion, that self-disclosure would illustrate both positive affect and affirmation. In each chapter I review evidence documenting that cross-sex friends supply one another with social support in the corresponding stage of life.

Sarason and her colleagues concluded that individuals with satisfying levels of social support deal better with stress and are generally healthier than those who lack sufficient social support (Sarason et al., 1997). Along similar lines, Ornish reviewed the literature on emotional support and concluded that individuals without such support have a three- to five-times greater risk of premature death and related diseases such as cancer, strokes, heart attacks and auto immune diseases (1998). Researchers do not know for sure why social support contributes to better health, but one theory is that people with a supportive network are more prone to seek medical attention and follow through on medical advice because members of their social support network insist that they do (Harvard Health Letter, May, 1999).

The unfortunate flip side of social support is social strain (Rook, 1992). Friends, family, and spouses are not always supportive and are sometimes viewed as unreliable, critical, and irritating (Walen & Lachman, 2000). Friendship scholars are careful to note that friendships are sometimes rife with difficulties (Berndt, 1996; Newcomb & Bagwell, 1996). Although the primary focus in this book is on the advantages of cross-sex friendships, potential disadvantages are periodically identified throughout the book as the need arises. Possible negative repercussions of cross-sex friendship can discourage individuals of any age from pursuing friendships with members of the other sex (Adams, 1985; Sroufe, Bennett, Englund, Urban, & Shulman, 1993).

Another generic benefit of cross-sex friendship, a corollary of the social support benefit, is that cross-sex friends throughout the life cycle can provide a buffer against loneliness (for old age see O'Connor, 1993; for young adulthood see Werking, 1997a; for toddlerhood see Whaley & Rubenstein, 1994). Severe cases of loneliness have been linked to serious consequences such as health problems, substance abuse, and even suicide (Jones, Rose, & Russell, 1990; Koenig & Abrams, 1999; Perlman & Landolt, 1999; Rotenberg, 1999; Snodgrass, 1989; Stack, 1998). In referring to the more extreme cases of loneliness, Duck bluntly stated "Loneliness is fatal" (1983, p. 16). Even when loneliness is not severe, it is still an unpleasant emotional experience related to a number of social and personal problems (Perlman & Landolt, 1999; Sullivan, 1953). For example, lonely individuals are viewed as being less likable and desirable as friends when compared to their nonlonely counterparts (Lau & Kong, 1999). However, scholars do not know for sure if loneliness causes one to be viewed as undesirable, or whether being viewed as undesirable causes one to feel lonely. Relatedly, loneliness can have a negative impact on a person's self-concept. Lonely people have a poorer self-image than the nonlonely (Duck, Pond, & Leatham, 1994; Inderbitzen-Pisaruk, Clark, & Solano, 1992). The stigma attached to being lonely interferes with a person's level of confidence in forming social bonds, thereby creating a vicious cycle in which the lonely become lonelier (Lau & Kong, 1999).

The loneliness construct is revisited in each of the remaining chapters of this book because of its pervasiveness throughout the life cycle (Rotenberg, 1999) and its hypothesized connection to friendships or lack thereof. In the upcoming pages I provide some basic information on (a) the definition of loneliness, (b) the types of loneliness, (c) the frequency of loneliness, (d) the major theoretical explanations of loneliness, and (e) how loneliness is viewed differently across the life cycle.

Most individuals, lay persons and professionals alike, the very old and the very young, have an intuitive understanding of what loneliness means (Perlman & Peplau, 1998). Lay definitions of loneliness have common ingredients. Lay persons focus on the thoughts and emotions related to loneliness such as anger, depression, paranoia, and feelings of isolation and rejection. Individuals also have a "cluster of images" about why people experience loneliness (Perlman & Peplau, 1998, p. 573). Despite the fact that most individuals have an intuitive understanding of what loneliness means, the loneliness construct is complex and does not easily lend itself to analytical dissection. A consensus on what loneliness means and what causes loneliness does not exist in the academic community. However, after a brief review of scholarly approaches to defining and understanding loneliness, Perlman and Peplau (1998) concluded that most experts agree that loneliness is unpleasant; that it is not synonymous with social isolation; and that it results from quantitative or qualitative deficiencies in one's social network.

The 1981 definition of loneliness offered by Perlman and Peplau (or some close variation of it) is frequently utilized by loneliness scholars and was adopted for this book. Loneliness is "the unpleasant experience that occurs when a person's network of social relations is deficient in some important way, either quantitatively or qualitatively" (1981, p. 31; also see Perlman & Peplau, 1998). As I demonstrate throughout this book, cross-sex friendships alleviate perceived deficiencies in a person's social network from early childhood through extreme old age.

The different types of loneliness are related to the duration and causes of loneliness and the definition of loneliness just presented (Perlman & Peplau, 1998). Loneliness scholars distinguish between trait and situational loneliness (Rook, 1988). Trait loneliness, also known as chronic loneliness, has been theoretically explained as resembling a personality trait (Shaver, Furman, & Buhrmester, 1985). Those who are chronically lonely are lonely regardless of the situation (Perlman & Peplau, 1998). Situational loneliness stems from the situation an individual is in. For example, a first-year college student attending a new school away from home may suffer from situational loneliness. Situational loneliness, although unpleasant, is often transitory as individuals form new social bonds (Rook, 1988). In each chapter of this book I explore ways in which cross-sex friendships help chronically and situationally lonely individuals.

Based largely on Weiss' seminal book, *Loneliness: The Experience of Emotional and Social Isolation*, loneliness scholars also distinguish between emotional and social loneliness (1973). Emotional loneliness results from the absence of intimate relationships (Sullivan, 1953). Similarly, some scholars argue for "functional specificity" (Litwak, 1985; Weiss, 1973). Functional specificity means that certain kinds of relationships meet needs that can only be met by that type of relationship. Social loneliness results from having an inadequate social network. For the socially lonely, loneliness does not mean a lack of a central, fulfilling relationship, but rather the lack of a satisfying network of social relationships. Throughout the book I review evidence that cross-sex friends in each phase of the life cycle relieve both social and emotional loneliness.

Just how common is loneliness in American society? Experts believe that loneliness afflicts the majority of people at least some of the time. Rotenberg began a recent edited volume on loneliness with the following observation: "After reviewing the literature, both academic and nonacademic (e.g., popular media), it has become obvious to me that loneliness is an inherent part of the human condition" (1999, p. 3). Other loneliness scholars have expressed similar sentiments concerning the inevitability and pervasiveness of loneliness across the life cycle (Perlman & Landolt, 1999; Rook, 1988). As suggested earlier,

chronically lonely individuals are lonely all the time. Whether chronic loneliness carries over from one stage of life to the next is not known because of a general lack of longitudinal studies.

Perlman and Peplau examined data from a National Council on Aging survey involving over 18,000 respondents between the ages of 18 and 85 (Perlman,
1991; Perlman & Peplau, 1998). Their goal was to explore how the frequency of
loneliness varies over the adult life cycle. Unfortunately, data on the friendship
patterns of those 18,000 individuals is not available. Nevertheless, when averaged across sex of respondent, 43% of respondents reported feelings of loneliness in the 18 to 24 age group, comparted to 35% of individuals in the 25 to 34
age group. Approximately 27% of women and men ages 35 to 44 reported feelings of loneliness. The percentage dropped to 25% of the respondents between
the ages of 45 and 64. For individuals in the 65 to 74, 75 to 84, and 85+ age
groups the percentages, respectively, were 26%, 28%, and 28%. A higher percentage of younger adults than any other group reported feelings of loneliness.
There were some differences between women and men. Approximately 20% of
males and 30% females in the 45 to 64 years age group reported feelings of loneliness. The gap between men and women narrowed in the 75 to 84 years age
group and disappeared for individuals over the age of 85.

What about loneliness during early childhood and adolescence? There is
some debate concerning how early in life a person might experience loneliness
(Perlman & Peplau, 1998), but the majority of loneliness scholars now agree
that children as young as kindergarten and first grade, sometimes younger, understand and experience loneliness (Burgess, Ladd, Kochenderfer, Lambert, &
Birch, 1999; Rotenberg & Hymel, 1999). Perlman and Landolt noted significant areas of overlap in the way loneliness is conceptualized by scholars studying adult loneliness and those investigating childhood and adolescent
loneliness (1999). For example, the two theories of adult loneliness that have
become prominent over the last 25 years (i.e., social needs theory and the cognitive processes approach; Perlman & Peplau, 1998; Terrell-Deutsch, 1999), appear to be equally applicable to children and adolescents (Rotenberg, 1999). In
a nutshell, proponents of a social needs explanation of loneliness contend that
people have basic social needs that can be met only in personal relationships
(Bowlby, 1973; Sullivan, 1953; Weiss, 1973). When those needs are not met,
loneliness results. The social needs approach emphasizes the emotional aspects
of loneliness (Terrell -Deutsch, 1999). Advocates of the cognitive processes approach argue that loneliness results not so much from unmet needs, but rather
from a cognitive realization of the difference between what one would like to
have in the way of relationships, and what one actually has (Peplau, Miceli, &
Morasch, 1982; Peplau & Perlman, 1979).

Although the definition of loneliness used in this book reflects more of a cognitive discrepancy approach to loneliness than a social needs approach, I incorporate both perspectives. The different approaches complement rather than

contradict one another (Terrell-Deutsch, 1999). My basic contention is that humans need personal relationship in each stage of life (i.e., the social needs approach), and cross-sex friendships can meet some of those needs in generic and unique ways. Additionally, the intellectual realization of loneliness (i.e., the cognitive discrepancy approach) could result from a lack of quality friendships and/or inadequate integration into social networks. Each of those relational deficiencies could be redressed through initiation and maintenance of close and casual cross-sex friendships. For example, children with poor social skills can rely on cross-sex friendships for benefits normally supplied in same-sex friendships (Kovacs, Parker, & Hoffman, 1996).

A life-cycle approach to the study of loneliness seems justified (Perlman & Landolt, 1999). A life-cycle perspective implies that the frequency of loneliness and the ways in which it is experienced depends on the stage of life being examined. Perlman and Landolt observe that the loneliness literature is divided into two general areas: research focusing on adult loneliness and research focusing on loneliness during childhood and adolescence (1999). There are important differences in the two literatures that are identified and discussed in subsequent chapters. For instance, in early childhood a friend of the other sex might relieve loneliness because he or she represents someone to play with (Whaley & Rubenstein, 1994). After the onset of puberty, a friend of the other sex might relieve loneliness because she or he is serving as a surrogate romantic partner.

The relationship between loneliness, stage of life, an individual's self concept, and the presence or absence of cross-sex friendships is a complex one that has yet to be investigated. I am not suggesting that having more and better cross-sex friendships is the solution for all lonely individuals. Nor am I suggesting that loneliness is a pathological condition that needs to be totally eliminated. I agree with some loneliness scholars that loneliness is a normal part of many of the developmental processes that occur throughout life (Sippola & Bukowski, 1999). Nevertheless, a strong case can be made that for some lonely people the solution to their loneliness lies in having a stronger network of friends. Although there are many ways of coping with loneliness (e.g., see Peplau & Perlman,1982; Perlman & Peplau, 1998; Rokach & Brock, 1998; Rotenberg & Hymel, 1999), having a supportive friend or network of friends is a viable option with convincing face validity and moderate to strong theoretical and empirical support (Burgess et al., 1999; Rotenberg & Hymel, 1999; Solano, 1986). Throughout this book I examine how cross-sex friendships or the lack of those friendships might contribute to or mitigate the effects of loneliness from early childhood through extreme old age.

Unique Benefits of Cross-Sex Friendships.   A second way in which cross-sex friendships enrich social networks is by providing unique benefits that same-sex friendships are unable to supply. Similar to generic benefits, unique benefits of cross-sex friendships may vary from one stage of life to the next, but several of them are available throughout the cycle of life. As will be documented in each chapter of this book, cross-sex friends in every stage of life provide each other with other-sex companionship and insider perspectives on how members of the other sex think, feel, and behave (Monsour, 1997). If there are biological sex and gender differences between women and men and girls and boys (Canary & Dindia, 1998), then cross-sex companionship and insider perspectives could make the behavior of the other-sex family members, coworkers, romantic partners, and peers more understandable (Monsour, 1988, 1997; Swain, 1992).

Now that I have opened the proverbial can of worms concerning sex and gender differences, this seems as good a place as any to get some nomenclature worries out of the way. Throughout this book I make reference to "gender" and "sex" differences and similarities between males and females. Unless otherwise stated, gender differences refer to differences between men and women or boys and girls that are a product of different socialization practices and histories. To borrow directly from Canary and Dindia's edited volume on sex differences and similarities in communication, "gender refers to the psychological and social manifestations of what one believes to be male and/or female, which might—or might not—reflect one's biological sex … sex refers to the genetic, biological differences between boys and girls, between men and women" (1998, p. 4) Simply stated, gender differences between women and men (and girls and boys) refer to differences that result from the different ways males and females are raised and socialized in American society. Sex differences are differences between women and men that are biologically and physiologically based, although the area between gender and sex differences is a gray one (Wood & Dindia, 1998)

Some scholars contend that women and men (starting off as girls and boys) are socialized so differently that they establish their own cultures early in life and that the different cultural experiences can make interaction and relationship formation difficult at times (Maccoby, 1990). Kunkel and Burleson noted, "The idea that men and women are so different that they should be regarded as members of different cultures is a perspective that has become widespread in both scholarly circles and the popular press" (1998, p. 102). Their assessment of the "different cultures perspective" is presented in chapter three of this book. For now, however, assuming there is at least some validity in the different cultures perspective, cross-sex friendships are beneficial to participants because partners teach each other the norms of their gender culture. Cross-sex friendship exposure to members of the other sex early in life should make cross-sex interactions later in life smoother and more inclusive (Leaper, 1994a; Yingling, 1994).

I do not wish to overemphasize the purported differences between men and women and boys and girls and how those differences might impact cross-sex friendships. Nor do I wish to completely dismiss those differences (if they do indeed exist). My position is very similiar to the one articulated by Dindia on a number of occasions (e.g., Dindia, 1997a). In contrast to Gray who contended that men and women are so dissimiliar that they seem to be from different planets (Gray, 1992), Dindia colorfully argued instead that women are from South

Dakota and men are from North Dakota. In other words, the differences between females and males are not so great as to justify a claim that they are from different planets, but may be great enough to justify a claim that they are from different but neighboring states. In every chapter of this book I make reference to how those differences, although small, are significant enough to cause problems for some potential and actual cross-sex friendships.

In summary of the first theme of the book, cross-sex friendships *can* and *do* enrich the social networks of participating members in generic and unique ways. The "do" part of my statement refers to actual empirical support for the claim that cross-sex friendships enrich social networks. Evidence documenting such enrichment has been slowly accumulating for years and can be observed, albeit unevenly and thinly, in every stage of the life cycle. That evidence is presented throughout the book. The "can" part of the statement refers to the potential of cross-sex friendships for enriching social networks. My hope is that cross-sex friendships will receive the academic and everyday-life attention they are due once this potential is more fully recognized by scholars and lay persons. Unfortunately, enrichment of social networks through formation of cross-sex friendships is often made difficult because of social and structural barriers to their formation, barriers that are the focus of the next section of the chapter.

Structural and Social Barriers to Cross-Sex Friendships Throughout Life

Although I believe that structural and social opportunities for cross-sex friendships will continue to increase in the 21st century, there is at the same time considerable evidence documenting the existence of structural and social barriers to the formation of those friendships. The second theme of this book, therefore, is that structural and social barriers inhibit the formation of cross-sex friendships throughout the life cycle (Monsour, 1997). Similarity in structural and social barriers exist between various stages of the life cycle, but there are also differences between and within life stages (Wright, 1989). The ways in which those barriers manifest themselves in each stage of life are treated in detail in the remaining chapters of this book. In the upcoming pages, I define and briefly describe social and structural barriers. A good place to begin is with an explanation of the relationship between the two types of barriers by giving an example illustrating both.

Marital status has structural and social implications for cross-sex friendships (Monsour, 1997; Werking, 1997a). Being married usually (but not always) puts a person at a structural disadvantage for initiating cross-sex friendships because the role obligations of marriage interfere with cross-sex interactions one might otherwise have if he or she were single (Booth & Hess, 1974; Monsour, 1997). Additionally, the expressed jealousy of a spouse can be a social barrier preventing the formation and maintenance of a cross-sex friendship (Rubin, 1985). The communicated jealousy of a spouse has structural implications for cross-sex friendship opportunities. For example, the wife or husband may strongly object to his or her spouse going places where there are opportunities for cross-sex interaction. As can seen from this example, there is a reciprocal relationship between structural and social barriers to cross-sex friendships. Social barriers often lead to structural barriers (and vice versa), and structural barriers perpetuate social barriers (and vice versa). Both types of barriers reinforce and reify one another.

Social Barriers to Cross-Sex Friendships Across the Life Cycle.   In the preface I identified a number of factors that increase the likelihood of cross-sex friendships becoming more prevalent as we move further into the 21st century. There are many such factors. For example, as women enter the workplace in larger numbers (Gini, 1998) and online friendships become more popular (Parks & Floyd, 1996), cross-sex friendships will almost certainly increase in number. Additionally, evidence presented in chapters four (on cross-sex friendships in adolescence) and five (on cross-sex friendships in adulthood), documents that male–female friendships in those age groups are quite common. Documentation already reviewed in the previous section of this chapter shows that cross-sex friends provide generic and unique benefits. Despite the fact that cross-sex friendships are beneficial and likely to become more commonplace in the near future, there are still considerable social and structural barriers interfering with their initiation and maintenance.

Social barriers to male–female friendships appear in a variety of forms and may originate from third parties or the cross-sex friends. Most commonly, social barriers are obstacles created by individuals in a person's social network that discourage or prohibit the formation of cross-sex friendships. As conceptualized in this book, social barriers are usually communicated in some way. For example, a romantic partner might strenuously object to her partner having a close cross-sex friend (Rubin, 1985). Or a youngster in middle childhood might be teased by his peers for having a friend of the other sex (Sroufe et al., 1993). Fear of being the subject of gossip among her friends may keep an elderly widow from initiating a cross-sex friendship (Adams, 1985). Social barriers might also originate from the social interaction of the participating members. Beginning with the landmark work of Maltz and Borker (1982), some scholars contend that from early childhood males and females develop different languages or at least different ways of using the same language (e.g., Leaper, 1994a; Mulac, Bradac, & Gibbons, 2001). Swain believes that differences in communication style between males and females make friendship initiation and maintenance difficult (1992; also see Tannen, 1990). The extent to which there actually are communication style differences between males and females is debatable (Canary & Dindia, 1998). That debate is revisited periodically throughout this book.

Social barriers to cross-sex friendship formation also reflect normative relational constraints in society existing in every stage of life. Normative relational constraints are norms that place constraints on where, when, and how cross-sex friendships may be initiated, developed, and maintained (Bell, 1981; Werking, 1997a). They may come from the larger social milieu (e.g., Mead's "generalized other," 1934), or from specific individuals or groups. Normative relational constraints can be conceptualized as both social and structural barriers. Before a normative relational constraint is communicatively expressed it is primarily a structural barrier. Once there is a communicative manifestation of a normative constraint, that constraint doubles as a social barrier.

The most pervasive and powerful relational normative constraint to cross-sex friendship formation is the "homosocial norm," which refers to the preference held by many individuals (and reinforced by society) to associate primarily with members of their own sex (Rose, 1985). Same-sex playmate and friendship preferences begin around the age of 3 or 4 (Maccoby, 1994) and continue throughout the life cycle (Monsour, 1997). The homosocial norm takes on a slightly different form as it materializes in various stages of life. For example, teenagers might favor members of their own sex because the verbalized norms of the clique or crowd to which they belong dictate that they should (Cotterell, 1996). Elementary school girls may prefer to play with other girls rather than boys because boys play much rougher than girls (Lewis & Phillipsen, 1998; Thorne, 1993). Older women may opt for same-sex friendships rather than cross-sex ones in order to prevent gossip about suspected romantic involvement (Adams, 1985).

Structural Barriers to Cross-Sex Friendships Across the Life Cycle. The possibility for cross-sex friendship formation is seriously compromised when females and males cannot interact. Indeed, communication is a necessary although not sufficient condition for any kind of friendship formation (Fehr, 1996). O'Meara labeled the lack of structural opportunities for cross-sex friendship formation as the "opportunity challenge" (O'Meara, 1994). Structural factors relevant to cross-sex friendship formation include, but are not limited to, residential proximity, the workplace, school setting, living in an urban or rural setting, social network structure such as crowd affiliation, and sex segregation (Blieszner & Adams, 1992; Cotterell, 1996; Fehr, 1996; O'Meara, 1994; Parks, 1997; Rubin, 1980). Structural factors also emphasize role demands and the different positions in society held by men and women that give them access to different kinds of power (Wright, 1989). Adams and Blieszner contended that having access to more power than women opens up more friendship opportunities for men (1994). Additionally, the role demands of being a parent and a spouse can interfere with friendship formation and maintenance (Carbery & Buhrmester, 1998; Rawlins, 1982).

Adams and Allan contended that individual structural factors are correlated with friendship formation but also with each other (1989; 1998). Therefore, researchers need to examine the "overall constellation of structural characteristics that constitute an individual's social location" (1989, p. 60) if they want to understand the structural constraints and facilitators of friendship. Along these same lines, Adams and Allan argued that relationship researchers in general have neglected to study how the different contexts in which relationships occur impact the dynamics of those relationships (1998; see also Duck, West, & Acitelli, 1997; Werking,1997a). They broadly defined *context* as anything external to the relationship that might influence how that relationship is viewed and conducted by the participants. Contextual factors would include structural constraints and facilitators on cross-sex friendship initiation, societal norms concerning appropriate male–female relationships, mass media influences on how individuals view cross-sex friendships, and a host of other variables. Although I agree with their observations concerning the importance of context (Adams & Allan, 1989; 1998), incorporating the overall constellation of structural characteristics and using such a broad definition of context would make proper empirical investigation of friendship processes a methodological nightmare. Of course, pointing out the difficulty of doing justice to context does not invalidate their claim that such contextualized analyses are needed. Perhaps, as observed by Duck (personal communication, October 2000), the *proper* study of friendship is a methodological nightmare.

Structural barriers make interaction between the sexes difficult primarily because of propinquity issues such as segregation of the sexes at work and school (Jacobs, 1989; Leaper, 1994a; McWilliams & Howard, 1993), and some older adults being housebound (O'Connor, 1993). Researchers have studied and established the relationship between physical proximity and social contact for more than 50 years (Adams & Allan, 1998; Festinger, Schachter, & Back, 1950). As noted by Fehr (1996), the first step in friendship formation is that individuals must come into contact with one another. The opportunity for interaction need not present itself in a face-to-face encounter, as demonstrated by online friendships (Adams, 1998; Parks & Floyd, 1996).

Individual level variables, such as biological sex, sexual orientation, level of education, physical mobility, and marital status, can also influence structural opportunities for friendship formation (Blieszner & Adams, 1992). Those variables influence the probability of people finding themselves in structural situations that facilitate or constrain the development of cross-sex friendship. For example, in the first empirical investigation of cross-sex friendship, Booth and Hess discovered that level of education, gender, and marital status influenced the likelihood of cross-sex friendship formation because they impact the opportunity for interaction with members of the other sex (1974). Others have noted that widowers are in a better structural position than widows for the initiation of cross-sex friendships because of the longer life expectancy of women (e.g., Wright, personal communication, June 24, 2000).

Although the primary focus in each chapter is on the social and structural barriers to cross-sex friendship, I also identify some of the structural and social factors that facilitate cross-sex friendship formation. Those factors are typically merely the reverse of the impediments. So for example, although voluntary sex segregation impedes cross-sex friendship formation during middle childhood (Gottman, 1986), sex desegregation during late adolescence can potentially facilitate cross-sex friendship formation through a process known as "channeling" that I discuss in detail in chapter four (Brown, Mory, & Kinney, 1994).

Cross-Sex Friendships Affect and are Affected by an Individual's Ongoing Social Construction of Self Throughout the Life Cycle

The third general theme of this book also serves as its central theoretical premise. I contend that cross-sex friendships in each stage of the life cycle affect and are affected by an individual's ongoing social construction of self. Explication of my premise requires a working definition of *self* and what it means to claim that the self is "socially constructed."

There are a number of different and legitimate ways of defining the self (Barrett, 1997; Lipka & Brinthaupt, 1992), and there is no general consensus among students of the self as to how that term should be defined (A. J. Wells, 1992). Barrett contended that because the self is not a single entity (a debatable point), then the "self" construct is not "amenable to a unitary definition" (1997, p. 82). Wells observed along similar lines that researchers, philosophers, and theoreticians have striven and struggled for centuries to adequately define the self and the self-concept (1992; see also Baumeister, 1987). Rather than incorporating the entire and decidedly amorphous construct of "self," I have simplified matters by concentrating instead on the "self-concept." In the interest of parsimony and relevancy to the central theme of this book, I have adopted Wells' conceptualization of the self-concept. As she noted "I began by thinking of the self-concept as a series of interrelated schemata about self, some conscious and some not so conscious, that are learned throughout life" (1992, p. 165). For purposes of this book, therefore, when references are made to the *self* I mean to reference a person's self-concept (A. J. Wells, 1992). An individual's self-concept is comprised of self-schemas, which are cognitive generalizations about oneself (e.g., "I am smart," "I make friends easily," etc; Baldwin, 1992), whereas the larger construct of self would include additional constructs and schemas not necessarily linked to self-schemas. To contend that a person's self-concept is socially constructed means that a person's conception of self is a product of his or her relationships (Markus & Cross, 1990).

Exploring the relationship between self-concept and cross-sex friendships is no easy task. As noted by Barrett in a chapter she wrote in the *Handbook of Personal Relationships* (1997), in order to cover the topic of self and relationship development thoroughly, "one would need an entire, very large book" (p. 81). Although "self-concept" is more manageable than the larger construct of "self," the self-concept construct itself is multi-dimensional, elusive, and has generated thousands of studies (Marsh, 1990). According to Marsh (1990), age and sex are two of the most commonly investigated correlates of self-concept, which dovetails nicely with my life-span approach (age) to the study of cross-sex friendships (sex).

I divided the upcoming section into three parts in hopes of more clearly articulating my central theoretical premise. First, I briefly describe the hypothesized relationship between cross-sex friendship and self-concept formation. I then lay out the particulars of the "interpersonal self perspective" (Markus & Cross, 1990) and the work of five theorists who exemplify that perspective. Finally, I explain the role of interpersonal communication in self and cross-sex friendship formation.

Cross-Sex Friendships and Self-Concept Formation.   Direct empirical support for the proposition that cross-sex friendships in each stage of the life cycle affect and are affected by an individual's ongoing social construction of self is thin at best. Although the cross-sex friendship literature is growing (Afifi & Faulkner, 2000), it is still underdeveloped and focuses heavily on young adulthood (Monsour, 1997; Werking, 1997a). Scholars know very little about the processes involved in the reciprocal relationship between cross-sex friendships and self-concept development. Consequently, parts of each chapter are exploratory and suggestive of new lines of research.

Much can be learned from an examination of the processes involved in the joint construction of self and cross-sex friendships in different stages of the life cycle. For instance, in chapter two I argue that cross-sex friendships or the absence of such friendships in early childhood can have a significant impact on developing gender schemas, schemas which in turn affect the self-schemas of children and influence the way they interact with others. Similarly, in chapter four I examine the role played by cross-sex friends in helping adolescents in their quest for self-exploration and self-discovery (Parker & Gottman, 1989). In each chapter I also examine developmental milestones and processes such as puberty and getting married and how those milestones and processes might impact self-concepts and cross-sex friendships.

The Interpersonal Self Perspective

According to Markus and Cross (1990), a considerable amount of theoretical speculation and some documentation has accumulated over the last century supporting the position that the "self" is socially constructed through an individual's personal relationships (e.g., Aron & Aron, 1997; Baldwin, 1911; Barrett, 1997; Bowlby, 1969; Cast, Stets, & Burke, 1999; Cooley, 1902; Mead, 1934; Sullivan, 1953; Tice & Baumeister, 2001). They refer to the socially constructed self as the "interpersonal self," as do Tice and Baumeister (2001), and observe that "Self-concept, identity, and personality researchers approach a consensus on the assumption that it is difficult—perhaps impossible—to escape the influence of others, or to extract a 'pure' self from the interpersonal context" (Markus & Cross, 1990, p. 576).

I contend that the socially constructed self-concept influences an individual's likelihood of initiating cross-sex friendships at various junctures of life and also affects thought and behavior within those friendships once they are established. Relatedly, the presence or absence of cross-sex friendships contribute to the ongoing process of self-concept construction. Like other significant social relationships, cross-sex friendships influence one's self-view, which in turn influences beliefs about cross-sex friendships and conduct in those relationships. As a case in point, some elementary school children who have difficulty forming same-sex friendships turn to members of the other sex for their friendship needs (Kovacs et al., 1996). Depending on a host of other variables, that cross-sex friendship could have a positive impact on a child's self-concept ("yes, I can make friends"), or a negative impact ("I have to settle for cross-sex friends because I can't make any same-sex ones").

The social construction of self begins in infancy via attachment with a primary care giver (Bowlby, 1969) and continues throughout life (Cross & Markus, 1991). There is a wide range of individual differences in the degree to which social relationships impact views of self (Markus & Cross, 1990). Additionally, as individuals go through the stages of life their self-concepts change to reflect those stages (Cross & Markus, 1991; Labouvie-Vief, Chiodo, Goguen, Diehl, & Orwoll, 1995). From an interpersonal self-perspective, the relationships formed and maintained during each phase of the life cycle have a significant impact on who that individual is, was, and will be.

Throughout this book I employ concepts and theories from the interpersonal self-perspective and closely related theoretical positions such as social constructionism (Berger & Luckman, 1966; Gergen, 1985). Specifically, the parallel perspectives of Gergen (1985; 1991), Cooley (1902, 1909), Mead (1934), Sullivan (1953), and Bowlby (1969), all interpersonal self theorists, are used to demonstrate how cross-sex friendships and self-concepts are connected. An examination of each perspective should help establish the theoretical foundation for subsequent arguments made throughout the book. The theorists are presented in chronological order starting with Cooley's 1902 work and ending with Gergen's 1985 perspective. Depending on degree of relevancy to a particular stage of life, some or all of these theorists are revisited in each of the remaining chapters. Each perspective and an amalgamation of all five are applicable in different ways to cross-sex friendship and self-concept formation in various stages of the life cycle.

A brief clarification concerning my use of the interpersonal self perspective is in order. As important as personal relationships are in the construction of self, other significant factors such as cultural and historical context impact an individual's evolving concept of self and the development of cross-sex friendships. As noted by Labouvie-Vief and her colleagues in their article *Representations of Self Across the Life Span*, "Recent interest in the self reflects a move of the field … toward a view of the self as a structure or set of processes characterized by multiplicity that is contextually (culturally, historically, and interpersonally) situated …" (1995, p. 404). Other scholars have similarly emphasized the importance of context (e.g., Adams & Allan, 1998; Blieszner & Adams, 1992; Duck et al., 1997; Sullivan, 1953). Clearly then, to conceptualize the self solely as the product of relationships would be an impoverished view. On the other hand, the interpersonal self perspective does not preclude consideration of cultural and historical contexts when unraveling the complexities of the relationship between self and cross-sex friendships (Markus & Cross, 1990).

Cooley and the Looking Glass Self (1902).   Cooley (1902) and Mead (1934) are symbolic interactionists (Cast, Stets, & Burke, 1999). Symbolic interactionism has been described as a general perspective or conceptual framework rather than one specific theory (Blumer, 1969; Longmore, 1998). Cooley and Mead believed that taking the role of the other toward one's own behavior is an essential characteristic of social conduct and that an individual's self is a product of social relationships and social interaction. Individuals gain knowledge about themselves through relationships and interaction, and they use that knowledge as the basis of their self-concepts (Bukowski & Hoza, 1989). Symbolic interactionism, in my view at least, is the embodiment of the interpersonal self perspective.

Cooley is possibly best known for his work on reflected appraisals and the "looking-glass self" (1902). The process of reflected appraisals has three elements: how a person imagines he or she appears to the other individual; how that person imagines the other individual is judging him or her; and then some kind of self-feeling based on the other person's reflected appraisal. Reflected appraisals constitute Cooley's symbolic interactionist notion of the looking-glass self in the following way:

> In a very large and interesting class of cases the social reference takes the form of a somewhat definite imagination of how one' s self—that is any idea he appropriates—appears in a particular mind, and the kind of self-feeling one has is determined by the attitude toward this attributed to that other mind. A social self of this sort might be called the reflected or looking-glass self … as we see our face, figure, and dress in the glass … so in imagination we perceive in another's mind some thought of our appearance, manners, aims, deeds, character, friends, and so on, and are variously affected by it (p. 183, 1902).

The imagined judgment of the other person triggers a feeling about oneself. As Cooley put it "We are ashamed to seem evasive in the presence of a straightforward man, cowardly in the presence of a brave one, gross in the eyes of a refined one, and so on." (p. 184). Just as others impact an individual's view of self, that individual's view of others impact the view that others have of themselves. For example, young heterosexual adults report that one of the benefits of having cross-sex friends is that they make each other feel like attractive members of the other sex (Monsour, 1988; Rubin, 1985). The mutual reflected appraisals occurring within the friendship becomes part of each person's self-concept. Cooley contends that as individuals go from childhood to adulthood they develop more resilient self-concepts that are not quite as susceptible to the changing attitudes of significant others.

Communication between individuals is a crucial part of Cooley's perspective (1902). Individuals see themselves as others see them, and those reflected appraisals are often inferred from verbal and nonverbal communication. A disapproving glance at one's attire, a seductive stare, a condescending tone of voice, a warm smile, are all nonverbal reflected appraisals from others that an individual might incorporate into her or his self-image. Reflected appraisals are often directly and verbally communicated. A cross-sex friend might say to her recently divorced male friend "I can't believe your wife filed for divorce, any woman would be lucky to have you as a husband." A recently widowed individual might be told by his female friend that he is a strong person and will get through the pain. A lonely middle-schooler might have his or her self-concept boosted by the friendly overtures of a sympathetic member of the other sex.

Mead and the Process of Role Taking (1934).   In a statement that made me feel better about my trepidation when reading Mead's original works, Duck admitted "The mention of G. H. Mead is usually enough to strike terror into otherwise alert and intelligent beings. Mead's published works are difficult reading, largely because his legacy of ideas was handed down through editions of notes taken by students at his lecture" (1994, p. 69). Although I agree with Duck's assessment, luckily there are sufficiently clear interpretations of Mead's work so as to circumvent most serious misrepresentations of his ideas (e.g., Blumer, 1969).

Mead and Cooley's theorizing laid the groundwork for the symbolic interactionist perspective (Blumer, 1969). According to Blumer, who in 1937 coined the term *symbolic interactionism*, that perspective rests on three premises: (a) people act toward things based on the meanings those things have for them, (b) those meanings are socially constructed through interaction with others, and (c) the meanings are handled through an interpretive process (Blumer, 1969). Blumer noted that the term *symbolic interaction* in part refers to the ability of humans, unlike other animals, to interpret or define each other's actions, rather than merely reacting to them.

Key to Mead's perspective is the tenet that people view themselves as objects much like they view others in their social network as objects. Consequently, an individual may have a view of herself, communicate with herself, and act toward herself, just as she might have a view of a friend, communicate with that friend, and act toward that friend. Because meanings of objects are socially constructed (the second premise of symbolic interactionism) and because one views oneself as an object, then the self becomes a social construction. The ability to take the role of the other, therefore, is central in the social construction of self. Taking the role of the other person involves taking the role of specific individuals, groups, and one's community and being able to see oneself as those individuals do. The role of the community is manifested as the "generalized other" (Mead, 1934). The generalized other is the perceived attitude of the whole social community toward an individual, an attitude that is instrumental in influencing a person's self view. The theoretical notion of taking the role of the other becomes particularly relevant in chapter four when I discuss teenage cliques and crowds and chapter five when I explore the workplace environment.

Communication or interaction is pivotal in Mead's view of symbolic interactionism and the construction of self. Mead emphasized the importance of communication with the following statement:

> The principle which I have suggested as basic to human social organization is that of communication involving participation in the other. This requires the appearance of the other in the self, the identification of the other with the self, the reaching of self-consciousness through the other. (1934, p. 253)

Communication involves participation in the other by taking the role of the other person and viewing the situation and oneself as the partner does. This perspective taking ability allows both individuals to monitor and adjust their communication. Blumer considered this mutual role taking as the *sine qua non* of communication and symbolic interaction (1969, p. 10). On a more cognitive than interactional front, Baldwin similarly argued that when individuals construct internal mental representations of their relationships (what he called *schemas*), those representations are comprised of self, partner, and the intermingling of the two (Baldwin, 1995).

Sullivan's Interpersonal Theory of Psychiatry and Chumships (1953).   Sullivan drew heavily from the work of Mead and is one of the central scholars in what is called *interpersonal psychiatry* (Greenberg & Mitchell, 1983). Like others who endorse the tenets of interpersonal psychiatry, Sullivan believed that the social and cultural context in which a person's self develops is fundamental to an evolving concept of self. He carefully laid out the part played by others in self-construction in each stage of the life cycle (1953). Although Sullivan's work is utilized to varying degrees in each chapter, for my purposes his theory is most relevant to the third chapter on middle and late childhood cross-sex friendships. Along those lines, Sullivan is best known in the community of friendship scholars for articulation of his *chumship* construct which is closely examined in chapter three.

Bowlby and Attachment Theory (1969). Throughout the book I repeatedly utilize Bowlby's Attachment Theory (Bowlby, 1969; 1973). Attachment theory has become very popular in recent years in the study of personal relationships (see Hinde, 1997, for a summary of that research). Attachment relationships are so fundamental to social organization that Weiss contended they constitute one of the two basic classes of human relationships-with "affiliations" being the other (1998). Periodically throughout the book I propose ways in which attachment theory might be used to shed light on the relationship between self-construction and cross-sex friendships in different stages of the life span.

The basic premise of attachment theory is that the relationship established between an infant and the primary care giver influences the personal relationships formed by the infant throughout life (Shulman, Elicker, & Stroufe, 1994). The primary care giver is usually the mother, but Bowlby was careful to specify that the "mother-figure" can be any individual who serves as the central provider of mothering behavior and to whom the child attaches (1969). A child is securely attached to the primary care giver if she or he is confident in the care giver's availability and responsiveness (Bowlby, 1969; Kerns, Klepac, & Cole, 1996). When a care giver is not responsive or available, the child begins to view him or herself as not being worthy of responsiveness or availability.

Researchers have established a category system for infant–caregiver relationships in which those relationships are classified as secure, anxious-resistant, and anxious-avoidant (Ainsworth, Blehar, Waters, & Wall, 1978). Scholars have also established that adults form attachment patterns, primarily with other-sex peers, that have significant impact on the formation and conduct of relationships (Weiss, 1982; Zeifman & Hazan, 1997).

Bowlby noted that "Although the growth of attachment behavior during the first year of life is reasonably well chronicled, the course it takes in subsequent years is not" (1969, p. 204). Attachment behavior occurs predominantly during the first 3 years of life, but it persists in "attenuated" form throughout the early school years and can be observed from the "cradle to the grave" as individuals form attachments with a range of others in their social network (Bowlby, 1969). For example, during adolescence and adulthood attachment behavior may be directed toward other individuals besides parents (Bowlby, 1969; Trinke & Bartholomew, 1997). Adults and teenagers can form attachment relationships with groups and even institutions, although those attachments are often mediated by some individual person in that group or institution (Bowlby, 1969, p. 207).

A key construct of attachment theory is Bowlby's notion of "internal working models." Based on early relationships and interactions with care givers, infants and toddlers develop internal working models of themselves, their care givers, and the relationship that exist between them (Bowlby, 1973). Referencing the theoretical work of Cassidy (1990), Verschueren and colleagues defined the internal working model of self as "a dynamic structure containing affectively charged cognitions about one's lovableness and worthiness" (Verschueren, Marcoen, & Schoefs, 1996, p. 2493). Internal working models are relationship schemas (Baldwin, 1992) that give the individual a framework within which to understand him or herself, the primary care giver, and relationship in general. The internal working models are based on recursive interactions that occur between the infant and care giver. Recursive interactions are scripted dyadic behaviors that regularly take place between the care giver and the child (Bowlby, 1969; Bretherton, 1985; Howes, 1996). They also occur between toddlers and adults other than the primary care giver that result in mental representations of those relationships as well (Schaffer & Emerson, 1964). Internal working models provide mechanisms for continuity in attachment style so that individuals exhibit styles of attachment behaviors that remain stable across the life cycle (Bowlby, 1973; Young & Acitelli, 1998). The stability of attachment styles, however, has recently been challenged (Baldwin & Fehr, 1995). That challenge is examined in the chapter on cross-sex friendships during young and middle adulthood.

Gergen and Social Constructionism (1985, 1991).   Although social constructionism was not highlighted by Markus and Cross as an interpersonal self theory, it clearly has the defining characteristics of that perspective (Berger & Luckman, 1966; Gergen, 1985; 1991; Gergen & Gergen, 1991). Gergen is one of the major proponents of social constructionism and noted (1985, p. 266) a strong link between it and Berger and Luckmann's seminal volume *The Social Construction of Reality* (1966). He contended that the self is no longer viewed as an essence in itself, but is instead, fundamentally relational (1991, see pp. 146–147). The intersubjective creation of reality through communication is one of the major areas of interest to social constructionists (Yerby, 1995). Social constructionism parallels the symbolic interactionist view of communication described earlier in this chapter. Gergen characterized communication as a fundamental way in which individuals establish a sense of relatedness, and not just a way of expressing what one might be feeling or thinking internally (1991).

Interpersonal Communication and the Construction of Self and Cross-Sex Friendships.   In a recent edition of *Human Communication Research*, Coover and Murphy succinctly summarized the importance of communication in the social construction of self by beginning their article with the observation "The essence of communication is the formation and expression of an identity. The formation of the self is not an independent event generated by an autonomous actor. Rather, the self emerges through social interaction" (2000, p. 125). Therefore, it would be difficult to discuss the reciprocal relationship between cross-sex friendships and development of self without including an examination of the interpersonal communication that makes those joint processes possible.

In addition to the interpersonal self theorists discussed in the preceding pages, a host of other scholars have established the importance of interpersonal communication in the construction of self and social relationships (Coover & Murphy, 2000; Baxter, 1987; Corsaro, 1985; Duck, 1997; Rawlins, 1992; Vygotsky, 1978; Wood, 1995, Yingling, 1994). For example, sounding very much like a symbolic interactionist and social constructionist, Wood argued that interpersonal communication is the process of creating meaning through the interpretation of symbols (1995; also see Baxter, 1987; Duck et al., 1997). The creation of meaning in a relationship and the interpretation of symbols is a joint endeavor as relational partners try to coordinate their interpretations (Duck, 1994). Communication in a relationship is impacted by the broader societal and cultural context in which it takes place (Sullivan, 1953; Wood, 1995). Part of the larger societal and cultural context would include the deep structures and societal practices explained later in this chapter (Hartup & Stevens, 1997), and the importance of context emphasized by Adams and Allan (1998). As cross-sex friendships adapt to differing developmental demands throughout the life cycle, they become both a product of and a contributor to communication that occurs between relational partners.

Throughout this book I argue that the social construction of self and the development of cross-sex friendships across the life cycle are cognitively and communicatively linked. Interrelationships between cognitive processes and communication have been understudied (Hewes, 1995). Nevertheless, based on schema theory (Arbib, Conklin, & Hill, 1987) I propose that starting in early childhood, self, gender, and friendships schemas begin to develop and co-mingle. The co-occurrence and co-mingling of these different and yet overlapping schemas represent the cognitive linkage between cross-sex friendships and views of self. Those cognitive couplings are influenced by communication (Planalp, 1985). Similarly, linkages are also apparent in the communication between friends that serves to build both the relationship (Wood, 1995) and a person's view of self (Coover & Murphy, 2000; Markus & Cross, 1990).

Thus far in the chapter I have previewed my arguments that cross-sex friendships enrich social networks (my first theme), that they are beset by social and structural barriers (my second theme), and that they affect and are affected by an individual's ongoing and socially constructed conception of self (my third theme). In the last two sections of this chapter I present a rationale for taking a life-cycle approach to the study of cross-sex friendships, and I offer a definition of those relationships.

EXPLANATION AND RATIONALE FOR
A LIFE-CYCLE AND DEVELOPMENTAL PERSPECTIVE
ON CROSS-SEX FRIENDSHIPS

Sherman, De Vries, and Lansford noted that life-cycle approaches to the study of friendship are very rare (2000, but see Rawlins, 1992). Life-cycle approaches to the study of cross-sex friendships are practically nonexistent (but see Monsour, 1997). Although there is really nothing simple about it, simply put, a life-cycle approach to the study of cross-sex friendship focuses on how cross-sex friendship experiences (broadly conceived) in earlier stages of life influence cross-sex friendship experiencs in subsequent stages of life. Those experiences encompass everything from the microlevel formation and development of cross-sex friendship and gender schemas, to macrolevel societal and group norms concerning the initiation of such friendships. Macrolevel experience would also include exposure to mass media portrayals of cross-sex friendships (Werking, 1995). Between the micro- and macrolevel experiences, are those on the mesolevel that involve interaction and communication between partners. All three levels of cross-sex friendship experiences affect one another. For example, mass media portrayals of cross-sex friendships (macrolevel) impact cross-sex friendship schemas (microlevel) which in turn impact actual conduct in those friendships (mesolevel).

I am not taking a hard-line, strictly deterministic "epigenetic" approach, but it is an epigenetic perspective nevertheless. According to Lewis and Feiring (1989), epigenetic theorists assume that "there is a direct relationship from one set of earlier social experiences to the next" (p. 248). In regards to cross-sex friendships, I do contend that cross-sex friendship experiences early in life are related to cross-sex friendship experiences later in life. Starting around the age of 2 and continuing throughout life, males and females individually and jointly have cognitive, emotional, social, and cultural experiences that contribute to an overall cross-sex friendship "gestalt."

A life-cycle approach to the study of cross-sex friendship illustrates that they occur in every stage of life and have a demonstrably protean nature (Monsour, 1997). Proteus was a sea god in Greek mythology who could assume different forms. The protean nature of cross-sex friendship reveals itself in a number of ways. Perhaps most important, cross-sex friendships transform themselves to reflect changes in society and to adapt to different developmental demands in each stage of life (Parker & Gottman, 1989). Developmental life-cycle milestones such as puberty, entering and leaving the workforce, marriage (or not getting married), having children (or not), coming out of the closet (or staying in it), and decreased mobility due to old age, have tremendous impact on the frequency, meaning, and viability of cross-sex friendships (Booth & Hess, 1974; Monsour, 1997; Rawlins, 1992; Savin-Williams, 1990; Wright, 1989). Cross-sex friendships change to accommodate different developmental milestones and the changing self-concepts of individuals who comprise those friendships. The self views of individuals change as they go through the life cycle (Damon & Hart, 1988; Labouvie-Vief et al., 1995), and cross-sex friendships change right along with them. Relatedly and reciprocally, as cross-sex friendships change, so do self-views.

There has been almost no attempt to take a developmental approach to the study of cross-sex friendships (Monsour, 1997) or a life-span perspective on communication (Nussbaum & Baringer, 2000). A developmental approach examines how cross-sex friendships develop and change over the life span and how those changes are related to underlying developmental processes. For example, teenagers conduct cross-sex friendships quite differently from their preteen counterparts. Whereas kids in middle childhood for the most part segregate into groups based on their sex (Leaper, 1994a), during the adolescent years those same individuals gravitate toward mixed-sex groupings and dyads (Brown et al., 1994). Those changes in social networks and dyadic composition can be explained by studying cognitive and pubertal developmental processes (Feldman & Elliott, 1990; Sippola & Bukowski, 1999).

There are many ways to view friendship from a developmental perspective (Newcomb & Bagwell, 1996), and a number of those views are employed to varying degrees throughout this book. Friendships may be seen as "developmental necessities," "developmental advantages," and even "developmental hindrances" (Newcomb & Bagwell, 1996). From a developmental necessity view, friendships are believed to be "vital to the acquisition of skills and competencies essential to a child's social, cognitive, and emotional development" (p. 290). The developmental advantage view does not conceptualize friendships as indispensable, but they are certainly beneficial in advancing cognitive, emotional, and social growth. Finally, there is the developmental hindrance view. From that perspective, not particularly championed in the developmental literature (so say Newcomb & Bagwell, 1996), friendships are not only unnecessary for positive developmental outcomes, but may actually hinder the attainment of such outcomes.

Hartup and Stevens contend that adopting a life-cycle perspective on friendship means assuming that friendships have a noticeable and significant impact on developmental outcomes. As developmental changes occur they "trigger" changes in the relationships of the involved individuals (1997). For example, friendships are unavoidably impacted by the developmental changes that accompany old age (Adams & Blieszner, 1989; Nussbaum, Thompson, & Robinson, 1989) and the onset of puberty (Ruble & Martin, 1998). As I examine cross-sex friendships in each stage of the life cycle I employ the conceptual framework developed by Hartup and Stevens (1997). Hartup and Stevens argued that a life-span perspective on friendships involves consideration of what they call "deep and surface structures." Deep structure refers to the broad societal meaning that has been attached to a particular type of relationship (such as cross-sex friendship), while surface structure refers to the social exchanges that occur between relational partners at any given point in time. One way of ascertaining deep structure is by asking individuals about the meaning of cross-sex friendship. Surface structure is determined by observing friendship interaction that tends to reflect and reinforce the underlying deep structure (see a similar analysis by Werking, 1997a, pp. 7–9).

A life-cycle approach to the study of any kind of relationship requires as a point of departure some determination of what the life stages are, what happens in those stages, and when they occur. There is a noticeable lack of consensus in the developmental literature concerning the best way to chronologically divide the life course; with the disagreement on such fundamental points as to what the phases of the life cycle are and when they occur (Rogers, 1982; Santrock, 1983). For example, although there is considerable agreement that adolescence begins with the onset of puberty, pinpointing when adolescence ends and adulthood begins is much more problematic. In the beginning of each chapter I briefly address difficulties associated with delineating the developmental time frame for that stage of life.

Despite a lack of agreement on the best way to chronologically partition the life cycle, the upcoming segmentation of the life course seems reasonable. A survey of the literature on cross-sex friendships from a life-cycle perspective reveals that those friendships occur with varying degrees of frequency during early childhood, middle and late childhood, adolescence, young and middle adulthood, and old age. A version of Santrock's (1983) life-cycle stages was utilized for the purpose of organizing cross-sex friendship studies (see also Monsour, 1997). The chronological time frame adopted for early childhood through adolescence is similar to Kerns (1996) and Parker and Gottman (1989). Early childhood encompasses ages 18 months through 6 years (toddlerhood through first grade); middle and late childhood includes ages 7 through 11 (elementary school years); adolescence spans ages 12 through 17 (middle school and high school); young and middle adulthood covers ages 18 through 34 and 35 through 64, respectively; and old age is any age over 65 years. This organizational scheme facilitates categorization of cross-sex friendship research because it parallels common patterns for entering and leaving the educational system and the workplace, which are the most common locations for cross-sex friendships and cross-sex friendship investigations (Monsour, 1997).

The age parameters given for each stage of the life cycle are rough approximations. Obviously, not all adolescents have become adults by the time they reach 18 or 19 years of age. Similarly, some 7-year-olds are developmentally behind their age cohorts and might be more appropriately placed in early childhood than middle childhood. Finally, some 75-year-olds (in my "older adult" category) may act, feel, and live in a younger way than a 55-year-old (my "middle adult" category).

DEFINING CROSS-SEX FRIENDSHIP

Due partly to the fragmentation of the cross-sex friendship literature (Monsour, 1997), and the inherent difficulty of defining friendship (Fehr, 1996), there is no generally agreed on definition of cross-sex friendship. Fehr noted that "Everyone knows what friendship is—until asked to define it. There are virtually as many definitions of friendship as there are social scientists studying the topic" (1996, p. 5). There is some agreement, however, that a cross-sex friendship is a type of friendship and therefore has many of the same defining characteristics as all friendships (O'Meara, 1989; Rawlins, 1992; Werking, 1997a; Wright, 1989). Defining friendship is therefore a necessary, but possibly not sufficient, condition for defining cross-sex friendship (Monsour, 1997).

Agreeing on a single scholarly or common sense definition of friendship is problematic because of the variations in how people in different life stages conceptualize it (Blieszner & Adams, 1992; Fehr, 1996; Hays, 1988; Tesch, 1989). Additional definitional difficulties arise because friendship may be described in many ways—as casual friendships, close friendships, good friendships, best friendships, and so on. Each type of friendship may bring to mind a different set of defining characteristics. Fehr observed a lack of consensus in the scholarly community concerning an exact definition of friendship (1996). She contended, as do I, that scholarly agreement on a single and precise meaning of friendship is unnecessary and possibly counterproductive because of the restrictive nature of such definitions.

Scholars use a number of methods for defining friendship (for a brief review of those methods see Monsour, 1997). The method I believe has particular merit is the paradigm case approach (Davis & Todd, 1982, 1985; Fehr, 1996; Roberts, 1982). Paradigm case formulations are generated by use of theory, by relying on past research, or by researcher intuition (Davis & Todd, 1985). There is variety among paradigm cases, such as genuine cases, or first cases, but the variant used by Davis and Todd (1982; 1985) is referred to as a *fundamental* or *archetypal case*. This is a case that best exemplifies the essence of the concept but does not need to be statistically frequent. A paradigm case formulation involves the construction of a complex paradigm case of the concept under investigation against which other cases can be recognized as variations of the paradigm case (Fehr, 1996; Ossorio, 1981). Alternative paradigm case formulations of the same concept are "possible because of legitimate differences in purposes and focus" (Davis & Todd, 1982, p. 83). For example, a researcher or theoretician might construct a paradigm case of cross-sex friendship and argue that those friendships have certain defining characteristics as exemplified by the paradigm case. But a different investigator would be well within her or his rights to construct an alternative paradigm case with different defining characteristics.

Although I did not conduct a formal paradigm case analysis in developing my definition of cross-sex friendship, I did adopt the flexibility allowed by that approach. A writer using the paradigm case approach has the freedom to argue that cross-sex friendships may or may not involve sexual attraction, that they may or may not provide insider perspectives, that they may or may not be reciprocal, or they may or may not have any other specific feature of a prototypical cross-sex friendship. That same writer can legitimately question whether a relationship is actually a cross-sex friendship if it is missing a key feature of his or her paradigm case, just as someone else can legitimately question the adequacy of the writer's paradigm case derived definition.

In this book a cross-sex friendship is defined as a voluntary, nonfamilial, nonromantic, relationship between a female and a male in which both individuals label their association as a friendship. In accordance with the spirit of paradigm case formulations, others are free to categorize family and romantic relationships as cross-sex friendships and their conceptualizations would be just as valid as my own. Finally when I use the term *cross-sex* (rather than *opposite-sex, other-sex,* or *cross-gender*) I mean simply, as does Werking (1997a), that the friends are of different biological sexes. I do not necessarily mean to imply that males and females *cross* some boundary between the sexes when they form a friendship, although they might in some cases (see Bukowski, Sippola, & Hoza's 1999 justification for using the term *other-sex* rather than *cross-sex,* p. 440).

Preview of Things to Come.   Each of the next five chapters (chaps. 2 through 6) follow the same organizational format. The three central themes of the book are developed and applied to the stage of life covered in that particular chapter. Although the themes are the same in each chapter, they unfold differently to emphasize the most salient developmental processes occurring in that part of the life cycle. In the final chapter I revisit the themes, summarize the literature, and offer two heuristic models of the relationship between self-concepts and cross-sex friendships.

2

Cross-Sex Friendships in Early Childhood
(18 months to 6 years of age)

The foundations for all adult relationships are laid in childhood.
—Steve Duck (1983, p. 114)

Duck's slightly paraphrased observation has particular relevance to the relational foundation of cross-sex friendships. From a life-cycle perspective, the cross-sex friendships an individual forms or fails to form during early childhood have long-lasting implications for similar friendships throughout life. Those early friendships provide the child with a cross-sex friendship schematic blueprint that guides behavior in subsequent cross-sex friendships. One of the major contentions of this chapter and book is that successful formation of cross-sex friendships early in life increases the probability of having those relationships and their attendant advantages in later stages of the life cycle. Additionally, cross-sex friendships and the quality of those relationships in early childhood impact socially constructed views of self. In turn, those views influence attitudes about cross-sex friendships and behavior in those relationships. These contentions and others are explicated and documented in the four sections of this chapter. The first three sections develop the central themes of the book and relate each theme to early childhood. In the final section I offer some concluding observations about cross-sex friendships in early childhood.

A number of preliminary observations need to be made before moving on to the first theme. In the next few pages I specify the age range encompassed by early childhood and briefly discuss the lack of scholarly agreement concerning the end of infancy and the beginning of toddlerhood. I also identify when cross-sex friendships first emerge and describe two major limitations of the early childhood cross-sex friendship literature.

Although not all developmentalists and friendship scholars agree with me (e.g., in Kerns, 1994, early childhood encompasses ages 3 to 7), for purposes of this book early childhood includes children roughly between 18 months and 6 years of age. This age range focuses attention on toddlers, preschoolers, kindergartners, and first graders. However, because individuals go through developmental stages at different rates (Schiamberg, 1988), some children may still show vestiges of early childhood when they are 7-year-olds and in the second grade (Howe, 1993). Indeed, Parker and Gottman categorize 7-year-olds as being in early childhood (1989). Similarly, some children may be developmentally ahead of the norm and show friendship capabilities before they are 18 months old (Howes, 1988). Individual differences in development are not particularly problematic for friendship researchers as long as we recognize those differences and resist temptations to over-generalize research findings and theoretical speculations.

There is a lack of agreement in the developmental and friendship literature concerning when infancy ends and toddlerhood begins, the importance of which I establish in the next paragraph. To illustrate the lack of consensus I pose the following question: Is a 14-month-old child an infant, a toddler, or both? In Schiamberg's textbook on child and adolescent development infancy includes the toddler period and encompasses ages 1 to 3 years of age (1988). A 14-month-old child is both an infant and a toddler according to Schiamberg's scheme. However, in an excellent chapter written by Rubin, Bukowski, and Parker in the *Handbook of Child Psychology* (1998, p. 633), infancy is identified as the first year of life, and toddlerhood starts approximately after the child's first birthday. A 14-month-old child is a toddler to those authors. However, in that same handbook Harter described infancy as occurring up to the age of 30 months (1998, p. 563), although she uses the term *toddler* when discussing infants in the 18 to 30-month-old category. For Harter, a 14-month old is an infant. For Howes, a well-respected and heavily published early childhood friendship researcher, a 14-month-old is in the second month of "early toddlerhood" (1988).

The apparent lack of agreement among scholars on when infancy ends and toddlerhood begins is important for several reasons. First, if children between the ages of 12 and 18 months are considered infants, rather than toddlers, then research documenting friendships in that age group (e.g., Howes, 1988; but note that she does not consider 12-month-olds as infants) implies that infants are more developmentally advanced than commonly assumed. Second, as a practical matter, developmentalists and friendship researchers will sometimes use the terms *infancy* and *toddlerhood* without clearly specifying when one ends and the other begins, making it difficult for interested readers to compare results and theoretical conclusions. Children of a particular age may be categorized as "toddlers" by one researcher and "infants" by another. The determination as to whether a child is an infant or a toddler should not be based on the age of the child, but rather on his or her level of cognitive, physical, and social development (Rubin et al., 1998). For example, one common sense marker of the transition from infancy to toddlerhood is that toddlers can walk, whereas infants can not. The increased mobility that walking affords makes friendship initiation an easier task than it might be for an infant who is confined to crawling.

Determining when infancy ends and toddlerhood begins is clearly relevant to the initial emergence of friendships. When do individuals form their first friendships? Infants by 6 to 9 months notice one another as indicated by mutual smiles and vocalizations (Hay, Pedersen, & Nash, 1982; Raymond, 2000). On the other hand, infant peer associations in the first 12 months of life typically lack characteristics indicative of relationships such as multiple, sustained interactions and reciprocity in social overtures (Hartup, 1983; Whaley & Rubenstein, 1994). Due to the absence of those relationship characteristics, infant peer associations in the first year of life are considered relationships in only a "nebulous sense" (Whaley & Rubenstein, 1994). However, friendship scholars apparently recognize that some infants are developmentally ahead of the norm and show the first signs of friendship before the onset of toddlerhood (Bukowski, Newcomb, & Hartup, 1996; see Howes, 1996, for a indirect treatment of that possibility). As noted by Bukowski, Newcomb, and Hartup "Mutually regulated ' friendships' can be identified among infants and toddlers, too, although the cognitive and linguistic concomitants of these relationships are not always obvious" (1996, p. 1). As I reviewed the literature on the initial emergence of friendships it became obvious that friendship researchers were hesitant to argue that friendship as a developmental phenomenon begins before children have their first birthday.

Things change in the second year of life. Children between the ages of 1 and 2 begin to notice regularities in interaction, and they use those regularities as guidelines for interaction (Miller, 1993). They also move from interpersonal contact centered around objects to more coordinated interchanges (Mueller & Lucas, 1975; Schiamberg, 1988). Interactions during the second year of life become progressively more complex and closer to what observers might consider friendship behavior (Howes, 1996). Howes (1988) documents that children as young as 12 to 18 months (whom she categorized as toddlers) establish friendships. By their second birthday children display advanced relationship building skills such as role reversal during play (Howes, 1996).

Identifying infancy (newborn to 12 months) rather than toddlerhood (1 to 3 years) as the developmental stage when friendships first emerge is potentially problematic and not without controversy. Hartup observes "Specifying an age when friendship first becomes visible in social interaction is extremely difficult" (1989, p. 47). Because infants/toddlers develop friendship and social skills in peer interaction simultaneously (Howes & Matheson, 1992), there is a problem determining if those early peer interactions represent the initial, behavioral manifestations of friendship, or whether those behaviors merely reflect the child's evolving social skills. Hinde (1979) and Howes (1996) have underscored the possibility that researchers might mistake emerging social skills of very young children as indications of friendship. For example, just because an 18-month-old has developmentally progressed from parallel play to interactive play does not necessarily mean he or she is engaging in friendship behavior. On the other hand, I believe it is equally plausible that scholars might label interactive behaviors as merely emerging social skills and mistakenly discount the possibility that those behaviors also represent the beginnings of friendship. How do researchers determine if interactions between extremely young children constitute friendship?

In order to conclude that the dyadic behavior of infants or toddlers constitutes a friendship one must be able to observe manifestations of friendship features such as intimacy and companionship (Howes, 1996; Rubin et al., 1998). Companionship is shown when infants or toddlers show a marked preference for spending time together and being in proximity. As noted by Howes, "There is a long research tradition of using preference or proximity as the definitive criterion for defining friendship ... when children prefer particular partners either by seeking them out for interaction or by maintaining proximity, the children are judged to be friends" (1996, p. 70). Along those lines, researchers have documented the tendency of children from 12 to 30 months to show preferential treatment toward a particular peer in their social group (Lee, 1973; Ross & Lollis, 1989). Well-acquainted children can engage in complementary and reciprocal games by 13 to 15 months of age (Howes, 1996). Sixty-eight percent of the children between the ages of 1 and 2 had what Howes considered to be reciprocal friendships (i.e., dyadic relationships in which both partners demonstrate mutual preference for and enjoyment of one another's company; 1988).

In summary, there is growing agreement among childhood friendship experts that children between the ages of 1 and 2 are willing, likely, and capable of forming friendships (Bullock, 1993; Howes, 1996; Rubin et al., 1998; Whaley & Rubenstein, 1994). Depending on how one defines infancy and friendship (which are major issues), even some infants form friendships. Those relationships may not be as sophisticated and intricate as the friendships of older toddlers and preschoolers, but they nonetheless display friendship characteristics. By the age of 3 or 4 the word *friend* has become part of a child's working vocabulary (Bukowski, Newcomb, Hartup, 1996; Erwin, 1998; Mannarino, 1980). Although using the word *friend* does not necessarily mean that a child knows what that word means, that usage at least shows that the label for the concept is available (Duck, personal communication, October 17, 2000). Along similar lines, from a social constructivist perspective "friendly" interaction between children at a very young age helps those children develop cognitive models of friendship before the word friend becomes part of their working vocabulary (Howes, 1996; Vygotsky, 1978; Yingling, 1994).

In addition to confusion over when infancy ends and toddlerhood begins, I encountered at least two limitations of the early childhood cross-sex friendship literature. First, very few researchers focus on those friendships, despite suggestions made by prominent scholars to increase the number of cross-sex friendship investigations (e.g., Bukowski et al., 1996). A second limitation of the literature was the quite persistent problem of researchers failing to distinguish between same-sex friendships and their cross-sex counterparts (e.g., Howes, Droege, & Matheson, 1994; Ladd, 1990; Ladd, Price, & Hart, 1988; Ladd, Kochenderfer, & Coleman, 1996; Park & Waters, 1989; Park, Lay, & Ramsay, 1993; Youngblade & Belsky, 1992). For example, Ladd and his associates examined the best friend relationships of 82 kindergartners to determine whether children's perceptions of those friendships were associated with their adjustment during the transition to first grade (1996). No information was given about the sex of the nominated best friends and no rationale was provided for the exclusion of that information. Such information might have been useful considering Gottman's belief that cross-sex friendships in that age group have a uniquely intimate quality (1986). Similarly, no real attempt was made to distinguish between same-sex and cross-sex friendships in Newcomb and Bagwell's impressive and often-cited meta-analytic review of childhood friendship studies (1995).

Cross-Sex Friendships and the Enrichment of Social Networks During Early Childhood

There is growing agreement among scholars that early childhood friendships are developmentally significant; although many of those same scholars admit that pinpointing the exact nature of that significance is problematic (e.g., Hartup, 1996a; Newcomb & Bagwell, 1995). Hartup argues that the kind and degree of developmental significance is often determined by the "identity of the child's friends and the quality of the relationships between them" (p. 10). Certainly, an important aspect of identity is a child's biological sex (Harter, 1998) and whether that sex is different from that of his or her friend.

One way of establishing developmental significance is through documentation of the generic and unique benefits provided by cross-sex friendships in early childhood. Before doing so, however, an important point needs to be acknowledged concerning benefits of cross-sex friendships in early childhood. Indeed, the point applies to friendships of all types in every stage of life. Friendships do not always lead to good things and can be costly endeavors (Bukowski et al., 1996, p. 10; Fehr, 1996). Early childhood cross-sex friendships are no exception. Although cross-sex friendships provide a number of benefits to participants in early childhood, those friendships can also have a downside. In the section on social and structural barriers to cross-sex friendships I identify some of the disadvantages of having friends of the other sex.

Generic Benefits.   Recall that generic benefits are benefits that can be supplied by both cross-sex and same-sex friends. The addition of a cross-sex friend to a child's social network enriches that network in much the same way as adding a same-sex friend. Many of the benefits that a child receives in a same-sex friendship, such as helping, intimacy, social comparison, and shared fantasies, are also available in cross-sex friendships (Ginsberg, Gottman, & Parker, 1986; Gottman, 1986; Howes, Droege, & Matheson, 1994; Whaley & Rubenstein, 1994). Early childhood friendships provide participants with enjoyment, companionship, social support, and a testing ground for the development of social skills imperative for a variety of other types of social relationships (Erwin, 1998; Howes, 1996). Friendships also give young children an opportunity to gain experience in encoding and decoding emotional displays (Howes, 1988; Parker & Gottman, 1989).

The primary generic benefit of having cross-sex friendships in early childhood is that those friendships can be a crucial source of social support. Social support involves interactions in which one or both friends provide affect, aid, or affirmation (Crohan & Antonucci, 1989). Studies have shown that cross- and same-sex friends in early childhood provide one another with positive emotional support and companionship (i.e., affect: Whaley & Rubenstein, 1994; Howes et al., 1994; Park, Lay, & Ramsay, 1993; Rizzo, 1989), aid (Rizzo, 1989; Whaley & Rubenstein, 1994), and ego affirmation (Ladd et al., 1996; 1997; Lewis & Feiring, 1989; Whaley & Rubenstein, 1994). Based upon his classic ethnographic study of first-grade friendships, Rizzo concluded "I observed often in the interactions among first-grade friends displays of reciprocal helping, sharing, ego reinforcement, loyalty (providing psycho social support), intimacy, and discovering and developing common interests" (1989, p. 117). Additional evidence of social support was revealed in Newcomb and Bagwell's meta-analytic review of childhood friendship studies. They concluded that friendships in childhood, unlike other types of peer relationships, provide supportive contexts for social, emotional, and cognitive growth (1995). Newcomb and Bagwell nevertheless judged that the "jury remains out" in regards to painting a complete picture of the developmental significance of children's friendships (1996, p.318).

A qualitative, one-year longitudinal study conducted by Whaley and Rubenstein of four toddler friendships is particularly insightful in showing how cross-sex friendships can enrich a young child's social network through the provision of social support (1994). I make note of the qualitative and longitudinal nature of the study because each methodological wrinkle adds strength to the study. Qualitative approaches are useful because they typically entail the accumulation of large amounts of descriptive data which are necessary for the development of theory (Berscheid & Peplau, 1983). The use of longitudinal designs in the study of friendship has been touted by a number of friendship researchers (e.g., Griffin & Sparks, 1990; Newcomb & Bagwell, 1996) because longitudinal studies are better able to track developmental changes in friendship than are cross-sectional investigations.

Several of the friendship dimensions inspected by Whaley and Rubenstein can be viewed from a social support perspective: *similarity* shows affirmation; *helping* and *sharing* shows aid; and *intimacy* shows affect. Two of the four friendships were cross-sex relationships between children 2 to 3 years old. Like their same-sex counterparts, the friendships of "Jed and Beth" and "Jed and Carly" displayed affection, loyalty, and work to sustain their relationships—enviable qualities for even adult friendships. When Jed's friend Beth could no longer continue daycare on a regular basis, Jed "roamed the room, frequently hitting others and playing alone rather than with other children" (p. 396). An interesting manifestation of affect possibly not seen in other stages of life, is what Whaley and Rubenstein referred to as *companionable silence*. In these interactions two children would lay close to one another, separate from the rest of the class, and mirror one another's nonverbals although not interacting verbally.

Another important manifestation of emotional support between friends in early childhood is gossip (Gottman, 1986). The function of gossip changes as the life cycle progresses (Gottman & Mettetal, 1986), but in early childhood its main purpose is to build solidarity (Gottman, 1986). Gossip in this stage of life is usually in the form of "we against others" and consist of "brief comments made in the context of play" (Gottman, 1986, p. 166). Interestingly, Gottman contended that gossip among preschoolers might be a precursor of self-disclosure, which presents an opportunity for another form of emotional support. Although never specifically documented to my knowledge, one can easily imagine a scenario in which first graders gossip about others in their social network who have teased them about their friendship. Such gossip would increase solidarity and help to create the perception of a shared reality.

One of the most obvious generic advantages of cross-sex friendships in early childhood is that they provide participants with someone to play with. Having a playmate is very important to young children (Rawlins, 1992). Indeed, Gottman contended that coordinated play is the central manifestation of peer interaction among children approximately 3 to 7 years old (1986). Park and her associates conducted a 1-year longitudinal study of same- and cross-sex best friends and documented that coordinated play increased over the year and was a major part of the interaction patterns of 4- and 5-year-olds (Park, Lay, Ramsay, 1993). Unfortunately, Park and colleagues did not distinguish between same- and cross-sex best friends. Coordinated play among cross- and same-sex friends involves self-disclosure, often done in the context of fantasy play (Gottman, 1986). Gottman documented a higher level of self-disclosure among 4-year-old cross-sex friends than among their same-sex counterparts (1986). Parker and Gottman argued that close examination of the themes of pretend play reveal that children use pretend play as a way of disclosing information about themselves that they may lack the conversational skills to otherwise reveal (1989; see also Howes, Matheson, & Wu, 1992).

Another generic benefit of friendships in early childhood, a corollary to the social support benefit, is that friendships serve as a buffer against loneliness (Burgess et al., 1999). Contemporary loneliness scholars agree that loneliness begins at an early age (Perlman & Landolt, 1999) and can be quite disturbing for young children who suffer from it (Asher & Parker, 1989; Erwin, 1998). Some experts even speculate that loneliness might be present during infancy (e.g., Parkhurst & Hopmeyer, 1999). Cassidy and Asher reported that about 10% of the 5- to 7-year-old children ($n = 440$) in their study felt very lonely or dissatisfied with their peer relationships at school (1992). Forty-six of the children were interviewed to probe further into their understanding of the loneliness concept. Nearly all of the children understood loneliness.

Burgess and colleagues drew the following conclusions in their review chapter on loneliness during early childhood:

> Thus, although only a small corpus of evidence has been assembled on the relation between young children's friendships and loneliness, the findings are consistent with the proposition that early friendships, because of the largely supportive provisions they can offer, inhibit feelings of loneliness. (1999, p. 114)

For example, in Corsaro's classic nursery school study of 3- and 4-year-olds he discovered that relationships served a very specific function: They helped children gain entry into playgroups, thus combating social loneliness (1985). In the earlier example of Jed and Beth's toddler cross-sex friendship, Jed was often observed playing alone once Beth had to leave the daycare center. Other early childhood friendship investigations have focused on friendship processes such as self-disclosure, aid, and validation that directly and indirectly block feelings of loneliness (Ladd, Kochenderfer, & Coleman, 1996; Parker & Gottman, 1989).

The relationship between loneliness and friendships in early childhood is complex. Although friendship features have been found to be correlated negatively with loneliness for young children (Coleman, 1993; Ladd et al., 1997), friendships can also exasperate loneliness. Early childhood friendships differ in quality, and friendships characterized by higher difficulty and less support may actually foster feelings of loneliness (Burgess et al., 1999). Burgess and her associates also contend that different kinds of relational partners and processes in early childhood influence loneliness. Specifically, friendships, peer-group acceptance, peer victimization, parents, and teachers, are each related to loneliness in distinct yet overlapping ways. What is clearly lacking from their analysis and other studies I surveyed is an explication of whether the sex composition of the friendship at such an early age has any noticeable impact on the dynamics of loneliness.

Unique Benefits. There are a number of unique and interrelated benefits available in cross-sex friendships during early childhood. Those benefits originate from the other-sex companionship made available in cross-sex friendships, companionship not possible in same-sex relationships. In this section I review evidence establishing that cross-sex friendships offer young children an opportunity to obtain an insider's perspective, to better understand members of the other sex and their culture, and to learn new ways of interacting. Although these benefits are available in later stages of the life cycle they take on added significance when a child is very young and developing initial beliefs about him or herself, cross-sex friendships, and members of the other sex.

Furnishing an insider's perspective on how members of the other sex think, feel, and behave has been recognized and well-documented as one of the unique advantages of adult cross-sex friendships (Monsour, 1997). However, the role of insider perspectives in early childhood development and cross-sex friendships has been virtually ignored. Although an insider's perspective is important to have as an adult (Werking, 1997a), it becomes even more valuable if made available at an early age so it can be incorporated into a child's developing gender schema. As soon as a child is able to differentiate between the sexes, usually around the age of 2 or 3 (Leinbach & Fagot, 1986; Martin, Fabes, Evans, & Wyman, 1999;), insider perspectives become relevant. Obviously, a 4-year-old may not be consciously aware that he or she is getting an insider's perspective from a cross-sex friend, but that lack of awareness should not prevent the information from being incorporated into the child's developing gender schema. As noted by Andersen (1993), information can become part of a person's relational schema without him or her being aware of it. However, the extent to which young children between the ages of 2 to 6 understand abstract manifestations of friendship like insider perspectives (e.g., "my friend tells me what it is like to be a boy/girl"), is debatable (Bigelow & LaGaipa, 1975).

A second unique advantage of cross-sex friendships in early childhood is clearly connected to the first. As a result of sex segregation and divergent socialization practices, girls and boys grow up in different worlds or cultures, so different that each group develops its own way of viewing reality and interacting in it (Corsaro, 1985; Leaper, 1994a; Maccoby, 1994; Rizzo, 1989). Maccoby contended that the segregated play groups that form for boys and girls at an early age exert powerful socializing effects. Boys and girls each develop and reinforce norms within their respective gender groups concerning appropriate behavior for their sex. Those sex-typed modes of interaction influence cross-sex relationships later on in adolescence and adulthood (Maccoby,1990). Leaper commented on and extended Maccoby's analysis when he observed "I shall argue that the patterns of behavior traditionally associated with girls' and boys' same-sex peer groups reflect differences in the expression of affiliation (interpersonal closeness, expressiveness) and assertion (independence, instrumentality) ..." (1994b, p. 68). Different norms that become progressively sex-typed in nature develop in the different gender groups concerning how and when to express affiliation and assertiveness.

After reviewing a number of studies focusing primarily on male and female preferences for different comforting strategies and ways of providing emotional support, Kunkel and Burleson concluded that there was no support for any predictions generated from the different cultures perspective (1998; see also Burleson, Kunkel, Samter, & Werking, 1996). On the other hand, however, they did acknowledge that there are significant differences between the sexes in certain aspects of their comforting behavior. As they noted:

> There is, then, a complex pattern of gender-related similarities and differences with respect to varied features of emotional support ... men and women both value the same things, see the same things as providing comfort, and prefer seeking comfort from females. Women, however, are more likely than men to provide comfort and use the message forms experienced as comforting. (p. 117)

As an alternative to the different cultures perspective they advocate their "skill deficit or skill specialization account." In their account they identify different social skills of boys and girls as originating from their different socialization experiences. So for example, girls are socialized and encouraged to a greater extent than boys to express and manage emotions. Boys are socialized and encouraged to a greater extent than girls to try to influence and direct the activities of others.

In line with the skill specialization account (Kunkel & Burleson, 1998), cross-sex friendships in early childhood provide participants with an opportunity to learn new ways of interacting. Those friendships can have powerful socializing effects on participants in much the same way as do sex segregated groups. Those socializing effects foster the acquisition of cross-sex interaction skills and understanding. Just as individuals learn norms and styles of interaction as they become socialized into groups comprised of members of their own sex (Serbin, Gulko, Powlishta, & Colburne, 1994; Smith & Inder, 1993), girls and boys in cross-sex friendships can learn different norms and behavioral styles. Cross-sex friendships can counteract the sex-typed behavior developed and reinforced in groups segregated by sex. How might this be done?

Research on early childhood friendships reveals that children construct and emphasize dyadic verbal and nonverbal similarity (Corsaro, 1985; Rizzo, 1989; Whaley & Rubenstein, 1994). Young friends model themselves after one another and in so doing learn new social skills, behavioral styles, and ways of viewing the world. Although modeling behavior of this type begins at an early age, friends of any age can learn from one another. There is some indirect evidence suggesting a connection between cross-sex friendships in early childhood and the acquisition of social skills (e.g., Howes, 1988; Serbin, Moller, Gulko, Powlishta, & Colburne, 1994, 1994). For example, Serbin and her associates concluded from their study of 2- and 3-year-olds that sex segregated toddlers are more behaviorally sex-typed than toddlers who freely interact with both sexes (1994). What is difficult to assess, however, is whether sex segregation leads to an increase in sex-typed behaviors, or whether sex-typed behaviors leads to sex segregation, or whether it is some combination of the two as Serbin and her colleagues suspected.

Howes studied social skills exhibited in play patterns of early toddlers (ages 12 to 23 months, $n = 34$) late toddlers (2- and 3-year-olds, $n = 99$), and pre-schoolers (4- to 6-year-olds, $n = 196$) who had or did not have cross-sex friends. Friends were identified and defined based on observations of play patterns. Howes concluded "Children in all three age groups who had cross-sex friendships engaged in more social play and showed more positive affect than did children without cross-sex friendships … these friendships may permit children greater access to diverse play groups, thus giving them the opportunity to practice social interaction skills" (1988, pp. 35–36). Howes offers a number of possible explanations why children with cross-sex friends might be more socially skilled than those without such friendships, but she does not specifically contend that they learn those expanded social skills from one another.

Adequately addressing the unique advantages of cross-sex friendships in early childhood would be difficult to do without acknowledging the pioneering research conducted by Gottman and associates during the 1980s. Gottman observed "It is my impression that, up to about age 7, cross-sex best friendships are very intense emotional relationships, not unlike some marriages" (1986, p. 156). Gottman's observation should not be taken lightly; especially considering his widely acknowledged expertise and research on marital relationships (Gottman, 1979; Gottman, Coan, Carrere, & Swanson, 1998; Kantrowitz & Wingert, 1999). He believed that cross-sex friendships among preschoolers have a uniquely intimate quality. Like many marriages, they contain a wide range of negative and positive emotions. Indeed, a common fantasy theme for young cross-sex friends is to pretend they are married (Gottman, 1986). Gottman bolstered his argument regarding the uniqueness of cross-sex friendships by citing Sherman's (1975) research on "glee." Glee is almost exclusively a cross-sex phenomenon among preschoolers, but clearly Sherman's 1975 research needs to be updated. The closeness exhibited in these friendships lends credence to the 55-year-old contention of Gesell that 3-year-olds often have a preference for members of the other sex (1945).

In summary, the studies reviewed in this section suggest that cross-sex friendships enrich the social networks of young children by providing them with relationships that broaden their interpersonal competencies and prepare them for a life of cross-sex interactions. Cross-sex friendships are particularly advantageous at a young age when social skills and gender schemas are just developing. When young children are given opportunities to play with members of both sexes, they are exposed to a wide range of behavioral practices and learn to appreciate the similarities and differences between boys and girls (Leaper, 1994b). Interactions in these early relationships can be instrumental in teaching toddlers and pre-schoolers how to be friends with members of the other sex further down the developmental road as children become adolescents and adults (Leaper, 1994b; Serbin et al., 1994; Whaley & Rubenstein, 1994; Yingling, 1994).

Structural and Social Barriers to Cross-Sex Friendships During Early Childhood

Social and structural barriers to cross-sex friendship formation in early childhood emanate from a variety of individuals in a child's social milieu such as parents, siblings, peers, friends, teachers, and daycare providers (Leaper, 1994b; Lewis & Feiring, 1989; Rawlins, 1992; Rubin, 1980). Social barriers can also originate from the friendship itself as young girls and boys struggle to communicate and connect. Throughout this section keep in mind that social and structural barriers to cross-sex friendship formation and maintenance are commonly intertwined. Structural barriers are closely akin to social barriers; often perpetuating or being perpetuated by those social impediments. For example, when verbal teasing (a social barrier) prohibits a cross-sex individual from entering a group comprised of members of the other sex, that prohibition puts structural constraints on the potential for cross sex interaction and subsequent friendship formation. Similarly, gender segregation (i.e., separation of individuals based on their biological sex, Leaper, 1994a) should be viewed as both a structural and a social barrier to cross-sex friendship because there are often social reasons (e.g., fear of being teased) for separating into gender based groups.

Before proceeding, a brief aside about nomenclature is in order. My use of the term *gender segregation* instead of *sex segregation* is deliberate. Although some scholars understandably distinguish between *biological sex* and *gender* (see Canary & Dindia's edited 1998 volume on gender and sex differences in communication), the separation of individuals based on their biological sex is routinely labeled by prominent experts as gender segregation (e.g., Fagot, 1994; Leaper, 1994b; Maccoby, 1994; Maccoby & Jacklin, 1987; Moller & Serbin, 1996; Serbin et al., 1994). So for purposes of this book, *gender* segregation refers to the separation of individuals based on their biological sex, rather than the separation of individuals based on different socialization histories and practices which is what the term *gender* might imply. Indeed, some scholars specializing in gender issues define gender as "the biological sex of the individual" (e.g., Cosse, 1992, p. 6). Similarly, when I make statements such as "Boys and girls are socialized into different gender groups," I mean that boys and girls are socialized into groups comprised primary of members of their own sex.

Social Barriers.   Social barriers to cross-sex friendship exist only minimally for children roughly 2 to 4 years of age. However, at some point in the developmental history of most children (around 2 to 4 years old) a preference for same-sex friendship and same-sex interaction slowly evolves, and give rise to social barriers to cross-sex friendships (Fagot & Leinbach, 1993; Maccoby, 1994). As previewed in chapter one, social barriers to cross-sex friendships often take the form of normative constraints (Wright, 1989). Perhaps the most prevalent norm of this type is the homosocial norm (i.e., the preference to spend time with members of one's own sex; Rose, 1985). The homosocial norm is an excellent example of the interplay between social and structural barriers and is particularly relevant to early childhood because it is there that the norm is first manifested. The preference to associate with members of one's own sex becomes a social barrier to cross-sex friendships when that preference is verbally reinforced by members of the child's social network and/or the child him or herself. The norm is so firmly entrenched in our society that it has structural ramifications. For example, social network structure, which is a contextual/structural feature impacting friendship formation (Adams & Allan, 1998), is influenced by the homosocial norm. An individual's social network reflects same-sex preferences and subsequently reduces structural opportunities for cross-sex interaction and friendship initiation.

Lipman-Blumen contended that the homosocial norm results from the promotion of homosocial behavior in early childhood and societal valuation of men over women (1976). Those two factors lead to the stratification of women and men in society in ways that give men access to more resources than women (Wright, 1989). Access to more resources and power could put males in a structural position for making more friends than their less powerful female counterparts (Adams & Blieszner, 1994). Commenting on Lipman-Blumen's analysis, Rose stated "Due to the encouragement of same-sex interactions among children, same-sex friendships may come to constitute a prototype for friendship by middle childhood or adolescence which is used to evaluate cross-sex interactions" (p. 64). The "prototype" referred to by Rose emanates from the deep structure of society and is revealed in surface level communicative manifestations of that structure (Hartup & Stevens, 1997). Although the homosocial norm does not begin to materialize until around the age of 3, by the age of 6 or 7 it is firmly in place with the vast majority of children openly preferring the company of same-sex others (Maccoby, 1994).

Social barriers to early childhood cross-sex friendships also take the form of relationship norms that regulate interaction between girls and boys and discourage the formation of cross-sex friendships. A relationship norm is a formal or informal guideline or rule establishing what kinds of relationships are permissible and the range of behaviors that are acceptable within those relationships. Relationship norms often originate from deep structure and are used to regulate behavior in relationships (Hartup & Stevens, 1997). Those norms, however, may be changed or negotiated in specific relationships as the deep structure is manifested as surface structure (Hartup & Stevens, 1997; Werking, 1997a). Relational norms are similar if not identical in meaning to relationship rules (Felmlee, 1999) that establish guidelines for acceptable thoughts, emotions, and behaviors in relationships (Argyle & Henderson, 1985; Bigelow, Tesson, & Lewko, 1996; Wood, 1995). From a "standard rule account" (Midwinter, 1992), "Knowing a rule is not only to know what one should do, but it also gives one some grounds for expectations one may have of the behavior of other people who accept the rule" (Harre & Secord, 1972, p. 183).

Relational norms and rules in cross-sex friendships often have relational expectations embedded in them which lead to the formation or dissolution of relationships (Felmlee, 1999). The norms and rules that exist in adult cross-sex friendship might have their origins in early childhood friendships, but I was unable to discover research investigating that possibility. Structurally, rules can facilitate or constrain certain types of interaction and communication. Following or deviating from relational norms and rules could put a person in a situation conducive or counterproductive to the formation of friendships. Rules serve as social barriers when individuals or groups orally impose the rules on others.

Similar to their adult counterparts, rules also govern the friendships of children (Bigelow, Tesson, & Lewko, 1996; Corsaro, 1985; Pataki, Shapiro, & Clark, 1994; Rizzo, 1989; Yingling, 1994). From Yingling's study of the conversations of 11 pairs of friends ages 3 to 10 she concluded that children within individual friendships cocreate friendship rules through interaction. Unfortunately, only one of the 11 friendships was a cross-sex relationship. Rizzo conducted an observational 5-month study of 16 children (8 boys and 8 girls) ranging in age from 6 to 7 and a half years (1989). Adopting a symbolic interactionist perspective (Mead, 1934), Rizzo surmised from his observations that first graders have a detailed knowledge of the rules of interaction and use those rules to guide their behavior with other children (1989; p. 123).

A potentially powerful impediment to cross-sex friendship formation in early childhood are the relationship norms and rules that accompany group membership. Verbal expression of group norms against cross-sex friendships constitute social barriers to friendship formation, whereas group membership itself is more accurately characterized as a structural barrier. Peer relationships between the ages of 3 and 6 are characterized by the formation of groups and attempts to include and exclude others from those groups (Corsaro, 1985; Martin et al., 1999; Rubin, 1980; Sims, Hutchins, & Taylor, 1998). In Corsaro's observational and longitudinal study of nursery school children (ages 3 to 4) he concluded that children are primarily concerned with social participation and protection of their interactive space. Protection of interactive space by a dyad or small group is often accomplished through employment of arbitrary rules, school rules, and social rules of pretend play. Arbitrary rules were sometimes related to characteristics of the child attempting entry into the group such as sex, size, dress, and so on. Corsaro noted "There was one pattern regarding sexual makeup of groups, sex of the child attempting access, and rate of resistance. While the rate of resistance was approximately 50% for access attempts by boys and girls to all girl groups and mixed groups, and for boys' access attempts to all boy groups, the rate of resistance was 75% for girls access attempts to all boys' groups" (p. 127).

Group membership is frequently dictated by obvious physical similarities among group members and potential group members (Rubin, 1980). The most obvious physical characteristic is an individual's sex. Additionally, girls and boys quickly learn that certain activities, behaviors, and interests are more appropriate for one sex than the other. This inculturation encourages a kind of in-group/out-group mentality among young children barely out of diapers (Martin et al., 1999; Rubenstein & Rubin, 1984; Yee & Brown, 1994). Leaper contended, for example, that girls encourage social sensitivity in their groups that tends to foster interpersonal closeness (1994b). Boys encourage competition and dominance, which tends to bring about individual assertiveness more than affiliation. The different ways that boys and girls characteristically behave could serve as social barriers because children, at least according to the behavioral compatibility hypothesis (Goodenough, 1934), prefer to play with others with similar behavioral styles.

Being ostracized, teased, or looked down on for having friends of the other sex is another social barrier to cross-sex friendships. Just how early these problems begin is difficult to pinpoint because of the scarcity of research in the area. As Rickleman documented decades ago, ostracization is so strong by the age of 7 that children hide their cross-sex friendships from other peers and go "underground" (1981). Additional research conducted in the 80's indicates that once a child enters the first grade he or she is at risk of being teased by peers for showing even a friendly interest in a child of the other sex (Best, 1983; Thorne & Luria, 1986). Research has also shown that as children get older they have increasingly negative attitudes toward peers who establish cross-sex friendships (Carter & McCloskey, 1984) and who display cross-gender behavioral characteristics (Erwin, 1998; Golombok & Fivush, 1994). In a recent study of 184 children between the ages of 41 and 82 months, most children believed that peers would be more likely to approve of their behavior if they were to play with same-sex, rather than cross-sex, others (Martin et al., 1999). Research by Yee and Brown revealed that when young children were asked how they "felt" about the different sexes they typically had more positive feelings about their own sex (1994).

In summary, playmate and friendship preferences of children before the age of 2 or 3 do not appear to be determined by a child's biological sex (Maccoby, 1994; Serbin et al., 1994). The absence of a noticeable, persistent, and pronounced same-sex friendship or play partner preference lessens the likelihood of social barriers being erected by the potential friends themselves or their peers. Social barriers to cross-sex friendship exist only minimally for children roughly

2 to 4 years of age. However, at some point in the developmental history of most children (around 2 to 4 years old) a preference for same-sex interaction and same-sex friendship slowly evolves and gives rise to social barriers to cross-sex friendships (Fagot & Leinbach, 1993; Maccoby, 1994).

Structural Barriers. The most obvious, powerful, and well documented (albeit indirectly) structural barrier to cross-sex friendship formation in early and middle childhood is gender segregation (Fagot, 1994). Conversely, gender desegregation in adolescence has an equally pronounced effect on cross-sex friendship facilitation (Sippola, 1999). In this section I devote considerable attention to gender segregation and will revisit the phenomenon in the next two chapters. In the upcoming pages I define and describe gender segregation, explain its relevance to cross-sex friendship formation, and present two theoretical explanations of why gender segregation occurs.

Recall that gender segregation is the voluntary and involuntary separation of individuals based on their biological sex (Leaper, 1994a; Moller & Serbin, 1996). Involuntary gender segregation in early childhood occurs when adults separate children based on their biological sex. Parents, daycare providers, and teachers may intentionally or unintentionally structure environments so that preschoolers have little opportunity for cross-sex interaction (Erwin, 1998; Lewis & Feiring, 1989; Monsour, 1997; Rubin, 1980). Voluntary gender segregation in early childhood is when children physically separate of their own volition into same-sex groups and dyads.

When does voluntary gender segregation begin to emerge, (i.e., when do children first begin to separate into groups or dyads comprised exclusively of members of their own sex?) The separation of girls and boys into same-sex dyads and groups does not occur overnight. Gender segregation begins in preschool and gradually intensifies during early and middle childhood (Leaper, 1994a; Martin et al., 1999). As Maccoby stated:

> Beginning sometime during the third or fourth year of life children more and more prefer to play with members of their own sex. The growing preference has been well documented in a wide variety of cultures and settings. What are not well understood are the causes and consequences of this powerful phenomenon of childhood. (1994, p. 87)

Voluntary, conscious, and deliberate gender segregation cannot occur until children have the ability to distinguish one sex from the other, which occurs around the age of 2 or 3 (Maccoby, 1994). Martin speculated that gender segregation may be set in motion as soon as boys and girls can tell the difference between the sexes. However, as she and her colleagues pointed out (Martin et al., 1999), researchers have not yet been able to link toddler gender segregation to their gender schemas. That implies they may segregate for some reason other than their perception of differences between boys and girls (Moller & Serbin, 1996). Moller and Serbin contend that gender segregation does not occur as soon as children recognize differences between the sexes, but rather once they realize that one's gender is constant and does not change (1996). In Corsaro's ethnographic study of 3- and 4-year olds he noticed a clear difference between the two age groups. The younger children tended to view members of the other sex as just playmates, not "boy" or "girl" playmates. The 4-year-olds, however, differentiated their same-sex playmates from their cross-sex ones, and by the end of the school year this recognition of gender differences impacted the way the children related to one another (1985). The 4-year-old children showed knowledge of appropriate sex-typed behavior and demonstrated tendencies to both approach and avoid other-sex peers.

Although the existence of gender segregation is well documented (Leaper, 1994a; Maccoby, 1990), the impact it has on cross-sex friendship formation and maintenance is not. Scholars have ignored the significance of gender segregation to cross-sex friendship formation in early childhood. Rather, they have focused their energies on other consequences and causes of gender segregation in childhood (Leaper, 1994a). But gender segregation is obviously and unquestionably related to cross-sex friendship initiation and maintenance because when girls and boys are physically separated the opportunity for friendship formation is seriously challenged (O'Meara, 1994). As succinctly summarized by Fagot (1994): "One concern with gender segregation throughout childhood is that boys and girls will meet in adolescence virtually as strangers, having learned different styles of interaction and coping skills" (p. 62). As will be seen in the upcoming chapters on middle childhood (chap. 3) and adolescence (chap. 4), Fagot's concern is well founded.

Researchers have indirectly established a connection between gender segregation and cross-sex friendships (e.g., Howes, 1988; Moller & Serbin, 1996; Serbin et al., 1994). Howes divided a sample of 329 children into three age groups. Sixty-eight percent of the youngest group (ages 12 to 23 months) had cross-sex friends, compared to 30% of children in the late toddler group (ages 2 to 3 years), and only 16% of those in the preschool group (ages 4 to 6). In a study investigating the initial emergence of gender segregation, Serbin and her colleagues videotaped 28 boys and 29 girls ranging in age from 26 to 40 months (1994). They defined "best friend" as most preferred play partner (1994). They concluded that gender segregation was slowly beginning to occur among children in that age range but it was not yet a dominant pattern. Although preschoolers played in mixed-sex groups more than same-sex groups, they played in same-sex dyads more. Forty percent of the dyadic play was in mixed-sex dyads, compared to 60% occurring in same-sex dyads. Significantly, the best friends of 44% of the girls and 65% of the boys were members of the other sex. Similarly, 34% of the girls and 54% of the boys played more often with a peer of the other sex. Interestingly, as a general pattern toddlers had more animated interactions with members of their own sex. In a study of the antecedents of toddler gender segregation (average age of 35 months), toddlers who were already gender segregating were compared to those who were not (Moller & Serbin, 1996). Although the children were able to accurately differentiate between the sexes (i.e., what is called "gender labeling"), "awareness of gender labels did not predict peer preferences" (p. 456). Twenty one percent of the males and 62% of the females played with same-sex peers at above chance levels during free play.

There are some documented sex differences related to gender segregation among preschoolers. Preschool girls appear to be "oriented" toward same-sex peers, adults, and little boys (Fagot, 1994). Boys, on the other hand, are primarily oriented toward same-sex peers. Orientation involves social proximity, interaction, and openness to influence. Although the difference in orientation indicates that boys in preschool would be more prone to gender segregation than girls, some studies have shown that girls segregate first (e.g., LaFreniere, Strayer, & Gauthier, 1984; Moller & Serbin, 1996; Serbin et al., 1994). Another example of sex differences in gender segregation is the dissimilarity in how 3-year-olds manage conflict in child care settings. Sims and her associates videotaped 50 3-year-olds during free play sessions at child care centers to discover when gender segregated behaviors began and if repeated exposure to members of the other sex encouraged gender-segregation (Sims, Hutchins, & Taylor, 1998). They concluded that gender segregation is identifiable in some aspects of conflict behavior, but that at age 3 there was still considerable overlap in the behavior of boys and girls. In general, however, boys were more aggressive in their mode of handling conflict and tended to use more "powerful" strategies than did the girls. The authors concluded that girls choose not to play with boys because doing so made them feel powerless (also see Maccoby & Jacklin, 1987). Their conclusion coincides with Corsaro's earlier finding that boy groups tended to block access attempts by girls more than girl groups attempted to block access attempts by boys (1985). The feeling of powerlessness identified by Sims and other colleagues might be incorporated into developing self and cross-sex schemas of young girls and carried into adult personal and work relationships. Moller and Serbin hypothesized that the tendency for girls to be more sensitive and boys more disruptive further contributes to gender segregation (1996; see also Maccoby & Jacklin, 1987; Maccoby, 1990). In their study of 57 toddlers ranging in age from 26 to 40 months, girls began segregating earlier than boys and also displayed higher levels of social sensitivity in their all girl groups than did boys in their all boy groups. On the other hand, boys tended to be more active and disruptive. Along similar lines, Gumperz claimed that boys and girls are socialized within different "speech communities" where they learn different ways of relating and communicating with others (1982).

Group boundaries clearly constitute structural barriers to friendship formation and are sometimes linked to gender segregation. Some researchers argue that boys in early childhood enjoy interacting in groups more than dyads, but girls display the opposite preference (Benenson, 1993). Young children who are not already part of an established group may have to "hover" outside the perimeter of the group looking for an opportunity to become part of it (Corsaro, 1985; Putallaz & Gottman, 1981; Ramsey & Lasquade, 1996; Rawlins, 1992). Attempting to enter an already established group accounted for over 50% of the conflicts observed among 50 3-year-olds during free play at child care centers (Sims et al., 1998). Group membership is also illustrated by the dialectical principle of judgment and acceptance that involves choices by young children concerning who will be included in or excluded from their groups (Rawlins, 1992). Choosing a cross-sex person as a friend might entail the cost of being excluded from other friendships and groups (Rawlins, 1992).

Identifying the many causes of gender segregation and adequately explaining its relationship to same-sex preferences in early childhood is no easy task (Maccoby, 1994). Simply stating that gender segregation is a result of same-sex preferences and adult-engineered separation of the sexes begs the question of why those preferences exist and why some adults encourage them. Additionally, the temporal sequence and causal relationship of gender segregation and same-sex preferences is not always clear (Maccoby, 1994). Do same-sex preferences cause gender segregation, or does gender segregation lead to the development of same-sex preferences? Perhaps it is a little of both. At this point in time scholars do not know for sure.

A number of theoretical explanations have been offered for same-sex preferences among individuals in early childhood; preferences that contribute to gender segregation and interfere with the initiation of cross-sex friendships (Monsour, 1997). Some explanations seem particularly relevant to cross-sex friendship formation in early childhood. One of those explanations, the "behavioral compatibility hypothesis," was originally formulated by Goodenough (1934) and Parten (1932) and has been championed by a number of researchers (e.g., Alexander & Hines, 1994; Fagot, 1994; Moller & Serbin, 1996). Proponents argue that gender segregation occurs because preschoolers are attracted to others who have similar interactional styles and toy preferences and that young children tend to be more similar to members of their own sex (Leaper, 1994a, p. 2). For example, boys tend to be rougher and more domineering than girls which encourages boys associating with boys and girls associating with girls (Maccoby, 1990). Some researchers have found reasonably strong support for the explanation (e.g., Fagot, 1994), whereas others have found mixed support (e.g., Maccoby & Jacklin, 1987; Moller & Serbin, 1996; Serbin et al., 1994). Maccoby reported inconsistent findings in her review of behavioral compatibility research and concluded "even though gender-differentiation in toy preferences and differentiation in playmate preferences proceed concurrently, they may not be causally connected" (1994, p. 89). However, she also believes that behavioral compatibility plays a role in encouraging same-sex playmate choices, and once those choices are made play styles within gender groupings become more differentiated.

The behavioral compatibility explanation has some interesting implications for cross-sex friendship formation in early childhood. For example, toddlers and slightly older children create similarity during the formation and development of their friendships and peer relationships (Corsaro, 1985; Rizzo, 1989; Whaley & Rubenstein, 1994). Behavioral compatibility, therefore, could be cultivated by children at a very young age before toy preferences and interactional style differences become noticeably pronounced and irreversible. Playing with members of the other sex from an early age might foster behavioral similarity and lead to higher levels of compatibility in that stage and later stages of the life cycle.

Another compelling explanation of voluntary gender segregation is the "social-cognitive" explanation of same-sex preferences, although the explanation has received only modest empirical investigation and support (Maccoby, 1994; Martin et al., 1999; Ruble & Martin, 1998). Proponents of this explanation posit that as children grow older they develop an understanding of gender and begin to value members of their own gender category and seek them out as similar others (Maccoby, 1988; 1990; Martin, 1994; Martin et al., 1999). For example, as girls come to learn what behaviors and beliefs are associated with being a girl and how those beliefs and behaviors are different from boys, they will seek out other girls. Boys undergo the same process. Furthermore, awareness of activities and behaviors appropriate for one's sex increases the likelihood of engaging in sex-typed behaviors (Maccoby, 1994). Along these lines, research conducted by Damon demonstrated that kindergartners were aware of which toys were girl toys and which were boy toys, although they did not see anything wrong with a child playing with a toy usually reserved for the other sex (1977). Damon argued that kindergartners may know that certain toys are boy toys, and certain toys are girl toys, but it is not until grade school that such information takes on a prescriptive quality where those children believe they ought not to play with toys reserved for members of the other sex (also see Maccoby, 1994). Moller and Serbin (1996) did not find support for the social-cognitive explanation in their study of 57 children ranging in age from 26 to 40 months. The social-cognitive explanation seems particularly relevant to cross-sex friendship formation in early childhood, or lack thereof, because cross-sex friendships might influence the formation and content of gender schemas. The possibility of the intermingling of gender, cross-sex friendship, and self-schemas is explored in the next section of this chapter.

Reviewing the rather large gender segregation literature leads me to conclude that there are no definitive and commonly agreed on explanations for same-sex playmate preferences (Monsour, 1997). I agree with Alexander and Hines that no single theory can adequately explain same-sex preferences and that some combination of theoretical approaches is warranted (1994). Their recommendation for theoretical pluralism, echoed by Serbin and her colleagues (1994), is a valid one, especially considering that same-sex preferences appear to have an "on–off" character as individuals go through the life cycle (Epstein, 1986).

In summary, there is considerable and convincing evidence that young children gradually gravitate to same-sex others during early childhood (see Leaper, 1994a, for an entire issue of a journal devoted to gender segregation). Fagot and Leinbach discovered that gender segregation developed slowly over a time period of 18 months to three years (1993). Studies documenting why children segregate are not conclusive (Leaper, 1994b). Physical separation of the sexes constitutes a structural barrier and makes other sex interaction and cross-sex friendship formation less likely than it would be if there was greater integration of the sexes. As boys and girls gravitate to same-sex dyadic couplings and same-sex group activities the differences between them that may have caused those gravitations in the first place become more pronounced (Fagot, 1994).

Cross-Sex Friendships Affect and are Affected by an Individual's Ongoing Social Construction of Self During Early Childhood

Recall that the third theme of this book also serves as its central premise, that is, cross-sex friendships affect and are affected by an individual's ongoing social construction of self throughout the life cycle. The relationship between self-concept and cross-sex friendships begins in early childhood. This part of the chapter is divided into two interrelated sections that lay the theoretical groundwork for continuation of similar arguments in subsequent chapters. First, I describe the hypothesized relationship between schemas and cross-sex friendship development in early childhood. In the second section I explain the role of communication in self-concept and cross-sex friendship construction in early childhood. In that section I apply the interpersonal self perspective (Markus & Cross, 1990) and accompanying theories to self and cross-sex friendship formation.

Schemas and Cross-Sex Friendships in Early Childhood.   There are a number of ways of linking cross-sex friendships to an individual's evolving concept of self. One way is through utilization of the schema construct. Before getting into an extensive elaboration of the types of schemas relevant to my argument, let me summarize and preview the positions I maintain and document throughout the book. I contend that gender, self, and friendship schemas simultaneously develop at a very young age. Self schemas begin to form earlier in life than gender and friendship schemas (Harter, 1998; Ruble & Martin, 1998), but eventually all develop concurrently. Those schemas influence one another through various types of cognitive connections and processes in every stage of life. The intermingling of these schemas constitute a major way that cross-sex friendships and self-views reciprocally affect one another. In order to adequately explain my position allow me to define and explicate a number of related constructs: *schema*, *self-schema*, *relational* and *friendship schemas*, and *gender schemas*.

According to Bem, a schema is "a cognitive structure, a network of associations that organizes and guides an individual's perception" (1981, p. 355; also see Andersen, 1993). In simpler terms, schemas are the thoughts, emotions, and beliefs a person has about people, places, things, events, and him or herself. Those thoughts, emotions, and beliefs determine how a person perceives the object of his or her schema. Schemas are both processes and representations that summarize experience and guide future behavior (Andersen, 1993; Arib, Conklin, & Hill, 1987). There are many types of schemas representing different stimulus domains (O'Meara, 1989), but the ones most relevant to the themes of this book are self-schemas, relational schemas, and gender schemas. Relational schemas include same-sex and cross-sex friendship schemas.

Recall from chapter one that I am focusing my attention on the "self-concept" construct, rather than the larger construct of "self". Wells equated a person's self-concept with his or her self-schema. Self-schemas are cognitive generalizations about oneself (e.g., "I am shy," "I am lazy," "I make friends easily"). Those generalizations are based on past experience and act as a framework for interpreting and organizing self-relevant information and experiences (Markus, 1983; A. J. Wells, 1992). From an interpersonal self and social cognitive perspective (Markus & Cross, 1990; Mintz, 1995), there is a reciprocal relationship between an individual's self-schema and his or her personal relationships (Andersen, 1993; Gergen, 1977; Markus, 1983). Relationships and their accompanying schematic representations impact and are impacted by a person's self-schema.

Cognitive representations of self (i.e., self-schemas) are believed to start in early infancy (Case, 1991) and to change over the life span (Cross & Markus, 1991; Harter, 1998; Labouvie-Vief et al., 1995). However, methodological constraints involved in studying self-concepts of preverbal infants make it difficult to draw hard-and-fast conclusions about the self-concepts of infants (Damon & Hart, 1988). Nevertheless, Case contended that the first sense of self is formed in the very earliest intimate relationships with care givers (1991). Cosse observed "Infant and early childhood theory and research show that a solid and enduring sense of self develops very early in the life cycle. However, disagreement exists regarding whether or not gender is at the core of the development of self" (1992, p. 8).

Baldwin (1992) noted in his review of the relational schema literature that different writers have discussed similar constructs employing analogous nomenclature such as interpersonal schemas (Safran, 1990), relationship schemas (Baldwin, Carrell, & Lopez, 1990) and internal working models (Bowlby, 1969). Following Baldwin's lead, I have adopted the label *relational schema* (Planalp, 1985). Planalp defined relational schemas as "coherent frameworks of relational knowledge which are used to derive relational implications of messages and are modified in accord with ongoing experiences in relationships" (1985, p. 9). In other words, relational schemas, in part, are the thoughts, emotions, memories, and expectations that a person has for specific relationships (e.g., a friendship with a next-door neighbor), as well as a person's set of beliefs about particular types of relationships (e.g., romances, friendships, parent–child relationships). A relational schema guides communication with the partner, and communication affects the content and structuring of the schema (Honeycutt & Cantrill, 2001; Monsour, 1994; Planalp, 1985). Individuals have different schemas for different kinds of relationships as well as specific schemas for particular relationships. So for example, Mary has a general friendship schema, a same-sex friendship schema, a cross-sex friendship schema, and a schema for her friendship with Bill. Individuals have schemas for particular types of relationships (e.g., a cross-sex friendship) even if they have never been in that kind of relationship. Information for the construction of relational schemas come from a variety of sources such as mass media, third parties, cultural norms, reading, and past and current relationships (Andersen, 1993; Honeycutt & Cantrill, 2001). Schemas can also change to incorporate new information (Arbib, Conklin, & Hill, 1987; Planalp, 1985).

Relational schemas involve three elements: representations of the self relevant to a particular relationship, representations of the partner, and representations of the interaction between self and partner (Baldwin,1992; see also Banse, 1999). For example, each child in the cross-sex friendship of two 4-year-olds would have a cross-sex friendship schema comprised of views of him or herself in the context of the friendship (part of their self-schemas), views of the partner (labeled by Baldwin as "other-schemas"), and views of the communication between self and partner. Baldwin drew a distinction between "declarative" and "procedural" knowledge (see also Arbib et al., 1987; Honeycutt & Cantrill, 2001). Declarative knowledge often is descriptive knowledge about things or people and is comprised of episodic and semantic memory (see also Harter, 1998). Whereas episodic memory focuses on specific occurrences (episodes) in the past, semantic memory is more abstract and based on repeated experiences. Declarative knowledge takes the form of self and partner schemas. Procedural knowledge is acquired information about rules and skills needed for the processing of information and is linked to the notion of "scripts." An interpersonal script is a cognitive structure specifying what to do and say in particular stereotyped relational activities (Baldwin, 1992, p. 468; also see Schank & Abelson, 1977). Interpersonal scripts also include a specification of the roles for members participating in the interaction. So the cross-sex friendship schemas of my hypothetical 4-year-olds would include declarative knowledge in the form of self and partner schemas, as well as procedural information (including scripts) about how to conduct themselves in that kind of relationship and in that specific friendship.

Gender schemas are knowledge structures containing information about what the sexes are like (Bem, 1981; Ruble & Martin, 1998). Chodorow contended from a feminist perspective that core gender identity is firmly established in both males and females by the age of three (1978). Bem argued over two decades ago that as a result of gender-role socialization, females and males cognitively organize information about the self according to the cultural definition of what it means to be male or female (1981). Developmental gender schema theorists contend that children's gender schemas guide how they think and behave in reference to members of the other sex (Martin, 1994), but the precise nature of the connection between gender schemas and behavior has yet to be established (Ruble & Martin, 1998). However, researchers have demonstrated that gender schemas impact preschoolers' preferences for sex-typed toys and activities (Carter & Levy, 1988). Martin and her colleagues have provided evidence that children ages 41 to 82 months are behaviorally influenced by their gender schemas and try to act in accordance with those schemas (Martin et al., 1999). Although it is debatable whether gender role socialization processes begin as early as preschool, part of the ongoing gender role socialization is internalization of the belief that cross-sex relationships are reserved for romantic couplings (O'Meara, 1989). That belief contributes to the formation of a "heterosexual subschema" that influences individuals to interpret cross-sex interactions and relationships in sexual and/or romantic terms (Bem, 1981).

Martin contended that gender schemas can be divided into explicit and implicit gender schemas (1994). The explicit gender schemas involve a "superordinate schema," an "own-sex schema," and an "other-sex schema" (1994). The superordinate schema supplies information necessary to categorize behaviors, traits, objects (like toys), and roles as related primarily to boys or girls. The own-sex and other-sex schemas are subordinate schemas that are more detailed than the superordinate schema and include plans for carrying out behavior individuals believe to be characteristic of their own sex (own-sex schema) or the other sex (other-sex schema). Martin believed that the more a child identities with his or her gender group, the more detailed that child's own-sex gender schema is likely to be (1994). Although not noted by Martin, one could reasonably argue that the amount of detail in the own sex and other sex schemas would also be influenced by having cross-sex friendships. Knowledge about gender can also exist in more abstract gender schemas that are the implicit theories of gender that people form (Martin, 1994). Those implicit theories of gender would typically lead children to assume that similarities exist between themselves and members of their own sex based on an abstract notion that members of their own sex are like them. As I have noted elsewhere (Monsour, 1994), perceptions of similarity often leads to interpersonal attraction between individuals.

Baldwin (1992) and others (Banse, 1999; Damon & Hart, 1988; Planalp & Fitness, 1999) have highlighted the importance of incorporating affect into models of relational and self-schemas. There is a vast literature on emotions, much of it relevant to the intersection of emotional and cognitive processes in personal relationships (Planalp & Fitness, 1999). Reviewing even a portion of that literature is beyond the scope and intent of this book. However, a number of observations made by Planalp and Fitness are worth repeating because of their relevance to my general argument that self-concepts and cross-sex friendships are interconnected. First, cognitive schemas (they use an example of a "friendship prototype") contain knowledge about emotions. For example, a general cross-sex friendship schema of a preschooler might contain knowledge that such friendships are exciting and fun. Second, cognitive and emotional processes in relationships are similar and serve somewhat complementary roles. Stated succinctly by Planalp and Fitness "Essentially, however, the cognitive system orients us to what makes sense, whereas the emotional system orients us to what matters. Stated this way, it is hard to imagine one system operating effectively without the other" (1999, p. 734). So for example, the cognitive component of a preschooler's cross-sex friendship schema could contain beliefs about those kinds of friendship, whereas the emotional component might contain affectively charged memories (good or bad) about those friendships. The cognitive beliefs and the emotional memories reciprocally influence one another.

A fascinating but yet-to-be studied phenomenon is the co-occurrence and possible merging of developing gender, self, and cross-sex/same-sex friendship schemas. Schema theory (Andersen, 1993; Arbib et al., 1987), common sense, and the "cognitive complexity" construct (O'Keefe & Delia, 1979; Honeycutt & Cantrill, 2001) all suggest that schemas can be combined to form new schemas. Theoretically, self, gender, same-sex and cross-sex friendship schemas could intermingle and lead to more complex and complete cognitive structures concerning members of the other sex and how they are related to self. As observed by Honeycutt and Cantrill "Cognitive complexity relates to the number, interrelationships, complexity, and variety of the schemes (note: by "schemes" they mean schemas) used when constructing messages" (p. 12). When early childhood communications are with members of the other sex, a cross-sex friendship schema can begin to develop at the same time as the formation of gender, self, and same-sex friendship schemas. A cross-sex friendship gender schema would guide communication with cross-sex friends and provide the young child with a model of cross-sex relationships that could become increasingly complex as he or she encounters different types of relationships with members of the other sex.

A number of cognitive processes are relevant to the connections that form between different schemas. A few of the more salient ones are priming (Baldwin, 1992; Banse, 1999), interactive cuing (Wegner, Giuliano, & Hertel, 1985), and transactive memory (Wegner et al., 1985). As explained by Banse, "The principle of priming is based on the idea that knowledge is represented as units or nodes of cognitive networks. If a unit is activated, this activation spreads along the connections of the network and activates related units"

(1999, p. 805). If certain parts of self, friendship, and gender schemas are "related units," then when one is activated the others might be as well. For example, if a 5-year-old boy disclosed to his 5-year-old cross-sex friend that he liked to play with dolls, the content of that disclosure (i.e., a knowledge unit) would be part of his self, gender, and cross-sex friendship schemas. The communicative act of disclosing that information would activate connections between all three schemas.

Similar to priming, interactive cuing is when communication from one partner serves as an interactive cue to stimulate and activate a cognitive structure such as a schema of the other partner. In the self-disclosure example just given, the disclosure from the 5-year-old boy would activate certain schemas of his 5-year-old female friend. The disclosure from her friend that he enjoyed playing with dolls would activate and become part of her gender schema (e.g., what is appropriate behavior for boys), her self-schema (e.g., if my friend plays with dolls maybe I can play with tanks), and her cross-sex friendship schema (e.g., girls and boys who are friends can talk about things they may not be able to talk about with their other friends).

Transactive memory involves a variety of processes that allow information to enter a relationship and be subsequently utilized by one or both relational partners (Wegner et al., 1985). It entails the individual and joint knowledge structures that each partner has concerning their relationship (Wegner et al., 1985) and is connected to an encoding phenomenon known as semantic elaboration (Anderson & Reder, 1979). Semantic elaboration occurs when inferences are drawn about incoming information and when that information is related to knowledge already stored. Going back to my self-disclosure example for a moment. From a transactive memory perspective, the self-disclosure of the 5-year-old boy and his friend's reaction to it were coded into various schemas of both individuals. Through semantic elaboration, the self-disclosure knowledge unit would be connected to information already existing in the gender, self, other, and friendship schemas of both children.

Not only does schema theory suggest that schemas can be combined (Arbib et al.,1987), other theoretical stances converge to support the view that self and cross-sex friendship schemas emerge from communication occurring between social actors (e.g., social constructionism, Berger & Luckman, 1966; Gergen, 1985; symbolic interactionism, Mead, 1934; social constructivism, Vygotsky, 1978; and Yingling's relational perspective,1994). Each of these theories can be used to hypothesize that when young cross-sex friends talk to one another, material is provided for the combination and structuring of gender, friendship, and self-schemas. Communication serves not only as the raw materials for the construction of self and cross-sex friendships, but the tool for putting those raw materials together. These ideas are more fully explored in the upcoming pages in which I explain the role of communication in schema and cross-sex friendship construction.

Communication and the Social Construction of Self and Cross-Sex Friendships. Early childhood friendship studies and theoretical treatises clearly establish the centrality of communication in the emergence and development of friendships (e.g., Cooley, 1902, 1909; Corsaro, 1985; Howes, 1996; Gottman, 1986; Parker & Gottman, 1989 Whaley & Rubenstein, 1994; Vygotsky, 1978; Yingling, 1994). By "emergence" I mean the first communicative, dyadic, and rudimentary schematic manifestation of what relationship scholars would label as friendship. Emergence also refers to the initial cognitive realization on the part of preschoolers that they are in a different kind of relationship from the ones they have with their parents and siblings (Monsour, 1997). There is an equally impressive body of work highlighting the importance of communication and language in the social construction of self (e.g., Coover & Murphy, 2000; Cooley, 1902; Gergen, 1977, 1991; Mead, 1934; Stern, 1985). Mintz noted that language for the very young child "provides a link between individual minds and social contexts … and permits the young child a means to reflect on, represent, and communicate about herself to other people" (1995, p. 61). Along those lines, one of the basic arguments presented in this book is that self-views and cross-sex friendships are established and linked through interpersonal communication.

Toddlers and preschoolers initially learn what friendship means through the verbal and nonverbal communication that occurs during coordinated play (Howes, 1996; Whaley & Rubenstein, 1994; Yingling, 1994). Howes, one of the foremost authorities on early childhood friendships, contended that toddlers and preschoolers form internal representations (i.e., schemas) of their developing friendships (1996). Those cognitive representations are a product of the interaction between the young children. Several prominent scholars propose that young children create friendships in a sophisticated fashion through communication, while at the same time internalizing what it means to be a friend (Corsaro, 1985; Rizzo, 1989; Yingling, 1994). This process of friendship formation can be explained by the social constructivist stance of Vygotsky in which intrapersonal phenomena, such as the formation of a model or schema of friendship, is a product of interpersonal interaction (Vygotsky, 1978; 1979).

Some empirical studies and conceptual pieces more recent than the theoretical work done by Vygotsky in the early 1900s have illuminated the intricate connections between dyadic communication and the formation of early childhood friendships (e.g, Corsaro, 1985; Howes, et al., 1994; Howes, 1996; Whaley & Rubenstein, 1994; Yingling, 1994). However, Yingling noted that few scholars have directly examined how young friends talk to one another and how that talk serves to both build and reflect developing friendships (1994; but she made note of Corsaro's 1985 work with preschoolers and Rizzo's 1989 work with first graders, as exceptions). Based upon her observations of naturally occurring friendship conversations of 3-to-10-year-old children, she presents a "relational perspective" on children's friendships. She proposed that "talk" between children is much more than a simple exchange of information. Talking frames the relationship and directly influences the evolving schematic representations of it. Children literally talk friendships into existence (1994). Communication between children not only expresses what the children are thinking, but shapes their thoughts as well (Yingling, 1994). The importance of everyday talk in the development and maintenance of personal relationships is receiving a growing amount of scholarly attention (see e.g., Duck, 1995, 1994; Spencer, 1994).

Echoing, extending, and reinforcing Yingling's position is the complementary observation made by Whaley and Rubenstein concerning the richness of early childhood interaction (1994). They contended that toddlers create a sense of understanding between themselves and then use that understanding as the basis for defining the nature of self and friendship. Whaley and Rubenstein observed four toddler friendships in a daycare setting over a 10-month period and concluded that communication in early childhood takes both verbal and nonverbal forms, molding and reflecting the child's conceptualization of friendship (1994). They noted that toddlers create similarity nonverbally by imitating one another's behavior. Personal relationship scholars have recognized the importance of similarity in building intimacy and relationships (e.g., Duck, 1994; see Monsour, 1994, for a review). Relatedly, Howes and Phillipsen found evidence suggesting that similarity in interaction style was a pronounced feature of cross-sex toddler friendships (1992; reported in Howes, 1996; see also Burleson, 1994).

In addition to playing a pivotal role in the construction of cross-sex friendships, interpersonal communication is also central to the social construction of self (Mintz, 1995). A child's developing self-schema is largely determined by the relationships he or she forms with other individuals (Markus & Cross, 1990). Those relationships are initiated, maintained, and modified through communication (Knapp & Vangelista, 1996; Wood, 1995). Different kinds of relationships such as peer, friendship, and primary care giver relationships, can have different effects on the child's evolving concept of self. In chapter one I introduced the work of five scholars whose writings are significant to the interpersonal self perspective (Markus & Cross, 1990) and the theoretical framework of this book: Cooley (1902), Mead (1934), Gergen (1977; 1985), Sullivan (1953), and Bowlby (1969). These interpersonal self theorists are relevant not only to the social construction of self, but also to the social construction of cross-sex friendships. Consequently, in this section I address how the perspectives of four of those scholars apply to early childhood cross-sex friendship and self-development. I postpone my discussion of Sullivan until the next chapter because of his belief, now known to be incorrect, that friendship does not begin until preadolescence (1953).

The social construction of self begins with the attachment between an infant and his or her primary care giver (Markus & Cross, 1990). Bowlby's attachment theory is therefore a good place to start (1969). Attachment theorists propose that the relationship formed between an infant and the primary care giver influences subsequent relationships established throughout the life cycle of the individual (Bowlby, 1969; Lewis & Feiring, 1989; Shulman, et al., 1994). Scholars have explored friendship and peer relationships from an attachment perspective (e.g., Kerns, 1994; Park & Waters, 1989), and the theoretical tenets of attachment theory can be used to explain the relationship between cross-sex friendships and a child's emerging self-concept. Kerns observed that "children learn within the mother-child relationship ways of thinking, feeling, and behaving that subsequently generalize to their own friendships" (1996, p. 142). She argues that in order for children to meet their goal of establishing coordinated interaction with one another (Gottman & Mettetal, 1986), they must have secure attachments to their primary care giver.

Because the infant or toddler establishes a close relationship with his or her primary care giver, attachment theorists contend that the cognitive and social processes that make friendship possible begin at a much earlier age than the emergence of the first friendship (Bowlby, 1969; Park & Waters, 1989; Shulman et al., 1994). Results from a number of studies indicates that the type of attachment between an infant or toddler and the primary care giver affects friendship quantity and quality. Sroufe found that preschoolers with a secure attachment to their mother during infancy had more friends than their insecure attachment counterparts (1993). Verschueren and her associates discovered significant and positive statistical relationships between the positiveness of 95 kindergartners' internal working models of self and their social competence and acceptance (Verschueren et al., 1996). In Fagot's longitudinal study of 156 children from 18 months to 7 years of age, she discovered a relationship between children's attachment classification at 18 months and their understandings and ratings of friendship at age 7. Insecure children, for example, rated their friendships as less positive than the children categorized as secure (1994).

Some attachment theory investigations are less relevant to cross-sex friendship than they could have been because experimenters failed to closely examine the sex composition of the dyad (e.g., Kerns, 1994; Park & Waters, 1989; Youngblade & Belsky, 1992; Youngblade, Park & Belsky, 1993). For example, in their study of 33 4-year-olds and their best cross-sex and same-sex friends, Park and Waters concluded that the dyads categorized as secure–secure were more harmonious, less controlling, more responsive, and happier than their secure–insecure counterparts. Unfortunately, they did not report on or examine differences in dyad sex composition on the investigated variables, nor did they report on within-group differences. Exploration of within-group differences and sex composition might have revealed interesting and useful information. For instance, although there were no differences in self-disclosure between the secure–secure dyads and the secure–insecure dyads, there could have been differences within those groups. It would have been useful to know if secure–secure cross-sex dyads self-disclosed more than secure–secure same-sex dyads; or if there was more or less harmony between cross-sex and same-sex dyads within the secure–insecure group. Existing research indicates that such differences might exist. Gottman has documented, for example, that 4-year old cross-sex friends self-disclose more than do 4-year-old same-sex friends (1986).

In a follow-up investigation of the study by Park and Waters (1989), Kerns (1994) examined the relationship between child-mother attachment security and children at two points in time (ages 4 and 5). Her sample consisted of 21 best friendship dyads (six boy/boy, seven girl/girl, and eight girl/boy). She found that at age 4 secure–secure dyads (meaning each friend was securely attached to his or her care giver) received higher scores on positive interaction than 3 secure–insecure dyads (meaning one friend was securely attached to his or her care giver but the other friend was not) but not higher scores on coordinated interaction. However, at the age of 5 secure–secure dyads scored higher than secure–insecure dyads on both positiveness of interaction and coordination of interaction. As was true in the study by Park and Waters, Kerns failed to examine or even remotely address possible differences between same-sex and cross-sex friendship pairings.

Two additional studies were designed to investigate associations between attachment history and friendship quality in preschoolers but also did not clearly examine differences between cross-sex and same-sex pairings (Youngblade & Belsky, 1992; Youngblade, Park, & Belsky, 1993). Although in the 1992 study Youngblade and Belsky were specifically interested in the same-sex friendships of 5-year-olds, 18% of their sample were cross-sex friendship dyads because target children were unable to name a close same-sex friend. Disturbingly, Youngblade and Belsky referred to the inclusion of cross-sex dyads as contributing "noise" to the sample. Regretfully, the investigators neglected to report direct findings on the cross-sex dyads. Nevertheless, they concluded that "positive and secure parent–child relationships are associated with more positive friendships and more negative family relationships with more negative friendships" (p. 700). Youngblade and her associates in a similar study were interested in discovering if mother–child and father–child attachment predicted friendship interactions at age 5 (Youngblade et al., 1993). Attachment styles were assessed at ages 1 and 3. As a general pattern with some exceptions, attachment history did not predict friendship interactions. However, as noted by Kerns (1996), both the 1992 and 1993 studies conducted by Youngblade and associates are compromised by the fact that Youngblade got attachment data for only one member of each dyad. A number of scholars have noted the importance of getting data from both members of a dyad (Duck, 1994; Hinde, 1979; Monsour, Harvey, & Betty, 1997), especially when examining connections between attachment theory and friendship quality (Kerns, 1994).

What conclusions may be drawn from the limited but growing number of studies conducted on attachment theory and early childhood friendships? Taken together, these studies suggest that attachment history, attachment style, and a child's internal working model of self do influence early childhood friendships. Children with a history of secure attachment to a primary care giver rate

their friendships as more positive (Fagot, 1994) and generally have more positive and coordinated interactions with friends (Kerns, 1994, 1996; Park & Waters, 1989; Verschueren et al., 1996). Disappointingly, there have been no
studies examining how attachment history impacts cross-sex friendships specifically in early childhood and later in life. Nor have there been studies addressing
how the internal working models of self and others (i.e., schemas) influences a
child's willingness and ability to form those friendships.

One need not have special insight to see how attachment theory might be
applied to early cross-sex friendship dynamics, or to pose provocative and important questions. For example, does the sex composition of the care
giver–child relationship influence the propensity of a child to form cross-sex
friendships? When a child forms an internal working model of his or her relationship with a primary care giver that internal working model might contain
assessments concerning the warmth and responsiveness of individuals of that
sex. For instance, if a female toddler forms a warm and secure attachment to her
father, might the internal working models of herself and her father make her
more likely to form subsequent friendship relationships with males than she
would if her attachment to her father was insecure? Another important question concerns whether attachment histories and styles have different effects on
the initiation and development of cross-sex friendships than they do on
same-sex ones in early childhood. Some scholars argue that children with
cross-sex friendships may be less socially competent than children without
cross-sex friendships (see Kovacs, Parker, & Hoffman, 1996, for a good analysis
of that argument). Perhaps children who pursue cross-sex friendships do so out
of a poor self-image related to insecure attachment with a primary care giver.
There is still much to be done with attachment theory as it relates to cross-sex
friendship development. My hope is that this book stimulates enough interest to
generate research and theoretical extension of attachment theory to cross-sex
friendship formation in early childhood.

The emergence of self in early childhood and the role played by others in a
child's view of self is a central theme in much of Cooley's work (Longmore,
1998). Nevertheless, there have been no empirical studies applying Cooley's
perspective and his looking-glass self concept to cross-sex friendship. However,
a number of points already delineated in this chapter have clear applicability to
the looking-glass construct. For example, much of the social feedback and reflected appraisals that impact self-development of a child take place in the context of primary group interaction (Cooley, 1909). Cooley described primary
groups as being "characterized by intimate face-to-face association and cooperation ... the family, the playgroup of children, and the neighborhood or community group of elders" (p. 179). Most relevant to our purposes are the playgroups
of children. After about the age of 3 children begin to slowly segregate into gender-based groups and dyads (Leaper, 1994a). If a child leaves the group to play
with a member of the other sex he or she takes the risk of being teased, ostra-

cized, and possibly excluded from the group (Best, 1983; Erwin, 1998; Rawlins, 1992; Thorne, 1986). A reasonable assumption is that those children see themselves as they imagine their peers might; that is, as individuals who are violating social norms by crossing gender boundaries. These negative reflected appraisals could have a number of consequences such as a poor self-image or a decision not to pursue cross-sex friendships out of a fear of unpleasant social repercussions.

Studies have shown that cross- and same-sex toddlers try to create verbal and nonverbal similarity between one another (e.g., Whaley & Rubenstein, 1994). The attempt to establish similarity could also be a product of reflected appraisals and the looking-glass self. Cooley contended that infants as young as 6 months old notice the influence they have on the behavior of others (1902, p. 196). When toddlers establish similarity by imitating one another, they are providing each other with social affirmation and positive reinforcement. Through their mutual imitations they are essentially reflecting back positive views of one another.

Reflected appraisals often take the form of direct and indirect feedback from members of one's social network (Cooley, 1902; 1909). Positive and negative feedback from peers, parents, teachers, and daycare providers directed at young children who cross gender boundaries contributes to a child's developing concept of self (Sroufe et al., 1993). Feedback from a cross-sex friend can also influence a child's emerging social self. One way in which this feedback is indirectly communicated is through fantasy play (Gottman, 1986). Early childhood friendship scholars, Gottman in particular, have emphasized the importance of fantasy play in dealing with fears and worries and learning to solve problems (1986). In his discussion of fantasy play among very young cross-sex friends, Gottman stressed that fantasy play enables friends to learn to deal with their fears and anxieties through social support. Fantasy play also helps to build confidence for young cross-sex friends because the repetition characteristic of fantasy play gives those friends a sense of control and mastery.

Mead's symbolic interactionist position identifies others in a person's social network as essential to that individual's self-view (Blumer, 1969; Corsaro, 1985; Harter, 1998; Mead, 1934). A person views herself or himself as a social object, and within that view is the incorporation of the views that others have of that individual. Identifying oneself as a social object means that an individual acquires a sense of self by appropriating the attitudes that others have toward him or her (Mead, 1934, p. 138). Symbolic interactionists believe that the meanings of things such as self and friendship are socially constructed through interaction with others (Blumer, 1969). Communication is the process that enables an individual to become an object to him or herself. Through communication with others and oneself an individual is able to see him or herself as others do. Part of the communicative process involving "participation in the other" is the mutual role-taking that occurs between partners during interaction (Blumer; Mead).

Each person needs to be able to view him or herself, the situation, and the partner from the perspective of the other individual. Blumer contended that "Such mutual role-taking is the sine qua non of communication and effective symbolic interaction" (p. 10).

Although untested, Mead's theoretical view of the self, communication, and others in an individual's social network has clear applications to the argument that cross-sex friendships impact and are impacted by a child's concept of self. Mead's observations concerning "imitation" and Corsaro's interpretation of those observations have interesting implications for early childhood cross-sex friendships. Imitation of another's behavior at a very early age is one of the ways that a child grows and learns new behaviors (Mead, 1934, p. 65). But imitation in Mead's view and other symbolic interactionists is more than mere automatic, near-mindless mimicking of another's behavior. Rather, imitation is a form of "incipient role-taking" in that when a child imitates the behavior of a partner he or she begins to see that behavior from the partner's perspective (Corsaro, 1985, p. 63). Imitation also fosters a sense of similarity between young friends, similarity that helps to establish solidarity even in the youngest of friends (Gottman, 1986). Gottman noted that fantasy play is the highest level of coordinated play among cross-sex friends and necessitates a willingness and ability to be involved with one's partner and be able to see things from his or her perspective (1986). Role-playing in fantasy land is a way of developing perspective-taking abilities.

Based largely on his ethnographic longitudinal study of 51 3- and 4-year-olds, Corsaro contended that when kids engage in role-playing (Gottman's fantasy play) they "begin to understand that mothers (or fathers, or babies, or firefighters) do not simply do certain things, but that they do certain things with others" (p. 64). Through fantasy play very young children begin to see themselves through the eyes of others in their own social group. Rizzo (1989) notes another Meadian application when he observes that children increase solidarity in their relationship by highlighting their similarities. He also interestingly observes that a friend could serve as the "agent of society or the generalized other" (p. 124) as friends mutually internalize by saying such things as "I like this, don't you?" To the extent that the child's friend represents society at large (i.e., Mead's generalized other, 1934), then the child feels a sense of belonging, not only to the dyad, but to the larger societal group as a whole (Sullivan, 1953).

Concluding Observations

In this final section I present a few concluding observations about cross-sex friendships in early childhood (ages 18 months to 6 years). My first observation focuses on the importance of taking a developmental and life-span approach in studying and understanding cross-sex friendships. As indirectly suggested by Bigelow and his colleagues in their endorsement of developmental approaches, the presence or absence of cross-sex friendships during early childhood and the quality and characteristics of those friendships lay the foundation for subsequent cross-sex friendships (Bigelow, Tesson, & Lewko, 1996, p. vii). A better understanding of cross-sex friendship processes in early childhood will lead to a better understanding of those processes later in life. I am not claiming that early childhood cross-sex friendships determine the form and function of cross-sex friendships throughout life in an absolute, causal sense. I do contend that much can be learned about early childhood cross-sex friendships by viewing them through a developmental lens. For example, gender segregation and homosocial friendship preferences slowly emerge around the age of 3 or 4 and continue until they become quite pronounced in middle childhood (ages 7 to 9). In order to discern why cross-sex friendships are a developmental anomaly in middle childhood, scholars must first understand what cross-sex friendship processes preceded that stage of development. Cross-sex friendships, like all relationships, include processes at the individual, dyadic, group, and societal levels (Bukowski, Sippola, Hoza, 1999; Rubin et al., 1998).

In the beginning of this chapter I tried to establish when friendships first emerge as a developmental phenomenon. Those beginning friendships are significant from a developmental and life-span perspective. Similarly, from a social constructivist (Vygotsky, 1978) and relational perspective (Yingling, 1994), the first cross-sex interactions and friendships that individuals experience could have significant impact on how they initially perceive members of the other sex and on the relational schemas that develop in conjunction with those initial perceptions. Those relationships set the schematic stage for cross-sex friendships that occur throughout the remainder of a person's life. The initial friendships formed at a very early age (e.g., Howes, 1988, documented friendships at 12 to 18 months) can leave an indelible impression on a child's developing friendship schema and can have an equally powerful impact on the young child's nascent self-concept. Howes contended that toddlers "form internal representations of peer and friendship relations in much the same way that they form internal representations of adult care givers and attachments" (1996, p. 66). If a toddler, for example, were to form an internal representation (i.e., a schema) of a particular cross-sex friendship, that schematic representation could influence the child's evolving schematic representations of self and gender. In reciprocal fashion, the child's self-schema and the incorporation of relationships into that schema (Markus & Cross, 1990) influences beliefs about and behavior in cross-sex friendships. In the final chapter of this book I present a heuristic model of the interconnections between friendship, gender, and self-schemas (see Fig. 7.1 in chap. 7, this volume).

My next conclusion centers around an irony in the early childhood friendship literature. Gender segregation in early childhood has inspired considerable empirical study and theoretical ruminations (e.g., Leaper, 1994a; Maccoby & Jacklin, 1987; Moller & Serbin, 1996). Scholars have extolled the virtues of mixed-sex peer interaction in early childhood and written extensively on the long-term relational consequences of gender segregation (Leaper, 1994a). Gender segregation is linked to other structural factors influencing cross-sex friendship formation such as proximity and group membership (Rubin et al., 1998). Indeed, the "overall constellation of structural characteristics" noted by Allan and Adams (1989) as having a major impact on friendships, probably has gender segregation as its focal point in early and middle childhood.

With all of the attention given to gender segregation one would think scholars would isolate and study the most noticeable outcome of that segregation (i.e., diminished cross-sex friendships). The gradual separation of the sexes beginning as young as 18 months (Fagot & Leinbach, 1993) impacts the likelihood of toddlers and preschoolers forming cross-sex friendships. Ironically, friendship scholars as a group have devoted little attention to cross-sex friendships of toddlers and preschoolers. Either by design or oversight, the majority of early childhood friendship researchers have ignored the friendships that boys and girls form with one another. The tacit rejection of cross-sex friendship as a topic worthy of scholarly investigation becomes even more mysterious when one considers that cross-sex friendships in early childhood are not uncommon. A significant percentage of the friendships in many of the studies reviewed for this chapter were cross-sex in composition (e.g., Gottman, 1986; Howes, 1988; Howes et al., 1994; Kerns, 1996; Park, Lay, & Ramsay, 1993; Whaley & Rubenstein, 1994; Youngblade & Belsky, 1992).

Another conclusion derived from the various literatures examined in this chapter is that the views of interpersonal self theorists such as Mead, Cooley, and Bowlby, complement the perspectives of many early childhood friendship scholars (e.g., Corsaro, 1985; Rizzo, 1989; Vygotsky, 1978; Whaley & Rubenstein, 1994; Yingling, 1994). Each of the parenthetical theorists, in his or her own way, makes the point that friendships and the concept of friendship emerge from interactions. Friendship and its cognitive representation are products of the communication occurring between participants, a view also supported by Gergen's social constructionism (1985; 1991). Interpersonal self theorists argue that self-views emanate from interactions and cognitive views of those interactions. Those self-views may be in the form of internal working models (Bowlby, 1969), reflected appraisals (Cooley, 1902, 1909), or viewing the self as a social object (Gergen, 1977; Mead, 1934).

When infants, toddlers, and preschoolers first begin to establish friendships those relationships form the basis of friendship schemas that interconnect with codeveloping gender and self-schemas. Theoretical intermingling of the interpersonal self (Markus & Cross, 1990) social constructivist (Vygotsky, 1978), and relational perspectives (Yingling, 1994) suggest that the self and cross-sex friendship schemas of children are partly determined by the relationships those children form with members of the other sex. The cross-sex friendships are a product of the communication that occurs between young girls and boys. When boys and girls first begin to interact with one another those interactions provide information for the formation of gender schemas, cross-sex friendship schemas, and an elaboration of their own self-schemas.

Although I engaged in occasional speculation when making certain points in the chapter, other observations are reasonably well documented. For example, the relatively small number of studies examining cross-sex friendships in early childhood have shown that those friendships provide benefits to the participating members (e.g., Corsaro, 1985; Gottman, 1986; Howes, 1988; Rizzo, 1989; Whaley & Rubenstein, 1994). The provision of social support in the form of affect, aid, and affirmation and protection against loneliness represent generic benefits that are also provided by same-sex friends. Other benefits, however, are quite unique to cross-sex friendship. For example, an insider's perspective provided by cross-sex friends can help children better understand members of the other sex and their culture. Indeed, cross-sex friendships can serve as a potential segue into that culture.

I close this chapter with the identification of a seldom acknowledged and never-studied developmental milestone that occurs in early childhood. The milestone is important because of its relevance to initial perception of cross-sex interaction and potential friendship. There has been no attempt to systematically study the first few occasions of extended cross-sex interaction between infants or toddlers—that is, what happens the first few times a very young child has an opportunity to interact with nonfamilial members of the other sex? Whether or not infants form friendships in general and cross-sex friendships in particular is a topic worthy of empirical and theoretical investigation. For the sake of argument let us assume for the moment that for many children "infancy" ends and toddlerhood begins at about the age of 15 months. As noted by Harter (1998) in her chapter on the development of self-representations, between the ages of 10 and 15 months infants begin to establish a sense of self as they differentiate themselves from their care givers. In Ruble and Martin's review chapter on gender development they observe that "Most infants are able to visually discriminate the sexes by 9 months of age … and by one year of age 75% of children can discriminate the faces of males and females" (1998, p. 944). Early peer cross-sex interactions before the age of 15 months help to form the beginnings of a cross-sex friendship schema, even if a friendship per se is only marginally established (Vygotsky, 1978). Along these lines, however, Howes suggested that because toddlers have limited awareness of their gender identities before about the age of 2 or 3 they may focus more on "friendship" availability than the gender of the partner (1988).

3

Cross-Sex Friendships in Middle and Late Childhood

(7 to 11 years of age)

At no other age do boys and girls behave as though one may be contaminated by mere interaction or proximity with members of the other gender. Claimed fear of 'cooties' and 'boy germs' conveys in a playful way the seriousness of the issues involved. So too do the swift and certain consequences that occur when gender boundaries are crossed.
—L. A. Sroufe et al. (1993, p. 455)

Cross-sex friendship processes begun in early childhood such as friendship schema development and gender segregation continue in modified fashion in middle and late childhood. Even some of the early childhood cross-sex friendships themselves continue (Gottman, 1986). However, I am not aware of any systematic attempts to longitudinally track specific cross-sex friendships as they go from early childhood into middle childhood. Although the cross-sex friendship processes in middle/late childhood are similar to the ones in early childhood, there are also noticeable differences as cross-sex friendships transform to reflect and accommodate developmental changes experienced by the participants. For example, as suggested in the above quotation, same-sex friendship preferences begun in early childhood become much more pronounced in middle childhood as children separate into groups determined primarily by biological sex (Sroufe et al., 1993).

The differences and similarities between cross-sex friendships in early and middle to late childhood are identified periodically throughout the four sections of this chapter. The first three sections develop the central themes of the book and relate each theme to middle and late childhood. In the final section I offer some concluding observations about cross-sex friendships that occur in this pivotal stage between early childhood and adolescence.

Before getting started a few preliminary observations are in order concerning the time frame covered by middle and late childhood, nomenclature, and some weaknesses I encountered in the middle and late childhood cross-sex friendship literature.

Middle and late childhood roughly encompasses ages 7 to 11 (the elementary school years) and culminates in preadolescence. In this chapter I use the terms *late childhood* and *preadolescence* interchangeably. I combined middle and late childhood into the same chapter for a practical reason (i.e., there were not enough cross-sex friendship studies to justify a separate chapter for each). However, empirical investigations (e.g., Gottman, 1986; Meurling, Ray, & LoBello, 1999) and theoretical positions (e.g., Sullivan, 1953) suggest there are developmental differences between friendships established in middle childhood and those formed in late childhood. Gottman offered an analysis of developmental patterns revealing that from age 8 to age 12 friendship goals shift from coordinated play to a concern about peer-group acceptance (1986). Meurling and his colleagues discovered that second and third graders (middle childhood) rate their friendships more positively than do fifth and sixth graders (late childhood); but that fifth and sixth graders draw greater distinctions between best friends and casual friends than do their younger counterparts (Meurling, Ray, & LoBello, 1999). In his interpersonal theory of psychiatry, Sullivan (1953) differentiated middle childhood from late childhood. Around the age of 10 (late childhood) a child develops a specific need for a close friend of the same-sex, what Sullivan called a *chum*, a need that did not exist during middle childhood. There is clearly a gray area between middle and late childhood, meaning that developmental processes and milestones that distinguish the two stages of life are often difficult to identify.

The literature on middle and late childhood cross-sex friendships is discouragingly sparse. Additionally, researchers often exclude cross-sex friendships from their investigations without giving reasons or explanations (e.g., Bagwell, Newcomb, & Bukowski, 1998; Lieberman, Doyle, & Markiewicz, 1999; Meurling et al., 1999; Ray, Cohen, Secrist, & Duncan, 1997). Investigators also often fail to address the biological sex composition of the friendship (e.g., Booth, Rubin, & Rose-Krasnor, 1998; Kerns, Klepac, & Cole, 1996; Parker & Asher, 1993; Ray & Cohen, 1996; Ray, Cohen, & Secrist, 1995). The biological sex composition of a friendship is an issue worthy of consideration. For instance, Ray and his associates' stated purpose was "to examine the size of children's best friend networks in the classroom, the playground, and nonschool setting, all in relation to the child's classroom sociometry" (1995, p.170). They also drew conclusions about popular and rejected status children. About 75% of their sample of 447 elementary school children were from Grades 2 through 6. Although children were not restricted to naming just same-sex friends, no attempt was made to examine cross-sex friendship pairings. They therefore overlooked the significant relationship between popularity and cross-sex friendships emphasized by other researchers (e.g., Bukowski, Sippola, Hoza, 1999; George & Hartmann, 1996; Kovacs, Parker, & Hoffman, 1996).

A year after their 1995 study, Ray and Cohen investigated children's behavioral and dispositional expectations for actual and prototypic classroom best friends (1996). Again, without offering an explanation, Ray and Cohen restricted the definition of best friend to a same-sex other who had been reciprocally nominated by the child. Twenty-eight children (15 girls and 13 boys) had no reciprocal best friends. The 28 children were not given an opportunity to nominate a cross-sex other as a best friend. Although it is difficult to know how many of those children might have had a cross-sex best friend, research by Kovacs and associates (1996) and Bukowski and colleagues (1999) has established that some children have only cross-sex friends and no same-sex ones.

A final example of a study in which cross-sex friendships were inexplicably excluded is an otherwise impressive attachment theory investigation conducted by Lieberman and her associates (Lieberman, Doyle, & Markiewicz, 1999). Two hundred and seventy-four elementary school students (ages 9 to 11) and 267 high school students (ages 12 to 14) participated in the study. One of the goals of their investigation was to examine relationships between attachment security, friendships, friendship quality, and popularity. Subjects were asked to list the names of up to eight of their same-sex best friends. No explanation was offered why best friends were confined to same-sex relationships, although other researchers had clearly established the centrality of cross-sex friendships for some children during middle childhood and the connection of popularity to those relationships (George & Hartman, 1996; Kovacs et al., 1996). Lieberman and her colleagues failed to investigate or acknowledge the possibility that the presence or absence of a reciprocated cross-sex friendship might be related to security of attachment to parents.

In addition to empirical investigators, reviewers of the childhood friendship and peer relationship literatures have also marginalized cross-sex friendships. In an otherwise excellent meta-analytic review of 82 preschool- to early-adolescence friendship studies comparing friends to nonfriends, Newcomb and Bagwell gave only token attention to cross-sex friendships (1995). In a similar fashion, in their otherwise outstanding review chapter on childhood peer interactions, relationships, and groups, Rubin, Bukowski, and Parker basically ignored cross-sex friendships and how those friendships might be related to central constructs in their review such as popularity (1998).

One more observation needs to be made concerning the literature on middle and late childhood friendships. Readers, researchers, and theoreticians must be careful not to confuse peer interaction studies involving same- and other-sex children with friendship investigations (Asher, Parker, & Walker, 1996; Rubin et al., 1998). There are well documented differences between friendship and nonfriend peer relationships (Newcomb & Bagwell, 1995). Therefore, conclusions drawn from studies about peer interaction are not necessarily applicable to friendships and vice versa. On the other hand, peer interaction studies provide interesting food for thought and do have relevance to cross-sex friendship. After all, friendship development has its beginnings in nonfriendship peer interaction. Although a comprehensive review of peer interaction studies is well beyond the scope of this chapter, selected studies are periodically cited as the need arises. For example, Ladd demonstrated that peer rejected third- and fourth-grade boys were more likely than their nonrejected peers to interact with girls, interaction that could serve as the foundation for a cross-sex friendship (1983).

Although many childhood friendship scholars tacitly discount the importance of cross-sex friendships by ignoring them in their research designs and literature reviews, some do not. Researchers studying middle and late childhood cross-sex friendships have documented how those relationships enrich the social networks of children. That documentation is examined in the upcoming section.

Cross-Sex Friendships and the Enrichment of Social Networks During Middle and Late Childhood

Enrichment of one's social network through the cultivation of cross-sex friendships occurs during middle and late childhood in much the same way as it did in the preschool years. Middle- and late-childhood friendships, like their early childhood predecessors, are developmentally significant when compared to nonfriend peer relationships (Newcomb & Bagwell, 1996). Although Newcomb and Bagwell recognized the developmental significance of childrens' friendships, they also noted that the "jury remains out" as to the exact nature of that significance (1996, p. 318). To extend their legal metaphor, I suggest that the jury has yet to convene on the developmental significance of cross-sex friendships because the bulk of the evidence has not been presented. Some of that evidence is reviewed in this section of the chapter in hopes of establishing a primae facie case concerning the developmental importance of cross-sex friendships.

Generic Benefits.   Cross-sex friends in middle and late childhood (ages 7 to 11) serve functions and provide benefits similar to those offered by same-sex friends (Parker & Gottman, 1989). A central benefit of middle and late childhood friendships is the mutual bestowing of social support. According to Crohan and Antonucci (1989), social support includes the provision of affect (e.g., closeness and intimacy), aid (e.g., help), and affirmation (e.g., validating a friend's values or beliefs). Researchers and theoreticians have demonstrated how middle and late childhood friendships serve social support functions (e.g., Bigelow, Tesson, & Lewko, 1996; Bukowski, Hoza, & Boivin, 1994; Parker & Asher, 1993; Rawlins, 1992; Sullivan, 1953).

Although researchers have shown that friends in middle and late childhood are supportive of one another, investigators rarely design studies for the express purpose of exploring social support functions of cross-sex friendships. Readers are implicitly encouraged to make generalizations about cross-sex friendships from samples of friendships dominated by same-sex pairings. For example, in Newcomb and Bagwell's meta-analysis they examined 82 studies where differences between friendship and nonfriend relationships were investigated (1995). In their summarizing "portrait of friendship," they concluded that friends provide a more efficacious context for social, emotional, and cognitive development than do nonfriends. One can infer that cross-sex friendships also provide a supportive environment for social, emotional, and cognitive development. However, it is impossible to determine with certainty if the identified benefits are equally and similarly available in same and cross-sex friendships because Newcomb and Bagwell did not clearly differentiate between the two types of friendship.

Social support in the form of "aid" (Crohan & Antonucci, 1989) includes the protection one child might give another against peer victimization (Hodges, Boivin, Vitaro, & Bukowski, 1999). Such aid overlaps with the provision of affect (i.e., protecting a friend shows that one cares for the friend) and affirmation (i.e., protecting a friend affirms that friend's self-image as being a person worthy of protection). Peer victimization is a specific type of peer relationship in which a child is frequently the target of various forms of abuse (Ladd, Kochenderfer, & Coleman, 1997). Targets of peer victimization also have higher levels of loneliness (Crick & Bigbee, 1998; Graham & Juvonen, 1998). Research has shown that targets of peer victimization during middle childhood are better protected from peer abuse if they have a best friend than children without a best friend (Hodges et al., 1999) What is unclear from the research (e.g., Hodges et al., 1999), is whether cross-sex friends offer such protection and if the protection differs in any significant way from protection provided by same-sex friends. In interviews conducted with children 8 to 10 years old (17 females, 13 males), Blomberg and I discovered evidence of cross-sex friends protecting one another from peer abuse in similar ways as their same-sex counterparts (1998). The following example illustrating the reciprocal nature of cross-sex friendship protection is from an interview with a 9-year-old boy.

> Sometimes when kids are making fun of her, because she's kind of chubby, I just say "stop that" or "it's ok Sarah" or "how would you feel," those kinds of things that would make them stop. Some kids will make fun of me because I'm not good at sports. Some kids make fun of me for other reasons and she stops them.

Friendships in middle and late childhood also provide social support through the facilitation of social and behavioral adjustment (Kovacs et al.,1996; Newcomb & Bagwell, 1996; Parker & Gottman, 1989). Helping a friend adjust behaviorally and socially can be viewed as a type of social aid. Friends can make behavioral and social adjustment easier for one another by providing an opportunity to practice interaction skills and to learn peer group norms (Rubin et al., 1998).

Social and behavioral adjustment is inextricably linked to peer group acceptance, otherwise known as popularity (Bukowski & Hoza, 1989). The importance of peer group acceptance to children during middle and late childhood is quite pronounced and difficult to overstate (Parker & Gottman, 1989). Researchers and theorists note that popularity is considerably more salient and significant to children during middle and late childhood than it is to their younger counterparts (e.g., Rubin et al., 1998; Sullivan, 1953). The importance and developmental significance of peer group acceptance warrants a closer inspection of popularity and its relationship to cross-sex friendship.

The popularity construct has dominated the literature on peer relationships for the last 15 years (Rubin et al., 1998). Additionally, as observed by Asher and his colleagues (Asher et al., 1996), although the distinction between friendship and popularity is often recognized, only recently has the relationship between those two constructs been empirically explored (e.g., George & Hartmann, 1996; Kovacs et al., 1996; Parker & Asher, 1993). Popularity refers to how well an individual child is liked and accepted by the members of his or her peer group (Bukowski & Hoza, 1989) and is typically operationalized through the use of sociometric methods. As customarily employed, sociometric methods allow for the categorization of a child as popular, rejected (unpopular), average, neglected, or controversial (Asher & Dodge, 1986; Duncan & Cohen, 1995; for reviews of sociometry and its limitations see Cillessen & Bukowski, 2000; Rubin et al., 1998, pp. 649–652, and Terry & Coie, 1991). Popular children are liked by most of their peers and disliked by few. Unpopular or rejected children are disliked by most and rarely liked. Children can be rejected by their peers for a number reasons such as having inefficient peer entry strategies and poor social problem-solving skills (Asher & Cole,1990; Erwin, 1998). Unpopular children "may appear self-centered, opinionated, and perhaps bossy; they may violate the rules of games or even try to change the game being played" (Erwin, 1998, p. 61; Stewart & Rubin, 1995). Because they are usually not even noticed by their peers, neglected children are neither liked nor disliked. Controversial children are highly liked by some of their peers and highly disliked by others. Average children are those who score around the mean on both the liking and disliking items on a sociometric instrument (Duncan & Cohen, 1995).

Researchers studying the relationship between popularity and friendship often neglect to provide sufficient information about the sex composition of the dyads being examined (e.g., Duncan & Cohen, 1995; Parker & Asher, 1993). For instance, Duncan and Cohen had 447 children (238 males and 209 females) from 16 classes in Grades 1 to 6 circle the names of three classmates who they "liked the most." Subjects also ranked each of their classmates on a scale of 1 (like very little) to 6 (like very much). Children were classified as popular, rejected, neglected, controversial, and average. As a general pattern, a basic homosocial preference was revealed with boys ranking boys higher than girls, and girls ranking girls higher than boys. Unfortunately, Duncan and Cohen did not provide data concerning the frequency that children included cross-sex others in their list of three best-liked classmates.

There have been a few noteworthy explorations of the relationship between popularity and cross-sex friendship (e.g., Bukowski et al., 1999; George & Hartmann, 1996; Kovacs et al, 1996). In their investigation of 227 fifth and sixth graders, George and Hartmann discovered that 17% of the children had one or more reciprocal cross-sex friends (1996).There was a statistically significant difference in the number of reciprocated cross-sex friendships of unpopular and popular children. Nineteen of the 64 popular children (30%) had a reciprocal cross-sex friend, compared to only 3 of the 41 unpopular children (7%). George and Hartmann speculated that popular children might have a higher level of social skills that enable them to successfully interact with members of the other sex. They also uncovered some interesting differences between girls and boys. Whereas 14% of the unpopular boys had at least one reciprocal cross-sex friend, none of the unpopular girls did. Along similar lines, 47% of the popular boys had at least one reciprocated cross-sex friendship, compared to 22% of the popular girls.

One of the laudable methodological design elements of the George and Hartmann study is that they did not restrict friendship nominations to the classroom or school. Children were allowed to report on friendships they had from a variety of locations. George and Hartmann contended that studies restricting friendship nominations to the classroom or school (e.g., Parker & Asher, 1993) might be underestimating the number of friendships because unpopular children often have friends outside the school environment (Smith & Inder, 1990). This might be especially true of cross-sex friendships in middle childhood because such friendships are sometimes forced "underground" out of fear of social reprisals (Gottman, 1986). George and Hartmann observed that 23% of unpopular children in their study did not have a reciprocal friend, compared to 55% of the unpopular children in Parker and Asher's study in which friendship nominations were restricted to the classroom. Opportunities for friendships to develop occur in a wide range of physical locales (Lewis & Phillipsen, 1998), although the most common locale for friendship studies has been in the classroom (Ray, Cohen, & Secrist, 1995).

Kovacs, Parker, and Hoffman (1996) improved on the George and Hartmann investigation in a well-designed and empirically rich exploration. They compared children with and without cross-sex friends on measures of social and cognitive competence, endorsement of sex-role stereotypes, and family composition. Kovacs and colleagues made a critical distinction between children whose cross-sex friends were their only or primary friends and children whose cross-sex friends were of secondary importance when compared to same-sex friends. Their sample consisted of 723 third and fourth graders (377 girls, 346 boys).

Ninety-two children (13%) had one or more reciprocal cross-sex friends. For 19 of the 92 children (about 3% of the entire sample of 723) cross-sex friendships were their only or primary friendships. Data analysis revealed that those children had poorer social skills than children with primarily same-sex friends. They were also rated as more aggressive and less helpful by their peers, were less well liked, and had lower self-esteem than those children whose primary friends were of the same sex. They also had fewer same-sex friends than children with only same-sex friends and children whose cross-sex friends were secondary to their same-sex ones. However, those 19 children were better adjusted than children without any friends and had less stereotypical views about sex roles than did other children.

A different and more encouraging profile emerged for the 71 children whose cross-sex friendships were secondary to their same-sex ones. They were as well adjusted socially and were generally viewed as more helpful and were better accepted by both boys and girls than those children with only same-sex friends (*n* = 572). In a telling statement complete with caveats and qualifiers, Kovacs and her colleagues observed:

> First, it seems clear that a cross-sex friend is better than no friend at all. If children can maintain primary relationships with same-sex peers, then cross-sex friendships do not appear to be detrimental to children's social skills and may possibly have a beneficial impact. However, having a primary same-sex friend is related to greater social and behavioral adjustment than is having a primary opposite-sex friend. It should be stressed, nonetheless, that further research is necessary to determine the long-term implications of these findings. (1996, p. 2284)

A reasonable conclusion from the Kovacs study is that the centrality of cross-sex friendships in a child's social network is connected to popularity, social support, and social and behavioral adjustment.

Bukowski, Sippola, and Hoza investigated cross-sex and same-sex friendships of 231 fifth-, sixth-, and seventh-grade girls and boys (ages 10 to 12). They discovered that children who were very popular or very unpopular were more likely than other children to have cross-sex friends (1999). For those children without a same-sex friend, having a cross-sex friend was linked to higher levels of perceived well being for boys but lower levels for girls. Recall that in the George and Hartmann study unpopular girls had no cross-sex friends, whereas unpopular boys did. Bukowski and colleagues contended that in some cases (usually for popular children) cross-sex friendships parallel same-sex friendships and that competent functioning in one domain is similar to competent functioning in the other. Other-sex peers can also function as a back-up system for those individuals who have problems establishing friendships in the same-sex domain. They observed "although there is clearly a link between low popularity and an orientation toward the other sex, it is not clear exactly how this process works ..." (p. 457). In a somewhat contradictory fashion, however, recall that George and Hartman discovered that popular children were much more likely to have reciprocal cross-sex friendships then were their unpopular counterparts.

Loneliness is associated with peer group acceptance (i.e., popularity) and friendships (Parker & Asher, 1993; Renshaw & Brown, 1993; Rotenberg & Hymel, 1999). The connection between loneliness and popularity is fairly obvious. Low- status and unpopular children generally report higher levels of loneliness and fewer friends than their more popular counterparts (Asher, Parkhurst, Hymel, & Williams, 1990; Crick & Ladd, 1993; Perlman & Landolt, 1999). Because popularity means how much a person is liked by his or her peers, being unpopular probably induces feelings of isolation and loneliness. Sullivan believed that loneliness might have its roots in the early school years if a child was ostracized and/or unable to form a close friendship. Parker and Asher found empirical support for their contention that having a friend, friendship quality, and peer group acceptance each make separate contributions to a prediction of loneliness (1993). Similarly, results from studies by Bukowski and his colleagues (1999) and Kovacs and her associates (1996) indirectly suggest that the companionship made available through cross-sex friendships, particularly for less popular children, offers protection against loneliness.

Unfortunately, in many studies of loneliness in middle and late childhood scholars either did not examine the sex composition of the dyad (e.g., Kerns et al., 1996; Parker & Asher, 1993) or they restricted friendship nominations to same-sex others (e.g., Parker & Seal, 1996; Renshaw & Brown, 1993). In those studies readers are implicitly encouraged to assume that cross-sex friendships are related to levels of loneliness in the same way as same-sex friendships. Sometimes making such an inference is justified, sometimes not. The point is that without access to data and analysis on the sex composition of the friendship dyads, interpreting studies is problematic and less than fully informative. For example, in one study third through fifth grade children ($n = 881$) were asked to identify their three "best friends" from a list of the children in their classroom (Parker & Asher, 1993). Participants were not restricted to naming only same-sex friends but they were also not allowed to name friends from outside their immediate classroom. Friendship quality, satisfaction, and levels of loneliness were assessed. Parker and Asher's results would have been more informative if they had separately examined cross-sex and same-sex friendships and allowed students to list friends who were not in their class. For instance, they concluded that some popular children did not have "best friends," whereas some unpopular children did. However, popular children without best friends might have had best friends who were not in their class. Also, readers of their study were not told if the unpopular children tended to gravitate toward cross-sex friendships. Knowing if friends of the unpopular children were members of the other sex, as some research indicates they sometimes are (e.g., George & Hartmann, 1996; Kovacs et al., 1996), would be useful information to have for intervention purposes and to contribute to the existing research base on cross-sex friendships in middle childhood.

Unique Benefits.   Cross-sex friendships during middle and late childhood offer a number of unique advantages that are not available in same-sex friendships. These special and overlapping benefits are a continuation and modification of those provided during early childhood: (a) an opportunity to obtain an insider's perspective, (b) an opportunity to learn new ways of interacting, (c) an opportunity to better understand members of the other sex and their culture, and (d) an opportunity to have a friend when same-sex avenues have not been successful.

One of the most significant advantages of cross-sex friendship at any stage of life is that the participating friends can provide each other with insider perspectives on how members of the other sex think, feel, and behave (Monsour, 1997). Insider perspectives are more salient and useful during middle and late childhood (ages 7 to 11) than they were in early childhood for a number of reasons. First, children in elementary school come to know for certain what they may have only suspected before, that is, girls and boys not only look different, but they think and act differently as well (Leaper, 1994b). The realization that the differences between boys and girls go beyond mere physical appearance, whether accurate or not, make insider perspectives more consequential in middle childhood than were in early childhood.

A second factor increasing the salience of insider perspectives is the intensification of gender segregation that occurs in middle childhood (Maccoby, 1994). As children spend more time with members of their own sex and correspondingly less time with members of the other sex, the social and behavioral differences between the two sexes are reinforced and amplified (Fagot, 1994). Gender segregation accentuates the need for children to have social contacts that enable them to see things from the perspective of members of the other sex. From the viewpoint of a symbolic interactionist, insider perspectives allow individuals to take the role of the other (Mead, 1934) and to see things from his or her world view. If the partner is a member of the other sex, seeing things from her or his viewpoint should increase understanding of how members of that sex see the world. Understanding how members of the other sex think, feel, and behave, should facilitate cross-sex interaction and decrease a child's degree of voluntary gender segregation. At a minimum, an insider's perspective could help a child understand why gender segregation occurs. For example, reflecting research showing that boys and girls have different play styles (Maccoby, 1994; Moller, Hymel, & Rubin, 1992), a young girl might tell her cross-sex friend that she generally plays with other girls rather than boys because "most girls don't like to play rough, and most boys do."

Despite the acceleration of gender segregation during middle and late childhood (ages 7 to 11; Leaper, 1994a), heterosexual children, toward the end of that stage of life, begin to view other-sex peers as potential boyfriends or girlfriends (Erwin, 1998). Having cross-sex friends and obtaining insider perspectives from those friends could be of great benefit to heterosexuals beginning to realize that they are attracted to members of the other sex for reasons other than friendship. Two 11-year-old cross-sex friends, for instance, could discuss their growing romantic interest in members of the other sex and provide each other with unique insider perspectives. The extent to which such conversations actually occur has not been investigated. A corollary to the insider perspective advantage is that young girls and boys could begin to see themselves as peers and friends first before becoming "known to one another as love interests" (Sagar, Schofield, & Snyder, 1983).

Friendships with members of the other sex give children an opportunity to develop new cross-sex interaction skills (or hone already existing ones carried over from early childhood) that will help them adjust to society's changing attitudes about appropriate sex-role behavior (Erwin, 1998; George & Hartmann, 1996; Maccoby, 1990). According to social learning theory, those skills are acquired by observing others and modeling one's behavior accordingly (Bandura & Walters, 1963). Such observational learning can lead to more adaptive behavior in novel situations and to new and different kinds of relationships (Cairns, 1979).

In 1994 an entire issue of a journal was devoted to exploring the causes and consequences of gender segregation (Leaper, 1994a). Contributors made the empirically based observation that boys and girls in middle school generally chose to engage in gender segregation, and as a result they develop their own gender-based norms of behavior and ways of viewing the world (e.g., Fagot, 1994; Maccoby, 1994). Interactions between cross-sex friends give those friends a window into the gendered world of their partner and a chance to be exposed to and possibly learn some of the behaviors characteristic of those worlds. Therefore, middle-aged children with cross-sex friends are privy to an important component of socialization that children without those friends are not. However, the acquisition of cross-sex behaviors might come at a cost. For example, 10-year-old boys who display play styles typical of girls are less accepted by their peers than boys who are more gender stereotyped in their styles of play (Moller et al., 1992). The lack of same-sex acceptance might explain why unpopular boys have cross-sex friends (i.e., they adopt play styles of girls that may make them more attractive to girls, but less attractive to boys). Similarly, girls who display play styles typical of their male counterparts are given the somewhat pejorative label of "tomboy" (Feiring & Lewis, 1989).

Although I believe that cross-sex friends can help one another become more effective in their social interactions, there is some controversy over whether middle-aged children with cross-sex friendships are more or less socially skilled than those without such friendships (Bukowski et al., 1999; Kovacs et al., 1996; Sroufe et al., 1993). Also open to debate is whether cross-sex friendships lead to higher levels of interactional skill, or whether the skills already exist and simply lead to more cross-sex friendships. If children with cross-sex friendships are more socially adept than those without such friendships, the greater level of communication skill could be either a consequence or a cause of having cross-sex friendships. Children with high levels of social skills are generally more popular than those with less skills and also tend to have more cross-sex friends than their less popular counterparts (George & Hartmann, 1996). Although popular children may have more cross-sex friends than unpopular ones, the reasons for having those friendships might be different. Popular children have friends of the other sex by choice, whereas some unpopular children who have been rejected by members of their same-sex peer group may be forced into such friendships (Bukowski et al., 1999; Carter & McCloskey, 1984; Kovacs et al., 1996). Perhaps the word *forced* is a bit too strong. Nevertheless, when children initiate friendships with other-sex peers because they are unsuccessful with members of their own sex the popular notion of friendships as being voluntary associations (Fehr, 1996; Rawlins, 1992), might need to be re-examined (see Blieszner & Adams, 1992, p. 2)

A third unique benefit of cross-sex friendships is that those relationships can increase understanding of the culture of members of the other sex, partly because of the insider perspective provided by those friends. Many friendship and peer relationship scholars believe that by middle childhood boys and girls have begun to develop their own separate gender cultures (Leaper, 1994a; Maccoby & Jacklin, 1987; Ruble & Martin, 1998; Thorne, 1986). For example, Leaper (1994b) reviewed evidence that boys' and girls' childhood peer groups emphasize different types of social skills and behaviors. Girls tend to focus on interpersonal sensitivity in small groups and dyads, whereas boys concentrate more on competition and activity in larger groups. Cross-sex friends can help each other understand how the respective gender cultures operate, which could reap immediate and long-term benefits. Immediate benefits would be the ability to form additional cross-sex friendships and to get along with cross-sex peers. Long-range benefits could be realized later in the life cycle as the child enters high school, college, and the workplace, equipped with a better understanding of the culture of the other gender (Leaper, 1994b).

The final and fourth unique benefit of cross-sex friendship was addressed in the previous section. For those children who have difficulty forming friendships with members of their own sex, cross-sex friendships offer relational refuge from the onslaughts of friendlessness and loneliness (Bukowski et al., 1999; Kovacs et al., 1996). However, some research indicates that boys are more successful than girls in forming cross-sex friendships when their same-sex avenues have been blocked (George & Hartman, 1996) and that cross-sex friendships have more positive effects on boys who have difficulty forming same-sex friendships than girls who have the same difficulty (Bukowski, et al., 1999).

In summary of this section, cross-sex friendships have the potential to enrich the social network of middle-aged children by supplying them with social support (George & Hartman, 1996), facilitating social and behavioral adjustment (Kovacs et al., 1996), and protecting them against loneliness (Bukowski et al., 1999). Uniquely, cross-sex friendships can also provide participants with insider perspectives and insights about cultural nuances and norms of the other sex and serve as a testing ground for learning different types of interaction skills (Leaper, 1994b). All of the benefits I identified need further empirical investigation and verification. Of course the advantages of cross-sex friendships can be reaped only if children can successfully overcome the social and structural barriers inhibiting their formation.

Social and Structural Barriers to Cross-Sex Friendship During Middle and Late Childhood

Social and structural barriers interfering with cross-sex friendship formation become more pronounced and formidable in middle and late childhood (ages 7 to 11) than they were in early childhood (ages 18 months to 6). As was true in early childhood, barriers to cross-sex friendships have structural and social components and are manifested in the surface and deep structures of society. Recall that the deep structure of society is where cultural definitions of relationships originate (Hartup & Stevens, 1997). The cultural definition of a cross-sex friendship in middle childhood has changed from what it was during early childhood. Societal views of cross-sex friendships in early childhood are typically not complicated by the knowledge that boys and girls can be boyfriends and girlfriends, whereas in middle childhood they are (Parker & Gottman, 1989). Surface structures, that is, behavioral and communicative displays of deep structure (Hartup & Stevens, 1997), are also subject to change as individuals move from early childhood into middle childhood. For example, gossip and self-disclosure have added significance and prominence during middle childhood when compared to the earlier stage of life (Parker & Gottman, 1989; Rubin et al., 1998).

The most obvious consequence of the amplification of social and structural barriers to cross-sex friendships is that middle-aged children have fewer of those friendships than they did in early childhood. Epstein characterized the changing frequency this way: "The literature suggests a curvilinear, developmental pattern of cross-sex choices of friends. Very young children make frequent cross-sex (sociometric) choices, children in elementary and middle school grades make almost no cross-sex choices, and adolescents increase their cross-sex choice of friends" (1986, p. 137). There is ample evidence that cross-sex friendships at any level of closeness are rare in middle and late childhood (Gottman, 1986; Kupersmidt, DeRosier, & Patterson, 1995; Rawlins, 1992). For example, Graham and Cohen estimated that about 90% of the friendships of school-aged children are same-sex (1997). In the study conducted by Kovacs and her associates (1996), 86% of the 723 third and fourth graders in their study did not have a cross-sex friendship. A recent longitudinal investigation documented that during middle childhood (Grades 1 to 3 compared to Grades 4 to 6, same children) the proportion of same-sex to cross-sex friendships increased (Graham, Cohen, Zbikowski, & Secrist, 1998).

Although cross-sex friendships in middle childhood are unusual, their rarity is sometimes grossly overstated. Schneider and colleagues claim that individuals in middle childhood make "virtually no cross-sex choices" (Schneider, Wiener, Murphy, 1994, p. 331). Similarly, Reeder (2000, p. 330) cited 20-year-old research (Rickelman, 1981) to support her observation that "by age 7 these relationships (meaning, cross-sex friendships) are virtually nonexistent." The assertions of Schneider and Reeder are clearly exaggerations. Recent studies have shown that children between the ages to 7 and 11 (my designation of middle childhood) do have cross-sex friends (e.g., Kovacs et al., 1996).

In the upcoming sections on social and structural barriers to cross-sex friendship there is considerable analysis of gender segregation and same-sex friendship and peer preferences. Gender segregation and its companion construct of same-sex peer preferences are inseparably related to structural and social factors inhibiting cross-sex friendships. Additionally, because of the overlapping and fused nature of social and structural barriers, I was unable (and perhaps unwilling), to cleanly separate the two concepts so that I could exclusively focus on each one in different sections. Therefore, parts of one section (e.g., social barriers) may seem to be just as appropriately placed in the other section (e.g., structural barriers), and vice versa. I ask for the reader's indulgence.

Social Barriers.   Recall from chapters one and two that social obstacles (real or imagined) to cross-sex friendship formation and maintenance come from third parties and the potential or actual cross-sex friends themselves. Social barriers to cross-sex friendship in middle and late childhood are related to other central constructs that are themselves interrelated: relational norms, normative constraints, and peer group acceptance (that is, popularity).

Social barriers to cross-sex friendships often appear as relational norms and normative constraints. The homosocial norm, for example, originates at the societal and group level and is then internalized at the individual level (Rose, 1985). Recall that the homosocial norm is the preference to associate primarily with members of one's own sex (Rose, 1985) and can be legitimately viewed as both a structural and social barrier. The homosocial norm becomes a social barrier when there is behavior expressed to establish or reinforce the norm. For instance, when someone is teased for having a friend of the other sex, that teasing is a communicative manifestation of the homosocial norm. Similarly, if an 8-year-old boy says or does something to discourage friendship overtures from a member of the other sex his behavior would also be an outward manifestation of the homosocial norm.

The vast majority of children in middle childhood prefer the company of same-sex peers (Leaper, 1994a). Why is the homosocial norm so much a part of the relational culture of children in elementary school? In the second chapter I reviewed some explanations for gender segregation and the related construct of same-sex preferences. I now add one more explanation that seems particularly relevant to middle childhood. Concern about peer group acceptance is a plausible explanation of same-sex preferences and is examined in the upcoming pages.

Homosocial preferences are revealed in sociometric ratings of peers that are essentially measurements of popularity. In middle childhood boys give higher ratings to boys than to girls, and girls give higher ratings to girls than to boys (Bukowski, Gauze, Hoza, & Newcomb, 1993; Duncan & Cohen, 1995; Sippola, Bukowski, & Noll, 1997). From their study of 326 second through ninth graders, Sippola and her colleagues concluded that same-sex preferences are due more to a positive bias toward one's own sex rather than a negative bias toward members of the other sex (Sippola et al., 1997; see also Bukowski, Hoza, & Boivin, 1993).

One of the putative developmental differences between early and middle childhood is that peer-group acceptance is more important to middle-aged children than it is to their younger counterparts (Parker & Gottman, 1989; Rubin et al., 1998). Children become increasingly concerned with fitting into their peer group and being liked by same-sex age-mates when they go from early to middle childhood. Friendship cliques begin to form during middle childhood and individuals "know, or soon come to know, that in-group and out-group membership is a volatile, occasionally capricious affair" (Parker & Gottman, 1989, p. 113).

Peer disapproval of interaction with members of the other sex in middle childhood can be a powerful impediment to friendship formation (Rubin, 1980; Thorne, 1986). Howe (1993) documented hostility between boys and girls by the time they reach the third grade. Paradoxically, however, some third graders also begin to establish boyfriend–girlfriend relationships (Howe, 1993). Children in middle childhood often erect social barriers to cross-sex interaction, barriers that make friendship formation based on that interaction difficult (Sroufe et al., 1993). Ostracizing, name calling, and teasing are such barriers. Girls who cross the gender boundary to play in boy groups are labeled "tomboys" (Feiring & Lewis, 1989). As noted in chapter two, fear of social disapproval is so strong in middle childhood that cross-sex friendships are sometimes forced "underground" (Gottman, 1986). Being ostracized and teased for having friends of the other sex is a risk that many middle-aged children are simply not willing to take. Sometimes the teasing is about the cross-sex friends being romantically involved even if they clearly are not (Parker & Gottman, 1989).

Ostracization is sometimes the result of children violating gender boundaries. In a study of gender boundary maintenance and violation at a summer day camp, 10-and 11-year-old children who violated gender boundaries were significantly less popular than those children who did not engage in such violations (Sroufe et al., 1993). Sroufe and his coresearchers concluded that respecting gender boundaries during middle childhood is a sign of social competence because it indicates knowledge of peer norms and a willingness to abide by them. Boundary maintenance correlated with other indices of social competence.

Children have rules governing when crossing gender boundaries is permissible (Maccoby, 1990; Sroufe et al., 1993; Thorne & Luria, 1986). For example, cross-sex contact is acceptable when it is accidental, incidental, or if accompanied with disavowal (Sroufe et al., 1993). Cross-sex friendships and the boundary violations they invoke are also acceptable if the friendships are of obvious secondary importance to same-sex ones (Kovacs et al., 1996). On the other hand, cross-sex contact is not typically acceptable if an individual joins a group of opposite-sex others (Sroufe et al., 1993). Boys engage in more gender boundary maintenance and violation than girls, and there are often greater sanctions against boys for such violations (Leaper, 1994b; Sroufe et al., 1993; Thorne & Luria, 1986). Relatedly, elementary school children who have primarily or only cross-sex friends are generally less well liked than children whose cross-sex friends are of secondary importance (Kovacs et al., 1996).

A social process closely related to boundary violations and peer group popularity is gossip (Rubin et al., 1998). Recall that in early childhood gossip is less frequent than in middle childhood, very brief, and normally done in the context of play (Parker & Gottman, 1989). Its main purpose is to establish solidarity between partners. In contrast, gossip in middle childhood becomes the centerpiece of interaction and is connected to a number of other social processes (Parker & Gottman, 1989). Indeed, Parker and Gottman contended:

> Gossip is far and away the most salient social process in friendship interaction at this age. Not only does gossip, primarily disparaging gossip, make up the great bulk of the content of conversation among middle childhood friends, but other social processes, such as information exchange, exploration of similarities, humor, and self-disclosure, occur almost exclusively in the context of gossip. (p. 114)

Gossip in middle and late childhood is a way of figuring out peer group norms and establishing dyadic solidarity between friends (Parker & Gottman, 1989). During this stage of life gossip is primarily negative-evaluation gossip about a third person often centering on how that person has violated group norms (Gottman & Mettetal, 1986). Because one of the dominant norms in this stage of life is that individuals associate primarily with members of their own sex (Sroufe et al., 1993) negative evaluation gossip might focus on children who engage in cross-sex friendships. Concern about peer group acceptance and the related worry of being the subject of negative gossip might be a major reason for same-sex preference and the general avoidance of cross-sex friendships that occurs in middle childhood. Casual, informal observation of my 8-year-old son certainly supports such a hypothesis.

Structural Barriers.

Gender is the most potent psychological determinant of friendship choice in middle childhood...whatever the origins, it is clear that as a result of the tendency for children to select same-sex friends boys and girls operate in very different reference groups throughout middle childhood. (Gottman, 1986, p. 140)

As the above quotation makes clear, same-sex friendship preferences and gender segregation begun in the early childhood continue in amplified fashion in middle childhood (Benenson, Apostoleris, & Parnass, 1998). More than any other structural barrier, gender segregation insures that many boys and girls will be strangers to one another when the pullings of puberty bring them back together again in adolescence (Fagot, 1994). Indeed, the sex of a child has been shown to be much more strongly associated with mutuality in friendship choice than the race of a child in both cross-sectional (e.g., Graham & Cohen, 1997) and longitudinal studies (e.g., Graham et al., 1998). Scholars contend that gender segregation in middle childhood is a contributing factor to later communication difficulties and power asymmetries in heterosexual romantic relationships (Gottman & Carrere, 1994; Leaper & Anderson, 1997). Although gender segregation is closely linked to social barriers to cross-sex friendship initiation and maintenance; that segregation is first and foremost a structural barrier. In the next few pages gender segregation is revisited along with related structural barriers such as proximity, group membership, and popularity.

Experts disagree as to why gender segregation occurs (Maccoby, 1994). I suggested on pages 77 to 78 of this chapter that same-sex preferences in middle childhood might be the product of peer pressure and the fear of being ostracized, teased, and generally shunned for crossing gender boundaries (Erwin, 1998; Sroufe et al., 1993). The social cognitive explanation of gender segregation explained in chapter two dovetails nicely with a peer pressure explication of same-sex preferences. From a social cognitive perspective, as children grow older they develop an understanding of what it means to be a girl or a boy and they begin to value members of their gender group, partly because they share obvious traits with those individuals which serve a self-validating function (Maccoby, 1994; Martin, 1994). As a child becomes socialized into a same-sex group he or she begins to internalize the norms and rules of that group. Some of those rules pertain to crossing gender boundaries and when such crossing is deemed acceptable (Sroufe et al., 1993). The fear of becoming less popular because one in associating too much with cross-sex others probably contributes to gender segregation.

Same-sex friendship preferences of middle schoolers has received a fair amount of research attention (e.g., Bukowski et al., 1993; et al., 1999; Sippola, Bukowski, & Noll, 1997). Bukowski and his associates investigated seven issues regarding children's preferences for same-sex peers and friends over cross-sex ones (Bukowski et al., 1993). Note that about half of the subjects were in early adolescence (i.e., 12 years of age). They gathered longitudinal data from two samples ($n = 292, n = 156$) and nonlongitudinal data from a third ($n = 236$). Students in all three samples were asked to list the names of their best friends of each sex and peers of each sex whom they did not like to play with. Their results indicated that same-sex preferences were based more on liking for same-sex peers than disliking of other-sex others (see similar results by Sippola et al.,1997). The preference for same-sex peers remained fairly consistent over time. A significant finding was that same-sex peer preferences were related to other-sex peer acceptance, that is, "the less that a child is accepted by other-sex peers, the more likely he or she is to display a preference for same-sex peers" (p. 260). Quite logically then, children who are not accepted by cross-sex others have little interest in playing with them or being their friends. Interestingly, re-sults also indicated that same-sex and other-sex popularity are closely related in that the impressions that one group has of an individual are "nearly identical" to the impressions of the other group. In support of a behavioral compatibility ex-planation of same-sex preferences (Fagot, 1994; Goodenough, 1934), boys who liked activities requiring gross motor skills (e.g., soccer) showed a stronger same-sex preference than boys who had less of an interest in those kinds of ac-tivities. Girls displayed just the opposite pattern, that is, there was a negative re-lationship between same-sex preferences and affinity for gross motor activities such as rough-and-tumble play. Considerable evidence has accumulated docu-menting that boys enjoy rough-and-tumble play more than girls (Lewis & Phillipsen, 1998; Pellegrini, 1990; Pellegrini & Smith, 1993; Thorne, 1993).

A noticeable shortcoming of the study was that Bukowski and associates (1993) equated "not wanting to play with a child" with "dislike for the child." In two out of three of the samples children were asked to list the names of those same-sex and other-sex peers they "did not like to play with" (p. 258). Only in the third sample were children asked to list peers they "did not like." Yet in the analysis of data and presentation of results and conclusions the peers that a subject did not want to play with were categorized as "disliked peers." Although Bukowski and others made a reasonable argument that "not liking to play with someone" was tantamount to disliking that person, there may be subtle but important differences between the two constructs. My 8-year-old son, for example, does not like to play with girls, not because he does not like them (so he tells me), but rather because they do not play the same way that he does.

In a study referenced earlier (i.e., Bukowski et al., 1999), researchers had 231 fifth, sixth, and seventh graders identify the three same-sex and the three other-sex peers that they liked the best from their class. Note that Bukowski and colleagues categorized subjects, many as young as 10 years old (whom I would categorize as being in late childhood), as adolescents. Peers were rated on a scale of 1 (dislikes a lot) to 5 (likes a lot). Overall, girls chose more same-sex peers as "best friends" than other-sex peers (4.4 compared to 3.1). Boys chose an average of 3.7 same-sex and 3.7 other-sex peers as "best friends". Bukowski and colleagues also examined the mean ratings of same and other sex peers by boys and girls. On average, girls gave same-sex friends a rating of 3.82 compared to a rating for cross-sex friends of a 3.05. Boys rated same and cross-sex friends respectively as 3.54 and 3.19. As observed on p.447 "The means presented show that the difference between girls and boys was larger on the same-sex measures (M = 3.82 and 3.54, for girls and boys respectively) than on the other-sex measure (M = 3.05 and 3.19)."

Same-sex preferences for communication partners were also revealed in a study conducted by Clark (1994). Eight hypothetical situations were read aloud and subjects ranging from the 4th to the 10th grade were asked to think of someone their own age they would like to talk to in that situation and to indicate if the person was a boy or a girl. For example, "Imagine that you were feeling a little lonely or left out …," and "Imagine that you needed to explain something that was really complicated …." When compared to the other grades, the fourth graders displayed a much stronger same-sex preference for a communication partner. Eighty percent of the choices made by girls and 74% of the choices made by boys were for a partner of the same sex.

Gender segregation in middle childhood is related to other structural factors influencing cross-sex friendship formation such as proximity and group membership. Except in cases of computer-mediated friendship initiation and maintenance (Adams, 1998; Parks & Floyd, 1996), physical proximity is a necessary (but not sufficient) condition for friendship formation (Fehr, 1996). Although it is conceivable that computer literate children in elementary school could form cross-sex friendships in the absence of physical proximity, to date there have been no empirical investigations of such anomalous relationships that I am aware of. Computer-mediated friendship in middle childhood is an unexplored and potentially rich area for study, especially examining how lonely and physically handicapped children might venture out into cyberspace to initiate friendships.

Group membership is a pertinent and potent structural factor that can interfere with cross-sex friendship formation in middle and late childhood (Thorne, 1993). As children congregate and segregate into same-sex peer groups they establish gender-based cultures. Indeed, the prevalence of gender segregation during middle childhood has led a number of experts to conclude that boys and girls live in different worlds during that stage of life (e.g., Maccoby, 1990; Maltz & Borker, 1982; Thorne, 1986; but see Kunkel & Burleson, 1998 for a critique of the different cultures perspective). Another related structural barrier to the development of cross-sex friendships in middle and late childhood is the well-documented preference of boys and girls to interact in groups and dyads, respectively (Belle, 1989; Benenson, 1994; Lewis & Phillipsen, 1998). Although some children do attempt to cross gender boundaries and enter into an other-sex group, such attempts are much rarer than attempts to enter a same-sex group (Luria & Herzog, 1991). Gaining admittance into a group of boys for the purpose of establishing a friendship with one of its members is difficult for a girl. Not only will the group probably not accept her as a member, but she might find it hard to interact outside of the dyadic context that she is more accustomed to and skillful at (Belle, 1989; Meurling et al., 1999; Rubin, 1980). Also, as observed by Maccoby (1990), boys engage in more rough-and-tumble play than girls. That fact coupled with the difficulty that girls often encounter when trying to influence boys makes girls hesitant to initiate cross-sex interaction (Erwin, 1998). In a similar fashion, because boys are more accustomed to group interactions, they may find dyadic interaction for the purpose of forming a friendship particularly demanding (Leaper, 1994b, p. 75).

The degree of status a child has within his or her peer network, (i.e., the child's popularity), is also structurally related to the formation of cross-sex friendships (George & Hartmann, 1996; Kovacs et al., 1996). Popularity can be conceptualized as the hierarchical status level or position occupied by a child in his or her social environment (Parker & Gottman, 1989; Rubin et al., 1998). As such, popularity is as much a structural barrier or facilitator of cross-sex friendships as it is a social one. Popularity is one determinant of access to others in a person's social network. By definition, unpopular children are less liked by peers of both sexes than their more popular counterparts and tend to be less socially skilled (George & Hartmann, 1996). Consequently, unpopular children might find themselves at a structural disadvantage for pursuit of friendships. Nevertheless, research has shown that unpopular children have cross-sex friendships (e.g., Kovacs et al., 1996), possibly as a result of being rejected by members of their own sex (Ladd, 1983). Some research suggest that popular children are more likely than unpopular children to have reciprocal cross-sex friends (George & Hartmann, 1996). Those friends provide structural network links to other potential cross-sex associations.

In summary of the second theme of this chapter, social and structural barriers to cross-sex friendships such as normative constraints, gender segregation, group membership, and concerns about popularity, all interfere with cross-sex friendships. Social and structural barriers are difficult to separate conceptually and on a practical level. Gender segregation can have detrimental effects later in the life cycle as boys and girls who were mostly separated in middle childhood are reunited as adolescents and young adults (Leaper, 1994b). Most friendship and peer relationship researchers have ignored the association between cross-sex friendships and popularity. This neglect is unfortunate. Research conducted by George and Hartmann, Kovacs and her associates, and Bukowski and his colleagues clearly indicate that the sex composition of a friendship dyad and the centrality of cross-sex friends in a child's social network impact peer-group acceptance and perceptions. As is shown in the next section of this chapter, constructs like popularity have a powerful impact on the self-concepts of children.

Cross-Sex Friendships Affect and are Affected by an Individual's Ongoing Social Construction of Self During Middle and Late Childhood

In the previous chapter the third theme and organizing premise of the book was developed by explaining two of the ways an individual's self concept and cross-sex friendships are related. A child's socially constructed self and cross-sex friendships are cognitively linked through schematic connections and communicatively linked through interaction. In this section I follow a similar topical scheme as the one employed in the parallel section in chapter two. I first examine the continuing role of interpersonal communication in the formation of cross-sex friendships and a child's developing concept of self in middle childhood. In the course of that examination I revisit the cognitive processes of gender, self, and cross-sex/same-sex friendship schema development. Second, I scrutinize a number of complementary theoretical positions from the interpersonal self perspective (Markus & Cross, 1990; Tice & Baumeister, 2001) to demonstrate how the social construction of self and the related communicative construction of cross-sex friendships are accomplished and related.

The role of interpersonal communication during early childhood in the development of an individual's self-concept and the emergence of cross-sex friendships continues through middle and late childhood. Just as they did during the toddler and preschool years, cross-sex friendships in middle childhood impact and are impacted by an individual's ongoing social construction of self, and communication plays a pivotal role in that process. Interpersonal communication theorists and researchers convincingly argue that communication is the *sine qua non* of personal relationships. As observed by one of the foremost proponents of this position, "communication is a generative process that creates understandings between people, defines relationships, composes rules for interaction, and establishes interpersonal climates" (Wood, 1995, p. xvi). The centrality of communication in the creation, maintenance, and understanding of relationships noted by Wood is recognized by leading scholars in the field of personal relationships (e.g. Duck, 1994) and has received empirical support from early and middle childhood friendship researchers (e.g., Corsaro, 1985; Parker & Gottman, 1989; Rizzo, 1989; Yingling, 1994). When applied to cross-sex friendships, communication is crucial to the dyadic construction of those relationships and the perception of a shared relational culture that accompanies that construction (Baxter, 1987; Monsour, 1994; Wood, 1995).

In addition to being the raw material of relationships, interpersonal communication makes an equally important contribution to an individual's developing view of self. An interpersonal self perspective on self construction contextualizes the "self" as an interpersonal creation (Tice & Baumeister, 2001). An individual's self is socially constructed through interactions with others. In a similar theoretical vein, from a social constructionism perspective (Gergen, 1977, 1991), the process of defining oneself is viewed as a series of communicative acts that take place in the context of relationships (Baldwin, 1992). Gergen contended that language is not just an outer expression of an inner reality, but rather is

> inherently a form of relatedness … in this way, meaning is born of interdependence. And because there is no self outside a system of meaning, it may be said that relations precede and are more fundamental than self. Without relationship there is no language with which to conceptualize the emotions, thoughts, or intentions of the self. (p. 157, 1991)

A large part of the social cognitive and communicative construction of self and cross-sex friendships is the ongoing development and evolution of relevant schemas. Interpersonal communication plays a pivotal role in the simultaneous construction of self, gender, and cross-sex/same-sex friendship schemas. Communication with others is directed by existing schemas, but at the same time it changes those schemas as well (Planalp, 1985).

In chapter two I proposed and described the co-mingling and codevelopment of gender, self, and cross-sex/same-sex friendship schemas during early childhood. When an individual enters middle childhood (i.e., second grade) he or she already has rudimentary gender (Ruble & Martin, 1998), self (Harter, 1998), and friendship schemas in various stages of development. Indeed, Howe contended that "Second grade is a very important year for self-concept development" (1993, p. 272). According to basic schema theory (Arbib, Conklin, & Hill, 1987), those preexisting knowledge structures influence the processing of incoming information. Depending on their experience with cross-sex friendships in early childhood, children in middle childhood will have different cross-sex friendships schemas. Even children who have never been in a cross-sex friendship still have nascent cross-sex friendship schemas (Honeycutt, 1993). Children with more extensive cross-sex friendship experiences have more complex and developed schemas. Because one of the functions of a relational schema is to guide communication behavior in relationships (Honeycutt & Cantrill, 2001; Planalp, 1985), cross-sex friendship schemas developed during early childhood would influence behavior in subsequent cross-sex interactions and friendship formation. Regretfully, the impact of preexisting cross-sex friendship schemas on the initiation and maintenance of subsequent cross-sex friendship has not received empirical attention.

Cross-sex friendship experiences and the schemas based on those experiences can have a significant impact on the evolving gender and self-schemas of children in middle and late childhood, just as those schemas can have an impact on cross-sex friendships and their accompanying schematic representations. A child's own-sex and other-sex schemas (Martin, 1994) are connected because part of a child's self-view is based on how that child perceives him or herself as being different from and similar to members of the other sex. Arguably, the own-sex and other-sex gender schemas of a child are linked to the child's cross and same-sex friendship schemas. All of those schemas are related in complex and sometimes redundant ways to a child's larger self-schema. For example, when an individual in a cross-sex friendship notices a similarity between herself and her cross-sex friend, that information would be added to many different schemas (e.g., her own-sex, other-sex, cross-sex friendship, and self-schemas). Similarity between relational partners has long been recognized as a basis for interpersonal attraction and the development of intimacy (Duck, 1994; for a review see Monsour, 1994).

Because a person's view of self is influenced by a wide range of relationships (Markus & Cross, 1990), the impact of cross-sex friendships or the lack of those friendships should not be overemphasized. On the other hand, nor should their influence on self-concept development be ignored. There are a number of theoretical perspectives relevant to my central argument that cross-sex friendships impact and are impacted by an individual's ongoing social construction of self throughout the life cycle. I begin my analysis with an examination of Sullivan's interpersonal theory of psychiatry and his chumship construct (1953), followed by a symbolic interactionist view (Cooley, 1902; Mead, 1934), and conclude with an application of Bowlby's attachment theory (1969).

The special saliency of Sullivan's speculations to cross-sex friendships in late childhood warrants inspection of the interpersonal theory of psychiatry and his chumship construct (1953). Sullivan (1892–1949) is one of the most often cited scholars in the area of preadolescent friendship. As a testimony to his notoriety, Furman observed that friendship studies share the same format, they invoke Sullivan's theory, and they stress the presumed importance of friendship (1993). Sullivan's self-labeled interpersonal theory of psychiatry is decidedly developmental in its approach to understanding personality and relationship development (Buhrmester & Furman, 1986). He believed that individuals have various interpersonal needs, and as they go through each stage of life those needs are satisfied via the formation of different types of relationships.

In what they labeled a "Neo-Sullivanian model," Buhrmester and Furman (1986) described Sullivan's five developmental stages and the central need in each stage: infancy (ages 0 to 2 years with a need for tenderness), childhood (ages 2 to 6 years with a need for companionship), juvenile era (ages 6 to 9 years with a need for acceptance), preadolescence (ages 9 to 12 years with a need for intimacy), and early adolescence (12 to 16 years with a need for sexuality). As a new need emerges it is added to the needs that already exist. Individuals attempt to create interpersonal situations that foster the fulfillment of their needs and avoid situations that might bring about fear, ostracism, loneliness, boredom, and anxiety (Sullivan, 1953).

Individuals also develop "interpersonal competencies" during each stage of life (Sullivan, 1953), primarily learned through interaction in different types of relationships (Buhrmester & Furman, 1986). For example, an only child not accustomed to sharing toys might learn that new skill (competency) from a friend.

The primary competencies acquired during middle and late childhood are the abilities to cooperate, compromise, collaborate, and compete. Children also develop perspective-taking and empathic abilities during late childhood. Sullivan's theory specifies that if an individual fails to establish a key relationship in a certain developmental stage he or she would be unable to acquire the new competencies necessary to function effectively in that kind of relationship.

Sullivan's juvenile era and the period of preadolescence roughly corresponds to my chronological designation of middle and late childhood (ages 7 to 11). Peer-group acceptance becomes increasingly important during the juvenile era, and an individual's level of self-esteem is determined by the degree of popularity achieved in the peer group. Being ostracized by one's peers, that is, not having one's need for acceptance met, is one form of "developmental arrest" (Sullivan, 1953, p. 217) that might occur during the juvenile era. Sullivan did not believe that children in the juvenile epoch (ages 6 to 9) were capable of forming full-blown friendships because their interactive strategies are concerned with figuring out what they must do in order to get what they want from their peers (Buhrmester & Furman, 1986; Sullivan, 1953). Obviously, I and many other students of early childhood friendships (e.g., Gottman, 1986; Howes, 1996; Whaley & Rubenstein, 1994) strongly disagree with Sullivan on this point.

During preadolescence the need for interpersonal intimacy begins to emerge and is added to the need for acceptance. That need for intimacy is met, according to Sullivan, by a friend of the same sex called a *chum*. As noted by Sullivan (1953):

> the beginning of preadolescence is equally spectacularly marked, in my scheme of development, by the appearance of a new type of interest in another person. These changes are the result of maturation and development, or experience … it is a specific new type of interest in a particular member of the same sex who becomes a chum or close friend. (p. 245)

According to Sullivan, male preadolescents are motivated to form a chumship with a particular same-sex peer between the ages of 8½ and 10 years of age. The chumship provides the preadolescent male with an opportunity to experience intimacy and consensual validation of all components of personal worth thru a merging of identities (1953; Youniss, 1980). The development of a chumship is theorized to prevent loneliness, validate self-worth, aid in the development of interpersonal sensitivity, and lead to healthier adult relationships later in life (Bagwell et al., 1998; Kerns, 1996; Sullivan, 1953).

Despite Sullivan's impact on the study of preadolescent friendships (Rawlins, 1992), his theory and writings have received considerable criticism. Allen characterized Sullivan as an "awkward and needlessly complex writer, who failed to leave behind a coherent accounting of his ideas" (1995, p.5). Similarly, Buhrmester and Furman described his written works as poorly organized and confusing (1986). The criticism most relevant to this book, curiously never mentioned in critiques and extensions of Sullivan's work (e.g.,

Allen, 1995; Buhrmester & Furman, 1986), is that Sullivan's chumship construct excludes cross-sex partners as possible chums. Chumships are by definition same-sex friendships. He never gave serious consideration to the possibility that individuals could form chumships with members of the other sex. He also confined his conclusions to his male patients because the female situation was more complicated and he had less information on it (1953, p. 248). Allen's contention that Sullivan was homosexual indirectly suggests that there may have been bias involved in his exclusion of cross-sex relationships as possible chumships (1995).

Although there have been investigations of cross-sex friendships that occur during middle and late childhood, none of those studies were theoretically conceptualized and methodologically designed as investigations of cross-sex chumships. However, in 1998 Blomberg and I conducted a preliminary, qualitative investigation into the possibility of cross-sex chumships. We interviewed 30 children (ages 8 to 10) about their "very good friends." Interviews were tape recorded, transcribed, and data organized and analyzed through N.U.D.I.S.T., a software program designed for analysis of qualitative interview data. In general, results reveal that preadolescent girls and boys do form cross-sex chumships that have many of the same defining characteristics as same-sex chumships. Most important, both cross-sex and same-sex chums provided one another with what Sullivan referred to as *consensual validation*. When consensual validation is given or received (usually via communication), friends are providing one another with affirmation of values, beliefs, and behaviors.

Symbolic interactionism is the embodiment of the interpersonal self perspective. A fundamental tenet of the symbolic interactionist viewpoint is that individuals come to see themselves as others see them (Cast et al., 1999; Kinch, 1963). Seeing themselves as others do is a result of the interactions they have with individuals in their social network. Knowledge about the self is gleaned from those interactions via the looking glass self (Cooley, 1902), and the process of role-taking (Mead, 1934). Mead and Cooley both emphasized how the social construction of self continues throughout childhood. Regretfully, there are no direct empirical investigations of the relationship between symbolic interactionist constructs and the development of cross-sex friendships. Still, there are some rather obvious ways in which a symbolic interactionsist perspective might be used to better understand how self and cross-sex friendship development in middle childhood are related.

A good place to start is with Cooley's notion of reflected appraisals (1902). In the reflected appraisal process, a child imagines how he or she appears to others and also imagines the judgments that others render of him or her based on that appearance. According to Cooley, the appearance of oneself to others involves not only one's physical appearance, but also one's attitudes, values, behaviors, and choice of friends (p. 184). The idea that children envision how others view them based on their choice of friends is relevant to several of the middle childhood constructs already addressed in the chapter. For example, I have already documented the existence of rules and norms regulating the crossing of gender boundaries during middle childhood (Sroufe et al., 1993). Children who cross gender boundaries are sometimes teased and ostracized. When a child crosses a gender boundary that transgression becomes part of his or her appearance to others. The child who makes that choice then imagines how others might be judging him or her because of that decision. Whether the imagined judgment is accurate or not, the child has an emotional reaction to those hypothesized evaluations, which would be incorporated into the child's view of self and his or her view of cross-sex friendships.

The popularity construct also has a number of conceptual linkages to Cooley's looking-glass self. For instance, as noted by Rubin and his colleagues in their examination of the popularity literature (1998), partly because of the favorable feedback they receive from peers, popular and average children usually have more positive views of themselves than do unpopular children. On the other hand, unpopular children routinely receive negative feedback from peers. Verbal and nonverbal feedback from peers is one of the ways in which reflected appraisals are manifested (Cooley, 1902).

Some of the results of the study by Kovacs and her associates can be interpreted from a reflected appraisal perspective (1996). They discovered that children with primarily cross-sex friends had lower levels of self-esteem than children whose primary friends were of the same-sex and those whose cross-sex friends were of secondary importance. Their lower levels of self-esteem could be partly accounted for by their views of how others might view them (i.e., as children who must cross gender boundaries in order to make friends). Kovacs and colleagues speculate that negative reactions from peers and teachers (i.e., negative reflected appraisals) for crossing gender boundaries could contribute to a poorer self-image than those children might otherwise have. Along similar lines, George and Hartmann found that popular children had significantly more cross-sex friends than did unpopular children (1996). Because popular children typically have high levels of self-esteem (Rubin et al., 1998, p. 660), they may imagine that others see them in a positive light because of their ability to be friends with both girls and boys. Bukowski, Sippola and Hoza discovered that "for boys who have no same-sex friends, having an other-sex friend is associated with more positive perceptions of competence ... in contrast, however, for the older girls (7th graders) who lacked a same-sex friend, having an other-sex friend was linked with less positive perceptions of well-being" (1999, p. 457). Bukowski and colleagues speculate that the gender difference can be explained by empirical findings that girls generally have a less positive view of boys than boys have of girls. Therefore, being friends with a boy when a girl has no same-sex friends might not be a viewed as a positive thing by girls who have to turn to boys for friendships. Those girls may believe that their peers have a negative view of them for having cross-sex friendships.

Mead and his particular version of symbolic interactionism is also relevant to views of self and cross-sex friendships. Recall that a key construct in Mead's theorizing is perspective-taking ability, that is the ability to see things, including oneself, from the perspective of others (1934). Seeing oneself from the viewpoint of others such as friends could impact a person's self-concept. That impact is clearly seen when the connection between popularity and self-concept is examined. Popularity is basically how much a person is liked by his or her peers. Popular children have more positive self-views than unpopular children (Rubin et al., 1998) partly because they see themselves as others do (i.e., as likable, friendly individuals).

Relatedly, Buhrmester and Furman speculate that in order to acquire the interpersonal competencies necessary to have a "chum" (actually, any close friendship), a child must develop perspective-taking abilities (1986). The child must be able to see things, including him or herself, from the perspective of his or her friend. From a symbolic inteactionist perspective, whether based on Cooley or Mead, the meanings of self and specific types of relationships (such as same and cross-sex friendships) are constructed through interaction with others (Blumer, 1969).

In theory, role taking (Mead, 1934), reflected appraisals (Cooley, 1902), and consensual validation (Sullivan, 1953) each contribute to the connection between views of self and cross-sex friendships in middle and late childhood. Cross-sex friends try to see things (including themselves) from one another's perspective. They internalize one another's reflected appraisals, and they provide mutual validation to one another as worthwhile human beings. Each of these constructs (i.e., role taking, reflected appraisals, and consensual validation) are interrelated. A somewhat different theoretical approach to the connection between cross-sex friendships and self concept construction, and yet still within the interpersonal self framework, is attachment theory.

Although attachment theory is more directly relevant to infancy than it is to middle and late childhood, Bowlby contended that attachment behavior continues to be strong throughout most of middle childhood (1969). The quality of attachment is theorized to influence "from the cradle to the grave" the child's self-concept, the way he or she views others, and subsequent personal relationships (Bowlby, 1969). A fundamental prediction of attachment theory, therefore, is that children with a history of secure attachment are more likely than those with a less secure attachment history to establish more and higher quality friendships in middle childhood. There has been relatively little research conducted on attachment security in middle and late childhood when compared to early childhood, adolescence, and adulthood (but see Booth et al., 1998; Lieberman et al., 1999; Kerns et al., 1996). Nevertheless, Cassidy and Berlin (1999) argued that attachment theory principles and loneliness in early and middle childhood are related. Citing a "sizable body of literature" establishing the relationship between peer relationships and loneliness, they conclude that to the extent that peer relationships are impacted by attachment history that history is indirectly related to loneliness.

The majority of investigators applying attachment theory to middle childhood friendships have either exclusively focused on same-sex friendship (e.g., Lieberman et al., 1999) or have neglected to distinguish between same- and cross-sex friendships (e.g., Booth et al., 1998; Kerns et al., 1996). The sex composition of a friendship is an important variable to consider when applying attachment principles to middle childhood friendships. For example, Booth and associates (1998) did not examine the sex of the nominated best friend of their 58 participants. Readers were not provided information about the percentage of the 58 eight-year-olds who chose a cross-sex other as their best friend. Perhaps there were none, perhaps many. A number of additional and important observations could have been made if cross-sex dyads had been separately examined and compared to same-sex friendship. For example, they surmised that securely attached children were no more likely than insecurely attached ones to include their best friends as sources of emotional support. But they did not examine, for instance, if securely attached children in same-sex friendships were more or less likely than securely attached children in cross-sex friendships to include best friends as sources of emotional support. Also, for girls but not boys, the less securely attached they were the higher they rated the effectiveness of the emotional support received from their best friend. But once again, they did not examine the possibility that there may have been differences between girls in same-sex friendships who were insecurely attached and girls in cross-sex friendships who were insecurely attached.

In a similar fashion, data gathered from 76 fifth graders revealed that children who reported a secure attachment to their mother had more reciprocated friendships and were less lonely than those reporting a less secure attachment (Kerns et al., 1996). Although children were allowed to list anyone they wanted from their class as a friend (i.e., they were not limited to same-sex friends), Kerns and her associates did not examine the possibility of differences or similarities between same-sex and cross-sex friendships and their relationships to loneliness and security attachment.

There have been a few studies that are at least suggestive of the relationship between attachment theory and cross-sex friendships (e.g., Lewis & Feiring, 1989; Sroufe et al., 1993). Lewis and Feiring's longitudinal investigation failed to uncover an overall relationship between attachment style (secure/insecure) and number of friends or best friends at age 9 (1989). However, the attachment style of boy's (secure/ insecure) but not girls was related to the number of same-sex but not cross-sex friends. Boys who were securely attached had more same-sex friends than boys who were insecurely attached. In a fascinating study on gender boundary violations during middle childhood, Sroufe and associates discovered that children with secure attachments to primary care givers were more likely to maintain and less likely to violate gender boundaries than those with less secure attachment histories (Sroufe et al., 1993). The investigators extrapolated from attachment theory that since boundary maintenance and violation is an important part of attachment behavior, children who were securely attached as infants and toddlers are similarly able to respect peer group boundaries in middle childhood.

Concluding Observations

Although there is moderate support for my contention that cross-sex friendships provide generic and unique benefits during middle and late childhood (e.g. Blomberg & Monsour, 1998; Kovacs et al., 1996), much more research needs to be done in the exploration of those advantages. For example, evidence that cross-sex friends provide each other with insider perspectives between the ages of 7 and 11 is sketchy at best. There is also limited and mixed empirical support for the proposition that cross-sex friendships facilitate social and behavioral adjustment. Relatedly, despite substantial evidence documenting the existence of gender segregation during middle childhood (Leaper, 1994a), investigations into the effect of segregation on cross-sex friendship formation and maintenance are rare. Nevertheless, I still offer a few summarizing observations about cross-sex friendships in middle and late childhood and review some of the important developmental milestones that impact friendship between girls and boys.

The generic and unique benefits provided by cross-sex friendships during middle childhood are manifested differently depending on the centrality of those friendships in an individual's social network (Kovacs et al., 1996). Research by Kovacs and her associates suggest that social support provided by cross-sex friends and the protection those friends afford against loneliness may be more pronounced and important for children whose primary friends are cross-sex rather than same-sex ones. The insider perspectives supplied by cross-sex friends also might be more readily available to individuals whose cross-sex friends are primary as opposed to secondary. The higher availability of insider perspectives could help explain why children with primarily cross-sex friends hold less stereotypical views about appropriate male and female behavior than children who have no cross-sex friends or whose cross-sex friends are secondary to their same-sex ones (Kovacs et al., 1996).

On the other hand, possible disadvantages of having cross-sex friends might be more likely for those children who have only cross-sex friends and no same-sex ones. For instance, children who have cross-sex friends because they are unable to form same-sex ones may experience feelings of social incompetence. Conversely, children who have only cross-sex friendships demonstrate what Kovacs and her associates refer to as "resilient adaptation" (1996, p. 2283). This means that they can adapt to a situation of not having same-sex friends by forming cross-sex ones (by being resilient). Relatedly, Bukowski, Sippola, and Hoza drew a similar conclusion about the ability of cross-sex friendships to act as a "backup system" for fifth- through seventh-grade girls and boys who had trouble establishing same-sex friendships (1999). That backup system, however, had different effects on boys than it did on girls. Boys who had cross-sex friends but no same-sex ones still had relatively positive self-views. Girls in similar situations had less positive self-views as a result of having only cross-sex friends (Bukowski et al., 1999).

The need to establish a cross-sex friendship typology (Monsour, 1997; Rawlins, 1994), was richly illustrated in the study conducted by Kovacs and her associates (1996). Their findings indicate that cross-sex friendships in middle childhood can be categorized into types of cross-sex friendships according to how central the friendships are to the participating members. For some individuals cross-sex friendships are their primary friendships. For other individuals cross-sex friendships are of secondary importance and located more at the periphery of their social networks. As a general pattern, children with primarily or exclusively cross-sex friends are less socially skilled and less popular than children whose cross-sex friends are not centrally located in their social network.

The developmental transitions from early childhood to middle and late childhood represent a dramatic change in the relational lives of most children. Entrance into elementary school brings about a significant increase in peer interactions which creates opportunities for friendship formation (Rubin et al., 1998). A number of developmental milestones important to cross-sex friendship processes occur during the elementary school years. Two of those milestones are gender segregation (Leaper, 1994a) and the overwhelming concern for peer group acceptance (Parker & Gottman, 1989; Sullivan, 1953).

Although gender segregation starts in early childhood (Leaper, 1994a), it intensifies in elementary school and becomes more complex and dialectical in nature. There is a tendency to voluntarily engage in gender segregation in the early part of middle childhood, but a contradictory proclivity in late childhood to be drawn to members of the other sex (Epstein, 1986; Howe, 1993; Rawlins, 1992; Rubin, 1980). To a greater extent than before, boys and girls in middle and late childhood notice they are different and segregate partly because of those differences. However, in a dialectical manner, preadolescents are also simultaneously drawn to and repelled by members of the other sex (Rawlins, 1992). Some scholars believe that gender segregation is a normal and appropriate developmental change in middle childhood (e.g., Sroufe et al., 1993; Sullivan, 1953). Others (myself included) strongly believe that gender segregation in early and middle childhood, "normal" or not, contributes to communication difficulties and power asymmetries in adolescence and adulthood (Leaper, 1994b). Empirical investigation of the connections between gender segregation and cross-sex friendships has barely begun and there is still much work to be done.

Youth in middle and late childhood are preoccupied with peer group acceptance (Bukowski & Hoza, 1989; Rubin et al.,1998; Sullivan, 1953). Although popularity in early childhood has been studied (see e.g., Howes,1990; Krantz & Burton, 1986) it has received much more research attention as a middle childhood phenomenon. Being accepted by one's peers becomes extremely important in middle childhood, and peer group feedback has significant impact on a child evolving concept of self (Cooley, 1902; Mead, 1934; Parker & Gottman, 1989). Despite the attention given to the importance of peer-group acceptance to children in middle childhood, the significance of being accepted by other sex peers in middle and late childhood is an understudied phenomenon.

Presenting empirically grounded arguments to support the claims advanced in this chapter has been difficult because the research base is so impoverished. With a few noteworthy exceptions, middle and late childhood friendship researchers have ignored cross-sex friendships. Throughout the chapter I gave examples of studies in which researchers either by design or oversight neglected to examine cross-sex friendships (e.g., Bagwell et al., 1998; Kerns et al., 1996; Lieberman et al., 1999; Newcomb & Bagwell, 1995; Rubin et al., 1998). In some of those cases an examination of cross-sex friendships was clearly warranted (e.g., Lieberman et al., 1999).

4

Cross-Sex Friendships
in Adolescence
(12 to 17 years of age)

Cross-sex relationships during adolescence are inherently ambiguous. Societal expectations, personal values, degrees of emerging sexuality, peer group pressure, and coordinated or clashing assumptions and perceptions all combine in shaping the dynamics of given relationships. Whatever occasions the shift, romantic involvement apparently alters adolescents' cross-sex friendships.

—W. K. Rawlins (1992, p. 93)

Processes related to cross-sex friendship formation and maintenance begun in early and middle childhood continue into adolescence. As was true of the transition from early childhood to middle childhood, specific cross-sex friendships from middle and late childhood might be carried over into adolescence. Rawlins contended in the above quotation that cross-sex friendships and cross-sex friendship processes are complicated and sometimes compromised by the onset of puberty, sexual identity development, and the complexity of the adolescent social network. Those complicating factors are explored in one or more of the four sections of this chapter. The first three sections develop the central themes of the book and relate each theme to adolescence. In the final section I offer some concluding comments about cross-sex friendships that occur in this strikingly dramatic stage of life. Before moving on to the first section, a few observations are in order concerning the significance and meaning of adolescence, its developmental relevancy to cross-sex friendship formation, the time frame it entails, and some weaknesses I encountered in the adolescent cross-sex friendship literature.

Adolescence is a monumentally important stage of life (Sippola & Bukowski, 1999). It occurs between childhood and adulthood and encompasses physical, social, emotional, intellectual, spiritual, and sexual maturation (Dyk, 1993; Feldman & Elliott, 1990; Rice, 1978), and can be subdivided into early, middle, and late adolescence (Elliott & Feldman, 1990) Individuals in adolescence are no longer children, nor are they adults. Adolescence is characterized by a peculiar set of competing demands and expectations. On one hand, adolescents are expected to conform to peer group norms, to have close friends, and to become romantically involved. On the other hand, being an adolescent is practically synonymous with establishing individuality and personal autonomy (Larson, 1999).

Friendship scholars agree there are quantitative and qualitative differences between childhood friendships and those formed during adolescence (see the excellent book on friendships in childhood and adolescence edited by Bukowski, Newcomb, & Hartup, 1996). On a quantitative level, the most striking statistic for our purposes is the increase in the number of cross-sex friendships from middle childhood to late adolescence. As teenagers go through the stages of adolescence cross-sex friendships become more normative and "adolescents turn equally toward same- and opposite-sex friends in times of need" (Kuttler, La Greca, & Prinstein, 1999, p. 358). In Feiring's investigation 9-year-olds averaged one cross-sex friend, compared to over five for 13-year-olds (1999). Kuttler and colleagues discovered that 47% of the 223 10th and 12th graders had a close cross-sex friend (Kuttler et al., 1999). Adolescent friendships are generally characterized by higher levels of intimacy and a greater emphasis on self-disclosure than friendships occurring in earlier stages of life (Rubin et al., 1998). Buhrmester discovered that intimate friendships were more important to adolescents than to preadolescents (1990). A distinctive qualitative difference is that most adolescents, unlike most of their younger counterparts, display abstract reasoning ability that influences the way they view and understand relationships (Hinde, 1979; Sippola & Bukowski, 1999). Adolescents are able to perceive friendships in a more holistic and self-reflexive fashion than are younger children (Sippola & Bukowski, 1999). The most striking qualitative difference between cross-sex friendships formed in middle/late childhood and adolescence is puberty.

The onset of puberty signals the beginning of adolescence (Feldman & Elliot, 1990). Dyk observed "From a medical perspective, pubertal development is the maturation of adult reproductive capabilities ... from another perspective, social scientists typically have viewed puberty as the biological, social, and psychological events that interact during early adolescence" (1993, p. 35). Puberty represents a turning point in the way boys and girls view one another and themselves (Rawlins, 1992). It is also the catalyst for the development of an individual's sexual orientation, which influences how adolescents view themselves and members of the other sex (Savin-Williams, 1990). And because girls usually start puberty a year or two earlier than boys (Brooks-Gunn & Reiter, 1990; Dyk, 1993), the effects of puberty on views of members of the other sex do not begin at the same time for age cohorts of different sexes. I contend that in regard to cross-sex friendship interest, initiation, and maintenance, puberty is the single most important developmental milestone occurring in the life cycle of an individual.

The multifaceted nature of the metamorphosis from childhood to adulthood makes the choice of a chronological time frame in which adolescence begins and ends somewhat arbitrary. Individuals mature in different areas at different rates, and though general patterns can be identified, there is considerable room for individual variation (Gottman & Mettetal, 1986; Rice, 1978). As noted by Schiamberg

> Puberty can begin as early as eight years for girls and nine and a half for boys or as late as thirteen years for girls and thirteen and a half for boys. In addition, rate of puberty can vary considerably, taking as little as one and a half years for girls and two years for boys to as long as six years for girls and five years for boys." (1988, p. 664)

There is near universal agreement that adolescence begins with the onset of puberty, with puberty defined as "a series of biological events that signals the coming of other changes" (Schiamberg, 1988, p. 592). Although the onset of puberty is easy to identify as the beginning point of adolescence (Cosse, 1992), pinpointing where adolescence ends and adulthood begins is problematic because of the many possible criteria for adulthood (Diamond, 2000). Scholarly extension of late adolescence into the early and mid-20s of research participants is not uncommon (e.g., Elliott & Feldman, 1990; Savin-Williams, 1990; Schiamberg, 1988). However, my informal observations as a college professor for 14 years has convinced me that the vast majority of college students in their early and mid-20s consider themselves adults and not adolescents and behave in accordance with their self-perceptions. In line with the self-views of many college students, some experts contend that late adolescence ends and young adulthood begins around the age of 18 (e.g., Harter, 1990). For purposes of this book, adolescence begins with puberty (roughly around the age of 11 or 12 years old) and ends with the completion of high school and entrance into college or the job market (roughly around the age of 18). Admittedly, some individuals display the physical and biological manifestations of puberty before the age of 12, and some individuals do not display the maturity level of an adult at the age of 18.

In my review of the adolescent cross-sex friendship literature I encountered similar difficulties to those which confronted me in my examination of childhood friendship studies. First, although cross-sex friendships are common among adolescents (Feiring, 1999; Kuttler, et al., 1999), investigations of those friendships are relatively rare (Furman & Shaffer, 1999; Sippola, 1999). The limited research has prompted a number of scholars to recommend further study of how cross-sex friendships impact adolescent development (e.g., Bukowski et al., 1996; Furman & Shaffer, 1999; Shaffer , 1999). Sippola perhaps put it best when she declared "currently we know almost nothing about the function of other-sex friendships in adolescent development" (Sippola, 1999, p. 411).

A noteworthy exception to the general lack of research on adolescent cross-sex friendships is a special issue of the *Journal of Youth and Adolescence* (see e.g., Sippola, 1999). Each article describes research on romantic relationships and/or cross sex friendships of adolescents. Unfortunately, the special issue displayed a disturbing methodological and conceptual oversight. Several contributors categorized individuals as young as 9 (e.g., Connolly, Craig, Goldberg, & Pepler, 1999) and 10 (e.g., Bukowski et al., 1999) as adolescents without offering any external evidence that those children had begun puberty. As stated previously in this chapter, there is considerable variability (i.e., individual differences) as to when puberty begins. Puberty (which signals the beginning of adolescence) starts roughly between the ages of 8 and 13 for girls and 9½ and 13½ for boys (Schiamberg, 1988). Please do not misunderstand me. The special issue and each of the contributions to it were excellent additions to the corpus of work on cross-sex friendships that occur between the ages of 9 and 17. However, some of the conclusions drawn in that issue about "adolescent" cross-sex friendships might be more appropriately applied to "preadolescent" or "late childhood" cross-sex friendships because there was no attempt made to demonstrate that 9- and 10-year-old respondents were indeed in adolescence. I also recognize that I have the same difficulty in this chapter, (i.e., my time frame for adolescence [12 to 17 years] is overly restrictive in that many individuals reach adolescence before their twelfth birthday).

The cross-sex friendships of adolescents are often unjustifiably excluded from the research designs and conceptual speculations of friendship scholars (e.g., Berndt, 1994; Buhrmester, 1996; Furman & Buhrmester, 1992; Laursen, 1996). For example, Berndt wrote an excellent chapter on "intimacy and competition in the friendships of adolescent boys and girls" in which he concluded (with caveats) that boy friendships are more competitive, and girl friendships are more intimate (1994; see also Hussong, 2000; Leaper & Anderson, 1997). However, he neglected to address what happens in cross-sex friendships where same-sex friendship behavioral routines of intimacy (which are more characteristic of girls) and competitiveness (which are more characteristic of boys) are enacted. Do the different styles lead to more or less satisfaction with cross-sex friendships when compared to their same-sex counterparts? Do the different styles clash with or complement one another? Similarly, Buhrmester wrote a provocative chapter on need fulfillment and interpersonal competence in adolescent friendships, but he failed to address how needs might be met and competence issues addressed in cross-sex friendships (1996). Finally, Laursen conducted a study in which different levels of intimacy in adolescent relationships were investigated (1996). Although mother, father, sibling, romantic partner, and best friend were examined using the *Relationship Closeness Inventory* (Berscheid, Snyder, & Omoto, 1989), no distinction was made between same-sex and cross-sex best friends. Perhaps the studies and chapters by Berndt (1994), Buhrmester (1996), and Laursen (1996), to name just a few, were designed to focus exclusively on same-sex friendships. If so, some attention should have been given to the possibility that the friendship processes examined in those writings might have been different in cross-sex friendships. Furman and Simon recently stressed the importance of studying a range of personal relationships within the adolescent social network, although curiously they did not mention cross-sex friendships (1998).

Another problem with some "cross-sex friendship" studies is that researchers do not clearly differentiate between cross-sex friends and romantic partners (Furman & Shaffer, 1999; Monsour, 1997). For example, in two related studies comparing same-sex and cross-sex best friend interactions best friends were identified according to how high school students responded to the questions "I spend the most time with ____," "I know ___ the best," and "I have lunch with ____ the most often" (Lundy, Field, McBride, Field, & Largie, 1998; McBride & Field, 1997). The individuals identified as cross-sex best friends were probably just that (i.e., friends and not romantic partners). However, because the researchers failed to introduce controls to insure that subjects did not list dating partners as best friends, conclusions drawn from those studies about cross-sex best friends should be made cautiously and viewed with suspicion. Along similar lines, adolescents will sometimes include romantic relationships when asked to report on cross-sex friendships (Furman & Shaffer, 1999), possibly because of the inherent ambiguity in cross-sex relationships during this stage of life (Rawlins, 1992).

Cross-Sex Friendships and the Enrichment of Social Networks During Adolescence

Adolescent cross-sex friendships supply benefits that are similar to and different from the benefits provided by same-sex friendships. Before examining those benefits a side note is in order. Like friendships in every other stage of life, adolescent cross- and same-sex friendships are sometimes a mixed bag of benefits and detriments. For example, Mechanic argued that intimate friendships with high levels of self-disclosure might be harmful to adolescents because such friendships and the conversations that occur in them focus too much attention on individual problems (1983). He contended that friendships can be most valuable when they distract attention away from the self. Scholars also distinguish between negative and positive adolescent friendships. Berndt and Keefe conducted regression analyses and discovered that adolescents who had supportive and intimate friendships became more involved in school than those who had friendships marked by conflict and competition (1992). The degree to which friendships have a negative or positive impact on a teenager's social environment depends on the quality of those friendships (Newcomb & Bagwell, 1996). High quality friendships generally improve the life of an adolescent. On the other hand, low quality friendships characterized by jealousy, competition, and destructive conflict, contribute to adolescent anguish.

Generic Benefits. Friends and peers during adolescence gradually replace parents as the main source of social support and intimacy (Frey & Rothlisberger, 1996). Social support comes in the form of affect, aid, and affirmation (Crohan & Antonucci, 1989). The provision of social support during the tumultuous times of adolescence often means meeting mutual needs. Researchers have observed for 50 years that one of the primary functions of relationships is that they meet a variety of needs (Buhrmester, 1996; Schutz, 1958; Sullivan, 1953; Weiss, 1974). Indeed, as noted by McAdams (1988), writings about human relational needs can be traced back to ancient Greece. Some theorists maintain that needs can be broken down into two broad categories. Based largely on Bakan's work (1966), McAdams contended that individuals have "agentic" needs for power, autonomy, and social control, and "communal" needs for intimacy and connectiveness (1988). Buhrmester (1996) reported empirical support for the validity of those two categories of needs.

Buhrmester (1996) and Maslow (1971) describe needs as being "preoccupying concerns." Individuals need to resolve basic concerns about food, shelter, and safety before they become preoccupied with more abstract matters such as social belongingness (Buhrmester, 1996). The acquisition of new needs as preoccupying concerns is one of the hallmarks of a developmental approach to understanding friendship. Individuals become concerned with additional needs when they enter a new stage of life. Negative repercussions and "developmental arrests" (Sullivan, 1953, pp. 217–218), occur when needs are not met. For example, loneliness is experienced when the need for companionship is not met (Sullivan, 1953).

In his chapter on need fulfillment, interpersonal competence, and the developmental context of early adolescent friendships, Buhrmester (1996) convincingly argued that female and male adolescent friendships meet different types of needs. Females focus more on communal needs for intimacy, connection, and emotional companionship. Males are more concerned with meeting agentic needs for enhancement of individual status and power. He further noted that "more frequent exposure to communal rewards in female same-sex friendships and agentic rewards in male same-sex friendships may strengthen the need for such rewards" and that "gender differences in the qualities of interactions with same-sex friends play an important role in the socialization of communal and agentic forms of competence" (p. 182). Noticeably absent from Buhrmester's otherwise excellent chapter is an analysis of how agentic and communal needs are manifested and met in cross-sex friendships.

Friendship, as a particular type of relationship, meets particular types of needs (Buhrmester, 1996; Sullivan, 1953; Weiss, 1974). Different needs become more or less salient in different stages of life (Sullivan, 1953). Buhrmester contended that the single most important and developmentally constant function of friendship is the provision of enjoyable companionship (1996; see also Cotterell, 1996). The need for enjoyable companionship is often met through communication. Rawlins observed that communicative companionship is a valuable part of adolescent friendship:

> One phrase summarizes the value of close friends for adolescents; 'he or she is someone to talk to'. Young people spend considerable time discussing their daily experiences in and out of school and during marathon evening telephone calls. While conversing, they joke and laugh, help each other with problems of all kinds, vent frustrations, and offer mutual encouragement. (1992, p. 83)

In a study of 223 adolescents in Grades 10 through 12 Kuttler and her associates had six items focusing specifically on companionship in close same- and cross-sex friendships (e.g., "How often do you and your friend go places together like a movie, skating, shopping, or a sporting event?"; 1 = never, 5 = every day). Forty percent of the boys and 50% of the girls had a close cross-sex friend. The average replies of girls and boys for companionship in their cross-sex friendships were, respectively, 3.68 and 3.23. It is interesting to note that the level of companionship reported in same-sex friendships by boys (3.49) and girls (3.67) was very similar to the level of companionship reported for cross-sex friendships.

In addition to meeting the need for enjoyable companionship, one of the most significant generic benefits of friendships is the provision of intimacy. Shulman and colleagues contended, erroneously I believe, that "Intimate close friendships, found across the life-span, *first appear* during early adolescence" (italics my own; Shulman, Laursen, Kalman, & Karpovsky, 1997, p. 597). Studies reviewed in chapters two and three clearly establish that children in early and middle childhood experience many of the traditional manifestations of intimacy. However, although intimacy is certainly a component of childhood friendships, intimacy needs are particularly important during adolescence (Rubin et al., 1998; Sullivan, 1953). For example, based on an aggregation of data spanning the second grade through young adulthood, Buhrmester concluded that having a confidant was more important in adolescence than it was in childhood or young adulthood (1990). Buhrmester and Furman believe that intimacy needs are met differently in male and female adolescent friendships. Males emphasize actions and deeds and females stress self disclosure (1987). Meeting intimacy needs differently may or may not cause problems in cross-sex friendships. Relatedly, in their study of 325 10th graders, Sherman and Thelen (1996) discovered that males, perhaps because of homophobia (Savin-Williams, 1990), reported a significantly higher fear of intimacy in their same-sex friendships than females reported in their same-sex friendships. However, in the study conducted by Kuttler and her associates (Kuttler, La Greca, & Prinstein, 1999) males reported almost as much intimacy in their same-sex friendships ($x = 3.6$; 5-point scale) as females reported in their same-sex friendships ($x = 4.39$).

Shulman and associates found support for their position that in the quest for intimacy same-sex adolescent friends try to balance both closeness and individuality (Shulman et al., 1997). Selman agreed that one of the distinguishing earmarks of adolescent friendship intimacy is the dialectical tendency for individuals to try and balance connectiveness and autonomy (1990; also see Rawlins, 1992). They want to be close to their friends but not so close as to compromise feelings of independence. The connection between friendship and adolescent strivings for autonomy will be more thoroughly discussed in a subsequent section of this chapter.

The need for friendship intimacy during adolescence can be met by cross-sex friends (Connolly et al., 1999; Johnson & Aries, 1983; Kuttler et al., 1999; Parker & Gottman, 1989; Rawlins, 1992; Sippola, 1999). One of the primary ways of showing intimacy is through the self-disclosure process (Dindia, 1997; Monsour, 1992). The process of revealing things about oneself is of central importance during the self-exploratory life stage of adolescence (Cotterell, 1996; Parker & Gottman, 1989). Individuals in adolescence develop a growing need (a preoccupying concern) for a intimate confidant with whom they can share and explore the feelings and attitudes they have about themselves and others (Buhrmester, 1996; Cotterell, 1996; Parker & Gottman, 1989; Rawlins, 1992). Establishing a safe environment in which self-disclosures are keep in confidence is very important to teenagers. Johnson and Aries discovered that 18- and 19-year-old boys (whom they categorized as being in late adolescence), preferred cross-sex friends as disclosure partners (1983). When compared to dating partners, some adolescents view their cross-sex friends as more suitable and understanding recipients of a range of personal disclosures (Werebe, 1987). On the other hand, in a study of junior high and high school students both males and females rated cross-sex friendships as lower in intimacy than their same-sex counterparts, yet there were no gender differences between boys and girls in how intimate they rated their cross-sex friends (Blyth & Foster-Clark, 1987). Relatedly, in Kuttler and colleagues' investigation of close cross-sex friendships of 223 adolescents in Grades 10 through 12, girls and boys gave similar responses when indicating on a 5-point scale how frequently they self-disclosed to their cross-sex friend (girls = 4.39; boys = 3.87).

Based on analysis of videotaped conversations of adolescent cross-sex and same-sex friends, Parker and Gottman concluded that a significant portion of self-exploration occurs through the mutual give-and-take of self-disclosure (1989). As straightforwardly summarized by Parker and Gottman "The salient social process at this age is honest, intimate, self-disclosure. Other social processes-notably humor, gossip, problem solving, social comparison, and mind reading-operate to prompt and promulgate self-disclosure" (p. 120). One of the conversational topics that differentiates adolescence from earlier life stages is that discussing the intimacy of the friendship becomes a legitimate topic of conversation (Gottman & Mettetal, 1986). Such discussions would be very important for young cross-sex friends trying to sort out the emotions they feel for each other (O'Meara, 1989).

Although the provision of social support through mutual self-disclosure is important to all adolescents, it might be especially significant to gay and lesbian teenagers. Data reviewed by Savin-Williams in his book *Gay and Lesbian Youth* show that gay and lesbian adolescents who are willing to self-disclose their sexual orientation do so to both same-sex and cross-sex friends (1990). Disclosing sexual orientation to a friend presents the dual possibilities of rejection or affirmation (Savin-Williams, 1990). The topic of sexual orientation and its relationship to views of self and cross-sex friendships is more thoroughly examined in a subsequent section of this chapter.

Implicit in many of my observations about social support, intimacy, and self-disclosure (all related concepts) is the corollary conclusion that cross- and same-sex friendships can provide protection against loneliness. A recently edited volume on loneliness in childhood and adolescence establishes that loneliness is a pervasive phenomenon (Rotenberg & Hymel, 1999). Adolescent friendships provide a buffer against loneliness (Bukowski, Hoza, & Boivin, 1993; Parker & Asher, 1993). Meeting needs for enjoyable companionship and intimacy, for example, have obvious connections to impeding feelings of isolation and loneliness.

Although loneliness can be particularly problematic during adolescence (Perlman & Landolt, 1999), some scholars consider it a result of normal adolescent developmental processes as individuals attempt to establish independence (Sippola & Bukowski, 1999). Loneliness also needs to be distinguished from being alone. Larson reported on data from 483 youths between the ages of 10 and 15 showing that they progressively spent more time with peers but also more time alone (1999). Privacy becomes increasingly important to teenagers, and they value that privacy to think, to concentrate on an activity, or to just "pull themselves together" (Larson, 1999). Interestingly, in Larson's data time spent alone was significantly correlated with loneliness for preadolescents, but not for adolescents. Similarly, Perlman and Landolt note that for children being alone might be "a sufficient antecedent of loneliness, whereas in adolescence, the causes of loneliness may be more complex and reflexive in nature" (Perlman & Landolt, 1999, p. 343). Significantly, the teens in Larson's study reported feeling lonely for 23% of their waking hours.

Some evidence indicates that adolescent males are lonelier than their female counterparts. In their review of 13 studies examining self-reports of adolescent loneliness, Koenig and Abrams uncovered five studies where males were significantly lonelier than females. Three additional studies documented marginal significance in the direction of males being lonelier, four studies found no gender differences, and only one was discovered in which adolescent females were lonelier (Koenig & Abrams, 1999). The connections, assuming there are some, between sex differences in adolescent loneliness and cross-sex friendship have not been directly investigated.

Sippola and Bukowski (1999) observed that an adolescent can experience loneliness because he or she feels alienated and/or isolated from his or her social group (which is how Weiss described social loneliness; 1973) and/or from particular others (which is how Weiss described emotional loneliness; 1973). Adolescent social networks are quite complex, comprised of cliques, crowds, and groups that are often mixed-sex in nature (Brown et al., 1994). If an adolescent has casual cross-sex or same-sex friends scattered throughout his or her social network, those casual friendships could help combat social loneliness (Larson, 1999). Emotional loneliness could be remedied through one or more close cross-sex friends (Rawlins, 1992).

Weiss contended that attachment theory principles can be applied to the emotional loneliness that so many adolescents experience. Indeed, emotional loneliness has been viewed as a developmental extension of attachment anxiety (Cotterell, 1996; Weiss, 1989). Attachment processes, through their hypothesized linkages to social support and companionship (Cotterell, 1996), can be seen operating in cross-sex friendships. To the extent that an adolescent relies on a cross-sex friend's availability and responsiveness, one could argue that an attachment relationship exists (Trinke & Bartholomew, 1997). For example, some unpopular adolescents who have trouble forming friendships with same-sex peers have been known to turn to cross-sex friends for companionship (Bukowski, Sippola, & Hoza, 1999).

Unique Benefits. Friendships between female and male adolescents provide benefits not obtainable in same-sex friendships. Adolescent cross-sex friends supply each other with insider perspectives (Sippola, 1999), other-sex companionship and validation as attractive members of the other sex (Rawlins, 1992), a broadening of interpersonal competencies (Furman & Shaffer, 1999), and preparation for romantic relationships (Connolly et al., 1999; Feiring, 1999). Cross-sex friendships and the advantages they supply provide "venues for learning about the other sex and may lay the groundwork for adult other-sex interactions" (Furman & Shaffer, 1999, p. 518). Each of these special benefits are examined in the upcoming pages.

Recall that receiving an insider's perspective from a cross-sex friend means that the friend provides insight on how members of his or her sex think, feel, and behave (Sapadin, 1988). Adolescents who had cross-sex friends in middle and late childhood might already be privy to an insider's perspective. However, many children spend the better part of their time in middle and late childhood avoiding members of the other sex (Sroufe et al., 1993). That avoidance contributes to gender segregation and the formation of separate boy and girl cultures in which the individuals learn different ways of viewing the world and interacting (chap. 3). Many children entering adolescence may not have been exposed to how peers of the other sex view the world, so when they finally come together in adolescence they meet "virtually as strangers" (Fagot, 1994, p. 62). Insider perspectives reach their highest level of importance in the life cycle of an individual during adolescence because they help lay the groundwork for mature romantic relationships (Swain, 1992) and more effective work associations later in life (Monsour, 1997; Sapadin, 1988; Sippola, 1999). Even if an adolescent had cross-sex friends and their accompanying insider perspectives as a child, the nature of those insider views might be quite different in adolescence once the insiders and their friends have entered puberty.

In addition to the provision of insider perspectives, cross-sex friends in adolescence also provide one another with other-sex companionship and validation as attractive members of the other sex. Based on their study of 1,755 adolescents, Connolly and her colleagues concluded that adolescents parallel adults in their views of romantic relationships and cross-sex friendships (but note, their "early adolescents" included children as young as 9 years old; 1999). Their findings suggest that if other-sex validation as an attractive member of the other sex is important in adulthood, such validation would also be important during adolescence. As I document in the next chapter, there is considerable evidence that cross-sex friends in young adulthood provide each other with validation as attractive members of the other sex (e.g., Monsour, 1988; Reeder, 2000; Rubin, 1985). Other-sex companionship supplied by a cross-sex friend may be very important to adolescents who do not have a dating partner and therefore need some kind of affirmation that they are attractive to members of the other sex (Sullivan, 1953). The self-view (i.e., self-schema) of an adolescent would be enhanced through reception of direct or indirect feedback from a cross-sex friend that he or she was an appealing member of the other sex. Wright's self-referent model of friendship (1984) and Cooley's notion of reflected appraisals (1902) suggest that such affirmation would be incorporated into the adolescent's view of self.

On a related issue, when heterosexuals enter puberty they soon develop a need (a preoccupying concern) to have a close relationship with a member of the other sex (Buhrmester & Furman, 1986; Sullivan, 1953). When that need is not met, perhaps because the adolescent does not have a romantic partner, loneliness is the likely result (Sullivan, 1953). Companionship with a member of the other sex via a cross-sex friendship could ameliorate the effects of loneliness precipitated by the lack of a romantic partner. Conversely, Sippola and Bukowski believe that because of differences in conversational style self-disclosure to members of the other sex may be difficult to achieve and actually contribute to increased feelings of loneliness (1999).

Buhrmester contended that same-sex friendships provide training for the development of interpersonal competencies (1996). He defines "interpersonal competencies" as the ability to "forge relationships that facilitate the fulfillment of both communal and agentic needs" (p. 182). If same-sex friendships can facilitate the development of interpersonal competencies, might not cross-sex friendships do the same? Those friendships would be ideal for meeting both types of needs and developing both types of competencies. Cross-sex friends could help each other develop interpersonal competencies such as agentic and communal skills that might be more characteristic of one sex than the other. If girls are generally more communally oriented, and boys more agentically oriented (Buhrmester), then each friend could learn from the other, resulting in higher levels of interpersonal competence for both.

Research by a number of investigators indirectly suggests that cross-sex friends can learn skills from one another such as building intimacy (e.g., Field, Lang, Yando, & Bendell, 1995; Leaper & Anderson, 1997). In a study by Field and associates, students with cross-sex friends displayed higher levels of intimacy with all of their friends than did students with exclusively same-sex friends (Field, et al.,1995). Along these same lines, Furman and Shaffer observe "Not only can they (meaning cross-sex friends) fulfill the typical functions of friendship, but because they are with members of the other sex, they can also provide the adolescent with experiences and perspectives that he or she had not encountered prior to adolescence" (1999, p. 515). Those experiences and perspectives could be helpful in development of interpersonal competencies. Similarly, Leaper and Anderson contended that adolescent girls and boys approach relationships differently (1997). Girls have been socialized to relate to others in a nurturing and supportive way, whereas boys have been socialized to focus more on independence and dominance. They propose that participation in platonic cross-sex friendships during adolescence enables girls and boys to develop different competencies. Boys can become more open and expressive, while girls can become more assertive.

Cross-sex friendships also provide a special benefit to heterosexual youth by preparing them for romantic relationships (Leaper & Anderson, 1997; Sippola, 1999). As succinctly stated by Leaper and Anderson, "Having close cross-gender friendships during childhood and adolescence may provide the basis for easier cross-gender romantic relationships during adolescence and adulthood" (1997, p. 97). In support of Leaper and Anderson's contention, Connolly and her colleagues discovered that the number of cross-sex friends in the 10th grade was a strong predictor of romantic relationships in the 11th grade. Adolescents with higher numbers of cross-sex friends were more likely to be involved in romantic relationships (Connolly, Furman, & Konarski, 1998).

A few other unique advantages of cross-sex friendships are worth noting, although not particularly pervasive or well documented. An advantage of cross-sex friendship for adolescent males is the higher level of emotional gratification available in cross-sex friendships than in their same-sex counterparts (Rawlins, 1992). Boys sometimes reap different advantages in their cross-sex friendships than in their same-sex ones. For example, in one study male high school juniors reported receiving more ego support from their best female friends than from their best male friends (Wright & Keple, 1981). Similarly,

Kuttler and her colleagues concluded that the cross-sex friends of adolescent boys were more likely to make those boys feel good about themselves than their same-sex friends (Kuttler et al., 1999). Some males prefer cross-sex friends over same-sex friends as disclosure partners (Johnson & Aries, 1983). Bukowski and colleagues observed that early adolescent boys without a same-sex friend had higher levels of perceived well being if they had a cross-sex friend than those boys with no friends at all (Bukowski, Sippola, & Hoza, 1999). Conversely, girls with no same-sex friends but cross-sex ones had lower levels of perceived well being. Clark discovered that for some conversational topics, an other-sex partner was preferred by adolescents (8th and 10th graders) as conversational partners (1994). Clark observed that "girls' selection of a male conversational partner rose from 20% in the fourth grade to 43% in eighth grade ... boys' selection of a female conversational partner increased from 23% to 50%" (p. 316). Unfortunately, no information was provided by Clark concerning whether other-sex conversational partners were cross-sex friends or romantic partners. Relatedly, the same-sex friendships of adolescent females are sometimes plagued with issues of jealousy and possessiveness over other same-sex friendships (Rawlins, 1992). Some high school girls reported that problems like jealousy and possessiveness were not a part of their close cross-sex friendships (Rawlins, 1992).

Social and Structural Barriers to Cross-Sex Friendships During Adolescence

The social networks of adolescents are exceedingly complex and involve variables from interactional, dyadic, and group experiential levels (Bukowski et al., 1999; Furman & Simon, 1998; Rubin et al., 1998). Social and structural barriers and facilitators to cross-sex friendship are an inherent part of the multilayered social environment of adolescents. However, those barriers and facilitators undergo changes from what they were during middle and late childhood, partly due to the elaborate nature of the adolescent network structure. The barriers from the previous life stage still exist, but they are often in attenuated or modified form. Despite the apparent loosening of structural and social constraints to cross-sex friendship formation that existed in middle childhood (Cotterell, 1996), new barriers emerge during adolescence. Although those barriers are mostly self-imposed by the cross-sex friends themselves, they are still a product of social and structural constraints and pressures.

O'Meara contended that one of the biggest "challenges" that potential cross-sex friends must overcome is what he labeled the "opportunity challenge" (1994). When girls and boys lack sufficient opportunities for interaction then friendship formation is unlikely. In middle and late childhood the opportunity for cross-sex interaction was structurally curtailed by gender segregation. However, the walls of gender segregation start to crumble during early adolescence (Kuttler et al., 1999).

Structural Barriers.   Although there is still some separation of the sexes, adolescence signals the beginning of a more balanced social network (Brown et al., 1994; Bukowski et al., 1999; Feiring, 1999; Richards, Crowe, Larson, & Swarr, 1998; Rubin et al., 1998). Transformations in the social landscape of girls and boys entering middle school and high school change the configuration of structural barriers to cross-sex friendship formation and maintenance. Additionally, social networks become more complicated than they were during middle childhood. As the walls of gender segregation begin to weaken, a social labyrinth takes their place, a maze in which potential cross-sex friends are embedded if they can only be found.

Cliques and crowds permeate the social environment of adolescents (Cotterell, 1996), becoming central features of the social topography that are rewarding but potentially hazardous. Cliques and crowds can give an adolescent a feeling of belonging and group acceptance, but they also can be sources of social frustration and anxiety if individuals are denied membership (Rubin et al., 1998). A clique is a small group of friends who are typically of the same age and sex (Cotterell, 1996). Cliques were a big part of the social world of kids during middle childhood and continue to be equally prevalent during adolescence (Rubin et al., 1998). Adolescent cliques are more likely than their preadolescent counterparts to transform into crowds (Rubin et al., 1998). Crowds and cliques and their relationship to cross-sex friendship formation and maintenance is clearly connected to gender segregation, or more precisely, gender desegregation. As adolescent boys and girls begin to spend considerably more time together than they did in middle and late childhood the possibilities for cross-sex friendships increase dramatically.

The research and scholarly interest in crowds can be traced back to the work of LeBon (1896/1908) and Hollingshead (1949), although the seminal observational fieldwork of Dunphy is more relevant to cross-sex friendship formation (1963; 1969). Dunphy concluded that one of the main functions of crowds was to give adolescents other-sex interaction experience (1969). Based on observations of 40 peer groups over a 2-year period, Dunphy described five stages in the transition from the gender-segregated groups of childhood to the more sexually integrated groups and cross-sex relationships of late adolescence. Brown and associates observed that crowds are "cultural evolutionary forms" that evolve to help adolescents adjust to the "momentous transformations" that occur in the peer social system as a child moves into adolescence (Brown et al., 1994). They described crowds as collections of adolescents who share commonalities in areas such as attitudes, dress, interests, and abilities (1994). Similarly, Cotterell characterized crowds as amalgamations of several cliques of teenagers (1996). Erwin portrayed a crowd as larger and more loosely knit than a friendship clique, often consisting of several cliques that associate on a regular basis in various locales (1998; see also Urberg, Degirmencioglu, Tolson, & Halliday-Scher, 1995).

Affiliation with a particular crowd gives a teenager a social identity that influences the kinds of relationships she or he forms with others (Brown et al., 1994). Depending on the type of crowd, all of the members of a particular crowd may or may not be friends with each other. Crowd "caricaturing" helps the adolescent determine if a person from another crowd would be willing to form a relationship. A crowd caricature is a somewhat exaggerated and distorted description of a crowd that has been mutually arrived at and consensually validated by adolescents (Brown et al., 1994). Brown and his associates took a symbolic interactionist perspective (Mead, 1934) and contended that adolescents cognitively and communicatively construct crowds and come to understand them through interaction with peers.

Based on data gathered from 905 adolescents (Kahn, 1989), Youniss and his associates provided excellent descriptions of crowd characteristics given by crowd members themselves (Youniss, McLellan, & Strouse, 1994). For example, Populars described themselves as having many friends, being well known, partying, and looking cool. However, they also described their fellow popular group members as being snobbish and superficial. The self-descriptions for Brains included academic ability, having high grades, being smart, and lacking other-sex companionship. All the major crowds (Populars, Normals, Jocks, Brains, Loners, Druggies) had both male and female members. The largest group was the Normals ($n = 247$). Sixty-one percent of that group was female, the other 39% were male. Of the 123 Populars, 72% were female and 28% were male. Of the 57 Jocks, 35% were female and 65% were male. The Brain crowd ($n = 51$) was the only one in which the sex composition was fairly equal. As a general pattern, females appeared more concerned with status and popularity than males, whereas males seemed more focused than females on physical prowess and deviance.

Structural factors related to crowds can impede and facilitate cross-sex interaction and friendship formation. Adolescent crowds "channel" teenagers into some relationships and away from others (Brown et al., 1994). Because there are different kinds of crowds with different sets of norms (Rubin et al., 1998), some crowds might encourage cross-sex friendships through channeling, while others might interfere with such formation. In their brief review of evidence in support of channeling principles, Brown and his colleagues concluded that although the evidence is "paltry," there is enough of it to lend credence to the general idea that channeling does occur (1994).

I propose that crowd membership can lead to cross-sex friendship formation in two basic ways. Cross-sex friendships could form between members of the same crowd, what I label as "intra-crowd cross-sex friendship formation," and cross-sex friendships could form between individuals from different crowds (i.e., "inter-crowd cross-sex friendship formation"). An extrapolation from the research of Brown and associates suggest that inter-crowd cross-sex friendship affiliations are probably more difficult than cross-sex friendship initiation within one's own crowd. Let us first examine cross-sex friendship formation potential between members of different crowds.

A complex interplay of factors combine to determine the probability of inter-crowd cross-sex friendship couplings. Although not specifically applied to cross-sex friendship associations, the three channeling principles identified by Brown and his fellow researchers have clear applicability: proximity, permeability, and desirability. Proximity refers to the "social distance" between crowds; permeability to the receptiveness of crowds to outsiders; and desirability to the anticipated negative or positive repercussions associated with affiliating with a different crowd or one of its members. An application of those principles to cross-sex friendship formation reveals that in order for a cross-sex friendship to have optimal conditions for formation, the two crowds need to be of approximately the same social status; the members of each crowd must be receptive to outsiders; and the two potential friends must believe that the advantages of associating with each other outweigh the disadvantages. Let us briefly examine each of these principles as they relate to cross-sex friendship formation.

The proximity principle pertains to crowd position in the status hierarchy. Crowd status is important because if two crowds are socially distant from each other (e.g.,Druggies and Populars), friendship formation is much less likely to occur than if the crowds are closer in social prestige (e.g., Populars and Jocks). If an adolescent decides to initiate a cross-sex friendship with a member of another crowd occupying a lower place in the status hierarchy, that friendship might effectively move him or her from one crowd to another. One can easily imagine the horror of a teenager discovering that because of a wrong friendship choice he or she was suddenly and socially demoted from the Populars to the Outcasts!

The permeability principle refers to how receptive crowd members are to outsiders. Social identity theory stipulates that entrance into a group by an outsider is often a formidable task (Tajfel, 1981). However, as noted by Brown and his colleagues, "the ambiguous, dynamic, and nonexclusive nature of crowd affiliations forces some modifications in the principles of this theory" (meaning, social identity theory; 1994, p. 142). In summarizing the mostly ethnographic research on crowd permeability, Brown and his associates concluded that certain crowds like Populars are open to overtures from certain other crowds like Normals, but closed to the entry attempts of individuals from other crowds, like Druggies.

Desirability is related to crowd status. The higher the crowd is on the status hierarchy the more desirable it is. Similarly, low status crowds are undesirable. The desirability principle would seem to preclude formation of cross-sex friendships between individuals from vastly different status groups because the higher status individual would not be willing to risk ejection from his or her group for associating with a member of a significantly lower status group. On the other hand, if a boy and girl are from two different crowds of approximately equal status the possibility for cross-sex friendship formation would be greater.

Unless the norms of a particular crowd discourage them, cross-sex friendship development is probably easier within a crowd (i.e., intra-crowd cross-sex friendship formation) than between crowds because of the similarity that characterizes individuals within the same crowd. Similarity is a strong basis for the development of intimacy in any relationship (Monsour, 1994). Descriptions by scholars of typical adolescent crowds do not include explicit information about cross-sex friendship norms. Information is provided, however, about friendships in general that bear some relevance to adolescent male–female friendships. For example, in their study of over 800 adolescents comprising five different crowds, Brown and his associates discovered that Druggies and Populars placed more emphasis than Brains on having romantic partners. That finding suggest that Brains might view cross-sex platonic couplings within their own crowd more favorably than Druggies and Populars because the latter groups might emphasize romance over friendship.

Other research indicates that high and low status groups place different levels of importance on friendship. As a general principle, higher status crowds like Populars, Jocks, and Preppies place more emphasis on maintaining status, even at the risk of losing friendships, than lower status crowds like Greasers, Burnouts, and Headbangers (Eder, 1985; Lesko, 1988). Therefore, cross-sex friendship formation within a high status group is more or less likely depending on perceptions as to what such a friendship might do to one's status within the group. Cross-sex friendship formation in lower status groups, on the other hand, might be determined more by perceptions of similarity and compatibility between a male and a female in a particular group.

Although crowds may facilitate and impede friendship formation, the bonds of friendship are more typically established through clique relationships (Cotterell, 1996). Because cliques are usually same-sex in composition, cross-sex friendship formation might occur between adjoining cliques of different sexes. Based on fascinating observational research in pedestrian malls, Cotterell explains how the process of inter-clique mingling is accomplished (1996). Two same-sex cliques, one male and one female, are in relatively close physical proximity, exchanging glances and smiles. Then one or more high-status members from one of the cliques approaches the other clique and contact is made. From that point there is a gradual formation of a subgroup comprised of both girls and boys which constitutes a crowd. The resulting crowd, in line with Dunphy's five-stage model of peer group formation (1969), may or may not dissipate into other-sex pairings with lower-status members modeling themselves after the heterosexual coupling patterns of the higher status members (Erwin, 1998).

The process of inter-clique mingling, amalgamation into a crowd, and eventual cross-sex pairings seems designed to facilitate and accommodate possible dating and romantic relationships more so than cross-sex friendships (Furman & Shaffer, 1999). To my knowledge there has been no research on how cross-sex friendships might form from Dunphy's five-stage model. Along these lines, as noted by Cotterell "Surprisingly few studies have traced the formation and disintegration of naturally occurring friendship cliques with any degree of precision" (1996, p. 52). However, in Feiring's longitudinal study of cross-sex friendships and romantic relationship of children and adolescents, she concluded that having larger networks of cross-sex friendships in early adolescence was related to a higher probability of being involved in romantic relationships in latter adolescence (1999).

Inter-clique cross-sex and same-sex friendships can be hard to establish because cliques are sometimes not willing to let an outsider join the group (Cotterell, 1996). This kind of group exclusionary behavior is perhaps a legacy from middle and even early childhood friendship groups that are often quite cliquish in their characteristics (Rawlins, 1992; Rubin, 1980). Indeed, Corsaro and Eder (1990) contended that adolescent cultures and groups are extensions of similar processes started in early and middle childhood. Once a friendship group or clique is formed, outsiders typically have a difficult time being accepted. Cotterell speculates that cliques may discourage an outsider's attempt to join their group out of fear that he or she might be trying to steal away one of its members.

Crowds and cliques and their impact on cross-sex friendship formation can also profitably be viewed from a systems perspective. Bukowski, Sippola, and Hoza recently argued (1999) that a systems perspective is based on two premises. First, relationship experiences in one domain (e.g., same-sex friendships) influence and are influenced by relationship experiences in another domain (e.g., cross-sex friendships). Second, "relationships are linked to phenomena at other levels of social complexity, specifically the individual and the group" (p. 440). They investigated same-and cross-sex friendships of 231 fifth, sixth, and seventh graders whom they categorized as being in early adolescence (1999). Although Bukowski and colleagues were not specifically interested in crowds or cliques per se, they were able to conclude that "children" (their words, not mine, which seems to contradict their labeling of the subjects as "early adolescents") of both sexes who were either very popular or very unpopular were more likely than other children to have cross-sex friends.

Social Barriers. Separating social barriers from their structural counterparts is difficult. Each type of barrier impacts the other. For instance, a certain structural channeling impediment to cross-sex friendship formation, for example, the potential cross-sex friend is part of the wrong crowd, gives birth to social barriers prohibiting the friendship (Brown et al., 1994; Youniss et al., 1994). Those social barriers, in turn, solidify the structural barrier. Therefore, many of the social barriers discussed in this section are inseparably related to their structural counterparts.

Norms and peer prohibitions against cross-sex friendship formation in adolescence are not nearly as powerful and pervasive as they were in middle childhood. Adolescents have cross-sex friendships (Bukowski et al. 1999), and it is generally "ok" from the peer perspective to have them. Because of the structural reconfiguration of the prevailing social networks (Dunphy, 1969), cross-sex interaction occurs more frequently and with considerably less opposition. However, individual friendship cliques and crowds still have norms concerning who members should or should not associate with. I suspect such norms have less to do with the sex of the potential friend and more to do with what crowd he or she belongs to. Adolescent group norms prohibiting the initiation of cross-sex friendships have not been documented. However, the normative expectation that adolescents have romantic partners (Rawlins, 1992) possibly has the unintended consequence of serving as an implicit norm against cross-sex friendship formation.

As explained in chapter one, society generates models of appropriate and/or ideal relationships. Hartup and Stevens contended that those models come from the deep structure of society and have surface level manifestations exhibited in communication between individuals (1997). The deep structure of society can be seen, for instance, in the way mass media portrays relationships. Messages from the media (books, situation comedies, films) suggest that the ideal male–female relationship is a romantic one (Werking, 1995, October). Similar messages are communicated to adolescents through their social networks and adult role models. Based on data gathered from 1,755 adolescents ages 9 to 14, Connolly and her colleagues concluded that the way adolescents conduct themselves in cross-sex friendships and romantic relationships is influenced by their knowledge of adult norms (1999). In a seeming contradiction of their purported strivings toward autonomy from adults, adolescents try to remain consistent with culturally endorsed views of male-female relationships. To the extent that adolescents internalize societal and peer group messages about proper and appropriate other sex relationships, they may devote their relational energy to the pursuit of romance rather than friendship. Connolly and colleagues concluded that there was no "discernible difference" between the way girls and boys described their cross-sex friendships (p. 492).

Recall that social barriers may originate from third parties, from the cross-sex friends themselves, or from a combination of the two. Along those lines, adolescents contend with a new set of social barriers to cross-sex friendship that existed only minimally in earlier stages of the life cycle. Those new barriers most likely reach their peak during young adulthood but exist in rudimentary form in adolescence. The barriers take the form of "challenges" that must be overcome in cross-sex friendship formation and maintenance. Rawlins introduced the challenges line of research in his landmark 1982 study. He portrayed cross-sex friendship as a "rhetorical challenge," contending that those friendships are characterized by rhetorical issues that must be negotiated in the friendship. In part, a man and a woman (or in this case, a girl and a boy), must communicatively establish a shared definition of the relationship in which romance is avoided, overt sexuality is de-emphasized, equality is fostered, personal freedom is permitted, and public portrayals of the friendship can be properly presented.

O'Meara (1989) restructured the rhetorical issues enumerated by Rawlins into four obstacles, or challenges, that cross-sex friends face. Women and men (adolescent girls and boys) must (a) confront the issue of sexuality, (b) determine the kinds of emotions they feel for each other, (c) present the correct picture of the relationship to relevant audiences, and (d) grapple with questions of equality is a society where men (boys) frequently have more power in cross-sex relationships than women (girls). O'Meara (1994) later identified a fifth challenge, the opportunity challenge, but it is clearly a structural impediment and was examined earlier in this chapter.

In the next few paragraphs I address the sexual and emotional bond challenge together because romantic feelings and sexual urgings for a member of the other sex often occur simultaneously (Reeder, 2000; Werking, 1997a). Following O'Meara's lead (1994), I refer to these two challenges as the "emotional challenge" and the "sexual challenge." For now I limit my discussion to heterosexual youth.

Confronting the sexual challenge means individually and jointly dealing with sexual tensions, desires, activities, and overtures that exist in the friendship. Although the sexual and emotional bond challenges appear to be self-imposed, they have their origins in a society and peer culture that socializes girls and boys to see each other as potential dating partners (O'Meara, 1989; Rawlins, 1994; Werking, 1997b). Heterosexual adolescents want to be accepted by members of the other sex as potential dating partners (Sullivan, 1953). That desire might heighten the need to conform to gender-role expectations such as dating members of the other sex rather than simply being friends (Katz, 1979; Ruble & Martin, 1998). Individuals in adolescence begin to view members of the other sex as sexual beings, and there is considerable peer pressure, especially among boys, to try to convert cross-sex relationships into romantic or sexual encounters (Bell, 1981; Rawlins, 1992). For example, high school girls reported that their male friends would try to change the relationship into a dating arrangement, which would often hurt the friendship (Rawlins, 1989). Sexual contact is part of some adolescent cross-sex friendships. Shaffer reported that 14% of her sample of cross-sex friends engaged in heavy petting, intercourse, or oral sex (1999).

The complex interplay of these two challenges present a number of questions that the cross-sex friends must address. For example, if an adolescent couple decides that they are friends and not romantic partners, does that definition preclude sexual involvement? If two friends decide to get sexually involved, does that mean that their relationship is really a romance and not a friendship? What about if one teenager has romantic feelings, but the other does not? Does that mean the relationship should be abandoned? As will be seen in the next chapter, some of these questions have been addressed in the adult cross-sex friendship literature, but thus far very little has been done in the adolescent friendship arena.

A third challenge facing adolescent cross-sex friends is trying to present the correct picture of the relationship to relevant audiences. The audience challenge first emerges during middle childhood when cross-sex friends are teased by peers about suspected romantic involvement (Parker & Gottman, 1989). It increases in relevance and perhaps difficulty during adolescence because the social networks are larger and more complex than they were during middle childhood (Cotterell, 1996). The increased number of cross-sex friends in adolescence also contributes to the audience challenge. When a larger social network is combined with more cross-sex friends the audience challenge becomes a more pervasive problem. The math is simple: There are more cross-sex friendships to explain to more audiences.

Relevant audiences would include romantic partners, crowds, cliques, family members, other friends, and even Mead's "generalized other" (which, according to Blumer, 1969, is the abstract social community). The crowd that an individual belongs to (e.g., the Preppie crowd or the Jock crowd) is a central audience that an adolescent may feel the need to explain his or her cross-sex friend to. For example, if having a dating partner is a sign of status in a certain crowd, then a member of that crowd may be more inclined to believe that an explanation of the relationship as "just a friendship" is necessary. On the other hand, however, because cross-sex friendships in adolescence are no longer considered anomalous aberrations, explanation of the friendship may not even be required.

The fourth challenge identified by O'Meara (1989) is the "power" or "equality" challenge. O'Meara contended that men generally have greater access than women to different types of power. Because same- and cross-sex friendships are theoretically based on equality (Davis & Todd, 1985; Fehr, 1996; Roberts, 1982) then women and men (or boys and girls) may have power struggles in their friendships. I was unable to discover direct research on the equality challenge as it applies to adolescent cross-sex friendships. However, there are studies suggesting that boys may have more power in cross-sex relationships than girls and also may be more competitive. Felmlee gathered strong empirical support documenting that in heterosexual dating relationships boys have more power (1994). Adolescent girls are more likely than boys to use compromise in conflict situations (Collins & Laursen, 1992). This raises the question of what happens when boys and girls form friendships and conflicts occur. Maccoby observed that male adolescent communication involves more interruptions and direct challenges than female adolescent communication (1990). Additionally, recall that research and theoretical speculations on early childhood friendships suggest that girls sometimes feel powerless in their interactions with boys (Maccoby & Jacklin, 1987; Sims et al., 1998). From a developmental perspective, the patterns established in early and middle childhood of boys being dominant in their interactions with girls and girls feeling powerless might carry over into adolescent interactions.

A potential social barrier to cross-sex friendship initiation and maintenance is the fear of being the subject of gossip. When individuals form relationships that are deemed inappropriate by society or members of their social network they run the risk of being the target of gossip (Duck & VanderVoort, 2000). Similar to gossip that occurs in middle childhood, adolescent gossip serves to promote solidarity within groups and to help discover and reaffirm the existence of same-sex peer norms (Parker & Gottman, 1989). Because different crowds and cliques have their own set of norms (Brown et al., 1994), the norms concerning cross-sex friendship would depend on the crowd or clique an individual belongs to. And the norms might not be as much against cross-sex friendship formation, although they might be, as they would be against affiliation with a member of another friendship clique or crowd. A girl or boy from the Druggie crowd might be hesitant to form a cross-sex friendship with a member of the Normal crowd for fear of being the subject of negative gossip.

A final social barrier to cross-sex friendship formation also existed in middle and late childhood. Basic differences between the way male and female adolescents interact might present social barriers to friendship. The extent to which such differences actually exist is open to debate (see the edited volume on sex differences and similarities in communication; Canary & Dindia, 1998; Mulac, Bradac, & Gibbons, 2001). If boys are indeed more aggressive than girls in their style of interaction (Maccoby, 1990), and if boys and girls are socialized in different cultural groups (Leaper, 1994a; Maltz & Borker, 1982), then it seems reasonable to hypothesize that such differences may lead to social and structural barriers to friendship formation. Some research does suggest that the conversations of adolescent boys and girls are different in tone. Tannen found that girls made more of an effort than boys to include their partner in the conversation and to build common understanding (1990b). Boys and girls tend to support each other differently, which Tannen believes might make communication between cross-sex friends difficult.

Cross-Sex Friendships Affect and are Affected by an Individual's Ongoing Social Construction of Self During Adolescence

My central premise that cross-sex friendships impact and are impacted by an individual's ongoing social construction of self was derived from the larger interpersonal self perspective in which individuals are theorized to be products of their social relationships (Markus & Cross, 1990; Tice & Baumeister, 2001). In the next few pages I extend and develop that premise through presentation of the following interrelated themes: (a) the adolescent's struggle for autonomy and individuation can be profitably viewed from an interpersonal-self perspective and is relevant to cross-sex friendship processes; (b) the emerging sexual identity of an adolescent impacts cross-sex friendship formation; and (c) interpersonal communication influences the construction of self-schemas, gender schemas, and friendship schemas.

Individuation and the Interpersonal Self-Perspective. Unlike self-views in childhood, in adolescence an important component of an individual's self schema is the view of self as independent and unique (Sippola & Bukowski, 1999). In their search for self, teenagers hope to find a person who is autonomous and special. They struggle to develop an internal and external sense of independence, while at the same time attempting to establish connectiveness to significant others in their social network (Larson, 1999). Scholars who study personal relationships have focused attention on the dialectic that exist between the processes of *relatedness* and *autonomy* (Baxter, 1988; Rawlins, 1992). According to proponents of the dialectical view, individuals struggle throughout life with the question of how much connection (i.e., relatedness) and independence (i.e., autonomy) they want in their personal relationships. The dialectic is particularly relevant in adolescence because being connected to peers and parents is still important but so is seeing oneself as an independent person separate from the influence of others. The struggle for personal autonomy and individuality rivals sexual maturation in developmental significance for the adolescent. Although peer group and crowd acceptance is important during early and middle adolescence, by late adolescence the desire for group acceptance is supplanted by a greater need view to see oneself as an individual with a unique world view (Sippola & Bukowski, 1999). My contention is that cross-sex friends can help an adolescent establish that sense of identity in generic and unique ways.

Part of the self-exploration of adolescents involves the process of individuation (Blos, 1967; Mahler, 1979). Individuation occurs when adolescents gradually begin to separate themselves from their parents in an attempt to establish autonomy and a sense of self. Friends help each other establish autonomy from peers and parents (Rawlins, 1992, p. 77). At first glance, the importance of individuation during late adolescence appears to challenge the interpersonal self-proposition that self-concepts are socially constructed. As noted by Sippola and Bukowski, "The notion that separation or individuation of the self from others is an important developmental task of adolescence is ubiquitous in the developmental literature" (p. 284). Rather than being contradictory and incompatible, however, the interpersonal self perspective and adolescent struggles for individuation can be seen as complementary. There are a number of ways in which the self might be viewed as an interpersonal creation (Markus & Cross, 1990). One of the central ways is through internalization whereby the thoughts, feelings, and behaviors of significant others are adopted so whole-heartedly that an individual comes to view them as her own (Markus & Cross, 1990). An adolescent, therefore, can still view herself as an individual and sepa-rate from others, although many of her values and beliefs may have originated from others in her social network. From a symbolic interactionist perspective (Blumer, 1969; Mead, 1934), the ability of humans to see themselves as objects gives them the capacity to differentiate themselves from other objects (i.e., to individuate).

The importance of individuation and its link to the interpersonal self per-spective is also seen in a provocative article written by Parker and Gottman (1989). They identified the underlying theme of adolescent friendship conver-sations as an attempt to discover the answer to two questions: "Who am I?," and "Who will I become?". Parker and Gottman contended that the process of self-discovery often occurs in the context of conversations with friends ranging from gossip to abstract discussions about the nature of self. Relatedly, the main goal of adolescent conversations, at least according to Gottman and Mettetal, is to understand the self in relationship to others (1986). The process of mutual self-exploration conducted in the safe context of a friendship is facilitated through self-disclosure, negative and positive gossip about others for social comparison purposes (Cotterell, 1996), problem solving, and the identification and analysis of similarities and differences between each other (Gottman & Mettetal, 1986). Cross-sex friends, like their same-sex counterparts, can help each other feel like unique and important individuals in their joint exploration of who they are and who they one day will be.

Friends and friendships influence self-concepts when they are conceptual-ized and contextualized as part of the self (Markus & Cross, 1990). As noted by Markus and Cross: "To the extent that maintaining certain relationships is criti-cal to self-definition, representations of these others will be continually active, integral parts of the self" (p. 576). For example, if a teenager in late adolescence goes against the norms of his crowd and forms a cross-sex friendship from an-other, lower-status crowd, that friendship might be viewed as a key part of the teenager's self-concept because it represents his individuation from the crowd. Individuation and friendship are connected in that friends provide affirmation to each other as independent and unique individuals (Wright, 1984).

Some feminist scholars suggest that the process of individuation in adoles-cence is different for girls and boys. Chodorow contended that adolescent fe-males like their male counterparts have a need to differentiate themselves from others, but they do so while being in relationships with others, rather than sepa-rating themselves from relationships as boys do (1978). Similarly, Gilligan (1990) believes that separation involves developing a sense of self while simul-taneously allowing one's partner to do the same thing within the context of the relationship. The views of Chodorow and Gilligan suggest that the cross-sex friendship schemas and self-schemas of females and males in late adolescence might be related to each other in different ways. In the last chapter of this book I propose that schemas overlap and influence each other. The overlap between cross-sex friendship schemas and self-schemas would be greater for adolescent females than their male counterparts.

Individuals develop cognitive skills during adolescence that are of great service in their search for self and in the quest for understanding their relationships, skills they did not have during middle childhood that allow them to construct more abstract self-portraits (Damon & Hart, 1988; Harter, 1990). Sippola and Bukowski (1999) clearly and colorfully described the developmental shift in cognitive acuity from middle childhood to adolescence: "The cognitive skills that emerge in adolescence are a powerful force—they free the adolescent from a concrete, quotidian existence and launch them into new realms of existence ... adolescents become capable of abstract representations, and they can engage in processes constructed entirely on abstract principles" (p. 283). Caricaturing crowds is a good example of how adolescents employ their increasing ability to engage in abstract thinking (Brown et al., 1994). And as noted by Brown and associates, the caricaturing reflects not only the ability to view reality less concretely, but also the ability to jointly construct reality with one's peers (Mead, 1934).

Bowlby's attachment theory (1969) can be applied to adolescence, cross-sex friendships, and the struggle for individuation. Savin-Williams noted the importance of attachment theory principles by citing a personal communication with L. A. Sroufe who said that early attachment relationships establish an "internal blueprint" for friendships in early adolescence and romance in adulthood (1994, p. 203). Attachment processes during adolescence are characterized by a growing attempt on the part of the adolescent to establish his or her autonomy from parental control and influence, to "detach" from parents (Cotterell, 1996). As they detach (i.e., individuate) from parents, adolescents form attachments with trusted others in their social network outside of their family, bonds that partially depend on perceived responsiveness and availability of trusted others (Cotterell, 1996). The trusted others include friends, but the extent to which those friends are members of the other sex has not been adequately investigated.

Emerging Sexual Identity and Cross-Sex Friendships.   In addition to the role played by cross-sex friendships in establishing autonomy from parental influence and control, those friendships are also related to sexual identity development (Sippola, 1999). By early adolescence most individuals have already begun to develop an emerging sense of their sexual identity (Katchadourian, 1990; Ruble & Martin, 1998). Although not the totality of an adolescent's self-concept, sexual identity is certainly an important component of it. Savin-Williams defined sexual identity as

> a consistent, enduring self-recognition of the meanings that sexual orientation and sexual behavior have for oneself. Although a public declaration of this status is not in-

herently necessary for sexual identity, there must be some level of personal recognition of this status. Affirmation, to varying degrees, may or may not follow. (1990, p. 3)

What impact does sexual identity and orientation have on cross-sex friendship formation during the adolescent years, and do cross-sex friendships uniquely influence the self-concepts of gay lesbian, and bisexual adolescents? Unfortunately, scholars do not know the answers to either of those questions. Identifying and studying the connections between cross-sex friendships and emerging sexual orientations is an important area of neglected research. From an interpersonal self perspective, the developing self-view of a gay or lesbian youth is influenced by the social feedback received from significant others. An important part of that feedback is the perception of being accepted by friends regardless of one's sexual orientation (Savin-Williams, 1990).

Unraveling the relationship of sexual orientation to cross-sex friendships is difficult for a number of reasons. First, gay, lesbian and bisexual adolescents are not easy to locate because they are frequently "invisible" to others and themselves (Savin-Williams, 1990; 1994). However, there are statistics available on the percentage of adolescents who self-describe themselves as gay, lesbian, or bisexual. In a study conducted in Minnesota public schools, almost 35,000 youths in Grades 7 through 12 were asked about their sexual orientation (Remafedi, Resnick, Blum, & Harris, 1992). Slightly less than 1% of the juniors and seniors defined themselves as bisexual, and .4% defined themselves as gay or lesbian. A surprising 11% said they were "unsure" of their sexual orientation.

Discerning the relationship between sexual orientation and cross-sex friendships in adolescence is also difficult because of a general lack of research. There is an apparent lack of interest on the part of most scholars to investigate adolescent cross-sex friendship (Monsour, 1997; Sippola, 1999) and/or the relationships of gay and lesbian youth (Savin-Williams, 1990). To differing degrees, cross-sex friendships and gay and lesbian youths have been marginalized by most of the scholarly community. Determining how cross-sex friendships are related to gay, lesbian, and bisexual youth is difficult to do when those relationships are routinely ignored by investigators. However, there is enough information available to make some reasonable inferences about cross-sex friendships and their relationship to youth with alternative sexual identities.

Savin-Williams (1990) reviews convincing evidence that gay and lesbian adolescents engage in "gender nonconformity" (i.e., gender atypical or cross-gendered behavior) more than their heterosexual counterparts. If homosexuals engage in behavior more typical of the other sex than their own, that behavior could form the basis for cross-sex friendships because similarity (in this case, similarity of personality traits and interactive behaviors) is a strong determinant of friendship (Monsour, 1994).

There is some information on cross-sex friendships in which at least one of the participants is gay or lesbian. For example, in a bizarre twist of the audience challenge, closeted gay, lesbian, and bisexual youths sometimes date heterosexual members of the other sex in order to keep up the appearance of heterosexuality (Zera, 1992). The dating partner of the gay or lesbian youth is actually more of a cross-sex friend than a romantic partner, although the dating partner might not define the relationship in that way or even realize that he or she is dating a homosexual. In a similar vein, Savin-Williams observed that closeted gay and lesbian youth might shy away from same-sex friendships for fear of being discovered, and may instead gravitate to the relative safety of cross-sex friendship in which others, at worst, might mistakenly assume heterosexual interest (1994).

Savin-Williams (1994) distributed about 300 questionnaires to adolescents ranging from age 14 to 23 for gay males and 16 to 23 for lesbians. Although I disagree with his categorization of individuals in their early 20's as adolescents, his data still warrant examination. Thirty-three percent of the gay adolescent males reported having a heterosexual female friend, although gay males had a greater number of same-sex than cross-sex friends, regardless of the sexual orientation of the friends (p. 83). Eleven percent of the lesbian sample reported having "lots" of gay friends. As a general pattern, lesbians had significantly more same-sex than cross-sex friends. Keeping in mind that most of his sample was over 18 years of age, Savin-Williams concluded that although having straight friends and being accepted by them was associated with positive self-feelings, they "are not sufficient factors to predict high self-esteem" (1990, p. 106). He also concluded that gay and lesbian adolescents who are willing to self-disclose their sexual orientation do so to same-sex and cross-sex friends. However, for adolescents struggling with sexual identity issues, having a close cross-sex friend to confide in might have advantages over a same-sex counterpart. Disclosing homosexual thoughts and urges to a friend might be more difficult and threatening if that friend is a member of one's own sex (Savin-Williams, 1990).

Interpersonal Communication and the Construction of Self and Cross-sex Friendships.   The role of interpersonal communication during childhood in the development of an individual's self-concept and cross-sex friendship formation continues throughout adolescence. The reciprocal influence between the cross-sex friendships of an adolescent and his or her ongoing social construction of self is also continued. Those friendships, admittedly along with a myriad of other relationships embedded in cliques, crowds, and families, impact and are impacted by an evolving concept of self (Ballard-Reisch & Seibert, 1993). In this section I examine how interpersonal communication contributes to the formation and maintenance of cross-sex friendships and self-concept development in adolescence. I also revisit the cognitive processes of gender, self, and cross-sex/same-friendship schema development.

Communication between adolescent cross-sex friends involves considerable self-disclosure and gossip, both employed in the service of self-exploration and defining the relationship (Gottman & Mettetal, 1986; Parker & Gottman, 1989). A lack of research makes it impossible to say for certain, but some of those self-disclosures probably involve telling each other what it is like to be a boy or a girl. These insider perspectives are particularly valuable because they help individuals establish gender identities and to recognize similarities and differences between themselves and their cross-sex friends. Gottman and Mettetal contended that gossip and self-disclosure in adolescent friendships concentrate on relationship problems, with intimacy development secondary to self-understanding. Although gossip between friends is typically about others in their social network and self-disclosures are about self, the processes are related. For example, if a cross-sex friend discloses to her partner "I don't like Mary because of the way she dresses," that communication is both gossip and disclosure.

Self-disclosures in same and cross-sex friendships have also been connected to the importance to adolescents of discrepancies between their outer and inner selves (Sippola & Bukowski, 1999). Sippola and Bukowski reported on a study of 239 students in Grades 7 and 9 (100 boys and 139 girls). They suggested that the degree of discrepancy between outer and inner selves would be correlated with the levels of self-disclosure in the friendship. They stated that "for a variety of reasons (see Maccoby, 1988) adolescents may feel a greater split between the true inner self and the false outer self that is presented to opposite-sex peers" (p. 292). Results indicated that adolescent males reported a greater sense of divided self with their cross-sex partners than did girls. What is not clear from their description, however, is whether participants were reporting exclusively on cross-sex friends, cross-sex peers, romantic partners, or some combination of all three.

By the time individuals enter adolescence their self (Harter, 1998), friendship (Sippola & Bukowski, 1999), and gender schemas (Ruble & Martin, 1998) have evolved beyond the rudimentary stage. A possible exception to this generalization would be the cross-sex friendship schemas of adolescents who had never been in a friendship with a member of the other sex. Unfortunately, there is no reliable longitudinal data on the percentage of adolescents who have never been friends with a member of the other sex. Until studies are done it is probably safest to assume that some adolescents have never had a cross-sex friend, although "some" must remain, for now, an undetermined amount. Adolescents without a history of cross-sex friendships would still have cross-sex friendship schemas (Honeycutt, 1993), but they would not be as detailed as the schemas of individuals who had actually had such friendships.

Although some adolescents may have cross-sex friendship schemas that have not gone beyond an elementary form because of a general lack of experience with those kinds of relationships, almost all adolescents have gender and self schemas that have evolved beyond the embryonic stage (Harter, 1998; Ruble & Martin, 1998). Those gender schemas influence the processing of gender related information and subsequent behavior (Ruble & Martin, 1998, p. 988).

Additionally, changing sex-role expectations are part of gender schemas and can impact self-schemas of adolescents and resulting communication behaviors (Ballard-Reisch & Seibert, 1993). As youths go through adolescence their gender schemas can follow any one of a number of different developmental pathways (Eccles & Bryan, 1994), and their self-schemas become more complex than they were in childhood as their abstract reasoning ability increases (Harter, 1998).

In previous chapters I emphasized that communication is a central feature of a number of theoretical formulations relevant to self-concept and cross-sex friendship formation (e.g., Cooley, 1902; Gergen, 1977; Mead, 1934; Vygotsky, 1986). For example, Hartup noted a similarity between Vygotsky and Mead who each believed that mind and self are products of social interaction (1996b). Earlier in this chapter I explained how cliques and crowds can impact views of self and views of cross-sex relationships and how crowds are essentially socially constructed in the minds and interaction of those who comprise them (Brown, Mory, & Kinney, 1994). Each of the aforementioned theorists has something to offer toward understanding the complex dynamics involved in communication, crowds, cliques, and cross-sex friendship and self construction.

Vygotsky believed that external processes such as group and dyadic interaction are the foundation for the formation of internal concepts and a key to understanding motivation—"everything internal was once external" (1981; Hartup, 1996b). Mental representations or caricatures of crowds, for instance, have their origins in communication within the crowd and between dyadic partners (Brown et al., 1994) Cooley's notion of "primary groups" is equally relevant (Cooley, 1909; 1998). He believed that individual identity is inseparably related to the primary groups an individual belongs to. In primary groups there is sometimes a fusion of individual identities into a common whole, although other dyadic relationships (such as friendships) might originate from the primary group (Cooley, 1909; 1998). Primary groups include (but are not limited to) friendship groups in early and middle childhood, cliques and crowds in adolescence, and families. Teenagers, at least according to Cooley's analysis, derive much of their sense of identity from primary groups (also see Brown et al., 1994).

The ability to view oneself as others do and seeing the other as he or she sees him or herself is fundamental to symbolic interaction (Blumer, 1969, p. 109). Taking the perspective of others toward oneself means taking the viewpoint of discrete individuals (a friend or a sibling for example), groups (such as crowds), and the more abstract community. Seeing things (including oneself) from the viewpoint of another person does not necessarily mean that one agrees with that viewpoint. A teenage girl's view of herself from the perspective of her cross-sex friend, for example, may or may not coincide with the view she has of herself. Meaning, her "metaperspective" (i.e., her view of her partner's view of herself; Laing, Phillipson, & Lee, 1966; Monsour, Betty, & Kurzweil, 1993) may or may not be the same as her view of herself (i.e., her direct perspective on herself). For a teenager concerned about figuring out who she is, viewing herself from all those different perspectives could be quite a cognitive challenge. Research by Gilligan and her colleagues indicate that as girls move from middle childhood through adolescence they progressively feel less secure in their identity (Gilligan, Lyons, & Hanmer, 1990). Blumer (1969) contended from a symbolic interactionist perspective that analysis of a group and its roles and norms must start with examination of dyadic interactions occurring within those groups (p. 108). Mead observed that interaction between members of functionally different groups can oftentimes be problematic, suggesting that the intercrowd cross-sex friendship formation speculated on earlier in this chapter might be particularly difficult if the crowds are functionally different.

If boys and girls think about and construct friendships in different ways (Berndt, 1982; Bukowski, Newcomb, & Hoza, 1987) and if relationships are a product of joint negotiation and construction (Gergen, 1991; Wood, 1995), it makes sense that cross-sex friendships might represent some amalgamation of perspectives. Tannen's conversational research on adolescent boys and girls suggest that they display different communication styles while interacting with friends (Tannen, 1990b). For example, the conversations that girls have with good friends are more relationally oriented and personal than the conversations of male same-sex friends. Boys generally appear more interested and focused on what they are saying, and less interested in the concerns of their partner. Girls, on the other hand, are more traditionally empathic and responsive to their partner than are boys. Tannen proposed that the apparent gender differences reflect less on a lack of concern on the part of boys, and more on merely a different way of showing concern. Commenting on Tannen's research, Cotterell observed that if communication styles of boys and girls are indeed different, then that difference might explain some of the frustration reported by cross-sex friends (1996).

Relatedly, a study conducted by McBride and Field showed that female high school juniors were less comfortable during interaction with a cross-sex best friend than with a same-sex best friend (1997). Females were also more "playful" with a female best friend than with a male best friend, but the reverse pattern revealed itself for the males in the study. Although the researchers should be commended for studying actual communication behavior, rather than self-reports of that behavior, interpretation of their results should be tempered with the recognition that a short videotaped conversation may not be representative of how same-sex and cross-sex friends interact in a more natural environment.

Although interpersonal communication competence is important during early and middle childhood, it becomes even more crucial in adolescence (Buhrmester, 1996). As children become adolescents, their friendships become more focused on talk and conversation than on play (Parker & Gottman, 1989). A reasonable conjecture is that part of the conversations of cross-sex friends would involve self-disclosures about the feelings they have for each other as well as feelings and thoughts that they have about themselves. These self-disclosures would help participants better understand themselves and their cross-sex relationships. In a similar fashion, positive gossip about the cross-sex friends of others might validate their own relationship.

Concluding Observations

Adolescence is a time of self-discovery and self-exploration (Parker & Gottman, 1989). It is perhaps the most crucial stage of life in the development of an individual's self-concept. Beliefs and values about the self and society are evolving into "a relatively stable system that will carry into adulthood" (Ballard-Reisch & Seibert, 1993, p. 283; Battle, 1982). From an interpersonal self-perspective, the exploration and discovery of self is accomplished at least partly through relationships with family, peers, same-sex friends, romantic partners, and cross-sex friendships.

The generic and unique benefits of cross-sex friendships during adolescence are mediated by crowd and clique membership. Like the adolescents who comprise them, cliques and crowds are sometimes capricious social entities (Cotterell, 1996). An adolescent may quickly and ruthlessly lose membership in a crowd or clique simply because he or she befriended the wrong person, precipitating feelings of social loneliness (Weiss, 1973). Alternatively, an adolescent may gain membership in a crowd because he or she befriended the right person. Membership in a particular crowd can facilitate or impede cross-sex friendship formation through various channeling principles (Brown et al., 1994). If belonging to a certain crowd leads to high levels of other-sex interaction, then the potential for cross-sex friendship formation is greater than it would be in a crowd characterized by less mixed-sex interaction. Once cross-sex friendships are formed, then unique benefits such as receiving insider perspectives and other-sex companionship can be reaped.

The impact of cross-sex friendships on self-views and vice versa is influenced by the larger social context in which those friendships occur (Adams & Allan, 1998; Bukowski et al., 1996). Crowds and cliques are an important part of the larger social context (Cotterell, 1996). The effect that crowds and cliques have on a teenager's view of self partially mediates and is mediated by the cross-sex friendships embedded in the various cliques and crowds. Therefore, the relationship between self-concepts and cross-sex friendships is influenced by the relationship between group membership and self-concepts, as well as group membership and cross-sex friendships. The complicated statistical and conceptual relationships between self-concepts, group memberships, same-sex friendships, romantic relationships, and cross-sex friendships are daunting—especially considering that those relationships might be different in each stage of adolescence (i.e., early, middle, and late adolescence). Several prominent scholars have noted the importance of including individual and group level analysis when studying same and cross-sex friendships in adolescence (e.g., Bukowski et al., 1999). However, researchers and theorists also conclude that the influence of those groups on self-concept formation begins to dissipate considerably as adolescents approach adulthood and start to value a sense of self-direction and autonomy more than peer approval (Cooley, 1902; Harter, 1998; Newman & Newman, 1986).

As observed in the previous two chapters, social and structural barriers to cross-sex friendships partially emanate from deep and surface structures (Hartup & Stevens, 1997). Deep structures suggest what form particular types of relationships such as cross-sex friendships should assume, while surface structures are the actual communicative manifestations of the deep structure. Brown and his associates contend that relationship guidelines coming from the deep structure of society are manifested as crowd norms concerning appropriate relationships. They conclude that"adolescents use crowds to construct a symbolic road map of prototypic peer relationships … and stipulates the ease or difficulty of interacting with certain peers, and what is risked, gained, or lost by nurturing particular peer relationships" 1994, p. 162). Similarly, Connolly and her colleagues proposed (based on their study of 1,755 early adolescents), that the conceptions adolescents have of cross-sex and romantic relationships mirror adult conceptions of those relationships, conceptions that originate from the deep structure of society.

Cross-sex friendships influence an adolescent's view of self by allowing for self-exploration in a relatively judgment free, self-affirming, and safe environment (Parker & Gottman, 1989). Research reviewed in this chapter established that conversations between cross- and same-sex friends involve consensual validation of each other's opinions about self and others (Buhrmester, 1996; Harter, 1990; Rawlins, 1992; Sullivan, 1953). I was also able to infer from Buhrmester's research (1996), although he did not do so himself, that cross-sex friendships provide adolescents with an opportunity to develop agentic and communal interpersonal competencies. The development of such competencies, arguably, would have a positive impact on an adolescent's self-image. Friends of the other sex can also act as cross-sex guides in an adolescent's journey of self-exploration by providing valuable insider information.

I conclude this chapter with a review of three *interrelated* developmental milestones that are particularly relevant to cross-sex friendship processes in adolescence: puberty, cognitive growth in abstract reasoning abilities, and personal strivings for individuation. Note that these milestones are not discrete events, but are instead complicated and interconnected processes that continue throughout adolescence. These milestones impact not only cross-sex friendship dynamics, but many other areas of adolescent life as well.

The quintessential developmental milestone in adolescence is the onset and maturation of puberty. And, not at all coincidentally, puberty is also the single most salient developmental process in cross-sex friendship formation. Unfortunately, researchers rarely investigate the relationship between puberty and cross-sex friendship processes. However, inferences are easy to make. Puberty profoundly and poignantly changes the way individuals view members of the other sex. Before puberty, members of the other sex were generally (but not always) avoided as evidenced by gender segregation and the formation of same-sex friendship dyads and groups (see chap. 3). After the onset of puberty, members of the other sex become potential friends and dating partners. Heterosexual boys and girls find themselves attracted to each other for reasons that might have their origins in sexual maturation, but also because members of the other sex can provide relief from loneliness, insider perspectives, other-sex companionship, and cross-sex guides in self exploration (Connolly et al., 1999; Parker & Gottman, 1989; Rawlins, 1992; Sippola, 1999).

Members of the other sex can be simultaneously attractive and intimidating to heterosexual adolescents (Erwin, 1998). The awkwardness of adolescence is no more acutely felt than during cross-sex interaction partly because most adolescents have had so little practice at it, and partly because sexual attraction is often a component of that interaction. Adolescents who are particularly shy around members of the other sex may find it especially difficult to initiate and maintain interaction (Erwin, 1998). Although I am not claiming that adolescent cross-sex friendships should be viewed as precursors to romantic relationships, those friendships can certainly enable adolescents to become more comfortable with members of the other sex, which could lead to more productive romantic relationships (Connolly et al., 1999; Furman & Shaffer, 1999).

Puberty has a different impact on cross-sex friendship potential for gay, lesbian, and bisexual adolescents. As sexual identities start to form with the onset of puberty, homosexual males and females begin to view members of their own sex in much the same way as heterosexual individuals view members of the other sex (Savin-Williams, 1990). One would think that *not* viewing members of the other sex as potential sexual and romantic partners would simplify matters immensely and make cross-sex friendship formation a relatively straightforward affair because those relationships would not be complicated by hidden and overt sexual and romantic agendas and tensions. This, unfortunately, is not the case, largely due to the "invisibility" of gay, lesbian, and bisexual youth (Savin-Williams & Rodriguez, 1993). Meaning, many gay and lesbian youth do not realize they are homosexual (thus, they are invisible to themselves), or they are not willing to reveal their sexual identity to others (thus, they are invisible to others). However, for gay and lesbian youth who are aware of their sexual preferences and willing to reveal them to selected others, cross-sex friendships provide an opportunity for those individuals to "come out" in the safe context of an individual friendship in which the partner would be less threatened by one's admittance of homosexuality (Savin-Williams & Berndt, 1990).

The connection between bisexuality and cross-sex friendships in adolescence is an unexplored one. Nevertheless, here are some observations that seem somewhat commonsensical. Assuming for the moment that a bisexual youth has recognized and accepted her or his bisexuality, relationships with members of the other sex might not be too terribly different from relationships that a strictly heterosexual adolescent might have with those individuals. Heterosexual adolescents can have romantic, sexual, friendship, and casual relationships with members of the other sex. Bisexual youth would have the same options. Heterosexual cross-sex friends of bisexual youth could provide the same kind of generic and unique benefits provided by the cross-sex friends of heterosexual adolescents. However, cross-sex friendships of bisexual youths might also have to confront some of the same challenges (O'Meara, 1989) that face strictly heterosexual cross-sex friends. The situation would be much more complex for bisexual youth who are still struggling with sexual identity issues. If an adolescent is vacillating between sexual identities, there might be considerable confusion in trying to decide how to relate to members of the other sex.

Another developmental milestone in adolescence centers around the desire to become an individual by establishing independence from the influence of others (Schinke McAlister, Orlandi, & Botvin, 1990). A recurring theme in much of the literature on adolescent development is that when adolescents get closer to young adulthood they become more concerned with seeing themselves as individuals with their own set of values and beliefs. This concern with individuality is revealed in research documenting that individuals in late adolescence become less focused on having the correct crowd connections, and more focused on developing their own set of values (Rubin et al., 1998). The developmental process of individuation is clearly connected to puberty and sexual identity realization and acceptance. Particularly for gay, lesbian, and bisexual adolescents, striving for individuality would involve acceptance of one's sexual orientation. For heterosexual adolescents, individuation might mean rejection of cultural pressures to view members of the other sex primarily as potential dating partners. Unfortunately, there has been little if any direct research on how the processes of individuation and cross-sex friendship formation and maintenance are related.

A third developmental milestone in adolescence is the growing ability to engage in abstract thinking (Sippola & Bukowski, 1999). This ability leads to more complicated and sophisticated views of self and others than existed in earlier stages of the life cycle. Self-schemas change from childhood to adolescence. A child is likely to think of him or herself in concrete, outwardly observable characteristics. Adolescents, in contrast, tend to have more complex and differentiated views of self and others (Harter, 1998). For example, an adolescent might come to appreciate and understand the various and sometimes contradictory roles or selves that he or she represents. Some experts have argued that as a result of normal cognitive development, such as increases in abstract reasoning ability, many adolescents become more flexible in their thinking about what constitutes "appropriate" sex-role behavior (e.g., Eccles, 1987). As noted by Ruble and Martin, however, empirical evidence documenting progressive flexibility from early to late adolescence is somewhat mixed (1998), and we know little about how such cognitive developments impact thinking about cross-sex friendships.

In conclusion, adolescence is a time when friendships between girls and boys can be of great benefit. After all, boys and girls in late adolescence are on the verge of becoming adults and having to deal with each other as men and women in a wide range of social, employment, and personal situations. Being friends with members of the other sex while simultaneously establishing a sense of identity and adulthood could lead to more informed, productive, and socially sensitive members of society.

5

Cross-Sex Friendships
in Adulthood
(18 to 64 years of age)

A survey of the burgeoning literature would lead one to believe that friendship is not only most common but also most possible between persons of the same sex, because the overwhelming majority of these studies have focused on same-sex friendship. By and large, friendship between the sexes has been overlooked by almost all researchers, regardless of their discipline.
—K. J. Werking (1997a, p. 2)

The above quotation from Werking's 1997 book is still an accurate assessment of the adult cross-sex friendship literature. Although in the last decade a handful of new studies have been added to the slowly growing list of adult cross-sex friendship investigations (e.g., Afifi & Faulkner, 2000; Kaplan & Keys, 1997; Werking, 1992, 1997a), friendship researchers still focus most of their energies on same-sex friendships. Despite the comparatively small size of the adult cross-sex friendship literature, it has much to offer in helping to explicate the major themes and theoretical premise of this book. As I have done in the preceding chapters representing earlier stages of life, presentation and review of the adult cross-sex friendship literature revolves around the three themes of the book. The final section of the chapter is reserved for concluding observations about male-female friendships in adulthood.

The stage of life identified as adulthood includes young (18 to 34 years old) and middle-aged (35 to 64 years old) individuals. Cross-sex friendships of *young adult* women and men have received quite a flurry of research attention in the last few years (e.g., Felmlee, 1999; Reeder, 2000), but the cross-sex friendships of *middle-aged adults* have been neglected (Sherman, De Vries, & Lansford, 2000). I concluded in an earlier review that young adult cross-sex friendships receive most of the research attention because university students are conveniently available to professors as research participants (1997). College also provides rich structural opportunities for formation of friendships between young women and men, surpassing even those of the much-touted workplace environment (O'Meara, 1994). Although I came across a number of friendship studies that included young and middle-aged participants (e.g., Bell, 1981; Bruess & Pearson, 1997; Duck & Wright, 1993; Lobel, Quin, St. Clair, & Warfield, 1994; Rubin, 1985; Sapadin, 1988; Werking, 1997a; Winstead, Derlega, Montgomery, & Pilkington, 1995), I was unable to discover any investigations conducted in the last 20 years focusing exclusively on cross-sex friendships of middle-aged adults. As I demonstrate periodically throughout this chapter, the dynamics of cross-sex friendships in middle-age might be different from those of their younger counterparts in early adulthood.

Cross-Sex Friendships and the Enrichment of Social Networks in Adulthood

Adult cross-sex friendships are different in some respects from their same-sex counterparts (Monsour, 1997), but there are also many similarities (Afifi & Guerrero, 1998; Wright, 1989). One way of viewing the similarities and differences between cross-sex and same-sex friendships is through an examination of generic and unique benefits of male–female friendships. Generic benefits reflect similarities between the two types of friendship, whereas unique benefits reflect their differences.

Generic Benefits.   Similar to life stages before and after adulthood, cross-sex friendships in young and middle adulthood provide participants with a number of generic benefits that are also available in same-sex friendships. Unlike friends in earlier and later stages of life, however, adult cross-sex friends can provide benefits in an environment not typically experienced by children, adolescents, and older adults (i.e., the workplace environment). In this section I review evidence documenting that cross-sex friends provide social support, important benefits in the workplace, and a protection against loneliness.

There is strong evidence that adult cross-sex friends provide one another with social support (e.g., Barbee, Gulley, & Cunningham, 1990; Carbery & Buhrmester, 1998; Gaines, 1994; Felmlee, 1999; Monsour, 1988; Patford, 2000; Winstead, Derlega, Lewis, Sanchez-Hucles, & Clarke, 1992). I start with Kathy Werking's book because she has conducted more research than any other single scholar on cross-sex friendships of young adults (Werking, 1997a). Based on her extensive knowledge of adult cross-sex friendships (she interviewed 190 individuals and collected survey data from another 636), Werking concluded "The benefits of cross-sex friendships are similar to those associated with same-sex friendship. Cross-sex friends offer comfort during difficult times, an outlet for the expression of fears, feelings, and fantasies, companionship, acceptance, and greater self-knowledge" (1997a, p. 162). Werking also observed that cross-sex friends provide each other with the same kind of social support normally given by same-sex female friends called *marriage work*. Oliker argued that female friends help each other with their marital problems by talking about the difficulties and providing feedback and possible solutions (1989). Werking suggested that the same kind of marriage work occurs in cross-sex friendships when friends act as sounding boards and provide feedback to each other on their respective marriages.

Implicit in Werking's observations about social support is the corollary conclusion that cross-sex friends serve many of the same functions as their same-sex counterparts. In one of the first studies of its type, Rose compared the functions of cross-sex and same-sex friendships of 90 young adults (1985). Cross-sex and same-sex friendships served basically the same functions, but as a general pattern same-sex friendships served them to a greater degree. Both women and men reported acceptance, loyalty, help, intimacy, and companionship most frequently to be the functions of same-sex friendship. Men but not women reported having the acceptance, intimacy, and companionship functions fulfilled to the same extent by cross-sex friendships. Interestingly, women but not men reported that the companionship function was met to a much greater extent by their cross-sex friends.

Barbee and her associates had 99 female and 103 male undergraduates indicate on a 7-point scale if they would prefer to talk to a same-sex close friend or a cross-sex close friend concerning two hypothetical "task" and "relationship" problems (Barbee et al., 1990; recall from chapter four a similar study by Clark, 1994, focusing on adolescents). Talking to a friend about a problem demonstrates an attempt to receive social support from that friend. Both men and women indicated a stronger preference for talking to a close same-sex friend about the two types of problems. Although the differences in preference scores were statistically significant, the average scores suggest a lack of practical difference ($x = 11.88$ for talking to a same-sex friend; $x = 10.53$ for talking to a cross-sex friend). Wright cautioned researchers against overemphasizing statistical significance at the expense of understating the lack of practical significance (1988).

In a study indirectly related to social support, 320 undergraduate students judged the appropriateness of a target friend's behavior in six hypothetical friendship vignettes (Felmlee, 1999). One of the purposes of the investigation was to discover norms and rules in cross-sex and same-sex friendships. Felmlee concluded that friendship norms were similar for both types of relationships. In the words of her respondents: "friends should try to support each other in times of sorrow," and "friends should feel comfortable enough to hug even if you haven't seen each other for a while." Both of these normative expectations relate to social support. An obvious shortcoming of the Felmlee and Barbee investigations is that both researchers incorporated hypothetical scenarios as part of their research design rather than having subjects report on actual events in their friendships.

Social support was investigated in a slightly different fashion by Gaines in 1994. He was interested in exploring the degree to which *affection* and *respect* were exchanged in same-sex and cross-sex friendships of young adults. Showing affection and respect in a friendship would meet the definition of social support used in this book, that is, giving and receiving affect, aid, and affirmation (Crohan & Antonucci, 1989). Sixty-two cross-sex friendships, 62 male friendships, and 64 female friendships were recruited for the study. Although there were cases in which participants withheld respect and affection in both same-sex and cross-sex friendships, men and women in cross-sex friendships generally showed trust in their partner, shared things with their partner, showed admiration for their partner, and praised their partner. On the other hand, disrespectful behavior was particularly likely to be reciprocated in cross-sex friendships. Gaines speculated that part of the disrespect might have originated from struggles that some men and women experienced in their cross-sex friendships about the nature of the feelings they had for each other (remember O'Meara's emotional bond challenge, 1989).

As discussed in chapter four on cross-sex friendships in adolescence, social support is also demonstrated when relational partners meet each other's needs (Knapp & Vangelisti, 1996; Rose, 1985). Unlike adolescence where individuals are not likely to be spouses or parents, marital and parental status in adulthood can influence the extent to which friends meet needs. Research with 180 young adults (ages 20 to 35) documented that friends meet needs to differing degrees depending on whether the young adults are single, married, or married with children (Carbery & Buhrmester, 1998). As noted by Carbery and Buhrmester, three of Weiss' nine social provisions (1974) involved types of social support (i.e., instrumental aid, emotional support, and guidance/advice). In general, results indicated that reliance on friends for meeting needs is greatest when a person is single, then it declines significantly during the marital and parenthood phases. Interestingly, 13% of the 90 men compared to 4% of the 90 women reported that their closest friend was a member of the other sex. Unfortunately, Carbery and Buhrmester did not reveal if there were any differences between same-sex friendships and cross-sex friendships in the provision of social support in each phase of young adulthood. Existing research leads me to believe that there might have been differences in the social provisions of "giving advice" and "getting emotional support." Some of the female subjects in my dissertation reported that their male friends gave them more objective advice than their female friends (Monsour, 1988). Also, female friends are often preferred over their male counterparts when someone, male or female, is seeking emotional support (Kunkel & Burleson, 1998, p. 112).

Another generic benefit of cross-sex friendships is that they provide the same kind of enjoyment normally associated with same-sex friendships. Cross-sex friendships can meet the need for everyday companionship. Relationship scholars, Duck in particular, believe that the everyday, commonplace, and routine interactions of relational partners such as friends add considerable quality and enjoyment to life (e.g., Duck, 1990, 1992; Wright, 1989). For instance, both men and women in their same-sex friendships get together primarily to "just talk" (Duck & Wright, 1993), a practice perhaps started in adolescence (Rawlins, 1992). The vast majority of time spent communicating with one's friend is not comprised of deep disclosures and exciting joint activities. Rather, much communication is just talk about nothing in particular, and yet the talking has a hidden significance in that it helps participants create a mutually understood and experienced reality (Duck, 1990, 1992, 1994; Duck, Rutt, Hurst, & Strejc, 1991).

Perhaps the most important manifestation of social support in adulthood is the relational refuge friends provide against social and emotional loneliness (Harvard Health Letter, May 1999). Although mass media often portrays old age as being the dominant stage of life for loneliness to occur, loneliness is actually most prevalent during young adulthood (Perlman & Landolt, 1999). Loneliness has similar deleterious effects in adulthood that it has in other stages of life. For example, Lau and Kong discovered that lonely subjects ($n = 96$ college students) rated themselves lower than nonlonely subjects in physical appearance, emotional stability, same-sex and other-sex relations, relations with parents, and general self-concept (1999). Subjects who read descriptions of lonely and nonlonely individuals rated the lonely ones less desirable as possible friends. Duck, Pond, and Leatham (1994) suggest that lonely people have a negative perceptual style, meaning that while communicating with others they tend to focus on the negative elements of their own communication style which leads to an overall dissatisfaction with their social interactions. Loneliness has also been connected to various types of physical health problems, although the "mechanisms linking the subjective experience of loneliness to physical health outcomes, are not well understood" (Perlman & Peplau, 1998, p. 579).

Recall that loneliness occurs when a person perceives a quantitative and/or qualitative deficiency in her or his social network (Perlman & Peplau, 1998). The two dominant theories of adult loneliness, that is, social needs theory (Bowlby, 1973; Sullivan, 1953; Weiss, 1973) and cognitive processes theory (Peplau & Perlman, 1979), propose at least a correlational link between loneliness and friendships—if not a causal one. In other words, loneliness and friendship scholars are confident that loneliness and friendships (or a lack of friendships) are related in some way (i.e., the correlational link), they just are not sure that a lack of friendships causes loneliness because multiple causal factors are likely at work (Rook, 1988). There is also confusion as to whether lack of friendships causes loneliness, or if loneliness causes a lack of friendships, or whether it is a case of reciprocal causality (Rook, 1988).

Knapp and Vangelisti indicate that there is a "vast body of literature" documenting that humans have basic interpersonal needs such as the need for affection and the need to be included in the activity of others (1996; see also Schutz,

1958). Proponents of a social needs approach to loneliness maintain that loneliness is the result of inherent interpersonal needs for relationships not being met (Sullivan, 1953; Terrell-Deutsch, 1999). Investigators have verified that cross-sex friends meet needs for affection (e.g., Afifi & Faulkner, 2000; Gaines, 1994). Supporters of cognitive processes theory maintain that loneliness results from the cognitive realization of a discrepancy between the quantity and quality of relationships one would like to have, and what one actually experiences (Terrell-Deutsch, 1999).

The definition of loneliness and the two major theories used to explain it suggest that having friends and high quality friends are effective ways of coping with loneliness. If loneliness means a perceived quantitative or qualitative deficiency in a person's social network (Perlman & Peplau, 1998), then friendship would seem to be a natural remedy for those deficiencies. Indeed, individuals who are lonely, when compared to their nonlonely counterparts, have fewer friends and fewer close friends (Bell, 1993). In 1998 I collected data from 188 college students (48 males and 140 females, average age of 22). Participants were asked to indicate on a 7-point scale how lonely they had been over the last 6 months (1 = not at all lonely, 4 = moderately lonely, 7 = extremely lonely). The average female and male responses were 4.27 and 3.88, respectively. Respondents were also asked "Do you think there is a connection between the loneliness you feel and a lack of enough quality friendships in your life?" Roughly 50% responded with a "yes," 40% with a "no," and 10% indicated they "did not know." From a broader life-span perspective, the last item on the survey was "Have you ever had a platonic friend who was a member of the opposite sex who was instrumental in keeping you company and making sure you weren't too lonely?" Dramatically, 75% of the males and 73% of the females responded with a "yes."

The workplace is an important context to examine when exploring generic benefits of cross-sex friendships (Furman, 1986; O'Meara, 1994). Lobel and her associates contended that a number of factors have increased the frequency and relevancy of male–female workplace friendships (Lobel et al., 1994). For instance, not only is there a higher proportion of women in the workplace now than there has ever been, but there is also a greater tendency for women and men to be working side by side in management strategies such as teambuilding, networking, and coalition building. Organizational friendships serve many of the same functions as friendships outside the workplace. They provide a buffer against stress, a source of enjoyment, and can stimulate individual creativity (Sias & Cahill, 1998; Yager, 1997). Friendship quality is also positively correlated with job satisfaction (Winstead et al., 1995). Sapadin's investigation is an excellent demonstration of some of the benefits of cross-sex friendships in the workplace (1988). The study deserves special attention because her 156 subjects were working professionals rather than college students and because her study included a fairly equal number of individuals from young and middle adulthood. Men rated their cross-sex friendships higher than their same-sex friendships in overall quality, nurturance, and enjoyment. Conversely, women rated their same-sex friendships higher than their cross-sex ones on those variables. Close examination of the mean ratings on 7-point scales given by men and women of their cross-sex friendships on enjoyment, intimacy, and nurturance reveals significant similarities, minor differences, and an overall pattern of moderately high ratings. As we see in the next section, though the generic benefits of cross-sex friendships in the workplace are important, it is the unique benefits of those friendships that give them a special quality not obtainable in same-sex friendships.

Unique Benefits.   The unique benefits of cross-sex friendships have been directly studied more in young adulthood than in any other stage of life. Similar to cross-sex friendships in earlier stages of the life cycle, adult cross-sex friends provide each other with insider perspectives (Monsour, 1988), other-sex companionship (Werking, 1997a), and they sensitize each other to gender differences in communication style (Swain, 1992). Each of these advantages and a few other less central ones are explored in this section. To start things off I review some of the findings from my dissertation (Monsour, 1988).

A central goal of my dissertation was to explore the special functions and unique rewards of cross-sex friendships when compared to same-sex friendships and romantic relationships (Monsour, 1988). Two hundred and eight undergraduate students completed an 11-page survey comprised of open- and closed-ended items. In general, survey responses revealed that cross-sex friendships provide other-sex companionship (also see Rubin, 1985), an insider's perspective (also see Sapadin, 1988; Werking, 1997a), and an opportunity to reveal sex-role discrepant information (also see Swain, 1992). When asked in open-ended format to list cross-sex friendship rewards that romantic partners could *not* provide, 25% of the males and 11% of the females listed receiving an insider's perspective. Although I did not have direct data to support my conclusion, I suggested that in some cases the insider perspective that one needs from a cross-sex friend concerns a romantic partner.

On the survey I listed cross-sex friendship characteristics gleaned from the literature, such as "cross-sex friends provide an insider's perspective on how members of the opposite sex think, feel, and behave" (Sapadin, 1988). Respondents indicated the importance of each characteristic on a 9-point scale. A particularly interesting finding was that women placed more importance than men on the cross-sex friendship characteristic of "providing other-sex companionship without the demands and expectations that normally accompany romantic relationships" ($X = 6.7$ for females, $X = 5.3$ for males, $p < .001$). Along these same lines, Swain contended that cross-sex friendships provide an arena in which individuals can explore the similarities and differences between men and women without the pressure that accompanies being a lover (1992). Recall that adolescents also indicated that their romantic relationships are often less open than are their good cross-sex friendships (Rawlins, 1992).

Men and women placed moderately high importance on the cross-sex friendship characteristic of providing other-sex companionship ($X = 6.3$) and providing validation as being an attractive member of the other-sex ($X = 4.7$) Providing validation as an attractive member of the other sex was also seen as an advantage by some of the participants in Rubin's study of friendship (1985). Afifi and Faulkner discovered along similar lines that 51% of their sample of college students had sex with a cross-sex friend whom they were not dating (2000). Although not specifically addressed in their study, one could assume (but perhaps mistakenly) that if cross-sex friends are having sexual intercourse with each other they are both receiving validation as attractive members of the other sex.

Respondents in my dissertation were also asked to respond to an item on a 9-point scale asking "To what extent does your cross-sex friend serve purposes and provide rewards that your same-sex friends do not?" (1 = to no extent, 5 = to a moderate extent, 9 = to a great extent). The average reply was a 4.2 for males and a 5.2 for females. The average reply to the item about rewards from a cross-sex friend that romantic partners could not supply was a 5.8 for the men and a 5.3 for the women. These findings support the argument that cross-sex friends can provide benefits that are not available in romantic relationships or same-sex friendships.

Swain (1992) made a number of observations about the unique benefits of cross-sex friendships. Based on interview data from a small sample of college students, he concluded that cross-sex friendships give women and men an opportunity to relate to each other as friends in ways that are less familiar but also less constraining than same-sex interaction. For example, some men feel freer to be more emotional and expressive in their cross-sex friendships than in their same-sex ones. Male respondents reported that cross-sex friendships gave them a chance to explore their feminine side and reveal sex-role discrepant information (e.g., "I cry during sad movies") without risk of appearing weak (see also Monsour, 1988; Rubin, 1985). Swain further contended that women, on the other hand, may find it easier to display competitive behaviors with close male friends than with close female friends (see also Monsour, 1988). As noted by Swain, "The cross-sex friends took on the role of an informant by sharing and sensitizing each other to the meanings of the other sex's style of intimacy" (p. 169). Swain argued (as I have in chaps. 2, 3, and 4) that one of the central benefits of cross-sex friendships is that participants can sensitize each other to gender differences in communication style. This advantage assumes that there are differences in communication style between males and females, an assumption I started to explore in the last chapter and will continue in the next few paragraphs (for some interesting treatments on the issue of gender differences see Burleson et al., 1996; Duck & Wright, 1993; Leaper et al., 1995; Mulac et al., 2001; Wood & Dindia, 1998).

Research findings point to language differences between women and men. Although not specifically focusing on differences between male and female friendships, Mulac and his associates found empirical support for the "gender-as-culture hypothesis" (Mulac, Bradac, & Gibbons, 2001). That hypothesis, in part, specifies that boys and girls learn to use language differently as they are socialized into their respective gender groups (Maltz & Borker, 1982). Once those differences are learned they contribute to communication difficulties between the sexes later in life (Maltz & Borker). Based on data gathered from over 300 undergraduates Mulac and his colleagues concluded:

> Results of the three studies demonstrated substantial and generally consistent support for the hypothesis that various features of male language are perceived as relatively (a) direct, (b) succinct, (c) personal, and (d) instrumental, whereas particular female language features are judged as relatively (a) indirect, (b) elaborate, and (c) affective. (2001, p. 141)

Mulac and his co-researchers were also careful to point out that although there are differences in the way men and women use language, "some men and women will have identical communication styles, which should facilitate mutual understanding" (p. 145).

In a fun and fascinating chapter on similarities and differences between men and women, two well known and highly respected communication scholars engaged in a friendly "dialogue" about purported gender and sex differences between women and men (Wood & Dindia, 1998). Wood cited numerous studies documenting differences in the communication styles of men and women and believes that differences between them are significant. She observed, for example, that women rely more than men on verbal communication, including personal disclosures, to build and maintain intimacy with friends and romantic partners. In contrast, Dindia labeled herself a "minimalist" because she believes the differences between men and women in personality traits and communication behaviors are small. Both scholars conclude by agreeing with Wright's assessment in the same book that especially in regard to friendships the differences between men and women are more a matter of degree than kind (Wright, 1998).

Similarly, Burleson and three of his colleagues concluded from their study of the perceived importance of eight communication skills in same-sex friendships ($n = 382$) that men and women were far more similar than different. However, as a general pattern men placed more value than women on instrumental skills and women placed more value than men are affectively oriented skills (1996). Relatedly, Leaper and Anderson contended that because of differences in socialization when they were boys and girls "Men may demonstrate a more domineering and autonomous communication style, whereas women may demonstrate a more accommodating and engaging communication style" (1997, p. 89). In a self-disclosure study of cross- and same-sex college friendships, Leaper and her colleagues audio-taped pairs of 18 female friendships, 18 male friendships, and 18 cross-sex friendships. Some of their findings contradicted traditional wisdom concerning male-female differences. For example, men made more disclosures than women regardless of whether they were in a same-sex or cross-sex friendship. On the other hand, in same-sex female friendships there were more elaborate supportive responses to the disclosures of their friends than there were in the other two types of friendship (Leaper, Carson, Baker, Holliday, & Myers, 1995).

Duck and Wright reanalyzed two sets of data collected in previous research endeavors in search of differences between male and female same-sex friendships (1993). Their study is relevant to cross-sex friendship because if men and women do conduct their same-sex friendships differently, those differences could be cause for concern and conflict when women and men get together as friends and enact different behavioral routines (Swain, 1992). On the other hand, differences in communication styles between women and men could also sensitize partners to those differences (Swain, 1992). A central conclusion of their reanalysis was that expressive and instrumental components of friendship are equally characteristic of both female and male same-sex friendships. Both men and women are expressive in their same-sex friendships, women just tend to be more overtly expressive than men. They also concluded that women are more instrumental in their same-sex friendships than they are stereotypically portrayed. Their self-report findings indicate that women put more into their same-sex friendships and get more back than do men in their same-sex friendships. Both women and men regard "talking for talking's sake" as a central feature of their friendships. Their findings suggest that if women and men do bring their same-sex friendship styles into their cross-sex friendship encounters, then those relationships would probably have expressive and instrumental components and be characterized by talking just for the joy of talking.

The sexual dimension of adult heterosexual cross-sex friendships can be problematic or pleasurable. In this section I focus on the positive aspects of sexuality in friendships between adult women and men. Later in the chapter I examine issues of sexuality that can potentially threaten the integrity of the friendship (i.e., O'Meara's sexual challenge, 1989). Unlike their same-sex counterparts, cross-sex friendships among heterosexuals offer the opportunity for sexual enjoyment ranging from flirtatious behavior to sexual intercourse (e.g., Afifi & Faulkner, 2000; Eyler & Baridon, 1992; Lobel et al., 1994; Sapadin, 1988).

Afifi and Faulkner had 309 college students (150 females and 159 males) complete a survey concerning sexual activity in nonromantic cross-sex friendships (2000). A surprising 51% of the respondents had sex with a cross-sex friend whom they had no intention of dating. I found that percentage to be astoundingly high, especially given my own research indicating that sexual overtones exist only minimally in cross-sex friendships (Monsour,

Betty, & Kurzweil, 1993). But according to more recent research than my own, sexual attraction is common in the cross-sex friendships of young adults (Kaplan & Keys, 1997). For about one-third of the participants in the Afifi and Faulkner study, having sex with a cross-sex friend was more than a one-time experiment. An interesting qualification to their findings, which they duly note, is that 44% of those who engaged in sexual activity eventually transformed the relationship into a romantic one. This finding coincides with Werking's position that sexual activity in a cross-sex friendship often changes the relationship into a romantic one (1997a).

Research conducted much earlier by Rubin (1985) and Sapadin (1988) provides additional documentation that sexual enjoyment is an important benefit in some cross-sex friendships. Both studies have added significance because part of their samples were middle-aged adults. Rubin interviewed 300 individuals ranging in age from 25 to 55 and representing various socioeconomic backgrounds (1985). She asked respondents "What do you get out of a friendship with a man (woman) that's different from a same-sex relationship?" Many heterosexual women and men reported that the sexual component often added a "zest" to the relationship that was absent in their same-sex friendships. Sapadin's investigation of 156 young and middle-aged professional men and women revealed that significant percentages of men (76%) and women (50%) enjoy flirting and sexual teasing with cross-sex friends. Sixty-two percent of the men and 50% of the women believed that "Having a sexual relationship adds deeper feelings and closeness to friendships." Six percent and 7% of women and men, respectively, mentioned sexual excitement as what they liked most about the friendship. Lobel and colleagues studied the psychological impact of intimacy between men and women at work in a sample of over 1000 organizational workers with a median age of 38 (1994). They contended that "employees are already confused about what constitutes appropriate male–female attitudes and behaviors at work—a confusion fueled by the sexual-harassment hearings conducted during the confirmation proceedings for Supreme Court Justice Clarence Thomas" (p. 5). Respondents were asked to describe their closest relationship with a person of the other sex. About 50% said there was sexual attraction in the identified relationship although sex itself was avoided. Men were more likely than women to perceive barriers to cross-sex friendships in the workplace and were more likely than women to see a sexual dimension to the friendship, possibly because men are more prone than women to misperceive friendly behavior as sexual interest (Abbey, 1982; Shotland & Craig, 1988). An important part of the article was their list of recommendations to managers on how cross-sex relationships, including friendships, should be viewed and handled. One of their conclusions was that sexual attraction between workers that is not acted on can either "energize employees or distract them, depending on their individual characters and needs" (p.15).

In the same vein as Lobel and her associates, Eyler and Baridon offered an interesting viewpoint on how sexual energy can contribute to a more productive working environment between members of different sexes (1992). They contended that sexual attraction between coworkers is natural even if those coworkers are in committed romantic or marital relationships outside of the workplace. Rather than denying such feelings and/or labeling them as destructive and counterproductive, men and women in organizational settings should recognize that sexual attraction does not need to be acted on, but it can nonetheless add energy and interest to projects in the workplace (Eyler & Baridon, 1992). Research on sexuality in the workplace (e.g., Eyler & Baridon, 1992; Lobel et al., 1994; Sapadin, 1988), especially as it relates to cross-sex organizational friendships, seems to be clearly relevant to intervention policies designed to prevent sexual harassment in the workplace. If women and men can learn to relate to one another as friends and colleagues, incidences of sexual harassment should decline.

Males and females sometimes differ in the extent to which they reap benefits in cross-sex friendships, as well as differing in the way their cross-sex friendships favorably or unfavorably compare to their same-sex ones. The relatively small body of research comparing cross-sex and same-sex friendships was nicely summarized by Werking when she observed "Friendship researchers have consistently reported that women rate their friendships with men lower than their same-sex friendships on amount of self-affirmation (Furman, 1986), intimacy (Rose, 1985), and closeness (Rubin, 1985); while men consistently rate their friendships with women higher than their same-sex friendships on these same dimensions" (1994, p. 9). Additionally, Aukett and colleagues discovered that males but not females derive greater emotional support from their cross-sex friendships than from their same-sex friendships (Aukett, Ritchie, & Mill, 1988). Buhrke and Fuqua concluded that females gave more support in cross-sex friendships than did males, and males felt closer to cross-sex supporters than the cross-sex supporters felt towards them (1987). Wellman (1992) reported that 73% of men and 82% of women claim to receive emotional support from their female friends—compared to just 27% of the females and 56% of the males who report getting such support from their male friends. Rubin (1985) found that two-thirds of the women identified by men as "close friends" disagree with their categorization of the friendship as close. Hacker (1981) discovered no differences in closeness between male same-sex friendships and cross-sex ones, but women in cross-sex friendships reported less intimacy than the men in those friendships. Bukowski and his colleagues discovered that men rated their cross-sex friends higher than their same-sex ones in enjoyability and goodness (1987). Parker and De Vries' investigation of 95 women and 95 men (average age 21) revealed that "when with women friends, men report greater appreciation, empathic understanding, deepened self-awareness, responsibility and connectedness" (1993, p. 623). The same pattern, however, did not hold true for women who generally reported higher levels of affect and connectedness in their same-sex friendships.

Women do not always receive fewer or lower quality benefits from their cross-sex friendships when compared to their same-sex ones. The women in Rose's study reported receiving more "companionship" from their male than from their female friends (1985). Females in my dissertation reported that their cross-sex friends served purposes and provided rewards that their same-sex friends could not to a greater extent than did males. For example, 13% of the female respondents but none of the male respondents indicated that their cross-sex friends provided an objective viewpoint that their same-sex friends could not provide (also see Rubin, 1985). Additionally, Sias and Cahill (1998) argued that cross-sex friendships in the workplace can potentially strengthen the informal networks of women in an organization, thereby leading to a more equitable distribution of power.

Based on her brief review of studies comparing cross-sex and same-sex friendships, Werking concluded that many researchers employ a "cross-sex friendship deficit model" (1994). In that model, men are seen as contributing significantly less to cross-sex friendships than their female partners, just as they do in the analogous "male deficit model" prevalent in heterosexual relationship research (Wood, 1994). In stark contrast to the cross-sex friendship deficit model, Werking's book on adult cross-sex friendship documents that the benefits of cross-sex friendship are more or less equally distributed among women and men (1997a). Because of Werking's extremely large data base, I tend to agree with her that women and men receive comparable benefits (and costs) in their cross-sex friendships.

In summary, adult cross-sex friends provide each other with a wide array of benefits ranging from simple companionship to not-so-simple sexual satisfaction. Many of those benefits are also present in same-sex friendships, although some, such as insider perspectives and other-sex companionship, are not. Some of the cross-sex advantages may also be available in romantic relationships, but the results of my dissertation suggests that some are not (1988). In order to glean the benefits of adult cross-sex friendships social and structural barriers must first be overcome. Unlike previous life stages, however, new and possibly more formidable barriers present themselves in young and middle adulthood.

Social and Structural Barriers to Cross-Sex Friendships in Adulthood

Despite the fact that cross-sex friendships are fairly common in adulthood (Wright, 1989), there are many social and structural barriers interfering with the initiation and maintenance of those friendships. In this section I examine six of the social barriers and three of the structural ones. As was true in previous stages of the life cycle, the social and structural barriers are related to each other. For example, being married can be both a social barrier to cross-sex friendship (e.g., a jealous spouse), and a structural one because married individuals typically have greater role obligations than single individuals which limit time and opportunity for cross-sex interactions.

Social Barriers.   Recall that social barriers may originate from members of the cross-sex friends' social network or from the cross-sex friends themselves. As such, there are so many barriers to cross-sex friendship that a common question to ask in the popular and scholarly literature has been "can a man and a woman be friends without sexual and romantic longings derailing the relationship?" (e.g., Ambrose, 1989; Cassel, 1989; Fehr, 1996; Margolis, 1988; Pogrebin, 1989; Simon, 1997; Walsh, 1997). Gaines observes that both academicians and lay persons are guilty of giving in to "common wisdom" concerning cross-sex friendships, that is "men and women cannot be friends; either they must become lovers or ultimately must terminate their relationships with each other altogether" (1994, p. 23). There was even a romantic comedy made in the late 1980s, *When Harry Met Sally*, that posed the question of whether women and men could be "just friends." Unfortunately, the movie reinforced the myth that male–female friendships are precursors to romantic relationships, which recent research has shown is often not the case (Afifi & Faulkner, 2000; Messman, Canary, & Hause, 2000). The movie is also an example of the enigma concerning whether mass media shapes societal views (in this case, about cross-sex friendships), reflects those views, or is some combination of the two (see Werking, 1995).

I doubt I will be able to, but before directly examining the social barriers to cross-sex friendships I would like to finally put to rest the question of whether a man and a woman can be friends without sexual and romantic stirrings sabotaging the friendship. The simple answer is that some can, some cannot. Recent research has shown that cross-sex friends can be sexually involved without that involvement damaging the friendship or being accompanied by romantic feelings (Afifi & Faulkner, 2000). My own research indicates that women and men can be platonic friends and experience very little if any sexual or romantic feelings (Monsour, Beard, Harris, & Kurzweil, 1994). Experts have also concluded that many cross-sex friends recognize the sexual feelings and enjoy them without letting them undermine the friendship (Lobel et al., 1994; Rubin, 1985; Sapadin, 1988). Relatedly, studies have shown that former romantic partners and spouses can redefine their relationship as a friendship (Kaplan & Keys, 1997; Masheter, 1997). The probability of romantic partners being friends after their romance has dissolved increases if they were friends before they got romantically involved (Metts, Cupach, & Bejlovec, 1989; Sheehan & Dillman, 1998), or if the man rather than the woman initiated the romantic breakup (Hill, Rubin, Peplau, 1976). On the other hand, I do not dismiss the possibility that sexual undertones, desires, and activity in cross-sex friendships can lead to their demise (Pogrebin, 1989; Sias & Cahill, 1998; Werking, 1997a). Even if the sexual and romantic desires of one or both of the partners do not end the friendship, a minority of cross-sex friends have considerable difficulty contending with underlying sexual and romantic issues (Monsour et al., 1994; 1997).

There are at least six social barriers interfering with the formation and maintenance of adult cross-sex friendships. The first four are the challenges identified by O'Meara in 1989 and were discussed in a preliminary fashion in the previous chapter. The four challenges are presented as social barriers to cross-sex friendships because they result from societal norms and expectations about appropriate male–female relationships and manifest themselves in communication between cross-sex friends and cross-sex friends and members of their social networks. I also direct the reader to an article written by Arnold in which she uses personal narratives to argue that same-sex friendships are plagued by similar types of tensions and challenges (1995). The fifth and most formidable social barrier to cross-sex friendship also doubles as a structural barrier (i.e., marriage or its equivalent). The sixth social barrier are difficulties emanating from the different styles of communication exhibited by women and men (Swain, 1992).

The emotional bond and sexual challenges are related and should be discussed together. The observation that romantic feelings for someone are accompanied by sexual attraction is almost axiomatic. Similarly, although sexual desires do not necessarily invoke romantic feelings (Rawlins, 1982), if those desires are acted on they often do (Werking, 1997a), but sometimes do not (Afifi & Faulkner, 2000). Although the two challenges are closely linked, I examine each one individually.

The emotional bond between a heterosexual woman and man can range from mild feelings of friendship affection to passionate feelings of romantic love (Reeder, 2000). In a landmark article that launched the challenges program of research, Rawlins offered a typology meant to "delineate certain possibilities in the interaction between friendship and romantic love" (p. 1982, p. 344). His category scheme gives an indication of the different types of bonds that might exist between two individuals: friendship, platonic love, friendship love, physical love, and romantic love. O'Meara contended that males and females have been socialized since preadolescence to see each other as potential romantic partners, which in turn increases the likelihood of viewing the emotional bond as one of romantic love (1989).

Studies have revealed that romantic undertones are present in some young adult cross-sex friendships (Monsour et al., 1994), that some individuals find those undercurrents intriguing (Rubin, 1985), and that it is not unusual for a romantic relationship to start out as a cross-sex friendship (Afifi & Faulkner, 2000; Metts et al., 1989). Flirtation behaviors occur in cross-sex friendships and romantic relationships, although they are usually displayed and interpreted differently in the two types of relationships (Egland, Spitzberg, Zormeier, 1996). Scholars have also noted that the possibility of "romantic escalation" in male–female friendships results in the avoidance of discussions about the state of the relationship (Afifi & Burgoon, 1998; Baxter & Wilmot, 1985; Monsour et al., 1994). The emotional bond challenge is probably not much of a challenge for cross-sex friends who are both happily married, or cross-sex friendships in which one or both partners are gay or lesbian. Those individuals would still need to negotiate the level of intimacy in their friendships, but at least those friendships would not be compromised or complicated by strong feelings of romantic interest.

My research indicates that the emotional bond challenge is not a significant barrier to cross-sex friendship formation or maintenance for most adults (Monsour et al., 1994; 1997). Percentages reporting "no emotional bond problem" in our 1994 study ranged from 57% of individuals involved in good cross-sex friendships to 94% of the individuals in casual cross-sex friendships. Overall, 66% of the females and 76% of the males reported no problems of that type. Additionally, participants kept a diary for 3 weeks. On average, respondents reported discussing the emotional bond challenge with their cross-sex friend slightly less than one time over that 3-week period. The general lack of discussion of the feelings cross-sex friends have for each other could mean that the emotional bond challenge was not really a problem at all. However, perhaps the topic was not discussed because the emotional bond issue was a problem. Along those lines, researchers have documented that some individuals in cross-sex friendships actively avoid discussion of relationally oriented topics because those topics are uncomfortable (Afifi & Guerrero, 1998). However, a small number of individuals reported having frequent discussions with their friend about their feelings for each other, with several participants having such discussions 20 or more times, and thinking about it even more frequently (Monsour et al., 1994).

In another study designed to investigate O'Meara's challenges, my colleagues and I (Monsour, Harvey, & Betty, 1997) utilized a variation of Heiderian Balance Theory (Heider, 1958) and Laing's Interpersonal Perception Method (Laing et al., 1966) to investigate the extent to which cross-sex friends agreed on the existence of the challenges. Seventy-three pairs of cross-sex friends completed a survey examining direct perspectives (DPs), metaperspectives (MPs), and meta-metaperspectives (MMPs) on the four challenges (Laing et al., 1966). We asked "To what extent have romantic feelings on the part of yourself or your friend caused problems in the relationship?" Each respondent gave his or her view on this item (the person's DP) as well as how he or she thought the partner would respond to that question (the MP of the primary participant). On a 7-point scale (1 = to no extent, 4 = to a moderate extent, 7 = to a great extent), the average female and male response was 1.6. Equally important, they understood the viewpoint of their partner concerning the emotional bond challenge (i.e., they not only agreed that the romantic "challenge" was not really a problem, but they also realized that they agreed).

On the other hand, some participants disagreed on the problematic nature of the emotional bond challenge and did not realize that they disagreed. For about 10% of the cross-sex friendship dyads the difference between male and female responses to the romantic feeling item was 3 or greater on the 7-point scale. In half of those friendships the male perceived a greater problem than the female (e.g., a female friend responded with a "2" whereas her male friend responded with a "5"). In the other half the female perceived a greater problem than the male. In friendships in which significant disagreement or misunderstanding occurred, women and men were equally likely to disagree with, and/or misunderstand, the perspective of their partner concerning the problematic nature of the emotional bond challenge.

The sexual challenge means that cross-sex friends must confront sexual tensions, feelings, and desires that exist in the relationship. In my 1994 study (Monsour et al., 1994), the vast majority of participants did not perceive sexual issues as a problem in their cross-sex friendships. However, 20% of the 52 males and 10% of the 86 females indicated that sexual tension in their friendship did present a problem. In my 1997 study (Monsour et al., 1997), participants were asked "To what extent has the sexual dimension of your friendship caused problems in your relationship?". Although the large majority did not perceive the sexual challenge as problematic, seven of the 73 cross-sex friendships (10%) displayed differences in male–female responses to that item of four or greater on a 7-point scale (1 = to no extent, 4 = to a moderate extent, 7 = to a great extent). Females identified the sexual dimension as a significant problem in three of the seven cases, whereas their male partners did not. The reverse pattern was discovered in the other three friendships.

Although not framed as a "challenge," a number of researchers over the last few years have investigated various aspects of the sexual component of young adult cross-sex friendships. Scholars have examined the impact of sexual activity on cross-sex friendships (Afifi & Faulkner, 2000); the role of sexual attraction in cross-sex friendships (Kaplan & Keys, 1997; Reeder, 2000); how former spouses and romantic partners might redefine their relationship as platonic (Masheter, 1997; Schneider & Kenny, 2000); motives for keeping a cross-sex friendship platonic (Messman et al., 2000), and flirting behavior in cross-sex friendships (Egland et al., 1996). Messman and her colleagues concluded that a primary motive many cross-sex friends have for keeping the relationship platonic is to safeguard its integrity and to keep it from disintegrating (Messman et al., 2000). Their conclusion indicates that some cross-sex friends do view the sexual challenge as potentially threatening to the status of their friendship, although some cross-sex friends view the sexual component as an advantage rather than a challenge (Afifi & Faulkner, 2000). These two apparently contradictory studies (i.e., Afifi & Faulkner, 2000 and Messman et al., 2000) are easy to reconcile. As noted by a number of scholars (e.g., Rawlins, 1994; Schneider & Kenny, 2000), not all cross-sex friendships are the same. In some cross-sex friendships sexual issues are problematic, in others they are not. Duck and VanderVoort (2001) offered an interesting analysis of how sexual activity in a cross-sex friendship can render that friendship "inappropriate" in the eyes of those who become aware of that activity. They concluded that although cross-sex friendship as a type of relationship may be considered "appropriate," if certain behaviors (e.g., sexual intercourse) occur in a friendship those behaviors might render that relationship an "inappropriate relationship of its type."

Depending on the specific friendship, sexual tension may be felt by one or both partners, it could be intense or mild, pleasant or unpleasant, acted on or ignored (Afifi & Faulkner, 2000; Messman et al., 2000; Sapadin, 1988; Werking, 1997a). For example, in Sapadin's study of workplace cross-sex friendships, 75% of the men and 82% of the women reported that 'Having a sexual relationship complicates a friendship in a way I dislike.' Sexual tension is often not openly discussed in cross-sex friendships (Afifi & Guerrero, 1998; Afifi & Burgoon, 1998; Monsour et al., 1994; Swain, 1992). In the Afifi and Guerrero study, 177 undergraduates completed a survey on topics they avoided with their female and male best friends. Individuals avoid discussing dating and sexual experiences more with cross-sex than same-sex friends even when those experiences involve parties other than the friend (see also Monsour et al., 1994). Felmlee (1999) contended there are norms about appropriate ways to display affection in cross-sex friendships that specifically address the sexual challenge. Along similar lines, Egland and her associates found evidence suggesting that college students apply different interactional rules when flirting with cross-sex friends as compared to romantic partners (Egland et al.,1996).

An excellent study by Guerrero (1997) suggested that the emotional bond and sexual challenges might be linked to impression management concerns within cross-sex friendships. In a observational, videotaped study of nonverbal involvement in cross-sex friendships, same-sex friendships, and romantic relationships, Guerrero (1997) discovered that "Anxious or shy individuals tended to exhibit nonfluency and tension when interacting with opposite-sex friends" (p.49). Guerrero concluded that the relatively elevated level of tension and nonfluency might be due to the ambiguity inherent in male-female friendships (Afifi & Burgoon, 1998; O'Meara, 1989). Interestingly, individuals in the cross-sex friendships seemed to be particularly focused on impression management as indicated by attempts to appear fluent and composed.

Despite my contention that the emotional bond and sexual challenges typically are not problematic (Monsour, 1997; Monsour et al., 1997; Monsour et al., 1994), I agree with Werking that when they are they can end the friendship because of the stress they put on the relationship. According to Werking's interview data on the dissolution of cross-sex friendships (1997a) when those two challenges do exist to a significant degree they can effectively cause the termination of the relationship (also see Sias & Cahill, 1998).

The third challenge faced by adult cross-sex friends is the power or equality challenge. Equality is a central element of friendship (Fehr, 1996; Rawlins, 1992) and is commonly associated with the concept of power (O'Meara, 1989). O'Meara argued that because men generally have more power in relationships than do women (also see Kuypers, 1999), the issue of friendship equality is potentially quite troublesome for cross-sex friends trying to maintain equality within a cultural context of gender inequality. Pogrebin similarly claimed that true friendships between men and women are near impossible to form because of the power inequity that is intrinsically part of male–female relationships (1989). Wood contended that the differences between men and women often reflect asymmetries in their social power (Wood & Dindia, 1998). Purported power differences in cross-sex relationships have also been linked to language and communication style differences between women and men (Tannen, 1994). Maltz and Borker (1982) argued that those differences can be traced back to early and middle childhood when boys and girls spent much of their time in gender-segregated groups (also see Leaper, 1994a and chaps. 2 and 3 in this volume).

On the other hand, Roberts' paradigm case formulation of cross-sex friendships suggest that equality does exist in the friendships between men and women. She characterizes cross-sex friendships as having "symmetrical eligibilities," meaning "Within the limits of their friendship, men and women have the same eligibilities to participate in social practices, and the same behavior is regarded as appropriate for both the man and the woman" (1982, p. 67). Robert's paradigm case formulation of cross-sex friendships represents an excellent point of departure for scholars interested in pursuing the position that females and males have relatively equal power bases in their friendships. Unfortunately, very little has been done with her theoretical framework.

The analysis of solidarity and hierarchy in cross-sex friendships offered by McWilliams and Howard provides an interesting theoretical perspective on power and equality in cross-sex friendships (1993). They maintain that solidarity and hierarchy are central dimensions of all relationships representing components of the closeness or distance between people. Relationships are hierarchically distinguished from each other on the basis of the extent to which one person has authority over another and the degree in which participating members have equal or unequal amounts of resources, influence, and prestige. Those relationships fall on a continuum of hierarchical differentiation with, for example, friendships between an employer and an employee at one end, and more egalitarian relationships like same-sex friendships between people of similar age and social positions at the other end. On the dimension of solidarity, relationships fall somewhere on a continuum from high solidarity (e.g., family, good friendships, some long-term work relationships) to low solidarity (e.g., acquaintances, short-term work relationships). They offer as an example the case of "giving advice." A man can get advice from his female friends and not suffer from a decline in relative status because that advice is likely to be interpreted, in gender stereotypic terms, as promoting solidarity, not hierarchy. However, when a woman gets advice from her male friend, that advice would be interpreted as promoting hierarchy because of the gender stereotype of men being more instrumental and status asserting than women (Wood & Dindia, 1998). To my knowledge, Mc Williams and Howard's solidarity/hierarchy framework has not specifically been applied to cross-sex friendships.

Empirical support for the power/equality challenge is not particularly strong but certainly worthy of inspection. Although not specifically focusing on friendships between women and men, Mulac, Bradac, and Gibbons (2001) contended that cultural differences in language use between women and may be linked to power differences in their relationships (also see Henley & Kramarae, 1991). They found fairly convincing evidence that young adult males have a more direct, succinct, and instrumental communication style than young adult females whose communication style is more indirect, elaborate, and emotional. But is one communication style more powerful than one other? In answering that question Mulac and his associates concluded that women and men both exercise power in their relationships through the use of language and that "it is not the case that the male style can be categorized as powerful and the female style as powerless. Things are less tidy than this" (p. 146).

Recall from previous chapters that in early and middle childhood girls when compared to boys are already beginning to suffer from a sense of powerlessness (Maccoby & Jacklin, 1987; Sims et al., 1998). Leaper (1998) audiotaped four different 5-minute conversations of adult female friendship dyads, male friendship dyads, and cross-sex friendship dyads. He discovered evidence documenting that in some cross-sex friendships males try to get the upper hand in decision making. Decision making is often viewed as a manifestation of power (Monsour, 1988). Leaper also found that male cross-sex friends were more likely than their female cross-sex friend counterparts to give negative responses to the suggestions of their friends (1998). In my own research (Monsour et al., 1997), the equality challenge was operationalized by asking respondents "To what extent has the question of who has more power and control in your friendship caused problems in your relationship?" In general, neither females or males considered the equality challenge as a problem in their cross-sex friendships. However, there were 11 friendships (about 15%) where the difference between male and female responses was 3 or greater. Women in those 11 friendships perceived a substantial problem in the area of power and control, whereas their male partners did not. *Standpoint theory* offers one explanation of the difference between men and women in their perception of the equality challenge in cross-sex friendship. According to a prominent standpoint theorist, in societies stratified by such things as race and gender, "the activities of those at the top both organize and set limits on what persons who perform such activities can understand about themselves and the world around them" (Harding, 1996, p. 240). Presumably, white males are at the top and therefore have an impoverished view of themselves, the world around them, and their cross-sex friendships. The activities of those men in their cross-sex friendships, such as performing what might be perceived as power moves, limits their ability to see things from the standpoint of their cross-sex friends.

Fehr (1996) suggested that one behavioral indication of the lack of equality are occasions when women conform to the interaction styles of male partners more than male partners conform to the styles of women (Bendtschneider & Duck, 1993; Gaines, 1994). But on the other hand, because men are sometimes more intimate with their female friends than with their male friends (Monsour, 1988), then perhaps men conform to the interaction styles of women as much as women conform to their styles (Fehr, 1996). Along similar lines in his empirical investigation of 62 cross-sex dyads, Gaines (1994) discovered that cross-sex friends are particularly likely to reciprocate disrespectful behavior and speculated that the reciprocity of disrespect might be part of the larger power struggle between men and women (O'Meara, 1989). However, showing disrespect was more the exception than the rule in cross-sex friendships. Those friendships were more typically characterized by showing both affection and respect. In their study of gossip in cross-sex and same-sex friendships, Leaper and Holliday found that men in cross-sex friendships were not more likely than women to make discouraging responses following gossip from their partner. They interpreted this finding as suggesting that males do not try to exert power and control in conversations any more than do their female counterparts (1995).

The equality challenge may be more pronounced in the workplace than other contexts because men are often older, more educated, and have a higher organizational ranking than females (Booth & Hess, 1974; O'Meara, 1994; Swain, 1992). The power differences between women and men in the workplace can also set up conditions for sexual harassment (Lobel et al., 1994; O'Meara, 1994). O'Meara observed that concerns over accusations of sexual harassment might discourage some "well-intentioned" men and women from initiating friendship contact (1994). Sandroff contended that as sex segregation in the workplace decreases, the potential for sexual harassment increases (1992). Along those lines, when asked what they disliked most about their cross-sex friendships, 9% of the women in Sapadin's workplace investigation but none of the men listed 'patronizing/sexist' attitudes and behaviors (1988). Situations in which women have more formal, organizational power than their male co-workers are also potentially fraught with power and sexual harassment issues (Roberts, 2000) that could interfere with cross-sex friendship formation.

Fehr concluded after her brief review of the equality issue in cross-sex friendships that the question of whether there is equality of inequality in cross-sex friendships largely remains unanswered (1996). Although her assessment was made 5 years ago, very little has been published since then exploring the equality challenge in cross-sex friendships (but see Monsour et al., 1997). In a recent book by Kuypers, *Men and Power,* contributors confirm the assumption that in American society men have more power than women, but that power comes at a price (1999). Whether part of that price is avoidance of cross-sex friendships by women is a question still open to empirical investigation.

The fourth social barrier to cross-sex friendship is the audience challenge faced by men and women in those relationships. Before O'Meara formalized the challenges facing cross-sex friendships (1989), Rawlins (1982) described the audience challenge as a continual one that is strategically met in different ways by trying to balance the public and private nature of the friendship. The first three challenges are concerned with the private and dyadic negotiation of the definition of the relationship, whereas the audience challenge is more public in nature. Public visibility of cross-sex friendships makes them vulnerable to relational misinterpretations. Reminiscent of what happens to children in middle school and high school, adults must carefully package the way their cross-sex friendships appear to outside audiences. The audiences with the highest level of relevance in adulthood are spouses, serious dating partners, and work associates. For individuals in the latter part of middle adulthood (early to late 50s) relevant audiences could also include their own children.

The audience challenge can present a clear social barrier to the initiation and maintenance of cross-sex friendships as others attempt to influence and control those friendships (Allan, 1989). Devine and Markiewicz contended that when a woman and a man in the workplace become close friends they are often assumed to be lovers by suspicious audiences (1990). Swain speculated that cross-sex friendships may also be threatening to some same-sex friends because cross-sex friendships offer something that same-sex relationships cannot, that is, other-sex companionship that is so highly valued in our society (1992). Jealousy over a cross-sex friend can be a source of serious conflict in marital and dating relationships (Allan, 1989; Cupach & Metts, 1991; Fehr, 1996; Lampe, 1985; Werking, 1997a). Because cross-sex friendships can threaten the status of an existing romantic relationship, some individuals are willing to abandon the friendship in order to eliminate the threat (Brenton, 1966; Swain, 1992), or the friendship might lead to the dissolution of the romantic relationship (Werking, 1997a). Werking is careful to point out that jealousy and possessiveness are not universal reactions of individuals to their romantic partners' cross-sex friends (1997a). Some individuals just accept that their romantic partner has friends of the other sex. On the other hand, she also notes that jealousy sometimes is a problem because of the physical attractiveness of the partner's cross-sex friend or because the audience member believes that serious dating partners should also be best friends so cross-sex friendships are unnecessary.

The fifth social barrier to adult cross-sex friendships is actually a special case of the audience challenge (i.e., marriage or its equivalent). Because of the tremendous time and role commitments involved, marriage affects a person's entire friendship network (Carbery & Buhrmester, 1998; Larson & Bradley, 1988; Milardo, Johnson, & Huston, 1983; Rawlins, 1992; Werking, 1997a). The impact of marriage on friendship becomes especially noticeable if the couple has children (Carbery & Buhrmester, 1998; Rawlins, 1992). Marriage has a more pronounced effect on cross-sex friendships than same-sex ones because of the taboo discouraging the initiation of cross-sex friendships by married individuals (Allan, 1989; Rubin, 1985; Werking, 1997a). Conventional wisdom and empirical evidence indicates that marriage represents a social and structural impediment to cross-sex friendship formation and maintenance (Bell, 1981; Block, 1980; Booth & Hess, 1974; Lampe, 1985; Bruess & Pearson, 1997; Monsour, 1988; Rose, 1985; Werking, 1997a). Some married men and women believe it is inappropriate to have close cross-sex friendships once they get married (Reid & Fine, 1992; Werking, 1997a). That sentiment is clearly exemplified in the following observation made by one of Rubin's male interviewees: "Friends with women? You've got to be kidding. It's nothing but trouble for anybody that cares about his marriage" (1985, p. 156). Research on communication rituals in friendships and marriage indicated that ritualizing behaviors such as "social/fellowship rituals" and "getting together" rituals were significantly less common among cross-sex friends when compared to same sex friends and married partners (Bruess & Pearson, 1997). Bruess and Pearson suggest that intimate rituals are less likely in cross-sex friendships because such rituals might be seen as a threat to the marriage.

Although married individuals do have cross-sex friends, those friendships often occur within the safe confines of marriage or work and usually involve mostly superficial interactions between the cross-sex friends (Allan, 1989; Bell, 1981; Booth & Hess, 1974; Lobel et al., 1994; Rawlins, 1982). As Fehr notes (1996, p. 149) "If a married person does have other-sex friends, certain "precautions" may be taken such as socializing in the presence of a spouse ... or limiting cross-sex friends to those met through one's spouse ...." Conversely, some cross-sex friendships of married individuals are quite close and do not pose a threat to the marriage (Werking, 1997a). None of the 14 married women interviewed by Werking who had cross-sex friends indicated that their husbands had problems with them having those friends. Instead, their husbands and cross-sex friends typically became friends. Nevertheless, women also reported that they carefully monitored what they did with their cross-sex friend so that the friendship would not be misinterpreted by their husband.

With the exception of Werking's 1997 book, there was very little empirical investigation during the 1990's of the impact that marriage has on cross-sex friendship initiation and maintenance. Recent studies comparing the cross-sex friendship patterns of large numbers of married to single individuals do not exist. My contention is that *initiation* of a cross-sex friendship by a married individual is quite different and more difficult than *maintenance* of one established prior to marriage. Although there is no direct research investigating those differences, there is data suggesting that cross-sex friendships are not a problem in a marriage if those friendships predate the marriage (Werking, 1997a). It also seems reasonable to speculate that casual cross-sex friendships among married individuals might be preferred over close cross-sex friendships because they would be less time consuming and less threatening to one's spouse.

Two somewhat dated studies in which cross-sex friendships and marriage were examined are those separately conducted by Rose and Rubin in 1985. Rose discovered that one-third of the married men and one-half of the married women in her study did not have a close cross-sex friend (1985), whereas over 70% of the single female undergraduates and all of the single male undergraduates reported having at least one cross-sex friend. In Rubin's interviews with 300 individuals from various socioeconomic and educational backgrounds she discovered that only 16% of the married women and 22% of the married men had cross-sex friendships (1985). Most of cross-sex friendships occurred between the college educated middle class. Part of the reason for the difference between numbers of cross-sex friends that professionals have as compared to members of the working class, at least according to Rubin's 1985 data, is that college educated individuals tended to marry late and therefore usually had cross-sex friendships at the time they got married. Members of the working class, on the other hand, tended to marry soon after high school and have not had the chance to cultivate many cross-sex friendships before they get married.

In summary, despite some excellent work by Werking (1997a), Bruess and Pearson (1997), and some older research by Rubin (1985), Rose (1985) and Booth and Hess (1974), cross-sex friendship scholars still know relatively little about the ways in which marriage impacts cross-sex friendships, and vice versa. More indepth qualitative interviewing of the type conducted by Werking(1997a) needs to be initiated with larger samples. Werking's study involved only 19 married individuals, 14 of whom were women involved with their cross-sex friend before they got married. Although the dynamics of cross-sex friendships in which the friendships predate the marriage are certainly important to understand, equally important are the strategies used by individuals to form new cross-sex friendships after marriage. I agree with Werking's conclusion that "For the most part, the positive influences of engaging in a close cross-sex friendship while married have been overlooked" (p. 145).

Recall from previous chapters that social barriers to cross-sex friendship include communication-based barriers that originate in the friendship. Maltz and Borker (1982) were among the first to articulate the position that girls and boys in early and middle childhood form separate gender-based cultures that lead to differences in the way each group views the world and communicates in it. The differences established in childhood and adolescence continue into adulthood and contribute to cross-sex communication breakdowns (Maltz & Borker, 1982; Maccoby, 1994). Swain argued that cross-sex friendships are more difficult to establish than same-sex ones because men and women have been socialized to interact in friendships differently (e.g., men focus more on shared activities and less on emotional expressiveness than do women; 1992). Based on in depth, qualitative interviews with 15 college-aged men and 6 women, Swain concluded that communication in cross-sex friendship can be difficult because young men and women have limited contact with members of the other sex during childhood adolescence, and therefore communication does not come as naturally as it does with same-sex friends. As a general pattern in his small sample, men and women said it was easier disclosing problems to their same-sex friends.

There are a number of individual personality variables that can make an individual less (or more) inclined to form cross-sex friendships. When an aspect of an individual's personality interferes with successful initiation or maintenance of a cross-sex friendship, that variable can be conceptualized as a social barrier to cross-sex friendship. One such personality variable is "social anxiety." Snell (1989) contended that women and men who are socially anxious are particularly prone to anxiety when around members of the other sex and when disclosing sex-role discrepant information (also see Guerrero, 1997). Therefore, he argued, socially anxious individuals make a concerted effort to present themselves to members of the other sex in a way that conforms to traditional gender-role expectations. He had 215 undergraduates (62 males and 153 females) complete a social anxiety scale and a masculine/feminine self-disclosure scale. Individuals who scored high on the social anxiety scale were less willing to discuss gender-role inconsistent information with cross-sex friends than were individuals who scored low on the social anxiety scale. Insightfully, Snell noted that socially anxious men and women may be "inadvertently perpetuating conventional gender-role values, values that can eventually limit their own well-being as well as others' freedom to act, think, and feel in self-fulfilling ways" (p. 123).

Another personality variable that influences communication and subsequently impacts adult cross-sex friendships is one's sex-role orientation (Monsour, 1988). Sex-role orientation is determined by the extent to which a person exhibits traditional masculine and feminine personality traits. According to Bem's original conceptualization (1974), individuals can be feminine, masculine, undifferentiated, or androgynous. Most relevant to our immediate concerns are androgynous individuals who display both male and female personality traits depending on the situation. In my dissertation (Monsour, 1988) I hypothesized that androgynous individuals would have more cross-sex friendships than their more traditional masculine and feminine counterparts because they had many of the same personality traits as members of the other sex which would lead to more effective communication. Androgynous males but not females had significantly more cross-sex friends than any other group ($X = 11$, compared to 6 and 7 for masculine and feminine males, and 4 to 6 for females in the categories of masculine, feminine, and androgynous). The upshot of this argument is that traditional males (i.e., men who score high on masculine personality traits), and traditional females (i.e., females who score high on feminine personality traits), might be at a communicative disadvantage when it comes to initiating cross-sex friendships because they lack a range of interpersonal competencies. Another possibility is that traditional females and males may be more inclined than androgynous males to see members of the other sex as dating partners and less inclined to see them as friends (also see Wright & Scanlon, 1991).

In summary of the section thus far, there are six social barriers that interfere with successful formation and maintenance of cross-sex friendships. Four of the barriers are the challenges to cross-sex friendships identified by O'Meara in his landmark 1989 article. Those four challenges—the emotional bond challenge, the sexual challenge, the audience challenge, and the equality challenge—are linked to the remaining two social barriers (i.e., marriage and communication based difficulties that are often linked to personality variables). All six of those social barriers are connected to the structural barriers discussed in the next section.

Structural Barriers.   In what has turned out to be a foreshadowing of one of the major themes of this book, O'Meara emphasized the importance of devoting more attention to the broader structural context in which cross-sex friendships take place (1994). When the structural context is taken into consideration a fifth "challenge" to cross-sex formation is apparent (i.e., the "opportunity challenge"). As described by O'Meara, the opportunity challenge refers to the general lack of structural opportunities for men and women to form cross-sex friendships. O'Meara believes that "opportunity structures" which can facilitate cross-sex friendship have four features: proximity, equality, a supportive normative structure, and a structure that provides time for interacting. As I review the structural barriers to cross-sex friendship I relate those barriers to O'Meara's opportunity structures.

There are three primary structural impediments to cross-sex friendship formation during adulthood: occupational sex segregation, marriage, and not attending college. According to Reskin (1993), the term *sex segregation* was coined and "placed into the sociological lexicon" in 1968 to refer to women and men's concentration into different occupations. The higher the level of sex segregation at work, the less likely it is for cross-sex friendships to form because males and females are not in the same proximity (O'Meara, 1994). Occupational sex segregation is still prevalent (Okamoto & England, 1999). Many men and women work in organizations or businesses comprised primarily of members of their own sex. Census data gathered in 1993 indicated that, on average, men worked in occupations that were 73% male and women worked in occupations that were 65% female (Okamoto & England, 1999). But the reverse of these statistics suggest structural possibilities for cross-sex friendships. For example, in occupations that are 73% male, the 27% who are female might have ample opportunity to form cross-sex friendships (demonstrating O'Meara's proximity opportunity structural feature, 1994), as long as status differences are not too

great between the males and females (demonstrating O'Meara's equality opportunity structural feature, 1994).

There have been very few studies specifically designed to investigate the impact of occupational sex segregation on cross-sex friendships (but see Booth &
Hess, 1974), although some have indirectly addressed the issue (e.g., Lobel et
al., 1994 Sapadin, 1988; Winstead et al., 1995). Most work in the area of
male–female organizational friendships have involved theoretical speculations
about those relationships (e.g., Fine, 1986; O'Meara, 1994; Safilios-Rothschild,
1981). For example, Fine contended that the workplace is a especially fertile
area for cross-sex friendships to develop because of the forced proximity of
workers (1986). Forced proximity can also lead to problems because sexual attraction between coworkers is inevitable (Eyler & Baridon, 1992). However, because organizational romances are generally frowned on (Collins, 1983; Lobel
et al., 1994), there is incentive for women and men to confine their social relationships to the friendship arena. As Fine (1986) so colorfully put it, "If the
company is a family, an organizational romance is incest" (p. 197).

Although the workplace is a potentially rich structural environment for the
cultivation of cross-sex friendships, it often does not meet the optimum criteria
for cross-sex friendship formation outlined by O'Meara (1994). For example,
occupational sex segregation (what O'Meara referred to as a macro-level trend)
impacts microlevel opportunities for cross-sex interaction. Without proximity,
it is unlikely that any kind of workplace friendship, cross-sex or otherwise, can
be formed (Sias & Cahill, 1998). And although occupational sex segregation
has decreased in the last 20 years (Jacobsen, 1994; T. Wells, 1999), the pace has
been "glacial" (Jacobs, 1989).

O'Meara noted that even if occupational sex segregation began to reverse itself faster than it currently is, there still would not be any guarantee that other
conditions necessary for cross-sex friendship formation would be met. For instance, because equality is a key ingredient of friendship (Blieszner & Adams,
1992; O'Meara, 1989), cross-sex friendships may be difficult to form in workplace environments in which either women or men have higher status. Men
typically have more status and power in organizations than do women
(O'Meara, 1994), but that appears to be changing. Eyler and Baridon observe
that it is becoming more common to see men and women working together,
side-by-side, as equals and professional peers in many organizations (1992; also
see Lobel et al., 1994). Relatedly, from a developmental perspective research by
Coats and Overman documented that women with boy playmates as a child
were more likely than women without such playmates to be in professions traditionally reserved for men (1992). A recent issue of *Scientific American* noted
that more women than men are now getting college degrees, which has led to
increasing numbers of females working in managerial positions (Doyle, 1999.)
Women held 46% of executive, administrative, and managerial positions in
1998, up from 34% in 1983 (Business Week, 1999).

Along with the proximity and equality criteria for cross-sex friendship formation, women and men in the workplace must also be operating within a set of organizational norms that allow cross-sex friendships to form (O'Meara, 1994). Several workplace friendship scholars have observed, however, that close friendships between men and women in the workplace are often viewed as either romantic relationships or precursors to romantic relationships (Devine & Markiewicz, 1990; Eyler & Baridon, 1992; Fine, 1986). Because organizational romances are usually viewed with unease (Lobel et al., 1994), there may be implicit norms discouraging cross-sex friendships that might change into romantic relationships.

The second major structural barrier to cross-sex friendship is marriage (Booth & Hess, 1974; Wright, 1989). Because about 95% of Americans marry at some time in their life (Seccombe & Ishii-Kuntz, 1994), marriage as a potential social and structural impediment to cross-sex friendship is highly salient. I was unable to find recent and specific information on the structural ramifications of marriage on cross-sex friendship formation. A few studies reviewed earlier document that married individuals have fewer cross-sex friendships than single individuals (Rose, 1985; Rubin, 1985). Wright expressed agreement when he stated "Marriage in and of itself seems to have the effect of reducing the number of cross-gender friends of both women and men" (1989, p. 210). Marriage curtails opportunities for cross-sex friendship formation because spouses spend most of their free time together rather than separately in social situations that might lead to cross-sex friendship formation. Additionally, once an individual gets married he or she generally becomes less dependent on friends for meeting social needs and becomes more dependent on the spouse (Carbery & Buhrmester, 1998). Marriage also might "raise the bar" for cross-sex relationships with other partners (Duck, personal communication, October, 2000); because individuals in satisfying marriages might develop higher expectations for cross-sex friendships.

I would remiss in my responsibilities if I failed to mention how marriage also presents structural opportunities for the formation and maintenance of cross-sex friendships. Married couples tend to form relationships with other married couples, resulting in what have been called "couple friendships"(Babchuk, 1965; Bendtschneider, 1994; Bendtschneider & Duck, 1993). Although the conversations that occur in couple friendships are usually less intimate that those that occur in individual ones, those friendships can be very satisfying (Bendtschneider, 1994). Couple friendships set up obvious possibilities for cross-sex friendship initiation and long-term maintenance. Next-door neighbors, for example, could establish couple friendships that last for decades (see for example, Babchuk & Anderson, 1989 and O'Connor,1993 in the next chapter on cross-sex friendships in old age).

The last structural impediment to cross-sex friendship formation in adulthood is mostly conjecture on my part, but a conjecture I believe is reasonable, somewhat documented, and worthy of further empirical investigation. Researchers have established, albeit indirectly, that young adults have more cross-sex friendships than do individuals in any other stage of life, with the possible exception of adolescence. Depending on what studies are examined, anywhere from 30% to 90% of young adults have at least one cross-sex friend (Monsour, 1997, 1998; Wright, 1989). There are a number of reasons why young adults *appear to have* more cross-sex friendships than most other individuals. I emphasize *appear to have* because the vast majority of studies of adult cross-sex friendships have focused on college students. College provides a wonderfully rich opportunity for initiation and maintenance of cross-sex friendships. All of the opportunity structures identified by O'Meara (1994) as necessary for workplace cross-sex friendships are present on college campuses: proximity, equality, a supportive normative structure, and a structure that provides time for interacting.

Therefore, when compared to young adults who go to college, individuals who do not attend college are at a structural disadvantage for the formation of cross-sex friendships (Rubin, 1985). The large number of individuals who never attend college or attend for only a short time have been disregarded by researchers who, I presume for the sake of convenience, have focused their research energies on more accessible college samples (I include myself in that critical generalization; see Rubin, 1985 and Sapadin, 1988, for exceptions). College affords significant structural opportunities for the formation of cross-sex friendships, especially colleges that offer housing on campus. Although 65% of the students who graduated from high school in 1998 attended college that same fall (Black Issues in Higher Education, July, 1999), it is not unusual for roughly one third of college freshman to not return to college the following year (Cravatta, 1997). On a related matter, because many young adults do not attend college, generalizing findings from college samples to the rest of the adult population should be done with caution (Gaines, 1994).

Cross-Sex Friendships Affect and are Affected by an Individual's Ongoing Social Construction of Self in Adulthood

Despite the fact that cross-sex friendships in adulthood have received more research attention than cross-sex friendships in other stages of the life cycle, the impact of those friendships on self-concepts has not been directly investigated. Also absent from the literature is a consideration of how a person's self-view in adulthood influences cross-sex friendship initiation and maintenance. In this section I resume my presentation begun in earlier chapters of a number of ideas concerning the cognitive and communicative connections between cross-sex friendships and views of self. My elaboration includes an application of some of the interpersonal self theories, an incorporation of two additional models (i.e.,

Aron & Aron, 1997 and Wright, 1984), and a brief examination of homosexuality and its relationship to cross-sex friendships and self-concepts.

In theory at least, by the time an individual enters young adulthood (age 18) his or her self, gender, and cross-sex/same-sex friendship schemas have already begun to intermingle and influence each other. That process begins regardless of the level of experience the person has had with cross-sex friendships. Additionally, interpersonal communications have a significant impact on self-schemas (Coover & Murphy, 2000), but those communications change and affect self-schemas differently as individuals go through the stages of life (Nussbaum & Baringer, 2000). Variations in self-concepts are related to a wide array of factors. Some of those factors reflect normal changes that accompany the gradual transition from young adulthood to middle adulthood (e.g., menopause for women and a general decline in physical abilities for both men and women). Some factors have nothing to do with the physical effects of aging and yet still impact self-concepts. A person might get married (or divorced), have children (or decide not to have them), reveal an alternative sexual identity (or make a decision not to), change careers, or move away from friends and family. All of those factors, and a host of other contextual ones (Adams & Allan, 1989), influence self-concepts and cross-sex friendships, which themselves influence each other. Of primary interest in this chapter is how cross-sex friendship and self-schemas influence each other and are both influenced by life-changing events in adulthood.

An obvious way in which cross-sex friendship schemas and self schemas impact each other is through the unique and generic benefits supplied by those relationships. For example, when an individual receives affirmation from a cross-sex friend as an attractive member of the other sex (Afifi & Faulkner, 2000; Monsour, 1988) that affirmation would be incorporated into the friend's self-concept (Rubin, 1985). Reciprocally, feeling good about one's attractiveness to members of the other sex might encourage a man or a woman to initiate communication in the pursuit of more cross-sex friendships. Recall that one of the manifestations of social support is affirming each other's sense of identity (Crohan & Antonucci, 1989). Cross-sex friends make each other feel good about who they are by validating each other's view of self and through acceptance of each other (Werking, 1997a).

Relatedly, insider perspectives supplied by cross-sex friends are relevant to the cognitive connections between self-schemas, cross-sex friendship schemas, and even gender schemas. Having insider information on how members of the other sex think, feel, and behave should make a person more confident in his or her interactions with members of the other sex (which would be part of the person' self schema), and more knowledgeable about members of the other sex (which would be a part of the person's gender scheme). This increased confidence could lead to initiation of cross-sex interaction and subsequent friendships, work relationships, or even romances. Recall from previous chapters that experts studying each stage of life have argued that effective cross-sex interaction in one type of relationship will lead to effective cross-sex interaction in other types (e.g., Connolly et al., 1999 for adolescence; Leaper, 1994b, for middle childhood; Gottman, 1986 for early childhood).

There are other ways in which cross-sex friendships and self-concepts are reciprocally related. Young adults in close cross-sex friendships have similar views of their relationship (Monsour et al., 1993). Similarity of relational schemas between two friends, as long as they recognize that similarity, is pivotal in the construction of a mutually understood and shared relational reality (Duck, 1994; Monsour, 1994). Part of that shared relational reality involves mutual affirmation of one another's identity (Wright, 1984). Social constructionism (Berger & Luckman, 1966; Gergen, 1991) and symbolic interactionism (Cooley, 1902; Mead, 1934) both stress the importance of interpersonal communication and socially constructed relational realities. Borrowing a basic tenet of postmodernism that reality is a social construction (Yerby, 1995), one can argue that relational realities are constructed by both partners who attempt to create a shared view of their joint experience and a shared view of one another (Duck, 1994; Monsour, 1994, Monsour et al., 1993; Wood, 1995). From a social constructionist perspective, reality within a relationship is intersubjectively created through interpersonal communication. Although theorists such as Gergen and Mead did not apply their perspectives to cross-sex friendships, that application is easily accomplished in the next few paragraphs through employment of concepts such as transactive memory, semantic elaboration, and interactive cuing.

Transactive memory (Wegner, Giuliano, & Hertel, 1985) is instrumental in the formation of similar relational schemas between friends and the construction of a joint relational reality (Monsour, 1994). It involves a variety of processes that allow information entering a relationship to be organized within that relationship and to be subsequently utilized by one or both relational partners (Wegner et al., 1985). Transactive memory entails the individual and joint knowledge structures that partners have concerning their relationship and "can be said to reside in the memories of both individuals—when they are considered as a combined system" (Wegner et al., 1985, p. 257). Communication between cross-sex friends is an essential element of transactive memory. For example, cross-sex friends reminiscing about some past event in their relationship might each remember different parts of that event. Through interactive cuing (Wegner et al., 1985), their individual memories serve as cues to stimulate more remembrances from each other concerning the event. They are able to reconstruct a joint perception of the event. For instance, positive displays by one or both partners of emotional support could become part of transactive memory and the cross-sex friendship schema for each individual. Both partners would share a version of dyadic reality in which each member of the friendship is a contributing, worthwhile, and admirable individual—all of which becomes part of their individual self-schemas.

A related cognitive process, semantic elaboration (Anderson & Reder, 1979), occurs when inferences are drawn about incoming information by relating that information to knowledge already stored. As noted by Duck (1994), when a similarity is communicated to a relational partner that partner might elaborate on the information by extending to other types of similarity, or to other layers of psychological organization (also see Monsour, 1994). Transactive memory is activated when friends talk about the meaning and importance of the noted similarity. For example, a person might say to a cross-sex friend who expressed anger about how others assume their relationship is romantic "I also get mad when people assume we are lovers rather than friends." The cross-sex friends would talk about the fact that they both noticed that others assume they are lovers and what that misinterpretation of their relationship means. As a product of talking about the noted similarity, partners encode the discussed commonality into their relational schemas in similar fashions—they interactively experience it in parallel form (Duck, 1994). The parallel encoding facilitates understanding of the way the partner thinks; and understanding the thought processes of a partner is an important part of connecting with that person (Kelly, 1969).

Self-disclosures that occur in cross-sex friendships are another way of having parts of one's self confirmed and validated by another (Reis & Shaver, 1988). Self-disclosure is the verbal revelation to a partner of information about oneself (Derlega, Metts, Petronio, & Margulis, 1993) and is conceptualized as a dialectical process involving and embedded in the larger processes of identity and relationship development (Afifi & Guerrero, 1998; Dindia, 1997; Rosenfeld, 1979). It sometimes can involve considerable risk to a person's self-concept if the disclosed informed is frowned on (Dindia, 1997). For instance, revealing an alternative sexual identity, an extra-marital affair, or a drug problem to a cross-sex friend would make a person vulnerable to criticism and subsequent damage to his or her self-concept.

There are some interesting theoretical models that can be applied to cross-sex friendship and self-concept construction (i.e., Aron & Aron's self-expansion model, 1997; Bowlby's attachment theory, 1969; and Wright's self-referent model of friendship,1984). Wright's friendship model is directly relevant to my basic premise that cross-sex friendships and self-concepts influence each other. One of his contentions is that because of the ubiquitousness of self, individuals develop a concern for the "well-being and worth of the entity he of she identifies as self" (1984, p. 118). Along these lines he further observed "to the degree that two people are friends, each provides the other with consensual validation concerning his or her sense of individuality … (p. 119) … (and) facilitates the expression and recognition of one's more important and highly valued self-attributes" (p. 120). According to Wright, the different types of rewards available in friendship can be thought of as "friendship values." Most relevant for my purposes are the friendship values of "ego support" and "self-affirmation." Ego support is provided when a friend helps an individual maintain a view of him- or herself as a competent, worthwhile person. Relatedly, a friend with self-affirmation value encourages and facilitates the expression and recognition of self-attributes that an individual places great value on. The cross-sex friendship schema that an individual has for a specific high quality cross-sex friendship would include friendship values like ego support and self-affirmation. That friendship schema would, in turn, impact the individual's self-view. Lea was able to garner reasonable empirical support for Wright's model as it applies to both same and cross-sex friendship (1989).

Aron and Aron (1997) proposed in their self-expansion model that "a central human motivation is self-expansion and one way people seek such expansion is through close relationships in which each includes the other in the self" (p. 251). Before entering a relationship an individual imagines how he or she might be after the incorporation of the other person (meaning, the other person's perspectives, resources, identities, etc). The self-expansion model has obvious similarities to other interpersonal self perspectives because each person is included in the self of the other. The model can be applied to cross-sex friendship initiation and subsequent impact on self-concepts. For example, when a person ponders whether or not he or she should initiate a cross-sex friendship in some specific locale such as the workplace, that person envisions the degree to which incorporation of the "other" into self would be advantageous. The possibility of acquiring an insider perspective, for instance, might make the prospect of a cross-sex friendship in the workplace enticing (Sapadin, 1988). On the other hand, the possibility that a friendship overture could be misinterpreted as sexual harassment might discourage an individual from trying to initiate such a friendship (O'Meara, 1994).

Some prominent scholars contend that friendships are not attachment relationships (e.g., Weiss, 1998). However, other researchers and theorists have argued quite persuasively that adults form attachments with other adults such as friends and romantic partners (e.g., Bowlby, 1969; Hazan & Zeifman, 1994; Trinke and Bartholomew, 1997). The argument that adults form attachments to other adults is straightforward. First, the components necessary for an attachment bond to exist are identified. Then one seeks to demonstrate that those components are observable in relationships other than those between primary caregivers and children. To the extent that attachment components exist in adult cross-sex friendships, one can argue that those friendships are essentially attachment relationships. For example, attachment figures are *safe havens* who offer a *secure base* from which the child can explore his or her environment (Bowlby, 1969). Infants and toddlers also strive to maintain *close proximity* to their caregiver and *mourn their loss* (Bowlby, 1969). Finally, attachment relationships are characterized by *strong emotional bonds*, though not always positive ones. Utilizing the five characteristic components of attachment relationships, Trinke and Bartholomew (1997) conducted a study in which they identified a hierarchy of attachment relationships for 240 young adults: romantic partner, mother, father, sibling, and platonic best friend (1997). They concluded that 77% of their sample were attached to their best friends, and a significantly higher proportion of females than males reported such an attachment. Unfortunately, no specific information was given on what percentage of best friendships were cross-sex in nature or whether there were any noteworthy differences between attachment relationships in cross-sex and same-sex pairings.

Bowlby's attachment theory is applicable to cross-sex friendships in other ways. Recall from earlier discussions that Bowlby believed infants and toddlers develop expectations about the *availability* and *dependency* of caregivers and that those expectations form the basis for internal working models or schemas of self and others (1969). Those expectations along with other factors lead to certain attachment styles that persist throughout life (Bowlby, 1969). The expectations and the internal working models within which they are embedded "tend to persist relatively unchanged throughout the rest of life" (Bowlby, 1973, p. 202; but see Baldwin & Fehr, 1995, who challenge Bowlby's assumption that attachment styles are relatively stable). The quality of attachment experienced by an individual in infancy and toddlerhood impacts the quality of that person's cross-sex friendships. Earlier in the book I concluded that the internal working models formed of primary caregivers could impact perceptions about the availability and dependency of members of that sex. For example, if the father of a 2-year-old girl is an undependable, unresponsive, and unavailable primary caregiver that young child might develop internal working models and gender schemas of opposite-sex others being less than reliable. Those expectations might generalize to other cross-sex relationships with friends and dating partners in adulthood.

The reciprocal influence between cross-sex friendships and self-concepts has another layer of complication added when one or both partners are homosexual. Scholars have stressed the importance of considering sexual orientation in studies of friendship because it is such a "potent organizing influence" on relationships (Nardi & Sherrod, 1994; see also Weston, 1991). Sexual orientation also has a significant effect on how a person views him or herself (Savin-Williams, 1990). Surprisingly, there have been very few investigations of gay and lesbian adult friendships (for an exception see Nardi & Sherrod, 1994) and even fewer that focus on cross-sex friendships in which one or both partners are gay or lesbian (e.g., Diamond, 2000). These kinds of cross-sex friendships take three forms: between gay men and heterosexual women; between lesbians and heterosexual men; and between gay men and lesbians. The small amount of research on these varieties of friendship has not specifically addressed how they influence and are influenced by the self-concepts or the participating members (Bell & Weinberg, 1978; Malone, 1980; Moon, 1995; Rubin, 1985). However, as I noted in the previous chapter, heterosexual cross-sex friends (and same-sex ones for that matter) who openly accept a lesbian or gay friend after she or he has "come out of the closet" can do much toward affirming that person's sense of social acceptance and personal identity (Savin-Williams, 1990).

Concluding Observations

Scholarly investigations of adult cross-sex friendships have increased significantly over the last 10 years and surpassed the number of cross-sex friendship studies in all other life stages combined. Most prominently, important advances have been made in understanding the sexual dynamics of young adult heterosexual cross-sex friendships. Although significant strides have been made in comprehension of some aspects of cross-sex friendships, other equally important issues have been ignored or minimally addressed. For instance, scholars have not examined developmental factors that impact cross-sex friendship formation and maintenance. In their study of the impact of marriage and children on friendships, Carbery and Buhrmester contended that scholars have a "disjointed understanding of adult friendships" (1998, p. 393; also see Sherman et al., 2000) because theory and research on adult friendships have not been integrated within a broader life-span perspective. I wholeheartedly agree with their assessment, especially as it applies to cross-sex friendships. Their research revealed that developmental changes in young adulthood such as getting married and having children significantly decreases the amount of dependency on friends for meeting needs.

Along similar developmental lines, in addition to getting married and having (or not having) children, other processes in young adulthood are relevant to cross-sex friendships but have not been adequately investigated. For example, self-concepts in early adulthood are characterized by a greater sense of autonomy and inward orientation than in previous stages of life (Labouvie-Vief et al., 1995). More self-reflection arguably leads to closer inspection of one's social relationships, including cross-sex friendships, and how those relationships are related to conceptions of self (Michaud, 1998). Additionally, researches of adult cross-sex friendship have only minimally addressed developmental links between adolescent cross-sex friendships and the cross-sex friendships of young adults. As an example of the developmental connection between life stages, Connolly and colleagues argued persuasively that adolescents get their conceptions of romantic relationships and cross-sex friendships from their parents and other adults (Connolly et al., 1999).

Researchers usually restrict their investigative efforts to young adulthood and overlook cross-sex friendships of middle-aged adults. The descriptive knowledge base on friendships in middle adulthood is generally underdeveloped (Blieszner & Adams, 1992; Sherman et al., 2000) and seriously impoverished in the specific area of cross-sex friendships. Perhaps cross-sex friendships of middle-aged individuals are not significantly different from their younger counterparts. For example, the marital and parenting demands faced by many middle-aged adults and young adults often results in a weakening of friendship ties (Rawlins, 1992). As a middle-aged man with a wife and three children I know that the demands of marriage and parenthood significantly curtails the time I have to spend with friends, or to establish new ones. On the other hand, social and structural barriers to cross-sex friendships might be more manageable for middle-aged adults who have had more practice contending with them than their younger counterparts.

Something else happens in middle-adulthood regardless of an individual's marital or parental status: the so-called midlife crisis. Part of the midlife crisis is a self-assessment of where a person is at the mid-way point of life—What he or she accomplished compared to the goals set in young adulthood. Jung (1933) suggested that an essential process in midlife is a reexamination of self, a process that has been empirically verified (Labouvie-Vief et al., 1995). Part of that self-assessment involves an appraisal of the friendships that one has or does not have in life (Michaud, 1998). Middle adulthood has its own special challenges that typically do not exist in young adulthood that take their toll on friend-ship—for instance, caring for an elderly parent can seriously curtail the time a middle-aged individual might have for friendship (Samuels, 1997). In summary, friendship scholars in general, and cross-sex friendship researchers in particular, have paid little attention to how middle-adulthood affects, and is affected by, cross-sex friendships.

Much of the adult cross-sex friendship research has been conducted with a heterosexist bias heavily influenced by an "ideology of heterosexual romanti-cism" (Werking, 1997b). Many cross-sex friendship researchers adopt what Rawlins astutely referred to as a heterosexist worldview (1994). That worldview is illustrated by the tendency of researchers to focus on sexual and romantic di-mensions of cross-sex friendships and to forget that heterosexuality is not uni-versal. This bias is especially obvious in recent studies focusing on issues dealing with the sexual component of cross-sex friendships (e.g., Afifi & Faulkner, 2000; Afifi & Burgoon, 1998; Kaplan & Keys, 1997; Messman et al., 2000; Schneider & Kenny, 2000). Please do not misunderstand me. The aforemen-tioned studies were solidly conducted and address important issues in cross-sex friendships. Nevertheless, those studies aptly demonstrate the heterosexist bias referenced by Rawlins and Werking. I am also aware that my own research (and indeed, even this chapter) is similarly infected with the heterosexist bias. There are a number of equally important topics that should be addressed more thor-oughly such as norms and rules in adult cross-sex friendships (Felmlee, 1999), cross-sex friendship between individuals in which one or both partners are gay or lesbian (Nardi, 1992; Rubin, 1985), cross-sex friendships of middle-aged in-dividuals, and interracial, intergenerational, and intercultural cross-sex friend-ships in adulthood.

Cross-sex friendship explorations reveal considerable variability between different types of adult cross-sex friendships. Some friends chose to have sex with each other (Afifi & Faulkner, 2000), some actively avoid sexual contact (Messman et al., 2000). Some men and women receive more social support from their same-sex friends than from their cross-sex ones (Barbee et al., 1990), whereas others, often males, report receiving more support from their cross-sex friendships (Aukett et al., 1988). Some cross-sex friends struggle with issues of power and control, others do not (Monsour et al., 1994). Some cross-sex friends recognize and value insider perspectives provided by their friends, others apparently pay them little heed (Monsour, 1988; Sapadin, 1988). The studies listed in this paragraph document that not all cross-sex friendships are the same and underscore the importance of developing a typology of those relationships (Monsour, 1997; Rawlins, 1994).

The question that was so popular in the latter part of the 20th century (i.e., "Can a man and a woman be friends?") can finally be put to rest in the beginning of the 21st century. Of course they can. The studies reviewed in this chapter indicate that women and men can and do form friendships with each other despite the social and structural barriers that get in their way. Those friendships provide social support (Gaines, 1994; Rose, 1985; Werking, 1997a), a buffer against loneliness (Monsour, 1998), insider perspectives (Sapadin, 1988; Monsour, 1988), other-sex companionship (Swain, 1992), excitement in the workplace (Eyler & Baridon, 1992; Lobel et al., 1994), and sometimes even sexual gratification (Afifi & Faulkner, 2000). Currently and in the immediate and long-term future we can expect to see more adult cross-sex friendships because individuals in earlier stages of the life cycle have already made them a natural part of their relational repertoire.

6

Cross-Sex Friendships
in Old Age
(65 years of age and up)

Cross-sex friendships in old age? What I am aware of so far, by way of both formal data and informal observation, gives me a renewed appreciation for the now-hackneyed paradox, "The more things change, the more they stay the same." About staying the same, it looks as if individuals who enjoy cross-sex friendships in earlier stages of adult-hood continue to do so as they age. But with the aging process, things do change in ways that make such friendships more difficult to form and maintain. Women, for example, tend to live longer than men and, in addition, usually have husbands who are several years older than them-selves. Thus, especially in "older" old age, there is a scarcity of appropriately aged men for women to form friendships with. And the men? They are inclined to continue a pattern that is more characteristic of men than women in earlier phases of adult life, particularly among so-called "working-class" men. That is, they rely on their spouses or other female kin for the kinds of confidence-sharing and emotional support that is generally associated with friendship. And the (relatively) rare older man who outlives his wife is more likely to remarry than to form a cross-sex friendship.

—Wright (personal communication, June 24, 2000).

The above quotation from Paul Wright is full of insightful opinions that I revisit throughout the chapter. I thought he would be the right person to use for my opening quotation for a number of reasons. First and foremost is the well-deserved reputation he enjoys in the community of friendship scholars. Second, unlike so many of his colleagues, Paul has actually written about older adult cross-sex friendships (1989). Furthermore, he developed a model of friendship that foreshadowed and inspired some of the ideas articulated throughout this book about the relationship between friendship and self-concept development (1984; see chap. 5, this volume). There is one more reason why Paul is eminently qualified to open this chapter, a reason I feel sure he would not mind me sharing with the reader. Three years ago Paul officially became part of the fastest growing segment of the U.S. population (i.e., older adults). Paul has plenty of company. At the age of 68 he has become one of 30 million Americans over the age of 65 (Harvard Health Letter, May 1999), a number that is expected to increase significantly by the year 2020 (Berry, 1993).

A few preliminary observations should be made before examining how the three themes of this book apply to cross-sex friendships in the final stage of the life cycle. In the next few pages I briefly address the diversity in old age and old-age friendships, the impoverished state of the literature on cross-sex friendships of the elderly, and the relative rarity of cross-sex friendships in our older population.

My choice of age 65 as the beginning of the final stage of the life cycle is somewhat arbitrary and traditional. Sixty-five is often chosen as the starting point of old age because it is the normal age of retirement and when social security payments begin (Rogers, 1982). Similar to other stages of the life cycle, old age can be subdivided into stages and typically is by social gerontologists and friendship researchers. As one indication of the inherent diversity of old age, experts partition older Americans into three age groups: the *young-old* (ages 60 to 74), the *old-old* (ages 75 to 84), and the *very old* (ages 85 and over; Hansson & Carpenter, 1994). Those over 84 are also referred to as the "oldest-old" (Johnson & Barer, 1997). Gerontologists have noted considerable variability in the effects of aging (Hansson & Carpenter, 1994). There are differences between groups (e.g., between the "young-old" and the "oldest-old") and within groups (e.g., not all people in the "old-old" category are the same). For example, the life styles of most 65-year-olds more closely resemble 45-year-olds than individuals over 84 (Allan & Adams, 1989; Johnson & Troll, 1994). Additionally, physical and mental decline is typically more pronounced for those over 84 than it is for younger individuals (i.e., the young-old and the old-old). On the other hand, some 85-year-olds seem younger both physically and mentally than others who are 15 years their junior (Johnson & Barer, 1997). The different age groups also have different views about aging. For instance, researchers divided 2,329 individuals into four age groups (55 to 64, 65 to 74, 75 to 84, and 85 plus) and discovered that those over 85 had the most positive perspective on aging (Seccombe & Ishii-Kuntz, 1991).

The conclusion that changes in friendship accompany changes that occur with increasing old age seems almost axiomatic from a developmental perspective (Wright, 1989). For example, partly because of decreased mobility caused by age-related health problems, many (but not all) individuals in late life are less likely than they were in earlier stages of life to take the initiative in forming new friendships (Allan & Adams, 1989; Johnson & Barer, 1997; Roberto, 1989). Similarly, some older individuals' who are losing friends to death and disability change their criteria for friendship and the value placed on those relationships (Field, 1999; Johnson & Troll, 1994). Furthermore, some scholars claim that as men and women progress through old age there is a loosening of traditional sex roles and each sex becomes more androgynous (Belsky, 1992; Guttman, 1987; Huyck, 1990). Belsky observed "The idea that women become more assertive and men softer and less stereotypically masculine in the second half of adult life has the distinction of being with us longer than practically any other concept in gerontology … " (1992, p. 165). Guttman in particular argued persuasively that as women and men age there is a shift in sex roles (1987). Recall from the previous chapter that an androgynous orientation for men was linked to higher numbers of cross-sex friendships for young adults (Monsour, 1988; also see Wright, 1989, p. 205; Wright & Scanlon, 1991).

Although old age brings about changes that eventually affect everyone who enters that stage of life, commentators emphasize the diversity of old age and old-age friendships and warn against making sweeping generalizations about either of them (Allan & Adams, 1989; Blieszner & Adams, 1992; Field, 1999; Johnson & Barer, 1997). Scholars have noted, for example, that some older Americans have many friends and seem to need them, some have smaller social networks and do not seem nearly as dependent on friends, and still others claim to not need friends at all (Blieszner & Adams, 1992; Field, 1999; Johnson & Troll, 1994). The view of those scholars are reminiscent of the position taken by Newcomb and Bagwell in regards to children's friendships (1996, see chap. 2, this volume). Recall they contended that the friendships of children could be viewed as developmental necessities, developmental advantages, or developmental hindrances. Adams, Blieszner, and De Vries suggested that the way older individuals define friendship is determined by their age, gender, and geographic location (2000).

Part of the diversity in old age and old-age friendships might be gender based. I use the word might because not all experts agree on whether or not there are significant differences between the friendships of older men and women. Generally speaking, the differences between older women and men in the way they conduct same-sex friendship is a continuation of modal differences that existed in young and middle adulthood, that is, men tend to be more instrumentally oriented and women tend to be more emotionally oriented (Wright, 1989). Although Wright was careful to note that there are exceptions to the modal patterns he identified and that gender differences between male and female friendships become smaller as friendships grow in duration (1982), he nevertheless outlined clear distinctions between the same-sex friendships of older women and men (1989). Along similar lines utilizing compelling longitudinal data from the Berkeley Older Generation study, Field identified important differences between women and men in the trajectories of friendship in old age (1999). For example, men in the old-old category were much less involved in their friendships than were women in that category. That gender difference, however, did not exist between men and women in the young-old category. Barer (1995) found that much larger percentages of women than men in their late 80s were willing to go to friends for instrumental and expressive support. Only 10% of the men compared to 38% of the women sought out a friend as a confidant. In commenting on the impact of structural and dispositional variables on the way older adults define friendship, Adams, Blieszner, and De Vries observe "The differing social structural locations and dispositions of men and women together may account for a wide range of differences in their friendship patterns and their perception of friendship" (2000, p. 129).

Despite documented differences between the friendships of older men and women, there are also similarities (Wright, 1989). For example, Matthews (1983) and Roberto and Kimboko (1989) found that older women and men had quite similar orientations toward friendship. Johnson and Troll contended that gender differences that exist between men and women in their friendships when they are in their 60s and 70s tend to disappear when individuals get into their 80s (1994), which is the opposite pattern reported by Field (1999). If the differences between women and men do in fact dissipate as they get older it may be because individuals in their 70s and 80s begin to depart from traditional sex-role behavioral patterns, that is, men become more like women and women become more like men (Belsky, 1992).

Although researchers are clearly interested in friendship gender differences in old age, their interest is restricted to differences in the same-sex friendships of men and women. Investigators have generally neglected studying gender differences within older adult cross-sex friendships (but see Wright, 1989, pp. 213–216). A number of interesting and potentially productive questions have yet to be addressed. For example, if older men and women conduct their same-sex friendships differently, which I am not totally convinced that they do, what happens when older men and women get together as friends? Do different styles of "doing friendship" cause problems for older men and women in cross-sex friendships? Do those problems, if they exist, unfold differently depending on whether the participants are in their mid-sixties as compared to their early 80s? And what about O'Meara's four challenges to cross-sex friendship (i.e., the emotional bond challenge, the sexual challenge, the audience challenge, and the equality challenge, 1989)? Do older women and men perceive and deal with those challenges differently? These questions and others like them have yet to be adequately addressed—a point I emphasize in the next paragraph.

The older adult friendship literature is embarrassingly small. Some studies that potentially could have been included in the cross-sex friendship literature are problematic because researchers did not ask respondents to indicate whether they were reporting on same-sex friendships or cross-sex ones (e.g., Blieszner & Adams, 1998; Dugan & Kivett, 1998; Dykstra, 1995; Gupta & Korte, 1994; Lamme, Dykstra, Broese, & Marjolein, 1996; Mullins & Dugan, 1990). Similarly, cross-sex friendships are implicitly discounted when investigators neglect to distinguish between same-sex and cross-sex friendships in their samples (e.g. Adams et al., 2000; Dugan & Kivett, 1998). With a few noteworthy exceptions reviewed in this chapter, investigations have not been conducted on cross-sex friendships of older Americans. There are a number of possible explanations for the lack of research attention, but I identify and briefly explain just two.

First, old-age cross-sex friendships represent the intersection of two marginalized groups (i.e., friendships of the elderly and cross-sex friendships).

Although old age as a stage of life receives ample research attention as evidenced by journals devoted to old age (e.g., *The Gerontologist* and *The International Journal of Aging and Human Development*), old-age friendships do not (Dugan & Kivett, 1998; but see Adams & Blieszner, 1989; Matthews, 1995). Similarly, friendships in general have received considerable empirical and conceptual attention, but cross-sex friendships have not (Werking, 1997a). A second explanation for the scholarly neglect of cross-sex friendships of older adults has its basis in the relative rarity of those relationships when compared to their same-sex counterparts. Uncommon relationships are difficult to locate in sample sizes large enough to allow for certain types of popular and powerful statistical procedures such as ANOVAS. Even moderately large sample sizes of elderly cross-sex friendships are difficult to come by because of the inclination of older people to associate primarily with members of their own sex. The homosocial norm (Rose, 1985) that began in elementary school (Maccoby, 1994) stretches into the twilight years of an individual's life. Older men and women typically select members of their own sex to spend time with, although this pattern is more pronounced for women than it is for men (Babchuk & Anderson, 1989; Field, 1999; Nussbaum, Thompson, & Robinson, 1989; Wright, 1989). Homosocial patterns and preferences established throughout life become entrenched and relatively resistant to change. Still, even individuals over the age of 80 sometimes depart from the same-age and same-sex norms of adult friendships (Jerrome & Wenger, 1999).

Just how common are friendships between women and men over the age of 65? The reported number of cross-sex friendships in old age varies from study to study, but the number usually represents less than 20% of an individual's friendship network. In Jones and Vaughan's study of best friendships among senior adults, none of the 53 women listed a male as her best friend (1990). Only 2 of the 23 males listed a female as a best friend. The low number of cross-sex friends might be explained by the decision of the researchers to study best friendships, rather than some other broader classification such as casual or close friendships. In Adams' classic 1985 investigation of the friendships of 70 elderly women, 17% listed males as friends. Similarly, in Babchuk and Anderson's study of 132 elderly women, 20% listed males as friends (1989). In a longitudinal study over a 14-year period (1978–1992), 100 women over the age of 64 at Time Two (1992) were asked to identify their closest friends (Roberto, 1997). Although the average number of close friends was five, only 4% of the sample named men as their closest friends. In Field's reporting of longitudinal data from the Berkeley Older Generation Study, women in both the young-old and old-old categories showed a stronger tendency than males to identify same-sex others as their close friends (1999). In O'Connor's qualitative investigation of same and cross-sex friendships of the frail elderly, only 16% of her 134 respondents ($n = 22$; 19 females and 3 males) included friends among those identified as very close. Nine of the 22 participants (6 women and 3 men) identified a member of the other sex as a close friend. So actually only 9 of the original 134 respondents (6%) identified a member of the other sex as very close. Wright (1989) gave four reasons why cross-sex friendships are rare in the older population: retirement from the workplace, women's longer life span, normative constraints against older women pursuing friendships with older men, and the likelihood of widowed men remarrying rather than forming cross-sex friendships.

Despite the fact that the vast majority of friendship scholars have ignored the friendships that older women and men form with one another, there have been enough investigations to draw some conclusions about how cross-sex friendships enrich the social networks of older Americans. Those investigations and my accompanying conclusions are presented in the next section.

Cross-Sex Friendships and the Enrichment of Social Networks During Old Age

Friendships between women and men in the final stage of the life cycle can be wonderfully enriching experiences (O'Connor, 1993). Those friendships might be long-standing ones dating back 30 or 40 years (Babchuk & Anderson, 1989; Field, 1999; Roberto, 1997) or, less likely, new ones initiated late in life (Field, 1999). In the interview data reviewed by Field (1999), over 70% of young-old and old-old individuals said most of their friends were old friends. Women's long-standing friendships were often 40 years old, compared to an average of closer to 20 years for men. However, the older an individual gets, the less likely it is that he or she will have surviving friends of comparable age (Johnson & Barer, 1997). Individuals who had cross-sex friends in earlier stages of life have already reaped the generic and unique benefits such friendships can provide and will probably continue to do so as an older adult (Wright, June 24, 2000, opening quotation in this chapter). Specific and clear data about cross-sex friendships spanning several stages of the life cycle are difficult to locate except for the occasional reference made to such friendships by researchers (e.g., Field, 1999; Goodman, 1986; O'Connor, 1993).

Like friendships in every other stage of life, friendships among those over the age of 65 can be sources of stress and strain as well as solace and satisfaction (Adams & Blieszner, 1998; Blieszner & Adams, 1998; Jones & Vaughn, 1990; Morgan, Carder, & Neal, 1997; Rook, 1989). Blieszner and Adams noted that adult friendship researchers have devoted very little attention to the problematic aspects of friendships (1998). Unfortunately, in their study of adult and older adult problematic friendships they did not clearly differentiate between same-sex and cross-sex friendship. Their failure to distinguish between the two types of friendship is surprising when one considers that some of the problems in heterosexual cross-sex friendships are qualitatively different from those that might present themselves in heterosexual same-sex friendships (remember O'Meara's challenges, 1989). For instance, the one example of a cross-sex friendship they did give revealed a problem with "interactive processes." In that case a 69-year-old woman had to fight off the sexual advances of a cross-sex friend of similar age.

Carstensen's theory of socioemotional selectivity predicts that problematic friendships in any stage of life, but particularly in old age, are discontinued (1993; 1995). He theorized that as individuals age and experience diminished energy and capabilities they become more selective about who they spend their time with. They focus their time and attention on relationships that have high emotional value and often disengage from less valuable ones (Johnson & Barer, 1992). Carstensen's theory has received a fair amount of empirical support (Lansford, Sherman, & Antonucci, 1998) and is revisited periodically throughout this chapter.

Generic Benefits.   Friendships between older men and women provide many of the same advantages they did in earlier stages of life, advantages that mirror those provided by same-sex friends (Wright, 1989). Older cross-sex friends help one another, exchange confidences, share interesting information, and provide emotional support (Babchuk & Anderson, 1989; Field, 1999; O'Connor, 1993). Individuals in late life describe friendships as involving understanding, devotion, and commonality (Patterson, Bettini, & Nussbaum, 1993). Similarly, older people define their friendships as including trust, loyalty, disclosures, shared activities, and mutual assistance (Adams et al., 2000).

The benefits of friendships in old age are so compelling that some individuals are willing to bend the rules, even their own, in order to insure the presence of friends. A longitudinal study over a 16-year period (1979–1995) revealed that older adults are willing to break away from friendship norms that were dominant during young and middle adulthood such as having same-sex and same-age friendships (Jerrome & Wenger, 1999). Researchers have documented that older adults form intergenerational cross-sex friendships (e.g., O'Connor, 1993), and older men who previously had only same-sex friendships are willing to initiate cross-sex ones (e.g., Field, 1999).

The largest category of generic benefits supplied by cross-sex friends is social support. Recall from previous chapters that social support involves giving and receiving affect, aid, and affirmation (Crohan & Antonucci, 1989). Proponents of the convoy model of social support posit that as individuals traverse the life span they surround themselves with others (i.e., convoys) who are close and important to them and who can provide necessary social support (Antonucci & Akiyama, 1995; Kahn & Antonucci, 1980). Those relationships develop over time and tend to reflect and be affected by changes that occur within an individual. Antonucci and Akiyama observed that family and friends serve different functions throughout the life cycle, with friends expected to provide companionship and family expected to provide long-term support for chronic needs (1995).

The connection between social support and physical and psychological health is widely acknowledged in the scientific community (see Sarason et al., 1997, for a review). Citing more than a dozen studies and providing empirical support of her own, Potts concluded that friends in old age provide one another with social support that often predicts lower levels of depression, better physical health, and higher life satisfaction (Potts, 1997; see also Adams & Blieszner, 1995). Unfortunately, studies in this age category often do not distinguish between social support provided by same-sex friends and support supplied by their cross-sex counterparts (e.g., Johnson & Troll, 1994). Social support provided by cross and same-sex friendship is sometimes not differentiated because there were so few cross-sex friendships in the study. For example, in a social support investigation of the best friends of 76 senior adults (53 females and 23 males), only 2 men and no women reported having a best cross-sex friend (Jones & Vaughan, 1990).

A number of investigators have specifically focused on social support provided by friends in old age (e.g., Adams & Blieszner, 1995; Dykstra, 1995; Johnson & Troll, 1994; Morgan et al., 1997; Rook & Ituarte, 1999). Morgan and colleagues noted that widowed women maintain friendships with both members of a married couple and depend on the male member for instrumental aid (Morgan et al., 1997). Johnson and Troll studied 111 women and men (77% women) over the age of 85 and concluded that friends provide little practical assistance (instrumental aid) but are relied on heavily for fun and recreation (1994). In their article *Aging Well With Friends and Family*, Adams and Blieszner argued that older individuals depend on friends and family for different types of social support and that older adults with many friends and strong family ties are better adjusted than those with fewer, lower-quality ties (1995).

Older women and men receive considerable social support from their immediate family (Rook & Ituarte, 1999). According to 1990 data from the American Association of Retired Persons, 80% of Americans over the age of 65 have adult children, and two-thirds of those children live within 30 minutes of the parent (Johnson & Barer, 1997). Another encouraging statistic is that 60% of older adults have weekly visits with their children, and 75% talk on the phone at least once a week. As wonderful as family can be, however, they often cannot take the place of friends in providing certain types of social support (Johnson & Barer, 1997). Furthermore, friendships take on added significance for the 20% of older Americans who have no children and the 5% who never marry (Rubinstein, Alexander, Goodman, & Luborsky, 1991). Friends become increasingly important as individuals grow old, more important in some ways than family. For example, friends are often more effective than children in improving morale (Blau, 1973), and they are a better source of fun and companionship than family (Johnson, 1983; Johnson & Troll, 1994). Wood and Robertson concluded that when older people need someone to comfort them, one good friend is more beneficial than a dozen grandchildren (1978). However, findings from the Berkeley Older Generation study revealed that friendship becomes less of a priority for some very old men who are less likely than old women to replace lost friendships (Field, 1999; Kessler, McLeod, & Wethington, 1985). Along similar lines, Barer found in her study of 150 women and men in their late 80s that significantly smaller percentages of men than women sought out instrumental (41% compared to 18%) and expressive (96% compared to 25%) social support from their friends (1994).

In an impressive longitudinal study of adults begun in 1928 (i.e., the Berkeley Older Generation Study), data was gathered about the friendships of young-old and old-old individuals (reported by Field, 1999). During extensive interviews lasting 4 to 6 hours, individuals in both age groups (who were the same individuals at different times in their lives) stressed the importance and frequency of "just talking" when asked "what do you do with your friends?" In addition to talking simply for the joy of talking, some older individuals also see one another as confidants. Forty-three percent of the participants at Time One (when they were "young-old") and Time Two (when they were "old-old") reported that they confided in a friend. However, 80% of the individuals who had confidants were women (Field, 1999), suggesting a continuation of modal patterns of slightly higher levels of self-disclosures for women than men in young and middle adulthood (Dindia & Allen, 1992; also see Barer, 1994). Talking for the sake of talking and self-disclosures illustrate the "affect" component of Crohan and Antonucci's definition of social support (1989). Self-disclosing to a friend can also give that friend a chance to provide social support through affirmation of what was revealed (Wright, 1984).

Social support is also manifested via reminiscing with friends. Investigators have shown that reminiscing among the elderly is a common communication behavior that provides important benefits, such as enabling an individual to cope with the fear of death (McMahon & Rhudick, 1964; Nussbaum et al., 1989) and helping the individual to defend his or her self esteem and beliefs (Priefer & Gambert, 1984). In Johnson and Troll's study of 111 women and men over the age of 85, sharing memories (reminiscing) was considered one of the most important characteristics of friendship (1994). The act of reminiscing is a fertile area for cross-sex friendship and communication researchers. For instance, cross-sex friends whose spouses have died may spend considerable time recalling what their marital relationships were like and trying to reconcile never-resolved problems.

Some older individuals form friendships with younger adults (Adams, 1985; O'Connor, 1993). Adams discovered that 11 of the reported 26 cross-sex friendships of elderly women were with men who were at least 10 years younger. As observed by Adams "These relationships, like the cross-sex friendships many of the women had earlier in their lives, were mediated by a friendship with another person or by involvement in a secondary organization" (1985, p. 609). Most of the younger men did favors for their female friend such as fixing things around the house and giving advice. In an investigation of the frail elderly, O'Connor found that one-third of the cross-sex friends named by her 22 respondents (19 females, 3 males) were young adults, and those friendships were more likely for individuals who were housebound. Intergenerational cross-sex friendships present interesting theoretical issues (O'Connor, 1993). From a traditional social exchange perspective (Thibaut & Kelley, 1959), older individuals may avoid intergenerational friendships because such friendships are perceived as one-sided, with the younger friend doing most of the giving and the older friend doing most of the taking (O'Connor, 1993). Such a situation may make an older individual feel overly rewarded, which is an uncomfortable arrangement from a social exchange perspective. The motive to have equity in relationships is partly due to older persons' desires to be independent and needed in some way (Nussbaum et al., 1989). Similarly, young people may feel the costs of such a relationship are too great (Chown, 1981; O'Connor, 1993).

Friends in old age can be bulwarks against loneliness (Bondevik & Skogstad, 1996; Mullins & Dugan, 1990). Loneliness among older adults has been empirically linked to shyness, lack of assertiveness, and an external locus of control (Hansson, Jones, Carpenter, & Remondet, 1986). Two of the leading national experts on loneliness, Perlman and Peplau, contended that friends in old age take on considerable importance in combating loneliness (1998). For example, a study of 208 elderly residents of 10 senior housing apartments revealed that loneliness was more prevalent among residents who had less contact with close friends (Mullins & Dugan, 1990). Surprisingly, having siblings, neighbors, children, or grandchildren did not impact the degree of loneliness. Unfortunately, no attempt was made to distinguish between same-sex friendships and their cross-sex counterparts. Research also indicates that widowed women and men report higher levels of loneliness than those who are married (Koropeckyj-Cox, 1998). However, in Dykstra's investigation of unpartnered women and men between the ages of 65 and 75, the absence of friendship rather than being single was an important determinant of loneliness (1995). Regretfully, Dykstra also did not distinguish between same-sex and cross-sex friendships.

Although same- and cross-sex friendships have the potential to provide generic benefits such as social support and protection against loneliness, some older men chose not to avail themselves of those benefits. Field concluded that some men lose interest in friendship when they get into their 80s, and even the categorization of friendship as a "close relationship" might change (1999). Some of those men are self-described loners who contend they do not need friends and find them annoying (Johnson & Troll, 1994). Data from the Berkeley Older Generation Study revealed that when young-old respondents were compared to old-old respondents, men but not women declined in 33% of the measures of casual friends (Field, 1999). Men also showed less of a desire than women for close friendships when the two age groups were compared. As for cross-sex friendships, measurements at Time One (when participants were young-old) and Time Two (when participants were old-old), showed that the closest friends of women were much more likely to be same-sex than the closest friends of men. Because men have a shorter life expectancy than women (Harvard Health Letter, December 1999), they tend to lose their male friends at a faster rate than women lose their female friends. Consequently, surviving males have fewer males to chose from (Johnson & Troll, 1994) and might turn to women for companionship and friendship—if they still value friendships, which sometimes they do not (Field, 1999). Research also indicates that women in their late 70s and early 80s are more likely than men to initiate new friendships, to engage in more activities and more intimate activities with friends, and to desire close friendships (Field, 1999; Roberto & Kimboko, 1989). Significantly smaller percentages of very old men seek out social support from their friends than women of comparable age (Barer, 1994).

Unique Benefits. Unique benefits of cross-sex friendships in old age are similar to those that existed in earlier stages of life. As I document in this section, whether they are in their mid 60s or late 80s, cross-sex friends provide each other with insider perspectives and other-sex companionship.

Existing research on cross-sex friendships in old age does not give a clear indication of the degree to which those relationships are valued because they provide other-sex companionship. Although the handful of studies on cross-sex friendships of the elderly document that friendships are valued because of the companionship they provide (e.g., Field, 1999; O'Connor, 1993), those studies do not unambiguously identify other-sex companionship as uniquely important. In fact, Adams' 1985 study indirectly proposes that the inherent presence of other-sex companionship in cross-sex friendships is what makes those relationships unappealing to many older women. Companionship with a member of the other sex for those women had unwanted romantic and sexual connotations. Conversely, O'Connor's interview data gathered from 22 frail elders indicates that cross-sex friendships are often "pseudospousal" in nature with the male and female friends assisting each other in gender-traditional ways. For instance, one man helped his cross-sex friend by doing the heavier domestic chores like washing windows and gardening. There was a "gender differentiated division of labor being maintained" in some of the cross-sex friendships (1993, p. 27).

A corollary to the other-sex companionship advantage is that elderly cross-sex friends provide one another with insider perspectives on how members of the other sex think, feel, and behave. Although this advantage has been well documented in young adulthood and middle adulthood (see chap. 5, this volume), its existence in old-age cross-sex friendships has not been explored. Also, insider perspectives might not be as useful in old age if men and women become less traditionally sex stereotyped as some scholars contend (Belsky, 1992) because those women and men may be more similar in disposition and behavior than they were in early and middle adulthood.

An important but unexplored benefit of intergenerational cross-sex friendships is getting an insider's perspective from one's older (or younger) cross-sex friend. Friends would be sharing two kinds of insider perspectives-gender and generational insider perspectives. For example, an older cross-sex friend might provide an insider's viewpoint on old age to her younger friend so that he could better understand his aging mother. However, because close friendships ordinarily involve age homophily (Babchuk & Anderson, 1989), the intergenerational friendships that do exist may be casual ones. Both Adams (1985) and O'Connor (1993) contend that intergenerational cross-sex friendships are characterized by the younger friend helping the older one by running errands and doing household chores. To my knowledge there has not been an attempt to explore the giving and receiving of intergenerational insider perspectives between cross-sex friends.

Reaping the generic and unique benefits that cross-sex friendships have to offer older adults can be made more difficult by the social and structural barriers interfering with their initiation and maintenance. In the next section I examine those barriers and some of the ways in which cross-sex friendships among older Americans might be facilitated.

Social and Structural Barriers to Cross-Sex Friendships During Old Age

Social and structural barriers to cross-sex friendship during old age display similarities and differences from those impeding friendship formation in earlier stages of the life cycle. As was true in previous phases of the life span, social and structural barriers in old age influence each other and are often overlapping. For example, Wright identified normative constraints as structural factors that might impede the formation of friendships (1989). A prevailing norm in the culture of many elderly women is to avoid cross-sex friendships (Adams, 1985). That normative constraint also doubles as a social barrier when elderly women say and do things to discourage their same-sex friends from forming male friendships. Although a lonely widow or widower might enjoy the other-sex companionship provided by a cross-sex friend (O'Connor, 1993), individuals in the widow's social network might erect subtle social barriers to those friendships (Adams, 1985).

Social Barriers.   One might think (and hope) that by the time an individual turns 65 she or he would no longer let mere social disapproval from network members interfere with the formation of cross-sex friendships. After all, one of the putative benefits of getting older is that individuals progressively become less concerned with what others think. As will be seen in this section of the chapter, however, individuals in old age pay attention to what others think about their friendships (Adams, 1985). Similar to earlier stages of the life cycle, social barriers also arise from the friends and the way they interact with one another. Throughout the book I have related those kinds of social barriers to purported but debated gender differences in the way men and women communicate and conduct friendships (Canary & Dindia, 1998).

Recall from chapter five that adults face six social barriers to the formation and maintenance of cross-sex friendships. Four of those barriers are the challenges identified by O'Meara (1989). The fifth social barrier is connected to marriage and the sixth to interaction difficulties flowing from different communication styles of the friends. In this chapter I treat the fifth social barrier, (i.e., marital status, which includes widowhood) as part of the audience challenge or barrier. The extent to which these social barriers are relevant to old age is difficult to assess because of the scarcity of cross-sex friendship studies. Nevertheless, in the next few pages I examine O'Meara's challenges, marital status, and communication based barriers to cross-sex friendships in old age.

There are no obvious reasons for believing that the challenges confronting cross-sex friendship in adulthood would magically disappear when individuals turn 65. Older women and men in cross-sex friendships must still decide how they feel about each other and deal with the potential specter of sexuality. They might also have power issues to contend with and be concerned with how their friendship appears to relevant audiences such as spouses, adult children, and other members of their social network. On the other hand, if the cross-sex friendship is one that is ongoing, (i.e., it was established years or even decades earlier), the challenges may have already been dispatched. The vast majority of evidence documenting existence of the challenges has been gleaned from studies of cross-sex friendships among college students. Friendship researchers do not know for sure if the challenges exist in the latter part of middle adulthood (ages 55 to 64) or old age. However, some existing research provides food for thought concerning the relevance to old-age friendships of the barriers to cross-sex friendships that existed in earlier stages of life (e.g., Adams, 1985; Blieszner & Adams, 1998; Babchuk & Anderson, 1989).

Babchuk and Anderson (1989) interviewed 132 women over the age of 65. Fifty-seven of the participants were married (43%) and 75 were widowed (57%). Roughly 20% of the married women and 20% of the widows had at least one close cross-sex friend. They did not specifically test their speculation, but Babcock and Anderson suggested that the relatively small number of cross-sex friendships could be partly attributed to potential jealousy from the spouse of the cross-sex friend. Foregoing cross-sex friendships because they might cause one's spouse (or the spouse of one's potential friend) to be jealous is an obvious manifestation of the audience challenge as a social barrier to cross-sex friendships.

Adams (1985) interviewed 70 elderly women living in the Chicago area in a landmark cross-sex friendship study. About 43% of her sample were 65 to 74 years old, 33% were 75 to 84 years old, and 20% were over the age of 85. The results of her study are pertinent to the emotional bond challenge/barrier, the sexual challenge/barrier, and the audience challenge/barrier (O'Meara, 1989). She allowed participants to use their own definition of friendship by stating "People have different ideas about what a friendship is. How would you describe what a friendship is?" Her 70 respondents identified a total of 678 friendships, some with males (3.6%, $n = 24$), some with females (90.6%, $n = 610$), and some with couples (6.1%, $n = 43$). Four of the cross-sex friendships were with men of similar ages but none of the women spent time alone with their male friend. Adams concluded that the vast majority of her sample preferred same-sex friends to cross-sex ones because they believed cross-sex friendships were the same thing as romantic relationships.

One of the more interesting findings of her study was that the definition of cross-sex friend for older women included a romantic dimension. Sexual and romantic encounters were considered inappropriate by most of her respondents. Additional research done at the time similarly suggested that societal norms more heavily discourage older women than older men from forming cross-sex friendships (Usui, 1984). Indeed, the provocative title of her article, *People Would Talk: Normative Barriers to Cross-Sex Friendships for Elderly Women*, suggests the salience of the audience challenge to older women. The audience challenge for cross-sex friends is to make sure that relevant audiences do not get the wrong idea about the friendship (O'Meara, 1989). About 80% of Adams' sample of elderly women dealt with the audience challenge by forgoing cross-sex friendships completely. The belief that cross-sex friendships were the equivalent of romantic relationships indicates that the women viewed friendships with men as involving sexual and romantic challenges.

Despite Adams' (1985) general finding that most women were not interested in cross-sex friendships because of their romantic and sexual connotations, 17% of the sample ($n = 12$) reported having one or more male friends. Interestingly, in 3 of the 14 couple friendships discussed by the respondents, the interviewee felt closer to the male member of the couple friendship. Adams noted that "of the 678 reported friendships, only about 2% were similar-aged, cross-sex friendships" (p. 607). Obviously, the interpretation of Adams' data depends on which statistic is emphasized. Two percent of the total number of 678 friendships sounds small (note, I did not say insignificant), whereas 17% of the sample of 70 women sounds much more impressive. I prefer incorporating both views and concluding that a small percentage (2%) of the overall friendship networks of elderly women are comprised of cross-sex friendships, although a sizable minority of elderly women (17%) have at least one such friend. Because most of the women in Adam's study were not interested in remarrying and tended to equate cross-sex friendships with romance, the prospect of a cross-sex relationship possibly brought to mind images of sexual and romantic issues (challenges) they did not care to contend with. When concern about how such friendships might appear to others is added to the mix, the result is a combination of social barriers (romantic, sexual, audience) that effectively block the formation of cross-sex friendships.

As interesting and provocative as Adams' study is, a major limitation must be noted. Although Adams was not totally clear on this point, it appears from her description on p. 607 that only 20 of the 70 respondents were specifically asked to discuss their cross-sex friendships (1985). And because those 20 were the first 20 she interviewed (rather than all subjects who reported having one or more cross-sex friends), conclusions about how elderly women define cross-sex friendship is more speculative than empirical in nature.

Many years after her landmark 1985 study, Adams conducted another investigation with her colleague Rosemary Blieszner (Blieszner & Adams, 1998). The main goal of their study of 42 elderly respondents was to explore the problematic aspects of friendships in old age. After extensive interviews with the participants they concluded that power and control issues were the source of many of the difficulties experienced by the friends. Unfortunately, information was not provided on how those power problems played out in similar or different ways in same-sex and cross-sex friendships. They did give an example of a cross-sex friendship that ended because of unwanted sexual advances of the male friend, but they gave no indication as to whether that kind of problem was common in cross-sex friendships.

In summarizing the applicability of O'Meara's challenges to older adult cross-sex friendships I cautiously conclude that the emotional bond, sexual, audience, and power challenges may be relevant. However, my conclusion is based on a few studies that were not specifically designed to investigate O'Meara's challenges. Researchers in those studies also did not focus on how males in cross-sex friendships viewed the potential challenges. The opening observation in this chapter by Paul Wright that "the more things change, the more they stay the same" implies that O'Meara's challenges might still be relevant in old age. Clearly, more research needs to be conducted to verify the extent to which O'Meara's challenges represent social barriers to cross-sex friendship among the elderly.

The audience challenge identified by O'Meara is directly relevant to a fifth social barrier blocking cross-sex friendship formation and maintenance among older individuals, (i.e., marital status). Although marital status as an impediment to cross-sex friendship was discussed in the previous chapter, there are interesting differences between young/middle adulthood and older adulthood in the way marital status might impact cross-sex friendships. Those differences are detailed in the upcoming paragraphs.

Married individuals with cross-sex friendships must carefully manage and monitor how those friendships appear to the most important audience member in their life (i.e., their spouse; Werking, 1997a). Babchuk and Anderson claim that cross-sex friendships are unlikely to exist between widows and married men unless the wives of those men are closely included (1989). The obvious and powerful social barrier at work here is jealousy from one's spouse. Just as it was throughout earlier stages of life, even in advanced old age the green-eyed monster (i.e., jealousy) can devour relationships (Atchley, 1985; Babchuk & Anderson, 1989; Pines & Aronson, 1983). Therefore, married individuals in their 60s,

70s, and 80s might have difficulty *initiating* cross-sex friendships, especially if the targeted new friend is single and attractive. On the other hand, marriage probably has little impact on cross-sex friendships of the elderly if those friendships were formed in adulthood and have survived the test of time. Instead, in situations where the cross-sex friendship predates the marriage, spouses often accept the friendship and frequently become friends with the person as well (Babchuk & Anderson, 1989; Werking, 1997a).

A closer examination of the study by Babchuk and Anderson (1989) reveals some of the issues involved in old-age cross-sex friendships in which one or both partners are married. The purpose of their study was to investigate the primary friendships of 132 married women and widows over the age of 65. About 20% of the married and widowed women had cross-sex friends. A slightly higher percentage of married women (14%) compared to widows (11%) had two or more primary cross-sex friends. This finding indirectly suggests that marriage is not an impediment to cross-sex friendships. But on the other hand, most of the married women who named men as friends were also friends with the wife of their cross-sex friend—indirectly suggesting that cross-sex friendships of married women are conducted within the safe confines of a triadic arrangement. They also noted that married women have a tendency to become at least casual friends with the husbands of their primary female friends.

Like in other stages of life, interaction difficulties originating from male—female communication style differences may produce social barriers to cross-sex friendships in old age. Field contended that one of the most robust findings on friendships in old age is that there are differences in the way women and men act in their same-sex friendships (1999; also see Wright, 1989; 1998). If older women and men do behave differently in their same-sex friendships, those differences could become problematic when those same men and women try to *initiate* friendships with each other because they are bringing different friendship expectations to those relationships. However, if the friendships are already established, perhaps dating back to early or middle adulthood (Field, 1999), differences in interactional styles between the cross-sex friends have presumably been worked out.

Although there is considerable research on sex and gender differences between women and men (Canary & Dindia, 1998), there has been no direct research that I am aware of on how sex- and gender-based communication differences may cause difficulties in interaction between elderly cross-sex friends. Scholars have suggested that when individuals get into their 70s and 80s they become less stereotypically sex-typed in their behaviors and attitudes and more androgynous (Belsky, 1992; Guttman, 1987). If older women and men do become more androgynous one would think interaction between them would be smoother because their behavioral routines during interaction would be similar. On the other hand, however, in their study of over 500 women and men between the ages of 70 and 103, Smith and Baltes discovered significant gender differences in 13 of 28 aspects of personality, social relationships, every-day activity patterns, and reported well being (1998).

In summary, the five social barriers hypothesized to interfere with formation and maintenance of cross-sex friendships in old age are in dire need of further empirical investigation. Evidence documenting the existence of the barriers is thin at best. Part of the problem is that there has not been a focused effort to investigate the extent to which the barriers exist. There are scattered pieces of data from different studies that, when combined, suggest that social roadblocks to cross-sex friendships between older men and women do exist and that they are worthy of further study. When friendships are interfered with by others or the communication differences of the friends themselves, reaping the benefits of cross-sex friendships becomes problematic.

Structural Barriers.   In the section on old-age friendships in their book *Adult Friendship*, Blieszner and Adams opened with a clear encapsulation of the nature of structural factors impacting friendships in old age: "Failing health, retirement, widowhood, and relocation modify the opportunities for some aging people to make and maintain friendships" (1992, p. 51). Note their use of the word modify. Sometimes those modifications constrain cross-sex friendship formation and maintenance. However, those modifica-tions may also facilitate friendship development between older men and women. For example, O'Connor highlighted the significance of structure in propagating cross-sex friendships when she noted that structural factors such as living in the same place, being housebound, or having previously been neighbors are important in promoting cross-sex friendships among the elderly (1993). Because of the dual ability of structural factors to facilitate and impede friendship formation, throughout this section I also address some of the ways in which old age might increase the likelihood of cross-sex friendships.

Three of the major structural barriers to cross-sex friendship formation and maintenance in old age are mobility problems caused by failing health and phys-ical decline, retirement, and marital status. Friendships are unavoidably af-fected by the developmental changes that normally accompany old age (Johnson & Barer, 1997; Nussbaum et al., 1989). Physical illnesses such as rheu-matism, bronchitis, and circulatory problems limit mobility, lessening the op-portunity for the initiation of new friendships and the continuation of old ones (Blieszner & Adams, 1992; Chown, 1981; Johnson & Troll, 1994). Simple things like driving a car or being able to walk a few blocks to visit a friend be-come increasingly difficult and then impossible as an individual ages. Addi-tionally, for those over about the age of 75, a combination of dying friends and increasing physical disability shrinks social networks and makes them less ac-cessible (Johnson & Barer, 1997). Conversely, if increased physical disability is occurring to both partners, those disabilities can strengthen the friendship because they give the friends one more thing in common and leads to mutual emotional support (Johnson & Troll, 1994).

One of the more obvious structural barriers to cross-sex friendship *initiation* is retirement from the workforce (Wright, 1989). When certain conditions are met the workplace can be a fertile environment for the formation of cross-sex friendships (O'Meara, 1994). Even taking into account the structural barriers of sex and occupational segregation identified in chapter five, organizations can give men and women opportunities for interactions that can lay the foundation for friendship formation (Sapadin, 1988). Retirement from the workplace effectively blocks possibilities for future cross-sex friendships. Disappointingly, the relationship between retirement and cross-sex friendships has been generally ignored.

Despite the lack of research attention, some fairly obvious inferences about the relationship between retirement and cross-sex friendships can be made. For example, once a woman or man retires from work he or she will no longer have the organizational cross-sex interaction opportunities enjoyed before that might have led to friendship. Therefore, the initiation of workplace cross-sex friendships is curtailed by retirement. But as noted by Allan and Adams (1989), retirement from the workforce is sometimes closely followed by participation in other types of social organizations that an individual might not have had time for while employed. Those social organizations could lead to structural opportunities for the formation of cross-sex friendships if the organizations are comprised of both women and men.

In addition to a weakening of opportunities for cross-sex friendship initiation, retirement from the workplace can lead to a gradual fading of already established friendships, because the individuals no longer have the opportunity for regular interaction (Blieszner & Adams, 1992; Roberto, 1997). On the other hand, close friendships formed in the workplace might continue well after retirement. Babchuk and Anderson (1989) discovered that elderly women who had been in the workforce had an average of 6 primary friends, compared to an average of 4 for those women who had not been in the workforce. Unfortunately, although 21% of their sample of 132 women had cross-sex friendships, no information was provided concerning how many of those friendships originated in the workplace. The sex of the retiree adds another layer of complication to unraveling the relationship between retirement and cross-sex friendships. Allan and Adams contended that retirement is a different experience for men and women because women base their sense of identity less on work than men do (1989), and women may be more likely than men to continue friendships that were established in the workplace after retirement. Bossé and colleagues discovered that the longer a man is retired from work the less likely he is to maintain friendships that originated there (Bossé, Aldwin, Levenson, Workman-Daniels & Ekerdt, 1990). Field, however, surmised that retirement did not significantly impact the amount of contact with friends or the intimacy level of those friendships (1999).

Marriage also potentially constrains structural opportunities for cross-sex friendship formation in old age because it generally restricts opportunities for cross-sex interaction with potential friends (Block, 1980; Booth & Hess, 1974; Wright, 1998). Wright made an obvious (but nonetheless astute) observation with clear applicability to marital constraints on cross-sex friendship formation: "Friendships probably will not flourish in sociobehavioral environments with strong, normative restraints against free, unstructured interaction ... therefore, friendships are relatively easy to put on hold, and sometimes to forego completely, in the face of expectations from more structured relationships and other role obligations" (Wright, 1998, p. 57). Marriages are more structured relationships with greater role obligations than are cross-sex friendships. Consequently, cross-sex friendship initiation and possibly even maintenance might be sacrificed in order to fulfill the more pressing duties, responsibilities, and pleasantries of marriage.

Conversely, marriage can also be a structural facilitator of cross-sex friendship because of the tendency of married couples to form couple friendships (Babchuk, 1965; Babchuk & Anderson, 1989; Rubin, 1985; Werking, 1997a). However, as noted in chapter 5, cross-sex friendships that emerge from couple friendships are typically characterized by more superficial interaction than same-sex friendships taking place in the context of the foursome (Bell, 1981; Bendtschneider, 1994; Booth & Hess, 1974). Along these same lines, older married women and widows to a lesser degree who have cross-sex friends are usually close friends with the spouse of their cross-sex friend. These friendships are often ones with a fairly long history in which the two couples got together as couple friends in middle and late adulthood (Babchuk & Anderson, 1989). The majority of research on cross-sex friendships originating from couple friendships is outdated or focuses on adult friendships rather than friendships of the elderly (but see Babchuk & Anderson, 1989; O'Connor, 1993).

Widowhood is an important structural factor impacting cross-sex friendship initiation and maintenance. Most of the 70 elderly women interviewed by Adams were widows, and the majority expressed no interest in having cross-sex friends. She contended that the culture established in the social networks of elderly widows discourages cross-sex friendship formation. Allan and Adams noted that network considerations should be a major element when analyzing structural influences on friendship (1989). For instance, a group of widows might get together once a week to play cards or have lunch and exclude males from their social gatherings. But research also indicates that individuals often form new relationships after the death of a spouse. In a study of 548 widowed women and men between the ages of 55 and 89, 28% reported establishing new and "important" relationships after their spouse died. Women were more likely than men to form new relationships, and relationships with neighbors were frequently cited (Lamme et al., 1996). Some of those relationships (10% of those for the women and 5% of those for the men) were friendships. Unfortunately,

Lamme and associates did not indicate how many of those new friendships were with members of the other sex. When Babchuk and Anderson discovered significant similarities in the friendships of elderly widows and married women they concluded that losing a spouse through death probably does not drastically change the friendship network of the newly widowed individual. They also observed that 19% of the 75 widows in their study established all of their friendships after their husbands died. How many of those friends were cross-sex ones was not revealed.

Widowhood has different ramifications for friendships depending on whether the surviving spouse is a man or a woman (Allan & Adams, 1989; Johnson & Barer, 1997). It generally seems to have less of an isolating effect on women than men (Allan & Adams, 1989). If a woman loses her spouse around the normal time of widowhood she will probably have same-sex friends who have also lost their spouses. Although most of the friends of widows are same-sex ones who are widowed themselves (Allan & Adams, 1989; Blau, 1961), some of those widows are friends with the husbands of their same-sex friends (Allan & Adams, 1989). Less often, widows may have cross-sex friends whose spouses have also died (O'Connor, 1993). Widowhood precipitates a change in the widow's social network as she increases the number of widows in her friendship network and decreases the number of married friends (Morgan et al., 1997). Decreasing the number of married friends restricts structural opportunities those widows might have for forming cross-sex friendships with the husbands of their married same-sex friends. Johnson and Barer (1997) noted that in the transition from marriage to widowhood, more than half of the women in their early 70s are still married, but that statistic drops to around 29% for women between the ages of 75 to 79 (for comparable statistics see Lamme et al., 1996). Those widows typically continue their same-sex friendships, often with friends who are also widowed. In contrast, because men tend to marry younger women and women live 6 or 7 years longer than men (Harvard Health Letter, December, 1999), when a man loses his wife to death he is not likely to have a number of other male friends who have experienced the same loss (Johnson & Barer, 1997). Some widowed men in their 60s and 70s may be willing to initiate new cross-sex friends to take the place of their deceased same-sex ones (Field, 1999), but it is not unusual for men in their 80s to lose interest in friendships (Field, 1999).

In addition to the primary structural barriers already identified (i.e., physical immobility, retirement, and marital status) other structural considerations impact cross-sex friendships. Those additional structural barriers are not independent of the primary structural ones. As noted earlier in this book, structural factors are interrelated (Allan & Adams, 1989). One of the additional structural factors is proximity. About one third of the 30 million older adults in America live alone (Harvard Health Letter, May, 1999). Living close enough to a friend to interact with him or her on a semi-regular basis is important for maintenance of the friendship. In Blieszner and Adams' (1998) investigation of problems in older adult friendships, one of the difficulties with friendships is that they sometimes just "fade away" because of geographic distance or physical immobility. However, research has also shown that when physical disability prevents face-to-face interaction older individuals compensate by using the phone and writing letters (Johnson & Troll, 1994). Physical proximity is also not an issue with online friendships (Parks & Floyd, 1996). However, research in the area of online cross-sex friendships of older adults is nonexistent.

Proximity issues are also relevant to intergenerational cross-sex friendships (O'Connor, 1993). Different social networks lead to different access to various kinds of people and relationships (Lamme et al., 1996). Older individuals living in age-segregated environments such as retirement communities, age-segregated housing, and long-term care facilities, have different social networks than older individuals living in age-integrated environments such as residential neighborhoods and age-integrated housing (Blieszner & Adams,1992). Those who are in age-segregated housing would have less structural opportunities for intergenerational cross-sex friendship development than those living in residential neighborhoods and age-integrated housing.

Wright noted that structural factors are sometimes as straightforward as the availability of certain kinds of potential partners (1989). Along these lines, overall life expectancies for women and men respectively are 79 and 73 (Harvard Health Letter, December, 1999). Because women live longer than men, males in late life have considerably more potential cross-sex friends to chose from than do women. The difference between women and men in life expectancy might explain why older men often have more cross-sex friends than older women (Booth & Hess, 1974; Jones & Vaughn, 1990; Nussbaum et al., 1989; Werking, 1997a). The fact that men tend to marry younger women coupled with the greater life expectancy of females helps to explain the disproportionate number of women when compared to men who are widowed (Talbott, 1998), and the greater number of studies done on widowed women when compared to widowed men (Bryant & Hansson, 1995).

Despite the structural impediments interfering with cross-sex friendships in old age, new structural opportunities also present themselves. Potts made note of an important and growing social trend, (i.e., healthy older adults living in different types of age-segregated retirement and housing communities; 1997). Two theories of aging have particular relevance to structural constraints and facilitators of cross-sex friendships during old age. Proponents of the "activity theory of aging" (Havighurst & Albrecht, 1953) posit that when people grow old they develop new roles and activities to take the place of the ones they no longer fill or do not fill to the same extent. For example, when an individual's children become adults and he or she retires from the workplace, that person will have freedom to pursue other roles and activities. On the other hand, proponents of the somewhat competing and contradictory "disengagement theory of aging" (Cumming & Henry, 1961) maintain that as individuals age they not only become less active in the roles they occupy but are also less likely to enact new roles. Potts (1997) observed that gerontologists have debated the comparative validity and relative merits of these two theories for decades. Both of these theories could be fruitfully applied to cross-sex friendship formation and maintenance but to this date no such research has been conducted. For example, the activity theory of aging suggest that with the decline in responsibilities of parental and organizational roles, individuals will have more time to establish same-sex and cross-sex friendships. Conversely, the disengagement theory of aging suggest that because of diminished energy and declining physical health, individuals might be less willing to take on new cross-sex friendships or exert much energy toward maintaining the ones that they do have (see also Carstensen's socioemotional selectivity theory, 1993).

Cross-Sex Friendships Affect and are Affected by an Individual's Ongoing Social Construction of Self During Old Age

According to the interpersonal self perspective adopted in this book (Markus & Cross, 1990; Tice & Baumeister, 2001), an individual's view of self in old age is influenced by his or her relationships and the cognitive and social processes that accompany those relationships. How large of a role cross-sex friendships play in an older person's self-concept is difficult to know because of a lack of research directly addressing the topic. Equally difficult is determining what effect, if any, an older person's socially constructed view of self has on the initiation and maintenance of cross-sex friendships. Nevertheless, inferences may be drawn from the rather anemic literatures on cross-sex friendships of older adults, the schemas representing those friendships, and the self-concepts of individuals who comprise those relationships.

Because a person can have a specific type of relational schema even if he or she has never been in that kind of relationship (Honeycutt, 1993), individuals who have never had a cross-sex friendship would still have mental representations of what those friendships are like. Therefore, regardless of the level of experience individuals have had with cross-sex friendships, by the time they turn 65 their cross-sex friendship schemas are well established. Note that I wrote well established rather than well developed (although the schema could be both). Just because a schema is well established does not necessarily mean that it is intricate or well developed. Like other relational schemas (Baldwin, 1995) cross-sex friendship schemas are the result of a lifetime of direct and indirect experiences with that kind of relationship. For some, a lifetime of experiences may amount to little more than handful of such experiences, for others it could entail thousands of interactions and dozens of relationships. Direct experience means involvement in actual cross-sex friendships. Indirect experience would include such things as observation of the cross-sex friendships of others and exposure to mass media portrayals of cross-sex friendships (Honeycutt & Cantrill, 2001; Werking, 1995).

Because cross-sex friendships in old age (or any age for that matter) are not all the same (Wright, 1989), one can reasonably infer that neither are the schematic representations of those friendships. Cross-sex friendship schemas, regardless of when they may have been initially formed, would include (among other things) beliefs about the advantages and disadvantages of cross-sex friendships, behavioral scripts to enact in those relationships (Schank & Abelson, 1977), value judgments about male–female friendships, and information about the possible relational trajectories of cross-sex friendship (Andersen, 1993). Some individuals might have had cross-sex friendships since they were in elementary school. Indeed, specific cross-sex friendships might have originated 40 years earlier (Field, 1999). Scholars know practically nothing about cross-sex friendships with such a rich history. Although researchers know that many older individuals have friendships dating back 20 to 50 years (Field, 1999; O'Connor, 1993; Roberto, 1997), they know nothing about cross-sex friendships that originated in early childhood and still exist in old age. Life history qualitative interviews conducted by Matthews suggest that life-long cross-sex friendships are very rare (1986).

There are no studies on cross-sex friendship schemas of the elderly, or if there are I was unable to discover them. However, one can make educated guesses about what those schemas might look like based on the self-reports of cross-sex friends and individuals without those friendships. Studies in which participants describe their cross-sex friendships (or explain why they do not have them) allow inferences to be drawn about the cross-sex friendship schemas of the participants. For example, the cross-sex friendship schemas of most of the elderly women in Adams' study apparently involved beliefs that such relationships were equivalent to romantic ones and therefore should be avoided (1985). Quite different from the older women in Adams' study, interview comments from the "frail elderly" in O'Connor's study suggested they had cross-sex friendship schemas portraying those relationships as essentially nonromantic, caring, and necessary friendships (1993). If schemas direct and guide behavior and communication in relationships as suggested by Baldwin's relational schema theory (1992, 1995), then a reasonable conjecture is that the cross-sex friendship behaviors and attitudes exhibited and reported by subjects in O'Connor and Adams' investigations were products of their cross-sex friendships schemas.

Because schemas can exist at varying levels of conscious awareness (A. J. Wells, 1992), an older person with only a few cross-sex friendship experiences dating back to an earlier stage of life might have a cross-sex friendship schema that is dormant. Furthermore, the cross-sex friendship schema that an individual carries into old age is not etched in stone or cast in cement. Despite the fact that relational schemas are sometimes stubborn and resistant to change (Fiske & Taylor, 1984), they are also dynamic and malleable (Andersen, 1993). Like other relational schemas, cross-sex friendship schemas can change even in advanced old age. Recall that some senior citizens change their criteria for friendship as they lose their existing friendships to death and relocation (Field, 1999; Jerrome & Wenger, 1999; Roberto, 1997). Hypothetically, for the better part of his life an 85-year-old man's cross-sex friendship schema might have contained beliefs that such friendships were "not appropriate" or "too much work" or "not necessary because I have plenty of (same-sex) friends." However, he might readjust his thinking (schema) about the value of a cross-sex friendship as his same-sex friends pass away. Indeed, some old men do initiate cross-sex friendships although they may not have had that kind of friendship before (Field, 1999). Close to 60% of men and women over the age of 65 establish new friendships (Johnson & Barer, 1997). However, remember that some men lose interest in friendship when they get very old (Field, 1999; Johnson & Troll, 1994). Losing or gaining interest in cross-sex friendships is evidence that cross-sex friendship schemas have changed.

In addition to a general cross-sex friendship schema in old age, individuals also have separate relational schemas for each cross-sex friendship. As observed by Baldwin (1992), "self schemas and other schemas (note: by other he means schemas for the other person in the relationship) can be defined as generalizations or theories about self and other in particular relational contexts that are used to guide the processing of social information" (p. 468). The comments of some of the participants in O'Connor's interviews with elderly people revealed bits and pieces of the cross-sex friendship schemas they had for particular cross-sex friendships. When commenting on a cross-sex friendship that had lasted 40 years, an 88-year old woman observed "He's about the closest friend I've got. I've known him so many years. He's not a stranger. We're like brother and sister" (1993, p. 26).

In summary, there is considerable variability in the cross-sex friendship schemas of older Americans. The variability is partly a product of the different cross-sex friendship experiences accumulated over a lifetime. Furthermore, as individuals go through the stages of old age (young-old, old-old, very old), there may be additional changes in the content and structuring of their cross-sex friendship schemas. Whatever form a cross-sex friendship schema has assumed in old age, that schema and the accompanying behavioral manifestation of it influences an older person's self-concept. In turn, the self-schema impacts the cross-sex friendship schema. In order to better understand the reciprocal influence between self- and cross-sex friendship schemas let me provide a little information about self-concepts (i.e., self-schemas) in old age.

Recall that a person's self-concept can be conceptualized as a set of interrelated self-schemas (A. J. Wells, 1992). Those self-schemas include core and role aspects of self—both of which are discussed in more detail a bit later (Markus & Nurius, 1986; A. J. Wells, 1992). Old age and changes in self-concept go hand-in-hand (Johnson & Barer, 1997; Labouvie-Vief et al., 1995). Even allowing for considerable individual differences, when a person begins to see him or herself as old, and/or is seen by others in that way via reflected appraisals (Cooley, 1902), that individual's self-concept changes (Hansson & Carpenter, 1994). How much change occurs and the nature of those changes is a common topic of investigation. For example, a recent survey of 150 adults over the age of 85 revealed that the majority did not see any significant change in their personality and believed they were pursuing a life style begun and developed in earlier stages of their life (Troll & Skaff, 1997). Similarly, research on the self-definitions of 516 older people documented that they saw themselves as active and present-oriented (Freund & Smith, 1999). Also increasingly apparent is that the self-views of those over the age of 84 (the "very old") are different from those in their late 60s and early 70s (the so-called "young-old"; Freund & Smith, 1999; Johnson & Barer, 1997). Many individuals over the age of 85 see themselves as "survivors" who have become accustomed to less social contact, and even enjoy it (Johnson & Barer, 1999). Some of these very old individuals deliberately withdraw from social relationships. As observed by Johnson and Barer in their book *Life Beyond 85 Years: The Aura of Survivorship*, "Our findings suggest that with advanced old age, the desired level of social involvements tends to decrease, and individuals develop the capacity to be alone. Thus they may cherish peaceful solitude rather than experience the discomfort of loneliness" (1997, p. 156). Johnson and Barer's observation is strangely reminiscent of Larson's similar point about adolescents savoring the time they had alone (1999).

From the interpersonal self perspective adopted in this book, an older person's self-concept is largely a product of his or her social relationships (Markus & Cross, 1990). That generalization might be less true for older individuals who have deliberately withdraw from personal relationships. However, many elderly persons maintain friendships and relationships with family members (Johnson & Barer, 1997; O'Connor, 1993). Furthermore, from a life-cycle perspective, the self-concept of an older person would be affected by past as well as present relationships. For example, an important cross-sex friendship from a previous stage of life might have changed the way an individual viewed herself and cross-sex friendships, although the friendship itself might have faded away.

The core aspects of a person's self-concept involve relatively stable generalizations and beliefs about oneself (A. J. Wells, 1992). By the time a person enters old age many of those core aspects are a product of decades of development. They may gradually change with age as individuals begin to see themselves differently than they did in adulthood, but some research indicates that individuals over 85 do not see themselves as changing in personality from adulthood (Troll & Skaff, 1997). However, when old age eventually catches up with them and their physical and/or mental abilities begin to noticeably decline their core beliefs about themselves might change. Some research suggest that cognitive self-representations of older individuals reflect less of an ability than middle-aged adults to think in terms of complexity and transformation

(Labouvie-Vief et al., 1995). If this is true, then older individuals who have not had cross-sex friends in their life may find it difficult to transform their thinking about those kinds of friendships.

The roles that a person occupies are part of his or her self-concept (Mead, 1934). For example, occupational roles (factory worker, medical doctor, grocery clerk), family roles (wife, son, sister, grandfather), community roles (volunteer, concerned citizen), and more informal roles (friend, next-door neighbor), all play a part in how a person views him or herself (A. J. Wells, 1992). Individuals undergo a restructuring and frequently a contraction of their roles as they age (Adams & Blieszner, 1989; Hansson & Carpenter, 1994; Rosow, 1985; Wright, 1989). Rosow argued that in old age the roles that a person occupied during adulthood, such as parent, school board member, wife, and employee, either no longer exist, or they exist in a modified form that renders them less vital, necessary, or fulfilling as they once were (1985; also see Cumming and Henry's disengagement theory of aging, 1961). If roles do influence an individual's self concept, then a restructuring or elimination of roles would certainly modify those self-concepts. Wright's (1989) observations about the fusion of roles is also applicable to changing self-concepts and their potential relationship to cross-sex friendships. A common fusion of roles is the combination of friendship and work relationship roles. When individuals retire from the workplace and subsequently lose their organizational role they may also inadvertently lose the friendship role that was attached to it.

Friendship scholars know very little about how the restructuring of roles that accompanies old age influences cross-sex friendship. We know even less about the interrelationships between restructured roles, cross-sex friendships, and changes in self-concepts. Earlier I proposed that retirement from the workforce could potentially end cross-sex friendships that originated in an organization and depended on it for their existence. Some individuals identify so strongly with their workplace persona that loss of that role could have a serious impact on their self-view. Recall that individuals value their friendships because they affirm positive characteristics of the individual (Wright, 1984). To the extent that workplace friendships validate an individual's sense of identity, that view of self might be impacted by the loss of the organizational role. Carstensen's socioemotional selectivity theory predicts that friendships (i.e., informal roles) that are more costly than beneficial are likely to be discontinued at any point in the life cycle, but especially during old age (1993, 1995). That same theory predicts that individuals may go out of their way to maintain friendships, including cross-sex ones, that originated from organizational roles if those friendships were instrumental in meeting emotional needs.

The symbolic interactionists examined periodically throughout this book took an active interest in the concept of roles and how roles impact a person's self-concept. Theorists like Cooley (1902; 1909) and Mead (1934) contended that the social world and oneself are quite puzzling until participants with the help of oth-

ers construct some kind of meaning and order from the chaos. Part of these socially organized systems of knowledge includes the roles that individuals occupy,
roles that are a product of social interaction and negotiation. As observed by A. J.
Wells, "Self is seen as an internal cognitive representation of a set of public characteristics and roles which are used in interaction with others" (1992, p. 162).
When roles are modified or eliminated as they commonly are in old age, changes
in self views are likely to accompanying those role changes.

Now that we have a little background information on cross-sex friendship
schemas and self-concepts of older individuals, we can proceed to the issue of how
self-schemas are related to gender and friendship schemas. Despite a rather large
(but fragmented) literature on gender schemas (for a good review of gender development see Ruble & Martin, 1998), investigators have not directly explored
the connection between gender schemas and same-sex and cross-sex friendship
schemas. Researchers have studied gender differences in friendships among the
elderly (e.g., Adams et al., 2000; Barer, 1994; Field, 1999; Roberto & Kimboko,
1989; Smith & Baltes, 1998; Wright, 1989), but they have not linked those differences to where they likely came from (i.e., the friendship and gender schemas of
older individuals). Relatedly, the purported loosening of sex roles that occurs in
old age (Belsky, 1992) has not explicitly been linked to changing gender schemas.

I make the same assumption about gender schemas that I did about cross-sex
friendship schemas (i.e., by the time an individual enters old age he or she has
fairly firm gender schemas in place), but those schemas are subject to change
(Belsky, 1992). Part of those cognitive representations would entail beliefs and
attitudes about appropriate male and female behavior and relationships. Gender schemas, like other types of cognitive structures and processes, would also
have emotional components (Planalp & Fitness, 1999). The gender schema of
an elderly person might be considerably more complex if the individual is gay,
lesbian, or bisexual, than if she or he was heterosexual. My contention is that an
older person's gender schema, just like the gender schemas of individuals in
other stages of life, influences that person's friendship schemas. Those schemas,
in turn, influence and are influenced by the older person's self-schema.

Not surprisingly, there have been no direct empirical investigations of the relationship between the self-concepts of the elderly and their cross-sex friendships. Researchers exploring the relationship of self-concepts to old-age
friendships have not distinguished between cross-sex and same-sex friendships.
For example, in Roberto's longitudinal investigation, 100 women were interviewed in 1978 and again in 1992 about their close friends (1997). The same 11
interview questions were posed at Time One and Time Two. Three of the questions were directly related to conceptions of self. Only three of the 74 women
named men as close friends. Roberto discovered that over a 14-year period
women became less willing to self-disclose negative things about themselves.
Unfortunately, no information was provided by Roberto concerning differences
between cross-sex and same-sex friendships on the identity questions. Ignoring

cross-sex friendships when they are already part of the established sample is reminiscent of similar oversights noted throughout this volume by researchers studying friendships in other stages of the life cycle.

Arguably, gender, self, and friendship schemas of older individuals are linked to communication occurring between those individuals. Social constructivists (e.g., Vygotsky, 1987), social constructionists (e.g.,Berger & Luckmann, 1966; Gergen, 1985), symbolic interactionists (e.g., Mead, 1934), and attachment theorists (e.g., Bowlby, 1969) each in different ways emphasize the role of communication in building mental representations of relationships. All the theorists stress that the schemas reflecting the relationships emerge from interaction with one's friend. Unfortunately, none of aforementioned theories has been applied to old-age cross-sex friendships. However, inferences may be drawn from existing work. For example, in Johnson and Troll's study of friendships of individuals over the age of 84 ($n = 111$), "good communication" was the most frequently mentioned characteristic of a close friendship (1994). Although the researchers did not report how many, if any, of the friendships were cross-sex ones, the friendship schemas of the participants apparently involved beliefs about the benefits of good communication in a friendship. Those beliefs would influence communication occurring in the friendship. Those communications would in turn influence the friendships and their accompanying schematic representations which would have an impact on the self-views of the participating friends.

Concluding Observations

Conclusions about benefits of cross-sex friendships in old age, social and structural barriers to their formation and maintenance, and the impact of those friendships on self-concepts must be cautiously drawn. The old age cross-sex friendship literature is woefully inadequate. After all, only about 10 studies have produced findings directly relevant to cross-sex friendships of the elderly. Most of those investigations were friendship studies in which cross-sex friendships were more of an afterthought than a central theoretical and methodological concern. To make matters worse, the majority of those studies concentrated on older women and ignored or marginalized their male counterparts. Many more studies need to be conducted before firm and empirically defensible conclusions can be confidently drawn. Additionally, future investigations should be longitudinal rather than cross-sectional in nature (Adams, 1989; Wright, 1989). As noted by Roberto (1997), most of what we know about older adult friendships is based on cross-sectional studies (but see Adams, 1987; Field, 1999; Roberto, 1997). From a developmental and life-span perspective, longitudinal studies are a necessity if we are to understand the complicated dynamics of cross-sex friendships in the last stage of life (Adams, 1989).

With the previously mentioned caveats in mind, I end this chapter with some conclusions about the cross-sex friendships of older Americans. Although conclusions derived from such a small data base must be seen as tentative, they are also suggestive of new avenues of research. I emphasize my first conclusion more heavily than the rest because of its relevance to the three themes and developmental approach of this book.

Although cross-sex friendships are somewhat of an anomaly in the *present generation* of older Americans (averaged across studies, roughly 15-20% of older Americans have cross-sex friends), results of investigations of earlier life stages suggest that cross-sex friendships will be considerably more common in *future generations* of older citizens. From the life-span perspective adopted in this book, the likelihood of having cross-sex friendships in old age is largely (but not exclusively) determined by the number and quality of cross-sex friendships individuals had in earlier stages of life. The older men and women comprising the samples of the studies reviewed in this chapter grew up in a time when cross-sex friendships were much rarer than they are today. Although statistical data prior to 1974 (Booth & Hess) is hard to come by, friendship experts seem to agree that cross-sex friendship is a relatively recent evolution in relationships (Werking, 1997a; Wright, personal communication, January, 2001). For example, Matthews (1986) conducted in depth, qualitative biographical interviews with 62 participants over the age of 60. She asked "Have you ever been friends with someone of the other gender?" As observed by Matthews "almost none of the informants cited as friends persons of the other gender" (p. 91). In stark contrast, when I asked a similar question in 1998 of 188 college students 75% of those students reported that they had a good cross-sex friendship at some point in their life that had provided protection against loneliness.

Cross-sex friendships are fairly common today in early childhood, adolescence, and adulthood (see chaps. 2, 4, and 5, this volume). When individuals who are now children, teenagers, and adults become older Americans they will be more likely than current and previous generations of older Americans to establish cross-sex friendships because they are accustomed to doing so. As cross-sex friendships become more common for future generations of older Americans, the unique and generic benefits of those friendships become more salient and the social and structural barriers become less daunting.

My second conclusion focuses on how older individuals define cross-sex friendships. A number of scholars whose work I reviewed made a point of addressing how older adults define friendship and how those definitions change over the life cycle and stages of older adulthood (e.g., Adams, 1985; Field, 1999; Johnson & Troll, 1994; O'Connor, 1993; Roberto, 1997). Adams claimed with some empirical support that elderly women define cross-sex friendships as romantic relationships (1985), and that older men and women emphasize different definitional qualities of friendship (Adams et al., 2000). In Roberto's longitudinal study of 74 older women she discovered significant changes in 7 of the 11 definitional qualities used to describe friends in 1978 when compared to 1992. Roberto's findings lend support to the claim made by scholars that friendships and the importance of certain friendship characteristics change across the life cycle (Hartup & Stevens, 1997; Hays, 1988). Along those lines, Field (1999) concluded that as individuals grow older they are more selective in what friends they retain, and that the general importance given to friendships may change. Similarly, in their study of 111 respondents over the age of 84 Johnson and Troll (1994) discovered that it was not uncommon for respondents to gradually change their definition of friendship so it could be extended to include acquaintances such as hired help. To sum it all up, in their study of friendship patterns of women and men ages 55 to 87 years old Adams and her colleagues concluded "It is not appropriate to assume that people share common criteria for friendship" (Adams et al., 2000). The problem with almost all of the aforementioned studies is that no attempt was made to systematically investigate differences and similarities in how older individuals view and define cross-sex and same-sex friendship and whether gender differences in those views exist and can be traced back to earlier stages of life.

Now let me directly address the central theoretical premise of the book. Although there is evidence suggesting that self-concepts are dynamic and can change in old age (Demo, 1992; Johnson & Barer, 1997; Labouvie-Vief et al., 1995), and documentation supporting the interpersonal self claim that relationships impact self-concepts (Markus & Cross, 1990), there is no direct substantiation of my claim that cross-sex friendships influence self-views of the elderly. By this I mean there have been no studies designed with the expressed purpose of investigating if cross-sex friendships impact or are impacted by the self-concepts of people over the age of 65. Nevertheless, studies establishing that cross-sex friends in old age give one another social support provides indirect validation of my claim that self-concepts and cross-sex friendships are related (e.g., Adams & Blieszner, 1995; Adams et al., 2000; Morgan et al., 1997; O'Connor, 1993; Potts, 1997). A reasonable inference is that the mutual social support given and received in any friendship would have positive influences on the self-concepts of both individuals. For instance, Wright (1984) proposed that good friends help each other maintain positive self-views through the giving and receiving of various manifestations of social support. Along similar lines, the act of reminiscing (itself a type of social support) among older people has been shown to be useful in defending self-esteem and belief systems (Priefer & Gambert, 1984).

I conclude this chapter with a brief reidentification of central developmental milestones in old age that are relevant to cross-sex friendship initiation and maintenance. These milestones typically occur gradually over the three sub-phases of older adulthood (i.e., young-old, 65 to 74 years old; old-old, 75 to 84 years old; and very old, 85+). Three of the more significant developmental milestones are retirement, widowhood, and diminishing physical and cognitive capabilities. All three have already been discussed so I will not repeat my analysis here. I do wish to reiterate, however, that there has been no direct research on the effect of retirement on already existing cross-sex friendships. Investigators employing longitudinal research designs, for example, could trace a group of cohorts from 5 years prior to retirement to 5 years after retirement to see if close and casual cross-sex friendships established in the workplace still existed 5 years after retirement and if the defining characteristics of those friendships differ at the two points in time.

Similarly, the impact of the death of one's spouse on cross-sex friendship initiation and maintenance has received no direct research attention. There have been a number of studies of how widowhood impacts an individual's social network, but none of them specifically focused on the cross-sex friendships in that network and most of them concentrated on widows rather than widows and widowers. Prevailing thought and some empirical research indicates there may be gender differences in how the death of a spouse influences cross-sex friendship initiation and maintenance (Hansson & Carpenter, 1994; Johnson & Barer, 1997). However, there is still much work to be done and many interesting questions to explore. For example, scholars do not know for sure if good cross-sex friends might be viewed by those with deceased spouses as surrogate spouses. No one has investigated if the other-sex companionship lost when a spouse dies can be replaced by cross-sex friendship companionship. Some of these ideas are hinted at in existing studies. For example, in O'Connor's study of the frail elderly, all of whom appeared to be widowed, she concluded that some of the cross-sex friendships were pseudospousal in nature (1993).

I believe the most relevant and powerful developmental milestone impacting cross-sex friendship initiation and maintenance is the gradual (or sudden) diminishing of physical and cognitive abilities. Recently the World Health Organization devised a new measure of longevity called "disability adjusted life expectancy" (AKA "DALE"; Economist, 2000). DALE is a estimate of how long a person can expect to live in good health, which is generally 7 years less than his or her total life expectancy. Assuming these statistics are correct, women with an average life expectancy of 79 can expect to be in good health until around the age of 72. Men, with an average life expectancy of 73, can expect to be in good health until about the age of 66. Therefore, as a general conclusion, women can expect to be in relatively good health for at least the first 5 or 6 years of "old age" (65 and older); whereas men have considerably less time. As the health of women and men decline and they subsequently become less mobile their opportunity to pursue friendships, cross-sex and otherwise, declines (Johnson & Barer, 1997). An interesting area of study would be to investigate how computer technology has been utilized by older individuals immobolized by physical infirmity to keep in touch with old friends and initiate new ones. The topic of online friendships is a provocative one, and although research in the area has only just begun it is an area bound to see more attention in the near future (see e.g., Adams, 1998; Parks & Floyd, 1996; Parks & Roberts, 1998). At a minimum, one would think that online friendships could help combat the effects of social loneliness (i.e., the feeling of being socially isolated; Weiss, 1973).

7

Cross-Sex Friendships and Self-Concepts From the "Cradle to the Grave"

Judy teasingly points out to John how he always likes to be right. John has never noticed this about himself; however, now that Judy has pointed it out to him he recognizes and accepts that this is indeed a feature of his character. Seeing himself through Judy's eyes changes his view of himself.

— D. Cocking & J. Kennett (1998, p. 505)

The friendship between John and Judy and the obvious impact it has on John's self-concept could occur in any stage of the life cycle. The near axiomatic proposition that friends impact one another's self-concepts would apply regardless of whether Judy and John were 2 or 82. Luckily for me, the example given by Cocking and Kennett in the above quotation just happened to be a cross-sex friendship. In their provocative article, *Friendship and the Self*, they explore some of the ways friendships and self-concepts are related from a philosophical perspective (1998). I conduct a similar theoretical exploration in this chapter from a cognitive, communication, and contextual perspective as briefly previewed in the next paragraph.

The cognitive and communicative construction of self and cross-sex friendships begins in late infancy with internal working models (Bowlby, 1969) and continues into the twilight years of a person's life (Markus & Cross, 1990). Whether through reflected appraisals (Cooley, 1902), social perspective taking (Mead, 1934), consensual validation (Sullivan, 1953), or identification with cliques and crowds (Brown et al., 1994), self-concepts (i.e., self-schemas) are largely determined by family, friends, and less intimate others in the surrounding social network. Relatedly, as argued by social constructivists (e.g., Vygotsky, 1978), social constructionists (e.g., Berger & Luckmann, 1966; Gergen, 1985), scholars adopting a relational perspective (e.g., Yingling, 1994), and interpersonal self theorists (e.g., Bowlby, 1969), self-schemas are a product of communication that individuals have with members of their social network. Additionally and importantly, the construction of personal identity via interpersonal communication (Coover & Murphy, 2000) occurs in a social and cultural context (e.g., mass media influence), which impacts the participants (Adams & Allan, 1998). I begin a more detailed theoretical exploration of the cognitive, communication, and contextual influences on cross-sex friendships across the life cycle momentarily. For now I digress in order to make a confession concerning the writing of this book and my unintentional enlistment of a co-author.

Throughout the 3-year process of writing this book someone was always looking over my shoulder and giving me advice about what to write and how to write it. More often than not, his recommendations were not based on knowledge of the empirical and theoretical literature or careful scientific observation. Instead, his suggestions were grounded in his own personal experiences and informal observations. Those personal experiences included not only his own, but those of his three young children, his father, his friends, his mother-in-law, his male and female neighbors, his work associates, his wife, ad infinitum. Sometimes his counsel was useful and even insightful. At other times his advice was unsolicited and disrupted my presumed social scientific objectivity.

As the reader has no doubt deduced by now, the person looking over my shoulder for 3 years was myself. How much of this book was written with the help of the "me" looking over my shoulder is unknown, but there is little doubt that he (me) was deeply involved. Social science researchers and theoreticians, whether they admit it or not, are intimately intertwined in their own scholarly endeavors (Gergen & Gergen, 1991). Steier noted in the introduction to his edited volume on *Research and Reflexivity*, "As inquirers and researchers, we create worlds through the questions that we ask coupled with what we and others regard as reasonable responses to our questions … we as researchers construct that which we claim to 'find' … "(1991, p. 1). He goes on to observe that research is a self-reflexive process in that "what I describe in my research is in no way existent apart from my involvement in it-it is not 'out there'" (p. 1).

In line with Steier's observation, the theoretical perspective developed for this book was based on formal and informal observation of others around me and my analyses of relevant literatures. Formal observation included my own empirical research on cross-sex friendships and systematic critiques of existing literatures. Informal observation, in many ways more productive than its formal counterpart, included casual consideration of the cross-sex friendship processes of those around me, including myself. I could not help but notice, for example, that my 8-year-old son and 4-year-old daughter displayed attitudes toward cross-sex friends that closely mirrored attitudes predicted by the research on early (my daughter) and middle (my son) childhood cross-sex friendships. Similarly, my 75-year-old widowed mother-in-law confirmed through her behaviors many (but not all) of the hypotheses of scholars studying old-age friendships. Analogously, my teenage nieces and nephews verified that cross-sex friendships do exist and are important, but romantic couplings with non-cross-sex friends are usually of higher priority. As for myself, being a husband and a father of three children, I did not need empirical studies to convince me that middle-aged adults have difficulty finding time for friendships.

My formal and informal observation of others as "objects" for study would seem to make me the "knower," and what I discover about those objects the "known" (Gergen & Gergen, 1991). However, from a social constructionist and interpersonal self perspective, it is difficult to maintain a clear distinction between myself (i.e., the "knower") and what I purport to "discover" (i.e., the "known"). Like others who are the objects of my inquiry, I am also a product of my social relationships. Thus, the way I view the world (and present some of that view in this book) is at least partly a reflection of how others view me and I view others. I realize that not being able to fully separate myself from what I do (i.e., writing this book) makes my analysis appear less than scientifically objective. However, as noted by Gergen and Gergen (1991), researchers and theoreticians can accept that there is "no means of removing the observer from the production of scientific accounts" and still productively and fairly engage in the joint construction of knowledge with fellow researchers who may or may share one's view of social reality.

In summary, the writing of this book was a joint endeavor accomplished by the social scientific me and the less than scientific casual observer of my immediate and broader social environments. The scientific part of myself recognizes that my analysis of cross-sex friendship and self-concept development was less than objective in the traditional, social scientific sense. After all, I was always part of the social landscape I was surveying. Even at the age of 47, I can still remember fantasy play as a preschooler, trying not to get cooties from girls in elementary school, gender segregation in middle school, cliques and crowds in high school, and having to explain as a young adult the nature of my cross-sex friendships. I believe those memories of the less than scientific casual observer enriched rather than detracted from my understanding of cross-sex friendship and self-concept construction. From a symbolic interactionist perspective, I was and am one of the objects in the social environment that I purport to study.

Now let us move on to the business at hand (i.e., reviewing and integrating the cognitive, communication, and contextual factors that impact cross-sex friendships and self-concepts across the life cycle). My goal can be accomplished by following the same general organizational format employed throughout the first six chapters of this book. Therefore, this final chapter is divided into four sections. I begin with a summarizing and integrating section on the generic and unique benefits of cross-sex friendships throughout the life cycle. To a greater extent than in previous chapters, I propose how benefits in one stage of life are related to benefits in subsequent stages. In the second section I similarly summarize structural and social barriers to cross-sex friendships and offer suggestions on how those barriers might be interconnected across the different phases of the life span. In the third section I return to the central premise of the book that cross-sex friends impact and are impacted by an individual's ongoing social construction of self. That premise is visually depicted and developed through the presentation of two conceptual models. The first model illustrates the interrelationships between self-schemas, gender schemas, same-sex friendship schemas, and cross-sex friendship schemas. The second model depicts the relationship between the cross-sex friendship schemas of two individuals and how the commonality in those schemas represents a mutually understood and shared relational reality (Duck, 1994). The final section of the book is a mercifully short one in which I tie up some loose ends and draw some conclusions about cross-sex friendships across the cycle of life. The last paragraph in the book is a brief description of the *kitchen sink* (i.e., those things that could have been—and possibly should have been—included in the book). After reading a rough draft of this book, Paul Wright wisely counseled me to leave the sink out.

Cross-Sex Friendships and the Enrichment of Social Networks Throughout the Life Cycle

To contend that cross-sex friendships offer generic and unique benefits from the "cradle to the grave" might be an exaggeration, but it is not one of hyperbolic proportions. After all, when a close cross-sex friend has a significant impact on a person's view of self, that impact would continue even after the death of the friend. On the cradle end, certainly by the time individuals are 2 or 3 years of age they are capable of forming rudimentary cross-sex friendships (Howes, 1996). In chapter two I explored the possibility that repeated interactions between cross-sex infants are precursors to cross-sex friendship, if not actual friendships themselves. Social constructivists maintain that the internal representation and understanding of a construct such as friendship originates from interpersonal interaction (Vygotsky, 1978). Initial interactions between infants form the basis for elementary friendship schemas (Howes, 1996). Seventy or 80 years later those same individuals might still be initiating and maintaining friendships with members of the other sex and reaping their benefits (Field, 1999).

Between the two anchors of the time continuum (for example, 2 to 102), cross-sex friendships manifest themselves differently to reflect the developmental stage in which they occur. In early childhood (ages 18 months to 6 years) coordinated play and fun are benefits at the center of cross-sex friendship interactions (Gottman, 1986). In middle and late childhood (ages 7 to 11) gossip and overlapping social phenomena such as self-disclosures become the central communicative processes of cross-sex friends that facilitate the bestowing of mutual advantages (Parker & Gottman, 1989). Cross-sex friends during adolescence (ages 12 to 17) serve as other-sex guides in self-exploration, identity development, and traversing the social labyrinths of crowds and cliques (Cotterell, 1996; Rawlins, 1992). Adolescent cross-sex friendships also pave the way for more mature romantic and work relationships in adulthood (Furman & Shaffer, 1999). Friendships between men and women in adulthood (ages 18 to 64) provide sexual gratification (Afifi & Faulkner, 2000), insider persp :ctives (Rubin, 1985; Sapadin, 1988), and various forms of social support (Wer.:ing, 1997a). Cross-sex friends in old age (ages 65 and over) take the place of deceased same-sex ones (Field, 1999), provide intergenerational perspectives (O'Connor, 1993), and serve as confidantes (Babchuk & Anderson, 1989). There are documented instances of cross-sex friends providing generic and unique benefits at both ends of the life cycle and every stage in between.

Even when working from a severely underdeveloped cross-sex friendship literature (Monsour, 1997; Werking, 1997a), giving examples of benefits provided by cross-sex friendships in various stages of the life cycle is not a difficult task. However, demonstrating that there are developmental connections between and within life stages that link those benefits together is considerably more challenging. There are dozens of interesting and important questions that need answers. For example, in what ways, if any, do insider perspectives and other-sex companionship provided by cross-sex friends before puberty impact the perception of those perspectives and companionship after puberty? Relatedly, if a child had one or more quality cross-sex friendships in middle childhood, would that child view subsequent cross-sex friendships in later stages of the life cycle differently from a cohort who did not have cross-sex friendships in middle childhood, but who now has them in adolescence? Are there gender differences in the perception of generic and unique benefits of cross-sex friendships, and are those gender differences a product of underlying developmental changes? Does success in cross-sex friendships during adolescence have anything to do with having successful cross-sex workplace relationships as an adult? For instance, are women and men who had quality cross-sex friendships in childhood and adolescence less likely to engage in sexual harassment in the workplace than those who did not have those friendships? How does perception of the unique benefits and challenges of cross-sex friendship change as a person goes from one stage of adulthood to another? Do the cross-sex friends of older individuals with recently deceased spouses offer a different kind of social support than their same-sex friends? Can the abilities of women and men (and girls and boys) to form successful cross-sex friendships be linked to their history of attachment with a primary caregiver? The lack of developmentally based longitudinal studies makes it difficult to provide answers to these questions and others like them.

Generic Benefits of Cross-Sex Friendships Across the Life Span.   There are important similarities in the generic benefits provided by cross-sex friendships in the different phases of the life cycle. Extant (although scant) literature on male–female friendships verify that those relationships provide an array of benefits such as social support, fun, companionship, and protection against loneliness. Social support in the form of affect, aid, and affirmation from cross-sex friends occurs at every juncture of the life span but has been better documented in young adulthood than any of the other stages. Many of the cross-sex friendship investigations reviewed in this book were not conducted as social support studies, but the central constructs explored by those scholars (e.g., companionship and intimacy) are manifestations of social support.

Friendship scholars have not specifically investigated how social support provided by cross-sex friends is manifested differently in the separate stages of the life cycle. Are affect, aid, and affirmation, the three broad categories of social support (Crohan & Antonucci, 1989), enacted differently by cross-sex friends in various stages of life? Knowing about such differences, if they do exist, is important if researchers are to unravel the complicated relationship between social support, cross-sex friendship, and health outcomes (Sarason et al., 1997). As reiterated throughout this book, the scientific and medical communities recognize the role of social support in promoting better physical and psychological health (Harvard Health Letter, May, 1999; Sarason et al., 1997). Friends are often the purveyors of social support. The convoy model of social support posits that individuals select certain relationships in life that will supply necessary support (Antonucci & Akiyama, 1987). Research reviewed in this book shows that cross-sex convoys are found in early childhood (Whaley & Rubenstein, 1994), middle childhood (Blomberg & Monsour, 1998), adolescence (Parker & Gottman, 1989), adulthood (Werking, 1997a), and old age (O'Connor, 1993).

Talking for the sake of talking, arguably a type of social support, is a generic benefit of cross-sex friendships across the life cycle. Talking serves somewhat different purposes depending on the stage of life in which it occurs, but the forms of talk are often similar. For example, gossip among cross-sex friends has been documented in early and middle childhood (Gottman, 1986; Parker & Gottman, 1989), adolescence (Parker & Gottman, 1989) and young adulthood (Leaper & Holliday, 1995). Although Adams did not specifically document gossip in older cross-sex friendships, she did imply through the title of her article, *People Would Talk: Normative Barriers to Cross-Sex Friendships for Elderly Women*, that the threat of gossip among elderly women might keep some of those women from forming cross-sex friendships (1985). In his book *Discreet Indiscretions*, Bergmann (1993) maintained that gossip is a form of social control in groups, an observation verified in the apparent attempts of some older women to control the cross-sex friendships of their peers through gossip (Adams, 1985). Gossip serves a slightly different function for cross-sex friends in each stage of life, but it always helps to solidify the friendship (for a comprehensive and insightful treatment of gossip as a social process see Bergmann, 1993).

Talking is how young cross-sex friends coordinate interactions for engagement in fantasy play (Gottman, 1986; Parker & Gottman, 1989). Rawlins similarly noted the importance of talking in the cross- and same-sex friendships of teenagers (1992) as did Duck and Wright in their analysis of adult friendships (1993). Field reported that many older individuals indicated that "just talking" was one of the joys of friendship (1999). Talking is the primary way that friends reap generic benefits of cross-sex friendship. It is also the means by which relationships are jointly constructed and mutually understood (Duck, 1994; 1995; Monsour, 1994; Spencer, 1994; Yingling, 1994).

Perhaps the most important generic benefit of cross-sex friendships is the protection they can provide against loneliness. Although some prominent early theorists maintained that children could not experience loneliness (e.g., Sullivan, 1953; Weiss, 1973), scholars now believe that loneliness is an inherent part of the human condition (Rotenberg, 1999) and that it impacts individuals in every stage of the life cycle (e.g., Perlman & Peplau, 1998). Parkhurst and Hopmeyer have recently theorized that loneliness as a developmental phenomena begins as early as late infancy (1999). The general position I have taken throughout this book is that cross-sex friendships serve as bulwarks against social and emotional loneliness. Casual cross-sex friendships are effective in helping an individual feel more integrated into his or her social network, which combats social loneliness. Good cross-sex friends provide the intimate connections that are necessary to ward off emotional loneliness. However, many individuals of varying ages (but especially in middle childhood, see chap. 3) do not have cross-sex friendships. Recognizing cross-sex friendships as a "viable interpersonal option" would double an individual's potential for establishing friendships and protecting him or her from loneliness (Rawlins, 1982, p. 351). Duck's empirically supported observation about loneliness, first cited in chapter one of this book, is worth repeating here: "Loneliness is fatal" (1983, p. 16).

I was unable to discover any studies specifically investigating the relationship between cross-sex friendships and loneliness. Meaning, there were no studies in which the *central goal* was to explore the association between cross-sex friendships and loneliness. However, there were a number of studies covering various stages of the life cycle in which friendships (both same and cross-sex) were directly or indirectly related to loneliness. For example, Whaley and Rubenstein's study of toddler friendships clearly demonstrated that losing a cross-sex friend can cause a toddler to display symptoms of loneliness (1994). Similarly, Kovacs and colleagues discovered that middle-aged children who have no same-sex friends will often turn to cross-sex ones for companionship and thus protection against loneliness (1996). Bukowski and associates (1999) make the same observation about individuals in early adolescence who form cross-sex friendships because they have no same-sex ones. Data that I collected in 1998 shows that young adults use cross-sex friendships as a protection against loneliness, as do some older adults (O'Connor, 1993).

Also missing from the literature are investigations focusing on developmental and life-cycle aspects of loneliness and cross-sex friendships. For instance, are children who form close cross-sex friendships in early childhood less susceptible to loneliness in middle childhood than children who do not form cross-sex friendships in early childhood? Similarly, are developmental changes such as

puberty and retirement related to loneliness and cross-sex friendship in different ways than they might be to loneliness and same-sex friendships? Are developmental milestones related in any systematic way to loneliness, self-concepts,
and cross-sex friendships? Can specific intervention programs aimed at mitigat-
ing loneliness in various stages of the life cycle increase their effectiveness by incorporating workshops on cross-sex friendship initiation and maintenance?
These questions and dozens more like them suggest areas of research that could
increase our understanding of the complicated dynamics involved in the relationship between loneliness, cross-sex friendships, and developmental issues.

Unique Benefits of Cross-Sex Friendships Across the Life Span.   Cross-
sex friends offer unique benefits in each stage of life. With some obvious exceptions such as sexual intimacy, the special advantages of cross-sex friendships are
more or less the same regardless of what stage of life is examined. What does
change, however, is the value placed on benefits like other-sex companionship
and insider perspectives. Although researchers do not know for certain, insider
perspectives on how members of the other sex think, feel, and behave may be
most valuable to heterosexual adolescents because of their increasing preoccu-
pation with members of the other sex (Buhrmester & Furman, 1986; Furman &
Wehner, 1993; Sullivan, 1953). Those same insider perspectives may be least
valued by kids in middle childhood who deliberately avoid members of the other
sex and are generally not interested in what makes them tick (Sroufe et al.,
1993). Preschoolers and toddlers may not even be cognitively aware that they
are getting insider perspectives, even once they reach the age where they can
differentiate between the sexes. The level of importance of insider perspectives
to older individuals is still open to question. Perhaps people in their 70s and 80s
believe they already understand how members of the other sex think, feel, and
behave, and thus do not need cross-sex friendships in order to acquire those
perspectives. If individuals do become less sex-typed and more androgynous in
old age than they were in earlier stages of life (Belsky, 1992; Guttman, 1987),
then insider perspectives may not be as needed as they were before.

Similarly, although other-sex companionship supplied by cross-sex friends
may be considered valuable for different reasons by heterosexual and homosexual adolescents and young adults (Monsour, 1988; Rawlins, 1992; Rubin, 1985;
Savin-Williams, 1990), it is actively shunned by many children in middle childhood (Sroufe et al., 1993), often not recognized for what it is by toddlers, and
not particularly cherished by many elderly women (Adams, 1985). On the other
hand, not all kids in middle childhood avoid cross-sex friendship (George &
Hartmann, 1996). Indeed, for some children cross-sex friendships may be the
only friendships they have (Kovacs et al., 1996). In those cases it may not be the
other-sex companionship that is valued so much as just companionship itself. In
like fashion, many elderly women do not place much value on having cross-sex
friends and the other-sex companionship they provide (Adams, 1985), but

some older men and women clearly appreciate the unique quality of their cross-sex friendships, illustrated by the tendency of those friendships to be "pseudospousal" in nature (O'Connor, 1993).

I have generally discussed protection against loneliness as a generic benefit of cross-sex friendship. However, those friendships could also offer a unique form of defense against the assaults of loneliness in certain stages of the life cycle. Heterosexual adolescents often have a preoccupying concern or need for companionship with members of the other sex (Buhrmester & Furman, 1986; Sullivan, 1953). Although that need might best be met by a romantic partner, cross-sex friends could serve as surrogate romantic partners by providing other-sex companionship and mutual validation as attractive members of the other sex (see Sippola, 1999 for a special issue of the *Journal of Youth and Adolescence*, that has some excellent articles on cross-sex friendships and romances in adolescence). Cross-sex friendships could also provide a unique kind of protection against loneliness for very old men who have lost their same-sex friends and spouses to death (Field, 1999; Matthews, 1986). Forming new same-sex friendships for men in their 80s may not be an option since most of their age-mates are dead (Johnson & Barer, 1997).

The unique benefits of cross-sex friendships have not been examined from a developmental or life-span perspective. For instance, scholars do not know to what extent the differing values placed on insider perspectives and other-sex companionship can be attributed to underlying developmental processes and change. If insider perspectives are more important to adolescents and young adults than they are to kids in early and middle childhood (which, by the way, investigators do not know for sure that they are), can the difference in importance be attributed to the onset of puberty? Relatedly, are those insider perspectives more, less, or equally important to homosexual adolescents just beginning to discover their sexual identities? Analogously, what impact do developmental milestones like getting married or entering the workplace have on the value placed on insider perspectives and other-sex companionship? Finally, how might insider perspectives and other-sex companionship differentially impact gender schemas of individual of different ages? These questions and many others like them suggest areas of research that could help expand our understanding of the special advantages that cross-sex friendship can offer throughout the life cycle.

Social and Structural Barriers to Cross-Sex Friendships Throughout the Life Cycle

Social and structural barriers inhibiting the initiation and maintenance of cross-sex friendships are relatively constant but only moderately documented features of the macro- and microlevel environments of individuals. The form and content of social and structural barriers might change from one stage of life to the next, but they always exist and typically are interrelated, overlapping, and jointly self-perpetuating. It is just as important, however, to acknowledge that there are also social and structural factors facilitating the formation of friendships between females and males of all ages (Blieszner & Adams, 1992). More precisely, those factors increase the likelihood of cross-sex interaction, which in turn augments the possibility of cross-sex friendship formation. Although one of the major goals of this book has been to identify and explain barriers to cross-sex friendships and not facilitators of those relationships, addressing one without acknowledging the other would misrepresent the impact of structure on friendship (Blieszner & Adams, 1992; Werking, 1997a).

At the larger, macrolevel of society, romantic couplings between heterosexual men and women are still considered the paradigmatic female–male relationship (Werking, 1997a). Expectations about the ideal form of male–female relationship flow from the deep structure of society and permeate every stage of the life cycle (Hartup & Stevens, 1997). The prevailing societal belief that the quintessential cross-sex relationship is a romantic one contributes to social and structural barriers to cross-sex friendships in different ways depending on the stage of life. In elementary school, girls and boys tease those with cross-sex friends about the suspected romantic nature of their relationship (Parker & Gottman, 1989; Thorne, 1987). Once youngsters leave childhood and enter adolescence, dramatically heralded by the onset of puberty, friendships with members of the other sex are generally of less developmental importance than romantic relationships (Sullivan, 1953). Although not quite as pronounced as it is in earlier stages of the life cycle, even in old-age, women and men may view relationships with one another as having undertones of romance (Adams, 1985; O'Connor, 1993).

Social Barriers to Cross-Sex Friendships Across the Life Span.   Social barriers to cross-sex friendships in every stage of life come from third parties and the cross-sex friends themselves. Barriers originating from third parties are potentially quite formidable. The formation of cross-sex friendships can be effectively blocked by the jealousy of a spouse (Rubin, 1985; Werking, 1997a), the taunting and teasing of middle-schoolers (Thorne, 1986), the suspicious glances of co-workers (Devine & Markiewicz, 1990; O'Meara, 1994), and the verbalized norms against cross-sex friendships common in some groups of elderly widows (Adams, 1985). Social obstacles flowing from the potential or actual cross-sex friends themselves include much-debated differences in the communication styles of females and males (see Wood & Dindia, 1998, for an example of that debate), O'Meara's four challenges (1989), and individual level variables such as social anxiety (Snell, 1989).

Despite my contention and earnest belief that social barriers to cross-sex friendships do exist, empirical verification of those barriers is relatively modest. Much more research needs to be conducted on how these barriers are manifested, the extent to which they actually impede cross-sex friendship formation, and the methods that individuals employ to overcome those stumbling blocks. A better understanding of the barriers interfering with cross-sex friendships is important so that strategies for dispatching those barriers can be formulated. Cross-sex friendships do provide important benefits, but those benefits are beyond reach if the friendships are not allowed to form and be maintained (O'Meara, 1994).

Social barriers to cross-sex friendship should be viewed from a life-span perspective. In a nutshell, cross-sex friendship experiences with social barriers in one stage of life influences cross-sex friendship experiences with social barriers in subsequent stages. Successful management of social barriers early in life should increase the probability of similarly successful negotiation of barriers later in life because an individual's self confidence and skill in overcoming obstacles has been bolstered. For example males and females who have positive cross-sex friendship experiences in early childhood (ages 18 months to 6 years) might handle social barriers to those friendships in middle childhood (ages 7 to 11) differently than individuals who had negative experiences in early childhood or no experiences at all. They would view and approach those barriers differently because their cross-sex friendship schemas would be different from individuals with negative or minimal cross-sex friendship experiences. Cross-sex friendship schemas would include (among other things) the benefits and disadvantages of those relationships (Baldwin's "declarative knowledge"; 1992), information about specific cross-sex friends (Baldwin's "other-schemas"; 1992), information about social barriers to those friendships (O'Meara's challenges), and strategies on how to deal with social barriers (Baldwin's "procedural knowledge"; 1992). Part of the cross-sex friendship experiential schema would also involve specific memories of interaction episodes with specific cross-sex others (Andersen, 1993).

What I am proposing (i.e., taking a life-span perspective on social barriers to cross-sex friendship), would in the best of all methodological worlds involve long-range longitudinal studies of the social barriers to cross-sex friendships. Ideally, a group of cohorts would be tracked from early childhood through old age. However, being a researcher myself, I know that such a life-long project might prove to be unmanageable and impractical for a number of reasons. Nevertheless, there is some precedent. The Berkeley Older Generation Study was started in 1928 with 470 young adults and continued through the 1980s with those participants who were still living (see Field, 1999). My proposal is much more modest; conducting longitudinal studies that cover the latter part of one life stage and the early part of the next. For example, tracking cohorts from age 4 to age 10 would cover the last 2 or so years of early childhood and the first 2 or 3 years of middle childhood. Data could be collected every 3 or 4 months (from age 4 to age 10) in order to capture the onset and demise of specific social barriers that are connected to specific life stages.

Social barriers to cross-sex friendships across the life-span may also profitably be viewed from a developmental perspective. A developmental perspective, in part, focuses attention on how underlying developmental processes in specific stages of the life cycle influence social barriers to friendships between men and women and boys and girls. As explained by Sippola and Bukowski (1999), developmental approaches to the study of relationships should account for the connections between "cognition, social needs, personal experiences, and the self" (p. 283). Each of these phenomena have been addressed throughout this book. Social barriers erected by cross-sex friends and members of their social network in particular stages of the life cycle reflect developmental processes occurring in those stages. An obvious example is how puberty, itself a developmental process, counteracts social barriers to cross-sex friendships that were erected during middle childhood when most children practiced gender segregation (which is also a developmental process). Although the pullings of puberty might encourage adolescent males and females to reinitiate contact with one another, puberty is also partly responsible for the sexual and romantic challenges that sometimes confront cross-sex friends in adolescence (Rawlins, 1992), adulthood (O'Meara, 1989), and even old age (Adams, 1985). Finally, as explained in chapter two of this volume, a developmental approach to the study of cross-sex friendships would be useful, perhaps even indispensable, in deciding when friendship as a developmental phenomenon first emerges in early childhood.

Structural Barriers to Cross-Sex Friendships Across the Life Span.   Structural barriers to cross-sex friendships in different stages of the life cycle have been only modestly investigated and verified. However, the impact of structure on friendship formation and maintenance is commonly acknowledged and written about by friendship authorities (for a few excellent examples, see Adams & Allan, 1998; Blieszner & Adams, 1992; Werking, 1997a). Scholars like Blieszner, Adams, and Allan contended, as do a host of others (e.g., Brown et al., 1994; Hartup & Stevens, 1997; O'Meara, 1994; Rawlins, 1992; Werking, 1997a; Wright, 1989), that structural factors are exceedingly important in understanding friendship processes. Structural constraints and facilitators determine the opportunities individuals have for interaction and friendship formation. However, as I repeatedly observed (and complained) throughout the book, for inexplicable reasons many friendship researchers have ignored explicit or detailed discussion of structural considerations in regards to cross-sex friendships (but see O'Meara, 1994; Werking, 1997a).

I identified a number of structural factors in this book; some more deterministic than others in facilitating and impeding cross-sex friendship formation across the life cycle. Additionally, certain factors are more relevant than others to specific life stages and cross-sex friendships within those stages. Foremost among those factors are gender segregation (in early and middle childhood; e.g.,

Leaper, 1994a), cliques/crowds and channeling (in adolescence; e.g., Brown et al., 1994), marital status and widowhood (in adulthood and old age; e.g., Booth & Hess, 1974; Rubin, 1985; Wright, 1989), sex and occupational segregation (in adulthood; O'Meara, 1994), physical immobility (in old age; Johnson & Barer, 1997), attending or not attending college (in young adulthood), and sexual orientation (across the life cycle; Savin-Williams, 1990, 1994). My list of structural factors is not comprehensive, but it does represent the major ones described in earlier chapters of the book.

I make the same life-cycle and development claim in regards to structural barriers that I made about their social counterparts (i.e., cross-sex friendship experiences with structural barriers in one stage of life impacts the experiences with structural barriers in subsequent stages). Similarly, developmental processes occurring in each stage of life that are relevant to cross-sex friendship processes affect and are affected by structural barriers and facilitators to cross-sex friendship formation. Although it is easy to give examples of structural barriers in different life stages and how they relate to cross-sex friendship initiation and maintenance, showing developmental connections between barriers crossing different life stages is quite another and more difficult matter. Once again, researchers need to conduct longitudinal investigations that track the rise and fall of specific structural barriers to cross-sex friendship formation. Scholars also need to focus more attention on what Adams and Allan referred to as the "overall constellation of structural characteristics" (1989). Meaning, in part, how are structural constraints and facilitators related to one another both within and across life stages?

Investigating how structural impediments in different stages of life are related to one another and cross-sex friendship formation has interesting potential. For instance, there appears to be some kind of continuity between gender segregation experienced in early and middle childhood and sex and occupational segregation in the workplace that occurs in young and middle adulthood. As observed by a number of scholars (Leaper, 1994b; Maccoby, 1994; Maltz & Borker, 1982; Mulac et al., 2001; Swain, 1992), one of the consequences of childhood gender segregation is that girls and boys develop different ways of relating to one another dyadically and in the context of their respective gender groups that can interfere with smooth interaction between the sexes later in life. There is also data suggesting that women and men in the workplace have different styles of interaction that are not that dissimilar from the patterns established years earlier in childhood (Tannen, 1995).

Cross-Sex Friendships and Self-Concepts Throughout the Life Cycle

The central premise of this book is that cross-sex friendships affect and are affected by an individual's ongoing and socially constructed concept of self throughout the cycle of life. As repeatedly reiterated throughout this book, my contention is that self-concepts and cross-sex friendships are cognitively linked through schematic connections and communicatively linked through interaction. Not only are self-concepts and cross-sex friendships connected through communication and cognitive schemas, but the schemas and communication are inseparably related as well (Planalp, 1985). The cognitive and communicative connections between cross-sex friendship and self-concepts take place in and are affected by broader contextual factors such as group memberships and mass media portrayals of cross-sex friendships.

In this section I present two conceptual models and describe how the models and the intermingling of schemas they represent change as individuals go through the life cycle. I also explain the relationship of communication to the cognitive processes depicted in each model and how the models adapt to reflect the accompanying stage of life. The conceptual models are designed as heuristic tools rather than comprehensive theoretical treatments. Wood offered a straightforward explanation of conceptual models and their strengths and limitations (1995). A conceptual model is a visual and/or verbal representation of a conceptual process (Wood, 1995). A good conceptual model clarifies a process by "defining and organizing important features and associations among them" (Wood, p. 41). The strength of conceptual models is also one of their primary weaknesses. Although conceptual models can simplify a labyrinthian process, the simplification can sometimes obscure or render invisible parts of the process they are designed to illuminate (Wood, 1995). Another inherent problem with conceptual models is that they cannot completely represent dynamics processes (Wood, 1995). Because schemas and relationships are processes and not static entities (Andersen, 1993; Arbib et al., 1987; Duck et al., 1997; Honeycutt & Cantrill, 2001), conceptual models of those processes are intrinsically limited.

Despite the limitations of conceptual models they are still quite useful if employed heuristically. A model has heuristic value if it is thought provoking and leads to insights about the phenomenon it represents (Wood, 1995). Empirical testing of some of the relationships suggested by the upcoming models is beyond the scope of this book. However, I have given examples of research projects that are indirectly supportive of the models. I have divided the rest of this section into two subsections. The first focuses on the model depicted in Fig. 7.1, and the second spotlights related cross-sex friendship processes depicted in Fig. 7.2.

Schematic Interconnections in a Cultural, Social, and Chronological Context.   Fig. 7.1 is a heuristic, Venn-like depiction (see Carroll, 1958, p. 175) of the interrelationships between self-schemas (see ellipse A), gender schemas (see ellipse B), cross-sex friendship schemas (see ellipse C), and same-sex friendship schemas (see ellipse D). The model indicates that the overlapping schemas occur in a cultural, social, and chronological context. More detail is given about these contextual factors at the end of this section. Before explaining how the model works and what it means, some basic review information about the four schemas should clarify my upcoming arguments and observations. Let me first give a reminder of a central limitation of conceptual models, (i.e., they can make a complicated process seem deceptively simple). Along these lines Planalp (personal communication, September, 2000) expressed a concern about my use of Venn diagrams because "they are so vague but look precise." I share her concern and therefore caution the reader that the relationships between the various schemas depicted in my conceptual models (as well as schematic relationships left out of the model) are not as tidy, neat, and clean as the diagrams might suggest.

Schemas are knowledge structures that "represent the mental organization of information ... " (Honeycutt & Cantrill, 2001, p. 14). They are internal, cognitive representations of selected parts of an individual's environment (Arbib et al., 1987). Just about anything that a person cares to name or think about has a schematic representation. Many of the concepts discussed in this book have a schematic counterpart existing in the minds of the individuals who are familiar with those concepts. For example, the caricatures that teenagers have for

Cultural, Social, and Chronological Context

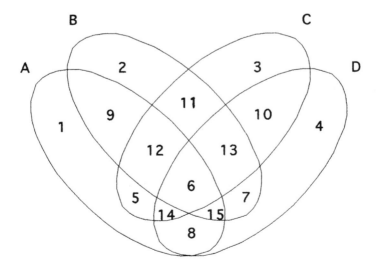

Fig. 7.1. Schematic Representation of the Connections Between Self-Schemas (A), Gender Schemas (B), Cross-Sex Friendship Schemas (C), and Same-Sex Friendship Schemas (D).

Cultural, Social, Chronological and Relational Context

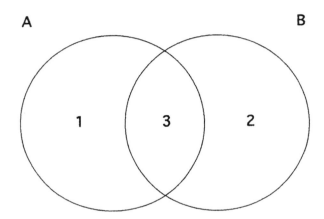

Fig. 7.2. Schematic Representation of the Connections Between the Cross-Sex Friendship Schemas of "Judy" (A) and "John" (B).

crowds are essentially schematic representations of those crowds (Brown et al., 1994). The schemas most relevant for my purposes are self-schemas (hereafter abbreviated SSs), gender schemas (hereafter abbreviated GSs), cross-sex friendship schemas (hereafter abbreviated CSFSs), and same-sex friendship schemas (hereafter abbreviated SSFSs). Those schemas are derived from prior experiences and play an active role in processing information and guiding behavior (Andersen, 1993).

According to relational schema theory (Baldwin, 1992), individuals have schemas for all types of relationships. Some of those schemas are relevant to the processes described in this part of the chapter, but they were not included in the model. Probably the most important relational schema left out of my model is the one that people have for romantic relationships (Honeycutt & Cantrill, 2001). Romantic relationship schemas and cross-sex friendship schemas are also overlapping, especially for unmarried individuals. Although not specifically studying schemas directly, Connolly and her colleagues surveyed 1,755 children and adolescents between the ages of 9 and 14 and discovered what could be interpreted as significant areas of overlap and nonoverlap between romantic relationship and cross-sex friendship schemas (Connolly, Craig, Goldberg & Pepler, 1999). Nevertheless, in the pursuit of parsimony, I decided against complicating the diagram with schematic representations of other relationships such as romances, sibling relationships, and relationships with parents. But the reader should recognize that although not depicted in the diagram, schemas such as the ones people have for romantic relationships impact cross-sex friendship schemas, self-schemas, and gender schemas.

Recall that a person's SS (Fig. 7.1; ellipse A) is the equivalent of that person's self-concept (Wells, 1992). The self-concept involves interrelated schemata about the self that are acquired throughout life. They exist at varying levels of conscious awareness and have both core and role aspects (Wells, 1992). Self-concepts are also characterized by change and stability throughout the life cycle (Demo, 1992). From a symbolic interactionist perspective, self-schemas include instances in which individuals engage in communication with themselves (Blumer, 1969). Gender schemas are knowledge structures containing information about what the sexes are like (Bem, 1981; Ruble & Martin, 1998). Martin contended that GSs (Fig. 7.1; ellipse B) are comprised of "own" and "other sex" subschemas (1994). Cross-sex and same-sex friendship schemas are types of relational schemas (Baldwin, 1992; Planalp, 1985). The CSFS in Fig. 7.1 (ellipse C) represents both a general cross-sex friendship schema and specific subschemas for particular cross-sex friendships. So for example, an older person might have a general CSFS that would include his general beliefs and feelings about cross-sex friendships. Knowledge of the generic and unique benefits (and costs) that flow from cross-sex friendships would be part of his CSFS (ellipse C), as would knowledge of social and structural barriers to those friendships. Some of those beliefs might be the product of a lifetime of experiences, while some might be much more recently acquired. Within the context of the general CSFS, he would have specific subschemas for particular cross-sex friendships. The SSFS in Fig. 7.1 (ellipse D) represents both a general same-sex friendship schema and specific subschemas for particular same-sex friendships.

The following is a brief explanation of how the model in Fig. 7.1 should be interpreted and a description of the most relevant compartments. The degree of overlap between the schemas and thus the size of individual compartments (1–15) in Fig. 7.1 is arbitrary and would change from individual to individual and life stage to life stage. For instance, compartment 5 represents the overlap and connection between a person's SS and his or her CSFS. The size of that compartment would vary according to the individual, the life stage he or she was in, and the extent to which cross-sex friendships impact his or her SS, and vice versa. The actual degree of overlap between a person's self-schema and his or her cross-sex friendship schema could be much larger or smaller than what is shown in the diagram.

Each compartment in the model corresponds to either an area of overlap between schemas (i.e., compartments 5–15) or nonoverlap between schemas (i.e., compartments 1–4). Overlap between compartments (schemas) suggest cognitive connections and similarities in both declarative and procedural content (Baldwin, 1992). Note that compartments 1, 2, 4, 7–9, and 15 do not overlap with a person's CSFS, whereas compartments 5, 6, 10, 11, 12, 13, and 14 do. The areas of nonoverlap represent those parts of a person's SSFS (4, 7, 8, 15), SS (1, 8, 9, 15), and GS (2, 9, 7, 15) that are relatively unaffected by the person's CSFS. Conversely, overlapping compartments represent those parts of a person's SSFS (6, 10, 13, 14), SS (5, 6, 12, 14), and GS (6, 11, 12, 13) that affect and are affected by a person's CSFS.

In the next few pages I systematically explain most of the compartments, starting with the four that are disconnected from the other 11 (i.e., compartments 1, 2, 3, and 4). Compartment 1 represents that part of an individual's self-schema (SS) that does not overlap with the individual's GS, SSFS, or CSFS. The lack of overlap in compartment 1 indicates minimal, if any, connection between that part of the individual's SS and that same individual's GS, SSFS, and CSFS. It represents that segment of an individual's self-schema (self-concept) that is independent of the way he or she the thinks and feels about gender (GS), same-sex friendships (SSFS), and cross-sex friendships (CSFS). Recall that from an interpersonal self perspective (Markus & Cross, 1990), a person's self-concept is largely a product his or her relationships. Compartment 1 would therefore also represent the impact that other relational partners such as parents, siblings, romantic partners, spouses, and coworkers, would have on the person's self-concept. Because compartment 1 occurs in a cultural, social, and chronological context (to be explained later in this section; see Fig. 7.1), that compartment would also include other factors, the media for example, which might impact the person's view of self.

Compartments 2, 3, and 4 represent those parts of an individual's GS (ellipse B), CSFS (ellipse C), and SSFS (ellipse D), respectively, that are independent of the other schemas. So for example, although parts of an individual's CSFS affects and is affected by the other schemas (e.g., compartments 5, 6, 10, 11, 12, 13, and 14), part of that schema (compartment 3) remains relatively unaffected by the SSFS, GS, and the SS. The same is true of a person's SSFS (i.e., parts of an individual's SSFS affects and is affected by the other schemas; e.g., compartments 6, 7, 8, 10, 13, 14, and 15), but part of that schema (compartment 4) is unaffected. Similarly, part of an individual's GS is affected by the other schemas (e.g., compartments 6, 7, 9, 11, 12, 13, and 15), but part of the GS is not (compartment 2).

Now that the reader is thoroughly confused (I thought models were supposed to simplify complicated processes!), let me move on to those parts of the model most relevant to the central thesis of the book. The most salient compartments are 5, 6, 12, and 14 because they depict overlap between a person's CSFS (ellipse C) and his or her SS (ellipse A). Each of those compartments represent cognitive connections between the way a person views him or herself and the way he or she views cross-sex friendships.

Compartment 5 represents overlap between a person's SS and CSFS and a lack of overlap with the other two schemas. More than any of the other 14 compartments, number 5 visually epitomizes the central thesis of this book because it represents the cognitive connections between a person's cross-sex friendships and his or her self-concept. The absence of overlap between the SS and CSFS with the GS and SSFS indicates that part of the amalgamation of a person's SS with his/her CSFS is separate from that person's GS and SSFS. What this means is that some of the connections between a person's view of self (SS) and his or her view of cross-sex friendships (CSFS) are (in theory) unaffected by gender and same-sex friendship schemas.

Compartment 5 would be relatively small if cross-sex friendships and self-concepts have little impact on one another. In contrast, if for any reason a person's self-concept is significantly impacted by a cross-sex friend (s) then the area of overlap would be quite large. For example, recall from the chapter on middle childhood that some children have only cross-sex friends (Kovacs et al., 1996). A reasonable hypothesis based on the interpersonal self perspective (Markus & Cross, 1990) is that for those children there would be greater overlap between their SSs and their CSFSs than there would be for children whose cross-sex friendships are less central. Another example is informative in a different way. According to Adams' 1985 research, most elderly widows do not have cross-sex friends. The absence of cross-sex friendships, however, does not mean that there would be no overlap between their SSs and CSFSs. Quite the contrary. Because those women tend to conceptualize cross-sex friendships as romantic relationships, their CSFSs would include those beliefs, beliefs which would have some kind of impact on their SSs. What kind of impact is a question for empirical investigation.

Compartment 5 is also relevant to the contention of some scholars that there are sex and gender differences in the degree to which others are incorporated into a person's self-schema and that women generally incorporate others into their self-concepts more than men do (e.g., Markus & Oyserman, 1989). The argument leads one to hypothesize that compartment 5 would generally be larger for females than it would be for males. From an interpersonal self perspective, one way in which relationships impact a person's view of self is when a person consolidates a partner into his or her self-concept (Aron & Aron, 1997; Markus & Cross, 1990). Because women are generally more relationally oriented than men (Chodorow, 1978; Gilligan, 1982; Miller, 1986; Tannen, 1990a), the relationships of women tend to be more central to their self-definition than are the relationships of men to their self-definition. In other words, women and men differ in the extent to which the relationships they are involved in become integrated with their self-views.

Other theoretical work suggest that compartment 5 (i.e., overlap between a person's SS and that same person's CSFS) would be larger for women than for men. Markus and Oyserman (1989), building from the writings of other theorists (Chodorow, 1978; Erikson, 1968; Gilligan, 1982) refer to the different self-schemas of women and men as "connectedness" and "separateness" schemas, respectively (p. 101). Relationships with others are a key element of a connectedness schema because others are see as part of self. On the other hand, separateness schemas of men incorporate others as not being part of the self but rather distinct and independent of it. The connectedness and separateness schemas of men and women are simiiar to cultural differences in the extent to which relationships with others are seen as central to self-definition. As noted by Markus and Oyserman (1989, p. 106) "The distinction between the self-as-connected and self-as-separate maps roughly onto the distinction between individualist and collectivist selves and onto the difference between Western and Eastern selves." Along similar lines, a recent study of language differences and similarities between women and men indirectly suggested that the more "socio-centric" language of women would lead to more connections between their self-schema and their cross-sex friendship schemas than the more "ego-centric" language of men (Mulac, Bradac, Gibbons, 2001).

Note that compartment 6 corresponds to overlap between all four schemas. It is at the center of the individual's schematic universe; representing the cognitive intersection of the person's SS, CSFS, GS, and SSFS. The intersection of the four schemas implies that each schema has connections to each of the other schemas. Compartment 6 potentially encapsulates a number of phenomena salient to cross-sex friendship and self-concepts. Belsky (1992) and Guttman's (1987) contention that as individuals age they become more androgynous has direct applicability to all four schemas.

The self-disclosure construct can be used to illustrate the intersection of all four schemas in compartment 6. Self-disclosure is a key component of friendship intimacy in every stage of life (e.g., Gottman, 1986 for young children; Field, 1999 for older Americans; Monsour, 1992 for adults). In adolescence, self-disclosure is a means of self-exploration and self-identity (e.g., "Who am I?" and "Will others accept who I am?"; Parker & Gottman, 1989). Self-disclosures are often emotional messages (e.g., "You don't know this, but I hate you"). Emotions are hypothesized to have important influences on cognitive (including schematic) processes (Planalp & Fitness, 1999). When cross-sex friends engage in self-disclosure the communicative process of message production and reception is relevant to all four schemas. The appropriateness of the self-disclosure might be judged using criteria from their GSs (e.g., is it appropriate for women to reveal unbridled ambition or for men to reveal paranoid weakness?). The appropriateness of a particular self-disclosure would also be assessed by how it compares to what is appropriate in same-sex friendships (which would be part of their SSFSs), and what might be deemed appropriate in that specific cross-sex friendship (which would be part of their CSFS). Finally, the self-disclosing reve-lation would impact the self-concepts (SSs) of both friends. The disclosing part-ner might be proud of her willingness to self-disclose. The recipient of the self-disclosure might be similarly proud for having been chosen as the receiver of an intimate disclosure. The self-disclosure would be particularly poignant if it involved a revelation of homosexuality (Savin-Williams, 1990). Such a revela-tion and the reaction to it would impact all four schemas of both individuals.

At a more theoretical level, because schemas can be combined to form new schemas (Arbib et al., 1987), compartment 6 represents not only the place where the four schemas intersect and overlap, but the place where a new schema is created. This new schema, representing an amalgamation of all four, might involve complex thoughts, emotions, and behavioral scripts for relating to others and oneself in a less gender stereotypical fashion. The new schema could fundamentally change the way an individual views him or herself and same-sex and cross-sex others.

To summarize where I am thus far, compartments 5 and 6 are two of the four compartments that reveal connections between a person's SS and his or her CSFS. Compartment 6 involves the other two schemas (i.e., GS and SSFS), whereas compartment 5 does not. Compartments 12 and 14 also correspond to areas of overlap between an individual's SS and his or her CSFS.

Compartment 12 represents overlap between a person's SS, CSFS, and GS, but does not involve the SSFS. The 12th compartment would be that part of an person's CSFS that is cognitively connected to his or her SS and beliefs about the different sexes (i.e., the gender schema), but not connected to his or her SSFS. Admittedly, this compartment might be quite small because there may be very little in the merging of the three schemas (SS, CSFS, and GS) that is not impacted in some way by an individual's SSFS. Similarly, compartment 14 rep-resents overlap between a person's SS, CSFS, and the SSFS, but does not in-volve a person's GS. Given the far-reaching impact of gender schemas (Ruble & Martin, 1998) it might be impossible to have a situation in which a person's GS does not impact in some way the fusing of a person's SS, CSFS, and SSFS. Wright's (1984) model of friendship and self-referent motivation seems particu-larly applicable to compartment 14 because an individual's SSFS and CSFS would include similarities and differences in the degree to which those respec-tive friendships contained important friendship values that facilitate a positive view of self (i.e., the SS).

As noted, compartments 5, 6, 12, and 14 correspond to the areas of schematic overlap most relevant to the central thesis of this book that cross-sex friendships impact and are impacted by an individual's self-concept. Other areas of overlap such as 10, 11, and 13 are also important. Compartment 10 represents the overlap between a person's SSFS and that same person's CSFS. If a person believed there was little difference between cross-sex and same-sex friendships there would be more overlap between those schemas than there would be if he or she saw significant differences. Relatedly, knowledge about generic benefits (i.e., benefits provided by same-sex and cross-sex friendships) would be found in compartment 10. On the other hand, the unique benefits of cross-sex friendship (like insider perspectives and other-sex companionship) would be located in compartments 3, 5, 11, and 12, but not in compartments 6, 10, 13, and 14.

The degree of overlap and connectiveness is also related to the stage of life an individual is in. For instance, there would probably be more overlap between the CSFS and SSFS of a 3-year-old who was just beginning to differentiate between the sexes (Howes, 1996) than there might be for elderly women or children in middle school who clearly differentiate between same-sex and cross-sex friends (Adams, 1985; Sroufe et al., 1993). Data from my dissertation also indirectly suggest that androgynous males, when compared to their more traditional masculine and feminine counterparts, might have larger areas of overlap between their CSFSs and SSFSs (1988). Belsky's (1992) contention that older men and women become more androgynous when they age also indirectly implies significant overlap between SSFs and CSFSs.

Compartment 11 represents the intersection of a person's GS and CSFS that is relatively unconnected to the other two schemas. A person's GS would influence how he or she viewed friendships with members of the other sex. In like fashion, a person's general CSFS as well as schemas representing specific cross-sex friendships would influence that person's view of what the sexes are like (i.e., would influence the person's GS). This process of reciprocal influence would begin as soon as a child could differentiate one sex from another (around the age of 2 or 3 according to some experts). Once a child could distinguish between a female and male playmate he or she would begin to form rudimentary cross-sex friendship schemas. From a social constructivist and symbolic interactionist perspective, those schemas would emerge from the communication that occurs between the young children (Mead, 1934; Vygotsky, 1978; Whaley & Rubenstein, 1994; Yingling, 1994).

Compartment 13 represents the intersection of a person's CSFS, SSFS, and GS that is unaffected by the person's SS. It seems obvious that the way a person views members of each sex, which would be included in his or her gender schemas, would influence the way that person viewed friendships with members of each sex. Similarly, the way a person viewed friendships with members of her own sex (SSFSs) and members of the other sex (CSFSs) would influence how she viewed the different sexes (GSs). This compartment might be quite small because there may only be a minuscule portion of the amalgamation of a person's CSFS, SSFS, and GS that is not impacted in some way by a person's SS. Indeed, the compartment may not exist at all because of the ubiquity of self (Wright, 1984).

There are a number of other questions that need addressing now that the key compartments in Fig. 7.1 have been examined. Most important are questions concerning life stage issues and how communication relates to what is primarily a cognitive model. Let us turn our attention to life stage issues first. How might the model change as individuals go through stages of the life cycle? My contention is that the degree of overlap and nonoverlap between the four schemas would change throughout the life cycle (referred to later in this section as "chronological context"). Theoretically, the change would be noticeable between and within stages of life. For example, although the degree of overlap between a person's SS and her CSFS might change as she goes from middle childhood to adolescence, it is also equally possible that the degree of overlap would change within each of those life stages. Not only would the degree of overlap and nonoverlap vary, but the content of the schemas themselves would change. As individuals go through the life cycle their self-schemas, relational schemas, and gender schemas change (Harter, 1998; Ruble & Martin, 1998). There may be periods of relative stability characterized by minimal change in one or more of the four schemas. For example, in a particular stage of life such as middle childhood, old age, or young adulthood, a person may have a fairly constant view of what the sexes are like. In similar fashion, a teenager may have a relatively stable mental representation (i.e., a schema) of what cross-sex friendships are like.

Despite my claim that schemas have relative periods of stability, developmental milestones would invariably affect the content and structuring of the schemas. For instance, whether heterosexual or homosexual, the onset of puberty has a significant impact on a person's view of self and members of the other sex (Brooks-Gunn & Reiter, 1990; Savin-Williams, 1990). Having children at the age of 30 might have an important effect on a man's view of himself (SS), and his attitudes about spending time with his cross-sex and same-sex friends (CSFS and SSFS; Cohen, 1992). If a healthy and active 80-year-old has a sudden stroke or heart attack that leaves her housebound, that "developmental milestone" (I am using that term loosely here) would impact the way she views herself (her SS) and her friends (her SSFS and CSFS; Johnson & Barer, 1997).

Another issue to address concerns the relationship of communication to what is primarily a cognitive model. Earlier in the book I summarized my theoretical position by stating that cross-sex friendships and self-concepts were cognitively linked through schematic connections and communicatively linked through interaction. What this means is that CSFSs impact and are impacted by SSs, but the impact occurs because of the communication that takes place between the relational partners. Relatedly, communication between partners affects the content and structuring of the schemas, which in turn affects the communication. The schematic links and communication are interrelated. As noted in earlier parts of this book, scholars see a clear association between communication (interaction) and cognitive schemas (Bowlby, 1969; Corsaro, 1985; Damon & Hart, 1988; Gergen, 1991; Hewes, 1995; Honeycutt & Cantrill, 2001; Mintz, 1995; Planalp, 1985; Planalp & Fitness, 1999; Vygotsky, 1978; Yingling, 1994). A number of the theoreticians and researchers who propose the link are guided by a belief in the connection between interaction and internal representations of friendship (e.g., Corsaro, 1985; Damon & Hart, 1988; Vygotsky, 1978; Whaley & Rubenstein, 1994; Yingling, 1994). Additionally, from an interpersonal self-perspective, the socially constructed self (which includes in large part a person's SS) is a product of interactions taking place in social relationships (Bowlby, 1969, Cooley, 1902; Gergen, 1991, Mead, 1934; Sullivan, 1953).

Note that in Fig. 7.1 the overlapping schemas are depicted as occurring in a cultural, social, and chronological context. Friendship scholars have emphasized the importance of contextualizing friendships and noted that contextual factors are often ignored in friendship investigations (Adams & Allan, 1998; Werking, 1997a). Cultural, social, and chronological contexts each have different implications for the overlapping schemas. Cultural context refers to the broader societal context within which schemas form and how that context might influence the content and structuring of a person's SS, CSFS, SSFS, and GS. Hartup and Stevens' deep structure (1997) is an example of the broader cultural context. They contend that society provides general guidelines for how to conduct oneself in various kinds of relationships such as friendship. Those guidelines originate from the deep structure of society and impact a person's SS, CSFS, SSFS, and his or her GS. Broad, cultural contextual factors would also include norms or beliefs that might be characteristic of a particular ethnic or racial group. For example, there may be differences between ethnic groups in the United States in their general attitudes about married individuals having close cross-sex friends. Those cultural differences would be reflected in the CSFSs, GSs, and SSs of individuals from selected cultural groups.

Social context is much more narrow in its focus than the cultural context. It includes the social groups an individual belongs to such as crowds, cliques, families, workgroups, and the social relationships he or she is involved in. The content and structuring of the schemas under examination would be influenced by the social context in which they occur. For example, if the overlapping schemas in Fig. 7.1 were those of a teenager, the social context in which the overlapping occurs would include relationships with parents, peers, romantic partners, coworkers, enemies, next-door neighbors, and so on. Different relationships in the social environment would influence the various schemas (i.e. SSs, CSFSs, GSs, SSFSs), and those schemas would influence the teenager's behavior in those relationships.

Social contextual variables would also involve communication that occurs in cross-sex friendships. For example, ellipse C in Fig. 7.1 represents an individual's general CSFS as well as specific subschemas for particular cross-sex friendships. The schemas in Fig. 7.1 would affect and be affected by communication in specific cross-sex friendships. Social contextual variables, like their cultural counterparts, are complicated and would impact the four schemas of interest.

Chronological context refers to the life stage an individual is in. The intermingling and coalescing of the schemas and the degree of overlap would take place in a particular life stage context. The life stage affects the schemas and the schemas impact events and processes occurring in that stage. For example, there may be more overlap between a woman's CSFS and her SS in middle age than there is in old age. More overlap might make her more likely to initiate and maintain cross-sex friendships in middle age than she does in old age. Fig. 7.1 represents a snapshot of what the overlapping schemas might look like at one point in time. However, the chronological contextual factors suggest that the configuration of the overlapping schemas would be constantly changing to reflect differences between and within life stages. My addition of chronological contextual variables in a small way addresses the developmental issues relevant to the central thesis of this book. If cross-sex friendships do impact and are impacted by an individual's evolving concept of self, developmental changes such as the onset of puberty or getting married would have an impact on the relationship between self-concepts and cross-sex friendships.

Before moving to an explanation of Fig. 7.2, let me briefly summarize where we are thus far. Fig. 7.1 is a visual depiction of the areas of overlap between four different schemas: self-schemas, cross-sex friendship schemas, same-sex friendship schemas, and gender schemas. Each of these schemas have subschemas. For instance, the general cross-sex friendship schema has subschemas for each individual cross-sex friendship. Gender schemas have subschemas representing "own-sex" and "other-sex" individuals (Martin, 1994). Self-schemas have subschemas for "ideal" versus "actual" selves (Harter, 1998). Overlap between one or more schemas implies that the schemas have some effect on one another. Overlap also implies that the content of the overlapping schemas may be similar. For instance, the content of CSFSs and SSFSs would be similar because cross-sex friendships and same-sex friendships have many of the same defining characteristics and provide many of the same generic benefits. Communication with partners (part of the social context) impacts the content of the various schemas and how they are structured. The intermingling of the four schemas takes place in a cultural, social, and chronological context. Finally, there are obviously schemas missing from the diagram that, if included, would also have degrees of overlap with those that are in the diagram (e.g., romantic relationship schemas, cross-sex sibling schemas, schemas for crowds, and so on).

Schematic Interconnections in a Cultural, Social, Relational and Chronological Context.   Fig. 7.2 is another heuristic, Venn-like diagram of the connection between schemas. In this section I explain the model with particular focus on compartments 1, 2, and 3 and the "relational context" in which the construction of the friendship takes place. This model, deceptively simpler than the first, represents overlap between the CSFSs of "Judy" and "John" (A and B). The warning I gave at the beginning of my discussion of Fig. 7.1 is worth repeating here. The model depicted in Fig. 7.2 is a simplified version of a very complicated process. The cross-sex friendship schemas of Judy and John could be influenced by a range of factors. Along those lines, as noted by Planalp in a comment she e-mailed to me in reference to Fig. 7.2, "knowledge of relationships is informed by other forms of knowledge (of conversations, of people, of oneself, of gender, and so on) and vice versa ... there are such huge bodies of knowledge that could potentially inform the (cross-sex friendship) schemas that there is virtually no limit" (Planalp, personal communication, September, 2000).

Information presented throughout this book documents that the relational schemas of two individuals are connected. The cross-sex friendship schemas of two young children, or two adolescents, or two older adults, overlap in meaning and result in a shared view of the relationship. That shared view is mostly a product of the communication that occurs between the two friends, although other things in addition to communication between partners contributes to a shared view of the friendship. For example, if the two friends independently observe other successful (or perhaps unsuccessful) cross-sex friendships and interpret what they see in the same way that information would be incorporated into their individual cross-sex friendship schemas and would contribute to a shared view of their friendship even if they never actually discussed what they saw. Or if members of their respective social networks say positive things to each of them about the platonic cross-sex nature of their friendship, those messages from network members could become part of the shared view of the friendships even if the friends never discussed those messages with each another.

The work of a number of scholars is relevant to the model depicted in Fig. 7.2 and the idea of creating a joint perception of the friendship. For instance, although not specifically highlighting cross-sex friendships, Duck made it clear that communication or "talk" between partners is the means employed in negotiating and establishing a joint version of the relationship (1994, see pp. 149–153; Monsour, 1994). Along those lines, childhood friendship researchers champion the position that children build friendships via communication (Corsaro, 1985; Howes, 1996; Rizzo, 1989; Whaley & Rubenstein, 1994; Yingling, 1994). The contention that interaction (talk, communication) between young children leads to a rudimentary friendship schema is also a principle of social constructivism (Vygotsky, 1978), and social constructionism (Berger & Luckmann, 1966; Gergen, 1985; 1991). Similarly, Bowlby argued that through interaction with primary caregivers children establish internal working models (i.e., schemas) of relationships (1969). Building on the work of Bowlby (1969), Trinke and Bartholomew established that young adults form attachment relationships with their best friends which implies an accompanying internal working model, or relational schema, representing those friendships (1997). At a more general relational level cutting across the life cycle, Wood contended that communication is the "primary way through which we create meaning as individuals and as partners in relationships" (1995, p. xvi).

Returning to Fig. 7.2, Judy has her schematic representation of the friendship ("A" in the model), and John has his ("B" in the model). The overlapping of their schematic representations of the friendship creates three compartments. In some ways they view their friendship in a similar fashion (compartment 3). However, there are also differences in how they view their friendship. Compartments 1 and 2 represent those parts of Judy and John's cross-sex friendship schemas that are not shared by the other person. In theory, compartments 1 and 2 represent the same thing; beliefs, memories, emotions, and expectations that one friend has about the cross-sex friendship that is not shared by the other. For example, in an adolescent cross-sex friendship Judy may believe that the relationship is very special because sexual contact is not part of the relationship. John may not share that belief, not necessarily because he believes the opposite, although he may, but because he simply has never thought about that aspect of the friendship. I will give examples only for compartment 1 (i.e., those parts of Judy's cross-sex friendship schema that are not part of John's schema). Keep in mind that compartment 2 similarly represents those things about the cross-sex friendship that John believes, feels, or remembers that are not shared by Judy (i.e., not found in compartment 1).

The differences between compartments 1 and 2 are often linked to underlying developmental processes such as puberty, more overt communicative processes such as gossip, or life-stage concerns such as increasing physical disability. Compartment 1 is clearly connected to the generic and unique benefits of cross-sex friendships and the structural and social barriers interfering with their formation. For instance, one partner may believe that the friendship provides a particular generic or unique benefit (such as providing an insider's perspective or protection against loneliness), whereas the other partner does not share that belief. Similarly, one partner but not the other may believe that social barriers will eventually derail the relationship. In the upcoming paragraph I provide several examples of beliefs that one partner (Judy) might have about their friendship that are not shared by her partner (John).

If Judy has entered puberty but John has not she might have sexual thoughts about the friendship, thoughts that are not shared by John. Or perhaps Judy who is now a young adult believes the friendship is lower in emotional intimacy than friendships she has with her same-sex friends. On the other hand, John believes that his friendship with Judy is just as intimate as the friendships she has with her female friends. In Rubin's interviews with over 300 young and middle-aged adults she discovered that it was fairly common for a man to name a woman as a close friend but for the woman to disagree and categorize the friendship as casual. Recall from chapter 3 that friendships in middle childhood are sometimes hidden from others in order to avoid teasing (Gottman, 1986). If John and Judy are in middle childhood, Judy might believe the friendship is not something that needs to hidden from others, but John believes the friendship should remain their secret. As suggested by my own research, during young adulthood Judy may believe there is a power imbalance in their friendship, while John does not (Monsour et al., 1997). Recall that O'Connor argued that some elderly cross-sex friendships are pseudospousal in nature (1993). If Judy and John are both widowed and in their 70s Judy might believe that their relationship is pseudospousal in nature , but John may not share that belief. O'Connor also suggested that intergenerational cross-sex friends may have different views on their friendship. If Judy is 75 and housebound, and John is her 25-year-old neighbor, Judy may view the friendship as lopsided because John is always doing chores for her but she can not reciprocate. John may not share that belief.

In addition to beliefs about the friendship that Judy and John may not share, compartment 1 also represents memories about the friendship and expectations for it that Judy has but John does not. Judy may clearly remember the first time John indicated a lack of romantic interest in her, whereas John may not. Andersen contended that relational schemas include relational trajectory information about where the person believes the relationship is headed (1993). If the friendship takes place in an organization, Judy may believe that it will eventually end because of workplace gossip about their relationship (Devine & Markiewicz, 1990). John might have a different relational trajectory as part of his schema for their friendship. Or maybe John and Judy started having intercourse in their cross-sex friendship (Afifi & Faulkner, 2000). Judy may believe such intimate contact is "inappropriate" (Duck & VanderVoort, 2001), but John may not share that belief.

Compartment 3 corresponds to the area of overlap between the cross-sex friendship schemas of Judy and John. Overlap implies similarities in beliefs, attitudes, emotions, expectations, and specific memories about their cross-sex friendship. Overlap is also the location of causal connections between the two schemas. The way Judy thinks and feels about the friendship impacts the way John thinks and feels about the friendship, and vice versa. A number of constructs already discussed in this book are relevant to the processes that result in compartment 3 (e.g., transactive memory, interactive cuing, and semantic elaboration; Anderson & Reder, 1979; Wegner et al., 1985). Recall that transactive memory refers to those memories about the relationship that reside in the schemas of both individuals. Sometimes those memories are constructed by the participants when they prompt each other's remembrances through the process of interactive cuing. Semantic elaboration is when Judy or John realizes they agree on something and then assumes that if they agree on that issue they must also probably agree on other issues that are similar. Duck argued in his model of the "serial construction of meaning" that individuals in relationships construct a joint version of reality through the recognition, evaluation, and extension of areas of commonality (in Monsour, 1994, I present a summary of the model that Duck presented in more detail in his 1994 book). For example, if Judy realizes that she and John agree that they should not have sex in their relationship, Judy might elaborate on that similarity and conclude (perhaps mistakenly) that John must also agree with her that romance should be avoided. Recall from chapter 5 that in the last 10 years there has been quite an influx of articles addressing sexuality in cross-sex friendships of young adults (e.g., Afifi & Faulkner, 2000; Eyler & Baridon, 1992; Kaplan & Keys, 1997; Sapadin, 1988).

Several of my research projects clearly establish that there is often considerable similarity between cross-sex friends in the way they view their relationship (Monsour et al., 1993; Monsour et al., 1997). In the 1993 study my colleagues and I utilized Heider's Balance Theory (1958) and Laing's Interpersonal Perception Method (Laing et al., 1966) to study the perception of intimacy in cross-sex friendships. We had 103 pairs of close cross-sex friends and gathered data from each partner in the friendship. As predicted by Balance Theory, there was considerable agreement, understanding, and realization of understanding between cross-sex friends concerning the level of intimacy of their friendship and how important the friendship was. In 1997 my associates and I conducted a similar analysis in which we once again utilized Heider's Balance Theory and Laing's Interpersonal Perception Method. This time we were interested in exploring to what extent cross-sex friends agreed on the existence of O'Meara's (1989) challenges. We compiled compelling evidence that individuals in young adult cross-sex friendships construct a shared perceptual reality in regard to the extent that certain challenges faced their relationship. Results from those two studies strongly suggest that cross-sex friends build a joint view of what the relationship means. That joint view is found in compartment 3. When individuals share meaning they have taken the first step toward establishing a "symbolic union," a union that promotes understanding and the perception of order in a relational universe that frequently is characterized by chaos and a lack of predictability (Duck & Barnes, 1992).

Compartment 3 also represents a manifestation of social constructionism (Gergen, 1991) symbolic interactionism (Cooley, 1902; Mead, 1934), and to a lesser degree, attachment theory (Bowlby, 1969). From those perspectives, a cross-sex friendship and what it means to the participants is socially constructed by the members of the relationship through communication. Sullivan's idea of consensual validation is also relevant to compartment 3. Sullivan contended that one of the most important functions of close friendships in late childhood is that the friends provide consensual validation to one another of their values, beliefs, and general self-worth. Although consensual validation is certainly important to the area of overlap between a person's self-schema and his or her cross-sex friendship schema (Fig. 7.1), it is also relevant to the overlap between the two cross-sex friendship schemas because that overlap represents similarity, similarity that often implies validation (Monsour, 1994). Recall from chapter 3 that Blomberg and I conducted a small study in which we interviewed 10-year-old boys and girls about their close friends (chums to use Sullivan's term). We garnered evidence from those interviews documenting that cross-sex friends do indeed provide each other with consensual validation (Blomberg & Monsour, 1998).

Baldwin and Fehr (1995) offer a perspective that is also relevant to compartment 3. They contended that a relational schema is comprised of a self schema, a schema for the other person, and a script representing the interaction between the two people (1995). Similarly, according to Baldwin (1992; see also Banse, 1999), relational schemas involve three elements: representations of the self relevant to a particular relationship, representations of the partner, and representations of the communication between self and partner. From an interpersonal self perspective, the overlap between Judy and John's cross-sex friendship schemas could involve partial incorporation of one anothers' self-schema as well as incorporation of views of the friend that would be included in each partner's cross-sex friendship schema.

The size of compartment 3 would vary depending on the two individuals involved, their stage of life, and where they are in the unfolding of their own relationship. Relational partners often become more similar in their views about their relationship (Duck, 1994; Monsour, 1994), implying that the size of compartment 3 might get larger as the friendship evolves. Recall the argument presented in chapter 2 that toddlers often construct similarity in their friendships (Whaley & Rubenstein, 1994). The realization that one is similar to one's partner typically makes one think better of the partner (because he or she shares your beliefs), and better of oneself (because one's view has been verified). If John and Judy's friendship has lasted for years or even decades the content and structuring and degree of overlap of their schemas would be quite different than it would be in they were in the beginning stages of their friendship. Long-range longitudinal studies tracking a cross-sex friendship schema from near its inception would be necessary in order to understand the cognitive, emotional, and interactional dynamics of cross-sex friendships that survive over multiple stages of life.

Many of the concepts and processes described in this book are at least tangentially relevant to compartment 3. The joint schematic representation of a cross-sex friendship by Judy and John is no doubt influenced by other factors "outside" of the relationship (Adams & Allan, 1989; Blieszner & Adams, 1992). For example, in chapter 4 I discussed the important role that cliques and crowds might play in cross-sex friendship formation during adolescence (Brown et al., 1994; Cotterell, 1996; Dunphy, 1969). If Judy and John both belonged to the same crowd, that similarity would impact their view of the friendship—especially if the crowd approves of the relationship. As another example, if John and Judy were both in their 80s and each fairly immobilized by their age, that similarity would become part of their joint schematic representation of the relationship. Recall that Johnson and Troll (1994; chap. 6, this volume) contended that mutual physical disability for individuals in extreme old age can make the friendship closer because it represents one more thing that they have in common.

As seen in Fig. 7.2, the overlapping schemas of Judy and John take place in a cultural, social, chronological, and relational context. The cultural, social, and chronological contexts depicted in Fig. 7.2 are very similar in meaning and effect as in Fig. 7.1. For example, the degree of overlap in Judy and John's schemas would be partly determined by social contextual factors like group memberships (e.g., families, crowds, work groups, church membership) and their relationships with other individuals (e.g., spouses, same-sex friends, parents), and the communication taking place in their friendship. One of the fundamental principles of many cognitive approaches to understanding communication and relationships is that communication is directed by relational schemas (such as CSFS), and it affects the content and structuring of the schema that is directing it (Honeycutt & Cantrill, 2001; Planalp, 1985). An individual's self-concept and his or her cross-sex friendships are linked through communication and relational schemas. The association between communication, self-concepts, and cross-sex friendships is no doubt a complex one. An additional complicating factor would be the life stage the individuals are in and the accompanying underlying developmental processes.

John and Judy's creation of a shared perceptual reality (depicted in compartment 3) would also be influenced by the stage of life each was in (i.e., the chronological context). If their cross-sex friendship was intergenerational (O'Connor, 1993) the chronological context might have different effects than if they were the same age. Cultural contextual factors would be of particular relevance if John and Judy were from different ethnic or racial groups with different views of gender and friendship issues (their GSs and CSFSs and SSFSs).

The relational context refers to a number of factors, but perhaps most important is the stage that the relationship is in. Developmental models of relationship–friendship formation posit that friendships go through certain developmental stages such as attraction, building, maintenance, and decline (Perlman & Fehr, 1986). The cross-sex friendship schemas and the amount of overlap between them takes place in the context of what stage of development or decline the relationship is in. For example, there is probably more overlap between schemas when a cross-sex friendship is growing than when it is deteriorating. Relational contextual factors would also include possible similarities and differences in how participants defined the relationship. For example, if Judy and John both defined the friendship as one on the road to sexual intimacy then that shared belief would influence both of their individual schemas as well as the similarity in their schemas.

Concluding Remarks

The main goal of this book was to offer a heuristic framework for viewing the reciprocal relationship between an individual's continually evolving concept of self and that person's equally dynamic conception and conduct of cross-sex friendships. I thought it was also important to emphasize the many advantages that cross-sex friendships have to offer, the relative neglect of those friendships by the scholarly community, the social and structural barriers inhibiting the formation of those friendships, and the likelihood that cross-sex friendships will become much more common as we go further into the 21st century. These were not disconnected goals. Advantages and disadvantages of cross-sex friendships can have positive and negative effects on a person's view of self. The benefits of cross-sex friendships, however, are possible only if social and structural barriers to their formation can be circumvented. The relative tokenism displayed by most friendship scholars toward the study of cross-sex friendships serves as a type of barrier to those friendships because it prevents adequate understanding of their dynamics. I lost track of the number of times I used the phrase "unfortunately, the researchers did not present data about the cross-sex friendships of the participants."

I hope the arguments presented in this volume have been thought-provoking. One of the reviewers of the preliminary proposal for this book was clearly knowledgeable about the state of the cross-sex friendship literature. She (or he) observed that I would need to do a great deal of "integrating and extrapolating." I believe I have done that. However, this book represents only the first step. I optimistically envision that scholars and students of friendship will take some of the ideas explored in this book and turn them into research projects and/or more detailed conceptual treatments. Cross-sex friendships in every stage of the life cycle need to be be studied more extensively in order to document and understand the benefits they have to offer and how developmental and life-span issues might influence those benefits.

The studies reviewed throughout this book have demonstrated the diversity existing in cross-sex friendships. Not all cross-sex friendships are the same, even those occurring in identical stages of life (Monsour, 1997). Some of those dissimilarities might have their roots in sex and gender differences in communication styles and ways of conducting relationships (Wood & Dindia, 1998). The fact that not all cross-sex friendships are the same means that different types of cross-sex friendships would affect self-concepts in different ways. Similarly, self-concepts would have a range of effects on cross-sex friendships, partly determined by life-stage and developmental issues.

Because of the fragmented nature of the cross-sex friendship literature (Monsour, 1997), locating every relevant study and writing would have been a herculean task doomed to failure. Luckily, providing a comprehensive life-cycle review of the cross-sex friendship literature was never a primary goal of this book. Instead, the goals all along have been to describe and document the three themes of the book, to relate those themes to individual stages of the life span, and to connect those themes in a holistic fashion to the entire cycle of life. Although my review is not encyclopedic, I believe it is representative of the cross-sex friendship literature. Literature reviews do not need to be exhaustive as long as they are representative of extant work on a subject (Cooper, 1989). I am confident that the cross-sex friendship work reviewed in this book represents 80 to 90% of the major relevant investigations and writings. I no doubt unintentionally overlooked the work of some scholars and to those individuals I offer my apologies (e.g., Lempers & Clark-Lempers, 1993).

THE KITCHEN SINK

During the 3-year process of writing this book I encountered numerous peripheral concepts, theories, and research projects that were indirectly related to cross-sex friendships and self-concept development across the life span. For the most part, those ideas and works of questionable relevance were excluded from the book because of their borderline salience. However, in the last 4 months of that 3-year process (with a deadline on the horizon) I became increasingly concerned (paranoid) that some of those "peripheral" concepts, theories, and research projects were actually more central than I had originally believed. That realization prompted me to consider adding a number of new theories and concepts so that my book would not only be comprehensive, but would include even the proverbial "kitchen sink." I asked my friend and colleague, Paul Wright, what to do and he wisely suggested that I leave out the "kitchen sink" and focus instead on what I already had. I took his advice. Nevertheless, I believe it is important to note that because of the inherent complexity of any relationship, no single book on a particular type of relationship can represent the full range of that complexity. The upshot of this concluding paragraph is that although I believe I have presented most of the relevant material given the goals of this book, there are certainly areas that I neglected to include that are important to the study and understanding of cross-sex friendships.

References

Abbey, A. (1982). Sex differences in attributions for friendly behavior: Do males misperceive female's friendliness? *Journal of Personality and Social Psychology, 42*, 830–838.

Adams, R. G. (1985). People would talk: Normative barriers to cross-sex friendship for elderly women. *The Gerontologist, 25*, 605–611.

Adams, R. G. (1987). Patterns of network change: A longitudinal study of friendships of elderly women. *The Gerontologist, 27*, 222–227.

Adams, R. G. (1989). Conceptual and methodological issues in studying friendships of older adults. In R. G. Adams & R. Blieszner (Eds.), *Older adult friendships: Structure and process* (pp. 17–41). Newbury Park, CA: Sage.

Adams, R. G. (1998). The demise of territorial determinism: online friendships. In R .G. Adams & G. Allan (Eds.), *Placing friendship in context* (pp. 153–182). Cambridge: Cambridge University Press.

Adams, R. G. & Allan, G. (1998). Contextualising friendship.In R. G. Adams and G. Allan (Eds.), *Placing friendship in context* (pp. 1–17). Cambridge: Cambridge University Press.

Adams, R. G., & Blieszner, R. (1989). *Older adult friendship: Structure and process.* Newbury Park, CA: Sage.

Adams, R. G., & Blieszner, R. (1994). An integrative conceptual framework for friendship research. *Journal of Social and Personal Relationships, 11*(2), 163–184.

Adams, R. G., & Blieszner, R. (1995). Aging well with friends and family. *American Behavioral Scientist, 39*(2), 209 (16).

Adams, R. G., & Blieszner, R. (1998). Structural predictors of problematic friendships in later life. *Personal Relationships, 54*(4), 439–447.

Adams, R. G., & Blieszner, R., & De Vries, B. (2000). Definitions of friendship in the third age: Age, gender, and study location effects. *Journal of Aging Studies, 14*(1), 117–133.

Afifi, W. A., & Burgoon, J. K. (1998). "We never talk about that:" A comparison of cross-sex friendships and dating relationships on uncertainty and topic avoidance. *Personal Relationships, 5*, 255–272.

Afifi, W. A., & Faulkner, S. L. (2000). On being "just friends": The frequency and impact of sexual activity in cross-sex friendships. *Journal of Social and Personal Relationships, 17*(2), 205–222.

Afifi, W. A., & Guerrero, L. K. (1998). Some things are better left unsaid II: Topic avoidance in friendships. *Communication Quarterly, 46*(3), 231–249.

Ainsworth, M. D., Blehar, M., Waters, E., & Wall, S. (1978). *Patterns of attachment.* Hillsdale, NJ: Lawrence Erlbaum Associates.

Alexander, G., & Hines, M. (1994). Gender labels and play styles: Their relative contributions to children's selection of playmates. *Child Development, 65,* 869–879.

Allan, G. (1989). *Friendship: Developing a sociological perspective.* Boulder, CO: Westview.

Allan, G., & Adams, R.G. (1989). Aging and the structure of friendship. In R. G. Adams & R. Blieszner (Eds.), *Older adult friendships: Structure and process* (pp. 45–64). Newbury Park, CA: Sage.

Allen, M. (1995). Sullivan's closet: A reappraisal of Harry Stack Sullivan's life and his pioneering role in American psychiatry. *Journal of Homosexuality, 29*(1), 1–18.

Ambrose, S. F. (1989). Men and women can be friends. In N. Bernards & T. O'Neill (Eds.), *Male/female roles* (pp. 207–212). San Diego, CA: Greenhaven.

Andersen, P. A. (1993). Cognitive schemata in personal relationships. In S. W. Duck (Ed.), *Individuals in relationships: Understanding relationship processes series: Volume 1* (pp. 1–29). Newbury Park: Sage.

Anderson, J., & Reder, L. (1979). Elaborative processing explanation of depth of processing. In L. S. Cermak & F. I. Craik (Eds.), *Levels of processing in human memory* (pp. 385–403). Hillsdale, NJ: Lawrence Erlbaum Associates.

Antonucci, T. C., & Akiyama, H. (1987). Social networks in adult life and a preliminary examination of the convoy model. *Journal of Gerontology, 42,* 519–527.

Antonucci, T. C., & Akiyama, H. (1995). Convoys of social relations: Family and friendships within a life span context. In R. Blieszner & V. H. Bedford (Eds.), *Handbook of Aging and the Family* (pp. 355–371). Westport, CT: Greenwood Press.

Arbib, M., Conklin, J. & Hill, J. (1987). *From schema theory to language.* New York, NY: Oxford University Press.

Argyle, M., & Henderson, M. (1985). The rules of relationships. In S. W. Duck & D. Perlman (Eds.), *Understanding personal relationships: An interdisciplinary approach* (pp. 63–84). London: Sage.

Arnold, L. B. (1995). Through the narrow pass: Experiencing same-sex friendship in heterosexual(ist) settings. *Communication Studies, 46* (3/4), 234–234.

Aron, A., & Aron, E. (1997). Self–expansion motivation and including other in the self. In S. W. Duck (Ed.), *Handbook of personal relationships* (2nd ed., pp. 251–270). New York: John Wiley & Sons.

Aronson, E. (1984). *The social animal.* San Francisco: W. H. Freeman.

Asher, S. R., & Cole, J. D. (Eds.). (1990). *Peer rejection in childhood.* Cambridge, UK: Cambridge University Press.

Asher, S. R., & Dodge, K. A. (1986). Identifying children who are rejected by their peers. *Developmental Psychology, 22,* 444–449.

Asher, S. R., & Parker, J. G. (1989). Significance of peer relationship problems in childhood. In B. H. Schneider, G. Atili, J. Nadel & R. P. Weissberg (Eds.), *Social competence in developmental perspective.* Dordrecht Netherlands: Kluwer.

Asher, S. R., Parker, J. G., & Walker, D. L. (1996). Distinguishing friendship from acceptance: Implications for intervention and assessment. In W. M. Bukowski, A. F. Newcomb, & W.

W. Hartup (Eds.), *The company they keep: Friendship in childhood and adolescence* (pp. 366–405). New York: Cambridge University Press.

Asher, S. R., Parkhurst, J. T., Hymel, S., & Williams, G. A. (1990). *Peer rejection and loneliness in childhood.* In S. R. Asher & J. D. Coie (Eds.), Peer rejection in childhood (pp. 253–273). New York: Cambridge University Press.

Atchley, R. C. (1985). *Social forces and aging* (4th ed., pp. 224–231). Belmont, CA: Wadsworth.

Aukett, R., Ritchie, J., Mill, K. (1988). Gender differences in friendship patterns. *Sex Roles,* 19, 57–66.

Babchuk, N. (1965). Primary friends and kin: A study of the associations of middle class couples. *Social Forces,* 43, 483–493.

Babchuk, N., & Anderson, T. B. (1989). Older widows and married women: Their intimates and confidantes. *International Journal of Aging and Human Development,* 28, 21–35.

Bagwell, C. L., Newcomb, A. F., & Bukowski, W. (1998). Preadolescent friendship and peer rejection as predictors of adult adjustment. *Child Development,* 69(1), 140–153.

Bakan, D. (1966). *The duality of human existence.* Boston, MA: Beacon Press.

Baldwin, J. M. (1911). *The individual and society.* Boston, MA: Boston Presss.

Baldwin, M. W. (1992). Relational schemas and the processing of social information. *Psychological Bulletin,* 112, 461–484.

Baldwin, M. W. (1995). Relational schemas and cognition in close relationships. *Journal of Social and Personal Relationships,* 12(4), 547–552.

Baldwin, M. W., Carrell, S. E., & Lopez, D. F. (1990). Priming relationship schemas: My advisor and the pope are watching me from the back of my mind. *Journal of Experimental Social Psychology,* 26, 435–454.

Baldwin, M. W., & Fehr, B. (1995). On the instability of attachment style ratings. *Personal Relationships,* 2, 247–261.

Ballard-Reisch, D. S., & Seibert, D. R. (1993). Academic self-concept, gender orientation, and communication apprehension in adolescents. In C. Berryman-Fink, D. Ballard-Reisch, & L. H. Newman (Eds.), *Communication and sex-role socialization* (pp. 283–310). New York: Garland Publishing.

Bandura, A., & Walters, R. H. (1963). *Social learning and personality development.* New York: Holt, Reinhart and Winston.

Banse, R. (1999). Automatic evaluation of self and significant others: Affective priming in close relationship. *Journal of Social and Personal Relationships,* 16(6), 803–821.

Barbee, A. P., Gulley, M. R., & Cunningham, M. R. (1990). Support seeking in personal relationships. *Journal of Social and Personal Relationships,* 7(4), 531–540.

Barer, B. M. (1994). Men and women aging differently. *International Journal of Aging and Human Development,* 38(1), 29(12).

Barrett, K. C. (1997). The self and relationship development. In S. W. Duck (Ed.), *Handbook of personal relationships* (pp. 81–97). New York: John Wiley & Sons.

Battle, J. (1982). *Enhancing self-esteem and achievement: A handbook for professionals.* Seattle, WA: Special Child Publications.

Baumeister, R. F. (1987). How the self became a problem: A psychological review of historical research. *Journal of Personality and Social Psychology,* 52, 163–176.

Baxter, L. A. (1987). Symbols of relationship identity in relationship cultures. *Journal of Social and Personal Relationships,* 4, 261–280.

Baxter, L. A., & Wilmot, W. W. (1985). Taboo topics in close relationships. *Journal of Social and Personal Relationships, 2,* 253–269.

Bell, A. P., & Weinberg, M. S. (1978). *Homosexualities: A study of diversities among men and women.* New York: Simon & Schuster.

Bell, B. (1993). Emotional loneliness and the perceived similarity of one's ideas and interests. *Journal of Social Behavior and Personality, 8,* 273–280.

Bell, R. R. (1981). Friendships of women and men. *Psychology of Women Quarterly, 5,* 402–417.

Belle, D. (1989). Gender differences in children's social networks and support. In D. Belle (Ed.), *Children's social networks and social supports* (pp. 173–188). New York: John Wiley & Sons.

Belsky, J. (1992). The research findings on gender issues in aging men and women. In B. R. Wainrib (Ed.), *Gender issues across the life cycle* (pp. 163–171). New York: Springer.

Bem, S. L. (1974). The measurement of psychological androgyny. *Journal of Consulting and Clinical Psychology, 42,* 155–162.

Bem, S. L. (1981). Gender schema theory: A cognitive account of sex typing. *Psychological Review, 88,* 354–364.

Bendtschneider, L. (1994). *"We all like to dance and play dominoes": The nature and maintenance of couple friendships.* Unpublished doctoral dissertation, The University of Iowa, Iowa City, IA.

Bendtschneider, L., & Duck, S. (1993). What's yours is mine and what's mine is yours: Couple friends. In P. Kalbfleisch (Ed.), *Interpersonal communication: Evolving interpersonal relationships* (pp. 261–291). Hillsdale, NJ: Lawrence Erlbaum Associates.

Benenson, J. (1993). Greater preferences among females than males for dyadic interaction in early childhood. *Child Development, 64,* 544–555.

Benenson, J. (1994). Ages four to six years: Changes in the structures of play networks of girls and boys. *Merrill-Palmer Quarterly, 40,* 478–487.

Benenson, J., Apostoleris, N., & Parnass, J. (1998). The organization of same–sex peer relationships. In W. M. Bukowski & A. H. Cillessen (Eds.), *New Directions for Child Development: Sociometry then and now: Building on six decades of measuring children's experiences with the peer group,* San Francisco, CA: Jossey-Bass Inc. (pp. 5–23)

Berger, P. & Luckmann, T. (1966). *The social construction of reality.* Garden City, NY: Doubleday.

Bergmann, J. R. (1993). *Discreet indiscretions: The social organization of gossip.* New York: Aldine de Gruyter.

Berndt, T. J. (1982). The features and effects of friendship in early adolescence. *Child Development, 53,* 1447–1460.

Berndt, T. J. (1994). Intimacy and competition in the friendships of adolescent boys and girls. In M. R. Stevenson (Ed.), *Gender roles through the life span: A multidisciplinary perspective* (pp. 89–110). Muncie, IN: Ball State University.

Berndt, T. J. (1996). Exploring the effects of friendship quality on social development. In W. M. Bukowski, A. F. Newcomb, & W. W. Hartup (Eds.), *Friendship in childhood and adolescence* (pp. 346–365). New York: Cambridge University Press.

Berndt, T. J., & Keefe, K. (1992). Friends' influence on adolescents' perceptions of themselves in school. In D. H. Schunk & J. L. Meece (Eds.), *Student perceptions in the classroom.* Hillsdale, NJ: Lawrence Erlbaum Associates.

Berry, J. (1993, February). Healthy, wealthy, and growing in numbers. *Brandweek, 34*(8), *32*(1)

Berscheid, E., & Peplau, L. A. (1983). The emerging science of relationships. In H. Kelley, E. Berscheid, A. Christensen, J. Harvey, T. Huston, G. Levinger, E. McClintock, L. Peplau, & D. Peterson (Eds.), *Close Relationships* (pp. 1–19). New York: W. H. Freeman.

Berscheid, E., Snyder, M., & Omoto, A. M. (1989). The Relationship Closeness Inventory: Assessing the closeness of interpersonal relationships. *Journal of Personality and Social Psychology, 57,* 792–807.

Best, R. (1983). *We've all got scars. What boys and girls learn in elementary school.* Bloomington: Indiana University Press.

Bigelow, B. J., & LaGaipa, J. J. (1975). Childrens' written description of friendship: A multidimensional analysis. *Developmental Psychology, 11,* 857–858.

Bigelow, B. J., Tesson, G., & Lewko, J. H. (1996). *Learning the rules: The anatomy of children's relationships.* New York: The Guilford Press.

Black Issues in Higher Education, Number of high school graduates attending college drops (1999, July). *16*(10), 18

Blau, Z. (1961). Stuctual constraints on friendship in old age. *American Sociological Review, 26,* 429–439.

Blau, Z. (1973). *Old age in a changing society.* New York: Viewpoints.

Blieszner, R., & Adams, R. G. (1992). *Adult friendships.* Newbury Park, CA: Sage.

Blieszner, R., & Adams, R. G. (1998). Problems with friends in old age. *Journal of Aging Studies, 12*(3), 223–238.

Block, J. D. (1980). *Friendship.* New York: Macmillan.

Blomberg, D., & Monsour, M. (1998, May). *Cross-sex chumships among preadolescent boys and girls: A qualitative extension of Sullivan's chumship construct.* Paper presented at the Interpersonal Network on Personal Relationships conference, Norman, OK.

Blos, P. (1967). The second individuation process of adolescence. *Psychoanalytic Study of the Child, 22,* 162–168.

Blumer, H. (1969). *Symbolic interactionism: Perspective and method.* Englewood Cliffs, NJ: Prentice-Hall.

Blyth, D., & Foster-Clark, F. (1987). Gender differences in perceived intimacy with different members of adolescents' social networks. *Sex Roles, 17,* 689–718.

Bondevik, M., & Skogstad, A. (1996). Loneliness among the oldest old, a comparison between residents living in nursing home and residents living in the community. *International Journal of Aging and Human Development, 43*(3), 181–197.

Booth, A., & Hess, E. (1974). Cross-sex friendship. *Journal of Marriage and the Family, 36,* 38–47.

Booth, C. L., Rubin, K. H., & Rose-Krasnor, L. (1998). Perceptions of emotional support from mother and friend in middle childhood: Links with social-emotional adaptation and preschool attachment security. *Child Development, 69*(2), 427–442.

Bosse, R., Aldwin, C. M., Levenson, M. R., Workman-Daniels, K., & Ekerdt, D. J. (1990). Differences in social support among retirees and workers: Findings from the normative aging study. *Psychology and Aging, 5,* 41–47.

Bowlby, J. (1969). *Attachment and loss: Vol. 1: Attachment.* New York: Basic Books Inc.

Bowlby, J. (1973). *Attachment and loss: Vol. 2: Separation, anxiety, and anger.* New York, Basic Books Inc.

Brenton, M. (1966). *Friendship.* New York: Stein & Day.

Bretherton, I. (1985). Attachment theory: Retrospective and prospective. In I. Bretherton & E. Waters (Eds.), *Growing points of attachment theory and research. Monographs of the Society for Research in Child Development, 50,* 1–2, Serial No. 209.

Brooks-Gunn, J., & Reiter, E. O. (1990). The role of pubertal processes. In S. Feldman & G. R. Elliott (Eds.), *At the threshold: The developing adolescent* (pp. 16–53). Cambridge, MA: Harvard University Press.

Brown, B. B. (1990). Peer groups and peer cultures. In S. S. Feldman & G. R. Elliott (Eds.), *At the threshold: The developing adolescent* (pp. 171–196). Cambridge, MA: Harvard University Press.

Brown, B. B., Mory, M. S., & Kinney, D. (1994). Casting adolescent crowds in a relational perspective: Caricature, channel, and context. In R. Montemayor, G. Adams, & T. Gullotta (Eds.), *Personal relationships during adolescence* (Vol. 6, pp. 123–167). Thousand Oaks, CA: Sage Publications, Inc.

Bruess, C. J. S., & Pearson, J. C. (1997). Interpersonal rituals in marriage and adult friendship. *Communication Monographs, 64,* 25–46.

Bryant, S. L., & Hansson, R. O. (1995). Widowhood. In R. Blieszner & V. H. Bedford (Eds.), *Handbook of Aging and the Family* (pp. 440–458). Westport, CT: Greenwood Press.

Buhrke, R. A., & Fuqua, D. R. (1987). Sex differences in same- and cross-sex supportive relationships. *Sex Roles, 17,* 339–351

Buhrmester, D. (1990). Intimacy of friendship, interpersonal competence, and adjustment during preadolescence and adolescence. *Child Development, 61*(4), 1101–1111.

Buhrmester, D. (1996). Need fulfillment, interpersonal competence, and the developmental contexts of early adolescent friendship. In W. M. Bukowski, A. F. Newcomb, & W. W. Hartup (Eds.), *Friendship in childhood and adolescence* (pp.158–185). New York: Cambridge University Press.

Buhrmester, D., & Furman, W. (1987). The development of companionship and intimacy. *Child Development, 58*(4), 1101–1113.

Buhrmester, D., & Furman, W. (1986). The changing functions of friends in childhood: A Neo-Sullivanian perspective. In V. Derlega & B. Winstead (Eds.), *Friendship and social interaction* (pp. 41–62). New York: Springer-Verlag.

Bukowski, W. M., Gauze, C., Hoza, B., & Newcomb, A. F. (1993). Differences and consistencies in relations with same-sex and other-sex peers during early adolescence. *Developmental Psychology, 29,* 255–263.

Bukowski, W. M., & Hoza, B. (1989). Popularity and friendship: issues in theory, measurement, and outcome. In T. J. Berndt & G. W. Ladd (Eds.), *Peer relationships in child development* (pp. 15–45). New York: Wiley.

Bukowski, W. M., & Hoza, B., & Boivin, M. (1994). Measuring friendship quality during pre- and early-adolescence: The development and psychometrics of the Friendship Qualities Scale. *Journal of Social and Personal Relationships, 11,*(3) 471–485.

Bukowski, W. M., & Hoza, B., & Boivin, M. (1993). Popularity, friendship, and emotional adjustment during adolescence. In B. Laursen (Ed.), *New Directions for Child Development: Close Friendships in Adolescence.* San Francisco: Jossey-Bass.

Bukowski, W. M., Newcomb, A. F., & Hartup, W. W. (1996). Friendship and its significance in childhood and adolescence: Introduction and comment. In W. M. Bukowski, A. F. Newcomb, & W. W. Hartup (Eds.), *Friendship in childhood and adolescence* (pp. 1–15). New York: Cambridge University Press.

Bukowski, W. M., Newcomb, A. F., & Hoza, B. (1987). Friendship conceptions among early adolescents: A longitudinal study of stability and change. *Journal of Early Adolescence, 7,* 143–152.

Bukowski, W. M., Sippola, L. K., & Hoza, B. (1999). Same and other: Interdependency between participants in same- and other-sex friendships. *Journal of Youth and Adolescence, 28*(4), 439–459.

Bullock, J. R. (1993). Lonely children. *Young Children, 48*(6), 53–57.

Burgess, K. B., Ladd, G. W., Kochenderfer, B. J., Lambert, S. F., & Birch, S. H. (1999). Loneliness during early childhood: The role of interpersonal behaviors and relationships. In K. Rotenberg & S. Hymel (Eds.), *Loneliness in childhood and adolescence* (pp. 109–134). New York: Cambridge University Press.

Burleson, B. R. (1994). Friendship and similarities in social-cognitive and communication abilities: Social skills bases of interpersonal attraction in childhood. *Personal Relationships, 1,* 371–389.

Burleson, B. R., Kunkel, A. W., Samter, W., & Werking, K. (1996). Men's and women's evaluations of communication skills in personal relationships: When sex differences don't make a difference and why. *Journal of Social and Personal Relationships, 13*(2), 201–224.

Business Week (1999, August 9) *Women in the workplace: Is parity finally in sight?*

Burleson, B. R., & Planalp, S. (2000). Producing emotional messages. *Communication Theory, 10*(2), 221–250.

Cairns, R. B. (1979). *Social development: The origins and plasticity of interchanges.* San Francisco: Freeman.

Canary, D. J., & Dindia, K. (1998). Prologue: Recurring issues in sex differences and similarities in communication. In D. J. Canary & K. Dindia (Eds.), *Sex differences and similarities in communication: Critical essays and empirical investigations of sex and gender in interaction* (pp. 1–18). Mahwah, NJ: Lawrence Erlbaum Associates.

Carbery, J., & Buhrmester, D. (1998). Friendship and need fulfillment during three phases of young adulthood. *Journal of Social and Personal Relationships 15*(3), 393–409.

Carroll, L. (1958). *Symbolic logic and the game of logic.* New York: Dover Publications.

Carstensen, L. L. (1993). Motivation for social contact across the life span: A theory of socioemotional selectivity. In J. E. Jacobs (Ed.), *Nebraska symposium on motivation: Developmental perspectives on motivation* (pp. 209–254). Lincoln: University of Nebraska Press.

Carstensen, L. L. (1995). Evidence for a life-span theory of socioemotional selectivity. *Current Directions in Psychological Science, 4,* 151–156.

Carter, D. B., & Levy, G. D. (1988). Cognitive aspects of early sex-role development: The influence of gender schemas on preschoolers' memories and preferences for sex-typed toys and activities. *Child Development, 59,* 782–792.

Carter, D. B., & McCloskey, L. A. (1984). Peers and the maintenance of sex-typed behavior: The development of children's conceptions of cross-gender behavior in their peers. *Social Cognition, 2,* 294–314.

Case, R. (1991). Stages in the development of the young child's first sense of self. *Developmental Review, 11,* 210–230.

Cassel, C. (1989, October/November). The final frontier: Other-gender friendships. *SIECUS report,* 19–20.

Cassidy, J. (1990). Theoretical and methodological considerations in the study of attachment and the self in young children. In M. T. Greenberg, D. Cicchetti, & E. M. Cummings

(Eds.), *Attachment in the preschool years: Theory, research and intervention* (pp. 87–119). Chicago, IL: University of Chicago Press.

Cassidy, J., & Asher, S. R. (1992). Loneliness and peer relations in young children. *Child Development, 63*(2), 350–365.

Cassidy, J., & Berlin, L. J. (1999). Understanding the origins of childhood loneliness: Contributions of Attachment Theory. In K. J. Rotenberg & S. Hymel (Eds.), *Loneliness in childhood and adolescence* (pp. 34–55). Cambridge, UK: Cambridge University Press.

Cast, A. D., Stets, J. E., & Burke, P. J. (1999). Does the self conform to the views of others? *Social Psychology Quarterly, 62*(1), 68–82.

Chodorow, N. (1978). *The reproduction of mothering: Psychoanalysis and the sociology of gender.* Berkeley: University of California Press.

Chown, S. M. (1981). Friendships in old age. In S. W. Duck & R. Gilmour (Eds.), *Personal relationships 2: Developing personal relationships* (pp. 231–246). New York: Academic Press.

Cillessen, H. N. & Bukowski, W. M. (2000). Recent advances in the measurement of acceptance and rejection in the peer system. *New Direction for Child and Adolescent Development, 88.*

Clark, R. A. (1994). Children and adolescents' gender preferences for conversational partners for specific communication objectives. *Journal of Social and Personal Relationships, 11*(2), 313–319.

Coats, P. B., & Overman, S. J. (1992). Childhood play experiences of women in traditional and nontraditional professions. *Sex Roles, 26* (7/8), 261–271.

Cocking, D., & Kennett, J. (1998). Friendship and the self. *Ethics, 108,* 502–527.

Cohen, T. F. (1992). Men's families, men's friends: A structural analysis of constraints on men's social ties. In P. Nardi (Ed.), *Men's friendships* (pp.115–131). Newbury Park, CA: Sage.

Coleman, C. C. (1993). *Relative contributions of classroom friendship and peer status to children's early school adjustment.* Unpublished master's thesis, University of Illinois at Urbana-Champaign.

Collins, N. W. (1983). *Professional women and their mentors.* Englewood Cliffs, NJ: Prentice Hall.

Collins, W. A., & Laursen, B. (1992). Conflict and relationships during adolescence. In C. U. Shantz & W. W. Hartup (Eds.), *Conflict in child and adolescent development.* New York: Cambridge University Press.

Connolly, J. A., Craig, W., Goldberg, A., & Pepler, D. (1999). Conceptions of cross-sex friendships and romantic relationships in early adolescence. *Journal of Youth and Adolescence, 28*(4), 481–494.

Connolly, J. A., Furman, W., & Konarski, R. (1998). *The role of peers in the emergence of romantic relationships in adolescence.* Unpublished manuscript. York University, Toronto.

Cooley, C. H. (1902). *Human nature and the social order.* New York: Scribner's. Published in 1964 by Schocken Books (Introduction by P. Rieff, Forward by H. G. Mead).

Cooley, C. H. (1909). *Social organization: A study of the larger mind.* New York: Schocken.

Cooley, C. H. (1998). *On self and social organization* (Edited by H. Schubert; A compilation of Cooley's major works). Chicago: The University of Chicago Press.

Cooper, H. (1989). *Integrating research: A guide for literature reviews.* Newbury Park, CA: Sage.

Coover, G. E., & Murphy, S. T. (2000). The communicated self: Exploring the interaction between self and social context. *Human Communication Research, 26*(1), 125–147.

Corsaro, W. A. (1985). *Friendship and peer culture in the early years.* Norwood, NJ: Ablex.

Corsaro, W. A., & Eder, D. (1990). Children's peer cultures. *Annual Review of Sociology, 16,* 197–220.

Cosse, W. J. (1992). Who's who and what's what? The effects of gender on development in adolescence. In B. R. Wainrib (Ed.), *Gender issues across the life cycle* (pp. 5–16). New York: Springer Publishing Company.

Cotterell, J. (1996). *Social networks and social influences in adolescence.* London: Routledge.

Cravatta, M. (1997). Hanging on to students. *American Demographics, 19*(11), 41.

Crick, N. R., & Bigbee, M. A. (1998). Relational and overt forms of peer victimization: A multi–informant approach. *Journal of Consulting and Clinical Psychology, 66*(2), 337(11).

Crick, N. R., & Ladd, G. (1993). Children' perceptions of their peer experiences: Attributions, loneliness, social anxiety, and social avoidance. *Developmental Psychology, 29*(2), 244–254.

Crohan, S. E., & Antonucci, T. C. (1989). Friends as a source of support in old age. In R. G. Adams & R. Blieszner (Eds.), *Older adult friendships: Structure and process* (pp.129–146). Newbury Park, CA: Sage.

Cross, S., & Markus, H. (1991). Possible selves across the life span. *Human Development, 34,* 230–255.

Cumming, E., & Henry, W. (1961). *Growing old.* New York: Basic Books.

Cupach, W. R., & Metts, S. (1991). Sexuality and communication in close relationships. In K. McKinney & S. Sprecher (Eds.), *Sexuality in close relationships* (pp. 93–110). Hillsdale, NJ: Lawrence Erlbaum Associates.

Damon, W. (1977). *The social world of the child.* San Francisco: Jossey-Bass.

Damon, W., & Hart, D. (1988). *Self-understanding in childhood and adolescence.* New York: Cambridge University Press.

Davis, K. E., & Todd, M. J. (1982). Friendship and love relationships. In K. E. Davis & T. O. Mitchell (Eds.), *Advances in descriptive psychology* (Vol. 2, pp. 79–122). Greenwich, CT: JAI.

Davis, K. E., & Todd, M. J. (1985). Assessing friendship: Prototypes, paradigm cases, and relationships descriptions. In S. W. Duck & D. Perlman (Eds.), *Understanding personal relationships: An interdisciplinary approach* (pp. 17–38). London: Sage.

Demo, D. (1992). The self-concept over time: Research issues and directions. *Annual Review of Sociology, 18,*(303), 24.

Derlega, V. J., Metts, S., Petronio, S., & Margulis, S. T. (1993). *Self-disclosure.* Newbury Park, CA: Sage.

Devine, I., & Markiewicz, D. (1990). Cross-gender relationships at work and the impact of gender stereotypes. *Journal of Business Ethics, 9,* 333–338.

Diamond, L. M. (2000). Passionate friendships among adolescent sexual-minority women. *Journal of Research on Adolescence, 10*(2), 191–209.

Dindia, K. (1997a, November). *Men are from North Dakota, Women are from South Dakota.* Paper presented at the Speech Communication Association Convention, Chicago.

Dindia, K. (1997b). Self-disclosure, self-identity, and relationship development: A transactional/dialectical perspective. In S. W. Duck (Ed.), *Handbook of personal relationships* (2nd ed., pp. 411–426). New York: John Wiley & Sons.

Dindia, K., & Allen, M. (1992). Sex differences in self-disclosure: A meta-analysis. *Psychological Bulletin, 112,* 106–124.

Doyle, R. (1999, October). Men, women, and college. *Scientific American, 28*(4), p. 40.

Doyle, A. B., & Markiewicz, D. (1996). Parents' interpersonal relationships and children's friendships. In W. Bukowski, A. F. Newcomb, & W. W. Hartup (Eds.), *The company they keep: Friendships in childhood and adolescence* (pp. 115–136). New York: Cambridge University Press.

Duck, S. W. (1983). *Friends for life: The psychology of close relationships.* New York: St. Martins.

Duck, S. W. (1990). Relationships as unfinished business: Out of the frying pan and into the 1990s. *Journal of Social and Personal Relationships, 7,* 5–28.

Duck, S. W. (1992). *Human relationships* (2nd ed.). London: Sage.

Duck, S. W. (1994). *Meaningful relationships: Talking, sense, and relating.* Thousand Oaks: Sage.

Duck, S. W. (1995). Talking relationship into being. *Journal of social and Personal Relationships, 12*(4), 535–540.

Duck, S. W. (1997). *Handbook of personal relationships: Theory, research, and interventions* (2nd ed.). New York: John Wiley & Sons.

Duck, S. W., & Barnes, M. K. (1992). Disagreeing about agreement: Reconciling differences about similarity. *Communication Monographs, 59,* 199–208.

Duck, S. W., Pond, K., & Leatham, G. (1994). Loneliness and the evaluation of relational events. *Journal of Social and Personal Relationships, 11,* 253–276.

Duck, S. W., Rutt, D. J., Hurst, M., & Strejc, H. (1991). Some evident truths about communication in everyday relationships: All communication is not created equal. *Human Communication Research, 18,* 228–267.

Duck, S. W., & VanderVoort, L. (2001). Scarlet letters and whited sepulchries: The social marking of relationships as "inappropriate." In R. Goodwin & D. Cramer (Eds.), *In appropriate relationships.* Mahwah, NJ: Lawrence Erlbaum Associates.

Duck, S. W., West, L., & Acitelli, L. (1997). Sewing the field: The tapestry of relationships in life and research. In S. W. Duck (Ed.), *Handbook of personal relationships* (2nd ed., pp. 1–23). New York: John Wiley & Sons.

Duck, S. & Wright, P. (1993). Reexamining gender differences in same-gender friendships: A close look at two kinds of data. *Sex Roles, 28,* 709–727.

Dugan, E., & Kivett, V. R. (1998). Implementing the Adams and Blieszner conceptual model: Predicting interactive friendship processes of older adults. *Journal of Social and Personal Relationships, 15*(5), 607–622.

Duncan, M. K, & Cohen, R. (1995). Liking within the peer group as a function of children's sociometric status and sex. *Child Study Journal, 25*(4), 265–287.

Dunphy, D. C. (1963). The social structure of urban adolescent peer groups. *Society, 26,* 230–246.

Dunphy, D. C. (1969). *Cliques, crowds, and gangs.* Melbourne, Australia: Cheshire.

Dyk, P. H. (1993). Anatomy, physiology, and gender issues in adolescence. In T. P. Gullotta, G. A. Adams, & R. Montemayor (Eds.), *Adolescent sexuality* (pp. 35–56). Newbury Park, CA: Sage Publications.

Dykstra, P. A. (1995). Loneliness among the never and formerly married: The importance of supportive friendships and a desire for independence. *Journal of Gerontology, 50B*(5), S321–S329.

Eccles, J. S. (1987). Adolescence: Gateway to gender-role transcendence. In D. B. Carter (Ed.), *Current conceptions of sex roles and sex typing: Theory and research* (pp. 225–241). New York: Praeger.

Eccles, J. S., & Bryan, J. (1994). Adolescence: Critical crossroad in the path of gender-role development. In M. R. Stevenson (Ed.), *Gender roles through the life span: A multidisciplinary perspective* (pp. 111–147). Muncie, IN: Ball State University.

Economist, June 10, 2000, Vol. 355, i85174, p.88.

Eder, D. (1985). The cycle of popularity: Interpersonal relations among female adolescents. *Sociology of Education, 58,* 154–165.

Egland, K. L., Spitzberg, B. H., Zormeier, M. M. (1996). Flirtation and conversational competence in cross-sex platonic and romantic relationships. *Communication Reports, 9*(2), 105–117.

Elliott, G. R., & Feldman, S. S. (1990). Capturing the adolescent experience. In S. Feldman & G. R. Elliott (Eds.), *At the threshold: The developing adolescent* (pp. 1–13). Cambridge, MA: Harvard University Press.

Epstein, J. L. (1986). Friendship selection: Developmental and environmental influences. In E. Mueller & Cooper (Eds.), *Process and outcome in peer relationships* (pp. 129–160). New York: Academic Press.

Erikson, E. (1968). *Identity. Youth and crises.* New York: Norton.

Erwin, P. (1998). *Friendship in childhood and adolescence.* New York: Routledge.

Eyler, D., & Baridon, A. P. (1992). Far more than friendship. *Psychology Today, 25,* 62–67.

Fagot, B. I. (1994). Peer relations and the development of competence in boys and girls. In C. Leaper (Ed.), *Childhood gender segregation: Causes and consequences: New directions for child development* (Vol. 65, pp. 53–66). San Francisco: Jossey-Bass Publishers.

Fagot, B. I., & Leinbach, M. D. (1993). Gender-role development in young children: From discrimination to labeling. *Developmental Review, 13*(2), 205–224.

Fehr, B. (1996). *Friendship processes.* Thousand Oaks, CA: Sage.

Feiring, C. (1999). Other-sex friendship networks and the development of romantic relationships in adolescence. *Journal of Youth and Adolescence, 28*(4), 495–512.

Feiring, C. & Lewis, M. (1989). The social networks of girls and boys from early through middle childhood. In DeBelle (Ed.), *Children's social networks and social supports.* New York: John Wiley & Sons.

Feldman, S., & Elliott, G. R. (1990). *At the threshold: the developing adolescent.* Cambridge, MA: Harvard University Press.

Felmlee, D. H. (1994). Who's on top? Power in romantic relationships. *Sex Roles, 31,* 275–295.

Felmlee, D. H. (1999). Social norms in same- and cross-gender friendships. *Social Psychology Quarterly, 62*(1), 53–67.

Festinger, L., Schachter, S., & Back, K. (1950). *Social pressures in informal groups.* New York: Harper.

Field, D. (1999). Continuity and change in friendships in advanced old age: Findings from the Berkeley older generation study. *International Journal of Aging & Human Development, 48*(4), 325 (2).

Field, T., Lang, C., Yando, R., & Bendell, D. (1995). Adolescents' intimacy with parents and friends. *Adolescence, 30*(117), *133*(8).

Fine, G. A. (1986). Friendships in the workplace. In V. J. Derlega & B. A. Winstead (Eds.), *Friendship and social interaction* (pp. 185–206). New York: Springer-Verlag.

Fiske, S. T., & Taylor, S. E. (1984). *Social cognition.* New York: Random House.

Fleming, R., & Baum, A. (1986). Social support and stress: The buffering effects of friendship. In V. Derlega & B. Winstead (Eds.), *Friendship and social interaction* (pp. 207–226). New York: Springer-Verlag.

Freund, A. M., & Smith, J. (1999). Content and function of the self definition in old and very old age. *The Journals of Gerontology, Series B, 54*(1), 55 (1).

Frey, C. U., & Rothlisberger, C. (1996). Social support in healthy adolescents. *Journal of Youth and Adolescence, 25,* 17–31.

Furman, L. G. (1986). Cross-gender friendships in the workplace: Factors and components. (Doctoral dissertation, Fielding Institute, 1986). *Dissertation Abstracts International, DEU87–03955.*

Furman, W. (1993). Theory is not a four-letter word: Needed directions in the study of adolescent friendships. In B. Laursen (Ed.), *Close friendships in adolescence* (pp. 89–103). New York: Cambridge University Press.

Furman, W., & Buhrmester, D. (1992). Age and sex differences in perceptions of networks of personal relationships. *Child Development, 63,* 103–115.

Furman, W., & Shaffer, L. A. (1999). A story of adolescence: The emergence of other-sex relationships. *Journal of Youth and Adolescence, 28*(4), 513–522.

Furman, W., & Simon, V. A. (1998). Advice from youth: Some lessons from the study of adolescent relationships. *Journal of Social and Personal Relationships, 15*(6), 723–739.

Furman, W., & Wehner, E. A. (1993). Romantic views: toward a theory of adolescent romantic relationships. In R. Montemayor, G. Adams, & T. P. Gullotta (Eds.), *Personal relationships during adolescence* (pp. 168–195). Thousand Oaks, CA: Sage Publications.

Gaines, S. O. (1994). Exchange of respect-denying behaviors among male-female friendships. *Journal of Social and Personal Relationships, 11,* 5–24.

George, T. P., & Hartmann, D. P. (1996). Friendship networks of unpopular, average, and popular children. *Child Development, 67*(5), 2301–2316.

Gergen, K. (1977). The social construction of self knowledge. In T. Mischel (Ed.), *The self, psychological and philosophical issues.* (pp. 139–169). Oxford, England: Blackwell.

Gergen, K. (1985). The social constructionist movement in modern psychology. *American Psychologist, 40,* 266–275.

Gergen, K. (1991). *The saturated self: Dilemmas of identity in contemporary life.* United States of America: Basic Books.

Gergen, K., & Gergen, M. (1991). Toward reflexive methodologies. In F. Steier (Ed.), *Research and reflexivity* (pp. 76–95). Newbury Park, CA: Sage.

Gesell, A. (1945). *The embryology of behavior.* New York: Harper.

Gilligan, C. N. (1990). Teaching Shakespeare's sister: Notes from the underground of female adolescence. In C. Gilligan, N. Lyons, & T. Hammer (Eds.), *Making connections* (pp. 6–29). Cambridge, MA: Harvard University Press.

Gilligan, C. N. (1982). *In a different voice: Psychological theory and women's development.* Cambridge, MA: Harvard University Press.

Gilligan, C. N., Lyons, P., & Hanmer, T. J. (1990). *Making connections: The relational worlds of adolescent girls at Emma Williard School.* Cambridge, MA: Harvard University Press.

Gini, A. (1998). Women in the workplace. *Business and Society Review, 99,* 3–17.

Ginsberg, D., Gottman, J. M., & Parker, J. G. (1986). The importance of friendship. In J. M. Gottman & J. G. Parker (Eds.), *Conversations of friends: Speculations on affective development* (pp. 3–48). Cambridge, MA: Cambridge University Press.

Golombok, S., & Fivush, R. (1994). *Gender development.* New York: Cambridge University Press.

Goodenough, F. (1934). *Developmental psychology: An introduction to the study of human behavior.* New York: Appleton-Century.

Gottman, J. M. (1979). *Marital interactions: Experimental investigations.* New York: Academic Press.

Gottman, J. M. (1986). The world of coordinated play: Same- and cross-sex friendship in young children. In J. M. Gottman & J. G. Parker (Eds.), *Conversations of friends: Speculations on affective development* (pp. 139–191). New York: Cambridge University Press.

Gottman, J. M., & Carrere, S. (1994). Why can't men and women get along? Developmental roots and marital inequities. In D. J. Canary & L. Stafford (Eds.), *Communication and relational maintenance.* Orlando: Academic Press.

Gottman, J. M., Coan, J., Carrere, S., & Swanson, C. (1998). Predicting marital happiness and stability from newlywed interactions. *Journal of Marriage and Family, 60*(1), 5–18.

Gottman, J. M., & Mettetal, G. (1986). Speculations about social and affective development: Friendship and acquaintanceship through adolescence. In J. M. Gottman & J. G. Parker (Eds.), *Conversations of friends: Speculations on affective development* (pp. 192–237). New York: Cambridge University Press.

Gottman, J. M., & Parker, J. G. (1986). *Conversations of friends: Speculations on affective development.* New York: Cambridge University Press.

Graham, J. A., & Cohen, R. (1997). Race and sex as factors in children's sociometric ratings and friendship choice. *Social Development, 6,* 353–370.

Graham, J. A., Cohen, R., Zbikowski, S., & Secrist, M. E. (1998). A longitudinal investigation of race and sex as factors in children's classroom friendship choices. *Child Study Journal, 28*(4), 245–265.

Graham, S., & Juvonen, J. (1998). Self-blame and peer victimization in middle school: An attributional analysis. *Developmental Psychology, 34*(3), 587(13).

Gray, J. (1992). *Men are from Mars, women are from Venus: A practical guide to improving communication and getting what you want in your relationships.* New York: Harper-Collins.

Greenberg, J. R., & Mitchell, S. A. (1983). *Object relations in psychoanalytic theory.* Cambridge, MA: Harvard University Press.

Griffin, E., & Sparks, G. G. (1990). Friends forever: A longitudinal exploration of intimacy in same-sex and platonic pairs. *Journal of Social and Personal Relationships, 7,* 29–46.

Guerrero, L. K. (1997). Nonverbal involvement across interactions with same–sex friends, opposite-sex friends and romantic partners. *Journal of Social and Personal Relationships, 14*(1), 31–58.

Gumperz, J. J. (1982). *Discourse strategies.* Cambridge, UK: Cambridge University Press.

Gupta, V., & Korte, C. (1994). The effects of a confidant and a peer group on the well-being of single elders. *International Journal of Aging and Human Development, 39,* 293–302.

Guttman, D. (1987). *Reclaimed powers: Towards a psychology of later life.* New York: Basic Books.

Hacker, H. (1981). Blabbermouths and clams: Sex differences in self-disclosure in same-sex and cross-sex friendship dyads. *Psychology of Women Quarterly, 5,* 385–401.

Hansson, R. O., & Carpenter, B. N. (1994). *Relationships in old age: Coping with the challenge of transition.* New York: Guilford.

Hansson, R. O., Jones, W. H., Carpenter, B. N., & Remondet, J. H. (1986). Loneliness and adjustment to old age. *International Journal of Aging and Human Development, 24,* 41–53.

Harding, S. (1996). Rethinking standpoint epistemology: What is "strong objectivity"? In E. Keller & H. Longino (Eds.), *Feminism and science.* Oxford, New York: Oxford University Press.

Harre, R., & Secord, P. F. (1972). *The explanation of social behavior.* Oxford: Basil Blackwell.

Harter, S. (1990). Self and identity development. In S. S. Feldman & G. R. Elliot (Eds.), *At the threshold: The developing adolescent* (pp. 352–387). Cambridge, MA: Harvard University Press.

Harter, S. (1998). The development of self-representations. In W. Damon & N. Eisenberg (Eds.), *Handbook of child psychology: Vol. 3. Social, emotional, and personality development* (5th ed., pp. 553–617). New York: John Wiley & Sons.

Hartup, W. W. (1983). Peer relations. In P. H. Mussen (Ed.), *Handbook of child psychology* (pp. 94–96). New York: John Wiley & Sons

Hartup, W. W. (1989). Behavioral manifestations of children's friendships. In T. J. Berndt & G. W. Ladd (Eds.), *Peer relationships in child development* (pp. 46–70). New York: John Wiley & Sons.

Hartup, W. W. (1996a). The company they keep: Friendships and their developmental significance. *Child Development, 67*, 1–13.

Hartup, W. W. (1996b). Cooperation, close relationships, and cognitive development. In W. M. Bukowski, A. Newcomb, & W. W. Hartup (Eds.), *Friendship in childhood and adolescence* (pp. 213–237). Cambridge, UK: Cambridge University Press.

Hartup, W. W., & Stevens, N. (1997). Friendships and adaptation in the life course. *Psychological Bulletin, 121*(3), 355–370.

Harvard Health Letter (May, 1999). *You're not alone when it comes to loneliness, 24*(8).

Harvard Health Letter (Dec, 1999). *Aging: Great expectations, 25* (3).

Havighurst, R. J., & Albrecht, R. (1953). *Older people.* New York: Longman.

Hay, D. F., Pedersen, J., & Nash, A. (1982). Dyadic interaction in the first year of life. In K. H. Rubin & H. S. Ross (Eds.), *Peer relationships and social skills in childhood* (pp. 11–40). New York: Springer-Verlag.

Hays, R. B. (1988). Friendship. In S. W. Duck (Ed.), *Handbook of personal relationships* (pp. 391–408). New York: John Wiley & Sons.

Hazan, C., & Zeifman, D. (1994). Sex and the psychological tether. In K. Bartholomew & D. Perlman (Eds.), Advances in personal relationships. Vol. 5. *Attachment processes in adulthood* (pp. 151–177). London: Jessica Kingsley.

Heider, F. (1958). *The psychology of interpersonal relationships.* New York: John Wiley & Sons.

Henley, J. M. & Kramarae, C. (1991). Gender, power and miscommunication. In N. Coupland, H. Giles, & J. M. Wiemann (Eds.), *Miscommunication and problematic talk* (pp. 18–43). Newbury Park, CA: Sage.

Hewes, D. (1995). *The cognitive bases of interpersonal communication.* Hillsdale, NJ: Lawrence Erlbaum Associates.

Hill, C. T., Rubin, A., & Peplau, L. A. (1976). Breakups before marriage: The end of 103 affairs. *Journal of Social Issues, 32*, 147–169.

Hinde, R. A. (1979). *Towards understanding relationships.* New York: Academic Press.

Hinde, R. A. (1997). *Relationships: A dialectical perspective.* Hove, UK: Psychology Press.

Hodges, E. V., Boivin, M., Vitaro, F., & Bukowski, W. M. (1999). The power of friendship: Protection against an escalating cycle of peer victimization. *Developmental Psychology, 35*, 94–101.

Hollingshead, A. (1949). *Elmstown's youth.* New York: John Wiley & Sons.

Honeycutt, J. M. (1993). Memory structures for the rise and fall of relationships. In S. W. Duck (Ed.), *Individuals in relationships: Understanding relationship processes series: Volume 1* (pp.60–86). Newbury Park: Sage.

Honeycutt, J. M., & Cantrill, J. G. (2001). *Cognition, communication, and romantic relationships.* Mahwah, NJ: Lawrence Erlbaum Associates.

Howe, F. C. (1993). The child in elementary school: The second grader. *Child Study Journal, 23*(4), 265–276.

Howes, C. (1988). Same- and cross-sex friends: Implications for interaction and social skills. *Early Childhood Research Quarterly, 3,* 21–37.

Howes, C. (1990). Social status and friendship from kindergarten to third grade. *Journal of Applied Developmental Psychology, 11,* 321–330.

Howes, C. (1996). The earliest friendships. In W. M. Bukowski, A. F. Newcomb, & W. W. Hartup (Eds.), *Friendship in childhood and adolescence* (pp. 66–86). Cambridge, MA: Cambridge University Press.

Howes, C., Droege, K., & Matheson, C. (1994). Play and communicative processes within long- and short-term friendship dyads. *Journal of Social and Personal Relationships, 11*(3), 401–410.

Howes, C., Matheson, C. C. (1992). Sequences in the development of competent play with peers: Social and social pretend play. *Developmental Psychology, 28,* 961–974.

Howes, C., Matheson, C. C., & Wu, F. (1992). Friendship and social pretend play. In C. Howes, O. Unger, & C. C. Matheson (Eds.), *The collaborative construction of pretend: Social pretend play functions.* Albany, NY: State University of New York Press.

Howes, C., & Phillipsen, L. C. (1992). Gender and friendship: Relationships within peer groups of young children. *Social Development, 1,* 232–242.

Hussong, A. M. (2000). Distinguishing mean and structural sex differences in adolescent friendship quality. *Journal of Social and Personal Relationships, 17*(2), 223–243.

Huyck, M. H. (1990). Gender differences in aging. In J. E. Birren & K. W. Schaie (Eds.), *Handbook of the psychology of aging* (3rd ed., pp. 124–132). San Diego, CA: Academic Press.

Inderbitzen-Pisaruk, H., Clark, M. L., & Solano, C. H. (1992). Correlates of loneliness in mid-adolescence. *Journal of Youth and Adolescence, 21,* 151–167.

Jacobs, J. A. (1989). Long-term trends in occupational segregation by sex. *American Journal of Sociology, 95,* 160–173.

Jacobsen, J. P. (1994). Sex segregation at work: Trends and predictions. *The Social Science Journal, 31*(2), 153–169.

Jerrome, D., & Wenger, C. (1999). Stability and change in late-life. *Aging and Society, 19*(6), 661 (16).

Johnson, C. L. (1983). Fairweather friends and rainy day kin: An anthropological analysis of old age friendships. *Urban Anthropology, 12,* 103–123.

Johnson, C. L., & Barer, B. M. (1992). Patterns of engagement and disengagement among the oldest-old. *Journal of Aging Studies, 6*(4), 351–364.

Johnson, C. L., & Barer, B. M. (1997). *Life beyond 85 years: The aura of survivorship.* New York: Springer Publishing Company.

Johnson, C. L., & Troll, L. E. (1994). Constraints and facilitators to friendship in late late life. *The Gerontologist, 34*(1), 79–86.

Johnson, F. L., & Aries, E. J. (1983). Conversational patterns among same-sex pairs of late-adolescent close friends. *Journal of Genetic Psychology, 142,* 225–238.

Jones, D. C., & Vaughan, K. (1990). Close friendships among senor adults. *Psychology and Aging, 5,* 451–457.

Jones, W. H., Rose, J, & Russell, D. (1990). Loneliness and social anxiety. In H. Leitenberg (Ed.), *Handbook of social and evaluation anxiety* (pp. 247–266). New York: Plenum Press.

Jung, C. G. (1933). *Modern man in search of a soul.* New York: Harcourt, Brace.

Kahn, C. M. (1989). *Family relationships and friendships in adolescence: Continuities and discontinuities.* Unpublished doctoral dissertation, Department of Psychology, The Catholic University of America.

Kahn, R. L., & Antonucci, T. C. (1980). Convoys over the life course: Attachment, roles, and social support. In P. B. Baltes & O. Brim (Eds.), *Life-span development and behavior* (Vol. 3, pp. 253–286). New York: Academic Press.

Kantrowitz, B., & Wingert, P. (1999, April 19). *The science of a good marriage (John Gottman researches what makes marriage works).* Newsweek, p. 52.

Kaplan, D. L., & Keys, C. B. (1997). Sex and relationship variables as predictors of sexual attraction in cross-sex platonic friendships between young heterosexual adults. *Journal of Social and Personal Relationships, 14*(2), 191–206.

Katchadourian, H. (1990). Sexuality. In S. Feldman & G. R. Elliott (Eds.), *At the threshold: The developing adolescent* (pp. 330–351). Cambridge, MA: Harvard University Press.

Katz, P. A. (1979). The development of female identity. *Sex Roles: A Journal of Research, 5,* 155–178.

Kelly, G. A. (1969). Ontological acceleration. In B. Maher (Ed.), *Clinical psychology and personality: The collected papers of George Kelly* (pp. 7–45). New York: John Wiley.

Kerns, K. A. (1994). A longitudinal examination of links between mother-child attachment and children's friendships in early childhood. *Journal of Social and Personal Relationships, 11*(3), 379–381.

Kerns, K. A. (1996). Individual differences in friendship quality: Links to child–mother attachment. In W. M. Bukowski, A. F. Newcomb, & W. W. Hartup (Eds.), *The company they keep: Friendship in childhood and adolescence* (pp. 137–157). Cambridge, MA: Cambridge University Press.

Kerns, K. A., Klepac, L., & Cole, A. K. (1996). Peer relationships and preadolescents' perceptions of security in mother-child relationship. *Developmental Psychology, 32,* 457–466.

Kessler, R. C., McLeod, J. D., & Wethington, E. (1985). The costs of caring: A perspective on the relationship between sex and psychological distress. In I. G. Sarason & B. R. Sarason (Eds.), *Social support: Theory, research, and applications* (pp. 491–506). Dordrecht Netherlands: Martinus Nijhoff.

Kinch, J. W. (1963). A formalized theory of the self-concept. *American Journal of Sociology, 68,* 481–486.

Knapp, M., & Vangelisti, A. L. (1996). *Interpersonal communication and human relationships.* New York: Allyn & Bacon.

Koenig, L. J., & Abrams, R. F. (1999). Adolescent loneliness and adjustment: A focus on gender differences. In K. J. Rotenberg & S. Hymel (Eds.), *Loneliness in childhood and adolescence* (pp. 296–322). New York: Cambridge University Press.

Koropecky-Cox, T. (1998). Loneliness and depression in middle and old age: Are the childless more vulnerable? *The Journal of Gerontology, Series B, 53*(6), 303.

Kovacs, D.M., Parker, J. G., & Hoffman, L. W. (1996). Behavioral, affective, and social correlates of involvement in cross-sex friendship in elementary school. *Child Development, 67,* 2269–2286.

Krantz, M., & Burton, C. (1986). The development of the social cognition of social status. *Journal of Genetic Psychology, 147,* 89–95.

Kunkel, A. W., & Burleson, B. R. (1998). Social support and the emotional lives of men and women: An assessment of the different cultures perspective. In D. J. Canary & K. Dindia (Eds.), *Sex differences and similarities in communication: Critical essays and empirical investigations of sex and gender in interaction* (pp. 101–125). Mahwah, NJ: Lawrence Erlbaum Associates.

Kupersmidt, J. B., DeRosier, M. E., & Patterson, P. C. (1995). Similarity as the basis for children's friendships: The roles of sociometric status, aggressive and withdrawn behavior, academic achievement and demographic characteristics. *Journal of Social and Personal Relationships, 12,* 439–452.

Kuttler, A. F., La Greca, A. M., & Prinstein, M. J. (1999). Friendship qualities and social–emotional functioning of adolescents with close, cross-sex friendships. *Journal of Research on Adolescence, 9*(3), 339–366.

Kuypers, J. A. (Ed.). (1999). *Men and power.* Amherst, NY: Prometheus Books.

Labouvie-Vief, G., Chiodo, L. M., Goguen, L. A., Diehl, M., & Orwoll, L. (1995). Representations of self across the life span. *Psychology and Aging, 10*(3), 404–415.

Ladd, G. W. (1983). Social networks of popular, average, and rejected children in school settings. *Merrill–Palmer Quarterly, 29,* 283–307.

Ladd, G. W. (1990). Having friends, keeping friends, making friends, and being liked by peers in the classroom: Predictors of children's early school adjustment. *Child Development, 61,* 1081–1100.

Ladd, G. W., Kochenderfer, B. J., & Coleman, C. C. (1996). Friendship quality as a predictor of young children's early school adjustment. *Child Development, 67,* 1103–1118.

Ladd, G. W., Kochenderfer, B. J., & Coleman, C. C. (1997). Classroom peer acceptance, friendship, and victimization: Distinct relational systems that contribute uniquely to children's school adjustment? *Child Development, 68*(6) 1181–1197.

Ladd, G. W., Price, J. M., & Hart, C. H. (1988). Predicting preschoolers' peer status from their playground behavior. *Child Development, 39,* 986–992.

LaFreniere, P., Strayer, F. F., & Gauthier, R. (1984). The emergence of same–sex affiliative preferences among preschool peers: A developmental/ethnological perspective. *Child Development, 55,* 1958–1965.

Laing, R. D., Phillipson, H., & Lee, R. (1966). *Interpersonal perception.* Baltimore, MD: Perennial Library.

Lamme, S., Dykstra, P., Broese, V. G., & Marjolein, I. (1996). Rebuilding the network: New relationships in widowhood. *Personal Relationships, 3*(4), 337–349.

Lampe, P. E. (1985). Friendship and adultery. *Sociological Inquiry, 55*(3), 310–324.

Lansford, J. E., Sherman, A. M., Antonucci, T. C. (1998). Satisfaction with social networks: An examination of socioemotioal selectivity theory across cohorts. *Psychology of Aging, 13*(4), 544–552.

Larson, R. W. (1999). The uses of loneliness in adolescence. In K. J. Rotenberg & S. Hymel (Eds.), *Loneliness in childhood and adolescence* (pp. 244–262). New York: Cambridge University Press.

Larson, R. W., & Bradley, N. (1988). Precious moments with family members and friends. In R. M. Milardo (Ed.), *Families and social networks* (pp. 107–126). Beverly Hills, CA: Sage.

Lau, S., & Kong, C. (1999). The acceptance of lonely others: Effects of loneliness and gender of the target person and the loneliness of the perceiver. *The Journal of Social Psychology, 139*(2), 229(1).

Laursen, B. (1996). Closeness and conflict in adolescent peer relationships: Interdependence with friends and romantic partners. In W. M. Bukowski, A. Newcomb, & W. W. Hartup (Eds.), *Friendship in childhood and adolescence* (pp. 186–210). Cambridge, MA: Cambridge University Press.

Lea, M. (1989). Factors underlying friendship: An analysis of responses to the Acquaintance Description Form in relation to Wright's friendship model. *Journal of Social and Personal Relationships, 6,* 275–292.

Leaper, C. (Ed.).(1994a), *New directions for Child Development: Childhood gender segregation: Causes and consequences, 65.* San Francisco: Jossey-Bass.

Leaper, C. (1994b). Exploring the consequences of gender segregation on social relationships. In C. Leaper (Ed.), *New directions for Child Development: Childhood gender segregation: Causes and consequences* (pp. 67–86). San Francisco: Jossey-Bass.

Leaper, C. (1998). Decision making processes between friends: speaker and partner gender effects. *Sex Roles: A Journal of Research, 39*(1/2), 125 (9).

Leaper, C., & Anderson, K. J. (1997). Gender development and heterosexual romantic relationships during adolescence. *New Directions for Child Development, 78,* 85–103.

Leaper, C., Carson, M., Baker, C., Holliday, H., & Myers, S. B. (1995). Self-disclosure and listener verbal support in same-gender and cross-gender friends' conversations. *Sex Roles, 33,* 387–404.

Leaper, C., & Holliday, H. (1995). Gossip in same-gender and cross-gender friends' conversations. *Personal Relationships, 2,* 237–246.

LeBon, G. (1896/1908). *The crowd: A study of the popular mind.* London: Unwin.

Lee, L. C. (1973). *Social encounters of infants: The beginnings of popularity.* Paper presented at the biennial meeting of the Society for the Study of Behavioral Development, Ann Arbor, MI.

Leinbach, M. D., & Fagot, B. I. (1986). Acquisition of gender labels: A test for toddlers. *Sex Roles, 15,* 655–666.

Lempers, J., & Clark-Lempers, D. (1993). A functional comparison of same-sex and opposite-sex friendships during adolescence. *Journal of Adolescent Research, 8,* 89–103.

Lesko, N. (1988). *Symbolizing society: Stories, rites, and structure in a Catholic high school.* Philadelphia: Falmer.

Lewis, M., & Feiring, C. (1989). Early predictors of childhood friendship. In T. J. Berndt & G. W. Ladd (Eds.), *Peer relationships in Child Development* (pp. 246–273). New York: John Wiley & Sons.

Lewis, T. E., & Phillipsen, L. C. (1998). Interactions on an elementary school playground: Variations by age, gender, race, group size, and playground area. *Child Study Journal, 28*(4), 309–320.

Lieberman, M., Doyle, A., & Markiewicz, D. (1999). Developmental patterns in security of attachment to mother and father in late childhood and early adolescence: Associations with peer relations. *Child Development, 70*(1), 202–213.

Lipka, R. P., & Brinthaupt, T. M. (1992). Introduction. In R. P. Lipka & M. B. Brinthaupt (Eds.), *Self-perspectives across the life span.* Albany: State University of New York Press.

Lipman-Blumen, J. (1976). Toward a homosocial theory of sex-roles: An explanation of the sex segregation of social institutions. In M. M. Blaxall & B. Reagan (Eds.), *Women and the workplace* (pp. 15–32). Chicago, IL: University of Chicago Press.

Litwak, E. (1985). *Helping the elderly: The complementary roles of informal networks and formal systems.* New York: Guilford.

Litwak, E. (1989). Forms of friendship among older people in an industrial society. In R. G. Adams & R. Blieszner (Eds.), *Older adult friendships: Structure and process* (pp. 65–88). Newbury Park, CA: Sage.

Lobel, S. A., Quinn, R. E., St. Clair, L., & Warfield, A. (1994). Love without sex: The impact of psychological intimacy between men and women at work. *Organizational Dynamics, 23,* 5–16.

Longmore, M. A. (1998). Symbolic interactionism and the study of sexuality. *The Journal of Sex Research, 35*(1), 44–58.

Lundy, B., Field, T., McBride, C., Field, T., & Largie, S. (1998). Same- and opposite-sex best friend interactions among high school juniors and seniors. *Adolescence, 33,* 130, 279 (11).

Luria, Z., & Herzog, E. W. (1991). Sorting gender out in a children's museum. *Gender & Society, 5,* 224–232.

Maccoby, E. E. (1988). Gender as a social category. *Developmental Psychology, 24,* 755–765.

Maccoby, E. E. (1990). Gender and relationships: A developmental account. *American Psychologist, 45,* 513–520.

Maccoby, E. E. (1994). Commentary: Gender segregation in childhood. In C. Leaper (Ed.), *New directions for Child Development: Childhood gender segregation: Causes and Consequences* (Vol. 65, pp. 87–97). San Francisco: Jossey-Bass Publishers.

Maccoby, E., & Jacklin, C. (1987). Gender segregation in childhood. *Advances in Child Development and behavior, 20,* 239–288.

Mahler, M. S. (1979). Thoughts about development and individuation. In M. S. Mahler, Selected papers: Vol. 2, *Separation and individuation* (pp. 34–55). NY: Jason Aronson (original work published in 1963).

Malone, J. (1980). *Straight women/Gay men.* New York: Dial Press.

Maltz, D. J., & Borker, B. A. (1982). A cultural approach to male-female miscommunication. In J. J. Gumpertz (Ed.), *Language and social, identity* (pp. 196–216). Cambridge, UK: Cambridge University Press.

Mannarino, A. P. (1980). The development of children's friendships. In H. C. Foot, A. J. Chapman, & J. R. Smith (Eds.), *Friendship and social relations in children* (pp. 45–63). New York: John Wiley & Sons.

Margolis, S. (1988). Some of my best friends are men. *Working Woman, 13*(6), 146(2).

Markus, H. (1983). Self-knowledge: An expanded view. *Journal of Personality, 51,* 543–565.

Markus, H., & Nurius, P. (1986). Possible selves. *American Psychologist, 41,* 954-969.

Markus, H., & Oyserman, D. (1989). Gender and thought: The role of the self-concept. In M. Crawford & M. Gentry (Eds.), *Gender and thought* (pp. 100–127). New York: Springer–Verlag.

Markus, H., & Cross, S. (1990). The interpersonal self. In L. A. Pervin (Ed.)., *Handbook of personality theory and research* (pp. 576–608). New York: Guilford.

Marsh, H. W. (1990). A multidimensional, hierarchical model of self–concept: Theoretical and empirical justification. *Educational Psychology Review, 2*(2), 77–172.

Martin, C. (1994). Cognitive influences on the development and maintenance of gender segregation. In C. Leaper (Ed.), *New directions for Child Development: Childhood gender segregation: Causes and consequences* (Vol. 65, pp. 35–50). San Francisco: Jossey-Bass.

Martin, C. L., Fabes, R. A., Evans, S. M., & Wyman, H. (1999). Social cognition on the playground: Children's beliefs about playing with girls versus boys and their relations to sex segregated play. *Journal of Social and Personal Relationships, 16*(6), 751–771.

Masheter, C. (1997). Former spouses who are friends: Three case studies. *Journal of Social and Personal Relationships, 14,* 207–222.

Maslow, A. (1971). *The farther reaches of human nature.* New York: Viking.

Matthews, S. H. (1983). Definitions of friendship and their consequences in old age. *Aging and Society, 3,* 141–155.

Matthews, S. H. (1986). *Friendships through the life course: Oral biographies in old age.* Newbury Park: Sage.

Matthews, S. H. (1995). Friendships in old age. In N. Vanzetti & S. W. Duck (Eds.)., *A lifetime of relationships* (pp. 406–430). San Francisco: Brooks/Cole.

McAdams, D. P. (1988). Personal needs and personal relationships. In S. W. Duck (Ed.), *Handbook of personal relationships* (pp. 7–22). New York: John Wiley & Sons.

McBride, C. K., & Field, T. (1997). Adolescent same–sex and opposite–sex best friend interactions. *Adolescence, 32*(127), 515(8).

McMahon, A. W., & Rhudick, P. J. (1964). Reminiscing: Adaptational significance in the aged. *Archives of General Psychiatry, 10,* 292–298.

McWilliams, S., & Howard, J. A. (1993). Solidarity and hierarchy in cross-sex friendships. *Journal of Social Issues, 49,* 191–202.

Mead, G. H. (1934). *Mind, self, and society.* Chicago, IL: University of Chicago Press.

Mechanic, D. (1983). Adolescent health and illness behavior: Review of the literature and a new hypothesis for the study of stress. *Journal of Human Stress, 9,* 4–13.

Messman, S. J., Canary, D. J., & Hause, K. S. (2000). Motives to remain platonic, equity, and the use of maintenance strategies in opposite-sex friendships. *Journal of Social and Personal Relationships, 17* (1), 67–94.

Metts, S., Cupach, W. R., & Bejlovec, R. A. (1989). "I love you too much to ever start liking you": Redefining romantic relationships. *Journal of Social and Personal Relationships, 6,* 259–274.

Meurling, C. J., Ray, G. E., & LoBello, S. G. (1999). Children's evaluations of classroom friend and classroom best friend relationships. *Child Study Journal, 29*(2), 29–95.

Michaud, E. (1998, April). Shoulda, coulda, woulda … *Prevention 50* (4), 120–129.

Midwinter, D. Y. (1992). Rule prescription for male-female interaction. *Sex Roles, 26,* 161–174.

Milardo, R. M., Johnson, M. P., & Huston, T. L. (1983). Developing close relationships: Changing patterns of interaction between pair members and social networks. *Journal of Personality and Social Psychology, 44,* 964–976.

Miller, J. (1986). *Toward a new psychology of women* (2nd ed.). Boston: Beacon Press.

Miller, J. B. (1993). Learning from early relationship experience. In S. W. Duck (Ed.), *Understanding relationship processes, 2: Learning about relationships* (pp. 1–29). Newbury Park, CA: Sage.

Mintz, J. (1995). Self in relation to other: Preschoolers' verbal social comparisons within narrative discourse. *New Directions for Child Development, 69,* 61–73.

Moller, L., Hymel, S., & Rubin, K. H. (1992). Sex typing in play and popularity in middle childhood. *Sex Roles, 26*, 331–353.

Moller, L., & Serbin, L. A. (1996). Antecedents of toddler sex segregation: Cognitive consonance, gender-typed toy preferences, and behavioral compatibility. *Sex Roles, 35*, 445–460.

Monsour, M. (1988). *Cross-sex friendships in a changing society: A comparative analysis of cross-sex friendships, same-sex friendships, and romantic relationships.* Unpublished doctoral dissertation, University of Illinois, Champaign.

Monsour, M. (1992). Meanings of intimacy in cross- and same-sex friendships. *Journal of Social and Personal Relationships, 9*, 277–295.

Monsour, M. (1994). Similarities and dissimilarities in personal relationships: Constructing meaning and building intimacy through communication. In S. W. Duck (Ed.), *Understanding relationship processes: Vol. 4. Dynamics of relationships* (pp. 112–134). Thousand Oaks, CA: Sage.

Monsour, M. (1997). Communication and cross–sex friendships across the life cycle: A review of the literature. In B. Burleson (Ed.), *Communication Yearbook 20* (pp. 375–414), Thousand Oaks, CA: Sage.

Monsour, M. (1998). *Loneliness and cross-sex friendships.* Unpublished manuscript. Denver, CO.

Monsour, M., Beard, C., Harris, B., & Kurzweil, N. (1994). Challenges confronting cross-sex friendships: "Much ado about nothing?" *Sex Roles, 31* (1/2), 55–77.

Monsour, M., Betty, S., & Kurzweil, N. (1993). Levels of perspectives and the perception of intimacy in cross-sex friendships: A balance theory explanation of shared perceptual reality. *Journal of Social and Personal Relationships, 10*, 529–550.

Monsour, M., Harvey, V., & Betty, S. (1997). A balance theory explanation of challenges confronting cross-sex friendships. *Sex Roles, 37* (11/12), 825–845.

Moon, D. (1995). Inclusion and exclusion: The term "fag hag" and gay male community. *Social Forces, 74*(2), 487–511.

Morgan, D., Carder, P., & Neal, M. (1997). Are some relationships more useful than others? The value of similar others in the networks of recent widows. *Journal of Social and Personal Relationships, 14*(6), 745–759.

Mueller, E., & Lucas, T. (1975). A developmental analysis of peer interaction among toddlers. In M. Lewis & L. A. Rosenblum (Eds.), *Friendship and peer relations* (pp. 223–257). New York: Wiley.

Mulac, A. Bradac, J. J., & Gibbons, P. (2001), Empirical support for the gender-as-culture hyptheses: An intercultural analysis of male-female language differences. *Human Communication Research, 27*(1), 121–152.

Mullins, L. C., & Dugan, E. (1990). The influence of depression, and family and friendship relations on resident's loneliness in congregate housing. *The Gerontologist, 30*(3), 377–384.

Nardi, P. M. (Ed.). (1992). *Men's friendships.* Newbury Park, CA: Sage.

Nardi, P. M., & Sherrod, D. (1994). Friendships in the lives of gay men and lesbians. *Journal of Social and Personal Relationships, 11*, 185–199.

Newcomb, A. F., & Bagwell, C. L. (1995). Children's friendship relations: A meta-analytic review. *Psychological Bulletin, 117*, 306–347.

Newcomb, A. F., & Bagwell, C. L. (1996). The developmental significance of children's friendship relations. In W. M. Bukowski, A. F. Newcomb, & W. W. Hartup (Eds.), *The company they keep: Friendship in childhood and adolescence* (pp. 289–321). Cambridge, MA: Cambridge University Press.

Newman, B., & Newman, P. (1986). *Adolescent development.* Columbus, OH: Charles Merrill.

Nussbaum, J. F., & Baringer, D. K. (2000). Message production across the life span: Communication and aging. *Communication Theory, 10*(2), 200–209.

Nussbaum, J. F., Thompson, T., & Robinson, J. D. (1989). *Communication and aging.* New York: Harper & Row.

O'Connor, P. (1993). Same-gender and cross-gender friendships among the frail elderly. *The Gerontologist, 33,* 24–30.

Okamoto, D., & England, P. (1999). Is there a supply side to occupational sex segregation? *Sociological Perspectives, 42*(4), 557.

O'Keefe, B. J., & Delia, J. G. (1979). Construct comprehensiveness and cognitive complexity as predictors of the number and strategic adaptation of arguments and appeals in a persuasive message. *Communication Monographs, 46,* 231–253.

Oliker, S. J. (1989). *Best friends and marriage: Exchange among women.* Berkeley: University of California Press.

O'Meara, D. (1989). Cross-sex friendship: Four basic challenges of an ignored relationship. *Sex Roles, 21,* 525–543.

O'Meara, D. (1994). Cross-sex friendship opportunity challenge: Uncharted terrain for exploration. *Personal Relationship Issues, 2*(1) 4–7.

Ornish, D. (1998). *Love & survival: The scientific basis for the healing power of intimacy.* New York: Haper Collins.

Ossorio, P. G. (1981). Conceptual-notational devices: The PCF and related types. In K. E. Davis (Ed.), *Advances in descriptive psychology* (pp. 83–104, Vol. 1.). Greenwich, CT: JAI.

Park, K. A., Lay, K., & Ramsay, L. (1993). Individual differences and developmental changes in preschoolers' friendships. *Developmental Psychology, 29*(2), 264–270.

Park, K. A., & Waters, E. (1989). Security of attachment and preschool friendships. *Child Development, 60,* 1076–1081.

Parker, J. G., & Asher, S. (1993). Friendship and friendship quality in middle childhood: Links with peer group acceptance and feelings of loneliness and social dissatisfaction. *Developmental Psychology, 29,* 611–621.

Parker, J. G., & Gottman, J. M. (1989). Social and emotional development in a relational context: Friendship interaction from early childhood to adolescence. In T. J. Berndt & G. W. Ladd (Eds.), *Peer relationships in child development* (pp. 95–131). New York: Wiley.

Parker, J. G., & Seal, J. (1996). Forming, losing, renewing, and replacing friendships: Applying temporal parameters to the assessment of children's friendship experiences. *Child Development, 67,* 2248–2268.

Parker, S., & De Vries, B. (1993). Patterns of friendship for women and men in same- and cross-sex relationships. *Journal of Social and Personal Relationships, 10,* 617–626.

Parkhurst, J. T., & Hopmeyer, A. (1999). Developmental changes in the sources of loneliness in childhood and adolescence: Constructing a theoretical model. In K. J. Rotenberg & S. Hymel (Eds.), *Loneliness in childhood and adolescence* (pp. 56–79). New York: Cambridge University Press.

Parks, M. R. (1997). Communication networks and relationship life cycles. In S. W. Duck (Ed.), *Handbook of personal relationships* (2nd ed., pp. 351–372). New York: John Wiley & Sons.

Parks, M. R., & Floyd, K. (1996a). Making friends in cyber-space. *Journal of Communication,* 46(1), 80–97.

Parks, M. R., & Roberts, L. D. (1998). "Making MOOsic": The development of personal relationships on-line and a comparison to their off-line counterparts. *Journal of Social and Personal Relationships,* 15(4), 517–537.

Parten, M. B. (1932). Social participation among preschool children. *Journal of Abnormal and Social Psychology,* 27, 243–269.

Pataki, S. P., Shapiro, C., & Clark, M. S. (1994). Children's acquisition of appropriate norms for friendships and acquaintances. *Journal of Social and Personal Relationships,* 11(3), 427–442.

Patford, J. L. (2000). Partners and cross-sex friends: A preliminary study of the way marital and defacto partnerships affect verbal intimacy with cross-sex friends. *Journal of Family Studies,* 6(1), 106–119.

Patterson, B. R., Bettini, L., & Nussbaum, J. F. (1993). The meaning of friendship across the life-span: Two studies. *Communication Quarterly,* 41(2), 145(16).

Pellegrini, A. D. (1990). Elementary school children's playground behavior: Implications for children's social-cognitive development. *Children's Environmental Quarterly,* 7, 8–16.

Pellegrini, A. D., & Smith, P. K. (1993). School recess: Implications for education and development. *Review of Educational Research,* 63, 51–67.

Peplau, L. A., Miceli, M., & Morasch, B. (1982). Loneliness and self-evaluation. In L. A. Peplau & D. Perlman (Eds.), *Loneliness: A sourcebook of current theory, research, and therapy* (pp. 135–151). New York: Wiley Interscience.

Peplau, L. A., & Perlman, D. (Eds.). (1982). *Loneliness: A sourcebook of current theory, research, and therapy.* New York: Wiley Interscience

Perlman, D. (1991). *Age differences in loneliness: A meta-analysis.* Vancouver, Canada: University of British Columbia. (ERIC Document Reproduction Service No. ED 3266767).

Perlman, D., & Fehr, B. (1986). Theories of friendship: The analysis of interpersonal attraction. In V. J. Derlega & B. Winstead (Eds.), *Friendship and social interaction* (pp. 9–40). New York: Springer-Verlag.

Perlman, D., & Landolt, M. A. (1999). Examination of loneliness in children/adolescents and in adults: Two Solitudes or unified enterprise? In K. J. Rotenberg & S. Hymel (Eds.), *Loneliness in childhood and adolescence* (pp. 325–347). New York: Cambridge University Press.

Perlman, D., & Peplau, L. A. (1981). Toward a social psychology of loneliness. In R. Gilmour & S. W. Duck (Eds.), *Personal relationships. Vol. 3: Personal relationships in disorder* (pp. 31–44). London, Academic Press.

Perlman, D., & Peplau, L. A. (1998). Loneliness. *Encyclopedia of Mental Health* (pp. 571–581). Academic Press.

Pines, A., & Aronson, E. (1983). Antecedents, correlates, and consequences of sexual jealousy. *Journal of Personality,* 51, 108–136.

Planalp, S. (1985). Relational schemata: A test of alternative forms of relational knowledge as guides to communication. *Human Communication Research,* 12, 1–29.

Planalp, S., & Fitness, J. (1999). Thinking/feeling about social and personal relationships. *Journal of Social and Personal Relationships, 16*(6), 731–750.

Pogrebin, L. C. (1989). Men and women cannot be friends. In N. Bernards & T. O'Neill (Eds.) *Male/female roles* (pp. 213–217). St. Paul, MN: Greenhaven Press

Potts, M. K. (1997). Social support and depression among older adults living alone: The importance of friends within and outside of a retirement community. *Social Work, 42*(4), 348–363.

Priefer, B. A., & Gambert, S. R. (1984). Reminiscence and life review in the elderly. *Psychiatric Medicine, 2,* 91–100.

Putallaz, M., & Gottman, J. M. (1981). An interactional model of children's entry into peer groups. *Child Development, 52,* 402–408.

Ramsey, P. G., & Lasquade, C. (1996). Preschool children's entry attempts. *Journal of Applied Developmental Psychology, 17,* 135–150.

Ramsey, P. G., & Lasquade, C. (1996). Preschool children's entry attempts. *Journal of Applied Developmental Psychology, 17,* 135–150.

Rawlins, W.K. (1989). *Boys and girls as friends versus boyfriends and girlfriends: Adolescent's conceptions of cross-sex relationships.* Paper presented at the meeting of the Speech Communication Association, San Francisco.

Rawlins, W. K. (1982). Cross-sex friends and the communicative management of sex–role expectations. *Communication Quarterly, 30,* 343–352.

Rawlins, W.K. (1992). *Friendship matters: Communication, dialectics, and the life course.* New York: Walter de Gruyter.

Rawlins, W.K. (1994). Reflecting on (cross-sex) friendship: De-scripting the drama. *Personal Relationship Issues, 2*(1), 4–7.

Ray, G. E., & Cohen, R. (1996). Children's friendships: Expectations for prototypical versus actual best friends. *Child Study Journal, 26*(3), 209–226.

Ray, G. E., Cohen, R., & Secrist, M. E. (1995). Best friend networks of children across settings. *Child Study Journal, 25*(3), 169–187.

Ray, G. E., Cohen, R., & Secrist, M. E., & Duncan, M. K. (1997). Relating aggressive and victimization behaviors to children's sociometric. *Journal of Social and Personal Relationships, 14*(1), 95–108.

Raymond, J. (2000, Fall/Winter). Kids, start your engines. Newsweek, pp. 8–18.

Reeder, H. (2000). "I like you … as a friend": The role of attraction in cross-sex friendship. *Journal of Social and Personal Relationships, 17*(3), 329–348.

Reid, H. M., & Fine, G. A. (1992). Self-disclosure in men's friendships: Variations associated with intimate relations. In P. M. Nardi (Ed.), *Men's friendships* (pp. 132–152). Newbury Park, CA: Sage.

Reis, H.T., & Shaver, P. (1988). Intimacy as an interpersonal process. In S. W. Duck (Ed.), *Handbook of personal relationships: Theory, research, and intervention* (pp.367–389). Chichester: Wiley.

Remafedi, G., Resnick, M., Blum, R., & Harris, L. (1992). Demography of sexual orientation in adolescents. *Pediatrics, 89,* 714–721.

Renshaw, P. D., & Brown, P. J. (1993). Loneliness in middle childhood: Concurrent and longitudinal predictors. *Child Development, 64,* 1271–1284.

Reskin, B. (1993). Sex segregation in the workplace. *Annual Review of Sociology, 19, 241*(30).

Rice, F. P. (1978). *The adolescent: Development, relationships, and culture.* Boston: Allyn & Bacon.

Richards, M. H., Crowe, P. A., Larson, R., & Swarr, A. (1998). Developmental patterns and gender differences in the experience of peer companionship during adolescence. *Child Development, 69,* 154–163.

Rickleman, K. E. (1981). *Childhood cross-sex friendships: An investigation of trends and possible explanatory theories.* Unpublished manuscript.

Rizzo, T. A. (1989). *Friendship development among young children.* Norwood, NJ: Ablex.

Roberto, K. A. (1989). Exchange and equity in friendships. In R. G. Adams & R. Blieszner (Eds.), *Older adult friendship: Structure and process* (pp.147–165). Newbury Park, CA: Sage.

Roberto, K. A. (1997). Qualities of older women's friendships: Stable or volatile. *International Journal of Aging & Human Development, 44*(1), *1*(14).

Roberto, K. A., & Kimboko, P. (1989). Friendships in later life: Definitions and maintenance patterns. *International Journal of Aging and Human Development, 28,* 9–19.

Roberts, D. (2000, February-March). Sexual harassment in the workplace: considerations, concerns, and challenges. *SIECUS Report, 28*(3), 8(4).

Roberts, M. K. (1982). Men and women: Partners, lovers, friends. In K. E. Davis & T. O. Mitchell (Eds.), *Advances in descriptive psychology* (Vol. 2, pp. 57–78). Greenwich, CT: JAI.

Rogers, D. (1982). *Life-span development.* Monterey, CA: Brooks/Cole.

Rokach, A., & Brock, H. (1998). Coping with loneliness. *The Journal of Psychology, 132*(1), 107–127.

Rook, K. S. (1988). Towards a more differentiated view of loneliness. In S. W. Duck (Ed.), *Handboook of personal relationships: Theory, research, and interventions* (pp. 571–589). New York: John Wiley & Sons.

Rook, K. S. (1989). Strains in older adult's friendships. In R. G. Adams & R. Blieszner (Eds.), *Older adult friendships* (pp. 167–194). Newbury Park, CA: Sage.

Rook, K. S. (1992). Detrimental aspects of social relationships: Taking stack of an emerging literature. In H. O. Veiel & U. Baumann (Eds.), *The meaning and measurement of social support* (pp. 157–169). New York: Hemisphere.

Rook, K. S., & Ituarte, P. (1999). Social control, social support, and companionship in older adult's family relationships and friendships. *Personal Relationships, 6*(2), 199–211.

Rose, S. (1985). Same- and cross-sex friendships and the psychology of homosociality. *Sex Roles, 12,* 63–74.

Rosenfeld, L. B. (1979). Self-disclosure avoidance: Why I am afraid to tell you who I am. *Communication Monographs, 46,* 63–74.

Rosow, I. (1985). Status and role change through the life cycle. In R. H. Binstock & E. Shanas (Eds.), *Handbook of aging and the social sciences* (2nd edition, pp. 62–93). New York: Van Nostrand Reinhold.

Ross, M., & Lollis, S. (1989). A social relations analysis of toddler peer relations. *Child Development, 60,* 1082–1091.

Rotenberg, K. (1999). Childhood and adolescent loneliness: An introduction. In K. Rotenberg & S. Hymel (Eds.), *Loneliness in childhood and adolescence* (pp. 3–8). New York: Cambridge University Press.

Rotenberg, K., & Hymel, S. (1999). *Loneliness in childhood and adolescence.* New York: Cambridge University Press.

Rubenstein, J., & Rubin, C. (1984). Children's fantasies of interaction with same and opposite sex peers. In T. M. Field, J. L. Roopnarine, & M. Segal (Eds.) *Friendships in normal and handicapped children* (pp. 99–124). Norwood, NJ: Ablex.

Rubin, K. H., Bukowski, W., & Parker, G. J. (1998). Peer interactions, relationships, and groups. In W. Damon & N. Eisenberg (Eds.), *Handbook of child psychology: Vol. 3: Social, emotional, and personality development* (5th ed., pp. 619–700). New York: John Wiley & Sons.

Rubin, L. B. (1985). *Just friends: The role of friendship in our lives.* New York: Harper & Row.

Rubin, Z. (1980). *Children's friendships.* Cambridge, MA: Harvard University Press.

Rubinstein, R. L., Alexander, B. B., Goodman, M., & Luborsky, M. (1991). Key relationships of never married, childless older women: A cultural analysis. *Journals of Gerontology, 46*(5), 270–278.

Ruble, D. N., & Martin, C. L. (1998). Gender development. In W. Damon & N. Eisenberg (Eds.), *Handbook of Child Psychology: Vol. 3: Social, emotional, and personality development* (pp. 933–1016). New York: Wiley.

Safilios–Rothschild, C. (1981). Towards a psychology of relationships. *Psychology of Women Quarterly, 5,* 377–384.

Safran, J. D. (1990). Towards a refinement of cognitive therapy in light of interpersonal theory: I. Theory. *Clinical Psychology Review, 10,* 87–105.

Sagar, H. A., Schofield, J. W., & Snyder, H. N. (1983). Race and gender barriers: Preadolescent peer behavior in academic classrooms. *Child Development, 54,* 1032–1040.

Samuels, S. C. (1997). Midlife crises: Helping patients cope with stress, anxiety, and depression. *Geriatrics, 52*(7), 55(7).

Sandroff, R. (1992). Sexual harassment: The inside story. *Working Woman 17,* 47–51.

Santrock, J. W. (1983). *Life-span development.* Dubuque, IA: William C. Brown.

Sapadin, L. A. (1988). Friendship and gender: Perspectives of professional men and women. *Journal of Social and Personal Relationships, 5,* 387–403.

Sarason, B. R., Sarason, I. G., & Gurung, R. (1997). Close personal relationships and health outcomes: A key to the role of social support. In S. W. Duck (Ed.), *Handbook of personal relationships* (pp. 547–573). New York: John Wiley & Sons.

Savin-Williams, R. C. (1990). *Gay and lesbian youth: Expressions of intimacy.* New York: Hemisphere Publishing Corporation.

Savin-Williams, R. C. (1994). Dating those you can't love and loving those you can't date. In R. Montemayor, G. Adams, & T. Gullotta (Eds.), *Personal relationships during adolescence* (Vol. 6, pp. 196–215). Thousand Oaks, CA: Sage.

Savin-Williams, R. C., & Berndt, T. J. (1990). Friendship and peer relationships. In S. Feldman & G.R. Elliott (Eds.), *At the threshold: The developing adolescent* (pp. 277–307). Cambridge, MA: Harvard University Press.

Savin-Williams, R. C., & Rodriguez, R. G. (1993). A developmental, clinical perspective on lesbian, gay male, and bisexual youths. In T. P. Gullota, G. R. Adams, & R. Montemayor (Eds.), *Adolescent sexuality: Advances in adolescent development* (Vol. 5, pp. 77–101). Newbury Park, CA: Sage.

Schaffer, H. R., & Emerson, P. E. (1964). The development of social attachments in infancy. *Monographs of the Society for Research in Child Development, 29,* 94.

Schank, R. C., & Abelson, R. P. (1977). *Scripts, plans, goals, and understanding.* Hillsdale, NJ: Lawrence Erlbaum Associates.

Schiamberg, L. B. (1988). *Child and adolescent development.* New York: Macmillan.

Schinke, S. P., McAlister, A. L., Orlandi, M. A., & Botvin, G. J. (1990). The social environmental constructs of social competency. In T. Gullotta, G. R. Adams, & R. Montemayour (Eds.), *Developing social competency in adolescence* (pp. 28–42). Newbury Park, CA: Sage.

Schneider, C. S., & Kenny, D. (2000). Cross-sex friends who were once romantic partners: Are they platonic friends now? *Journal of Social and Personal Relationships, 17*(3), 451–466.

Schneider, B. H., Wiener, J., & Murphy, K. (1994). Children's friendship: The giant step beyond peer acceptance. *Journal of Social and Personal Relationships, 11*(3), 323–340.

Schutz, W. C. (1958). *FIRO: A three-dimension theory of interpersonal behavior.* New York: Holt, Rinehart, & Winston.

Seccombe, K., & Ishii-Kuntz, M. (1994). Gender and social relationships among the never–married. *Sex Roles: A Journal of Research, 30*(7/8), 585–604).

Seccombe, K., & Ishii-Kuntz, M. (1991). Perceptions of problems associated with aging: Comparisons among four older age cohorts. *The Gerontologist, 31*(4), 527(7).

Selman, R. L. (1990). Fastening intimacy and autonomy. In W. Damon (Ed.), *Child development today and tomorrow.* San Francisco: Jossey-Bass.

Serbin, L. A., Moller, L. C., Gulko, J., Powlishta, K. K., & Colburne, K. A. (1994). The emergence of gender segregation in toddler playgroups. In C. Leaper (Ed.), *New directions for Child Development: Childhood gender segregation: Causes and consequences* (Vol. 65, pp. 7–18). San Francisco: Jossey-Bass Publishers.

Sheehan, M. A., & Dillman, L. (1998). *Why can't we be friends? The development of cross-sex friendship following romantic dissolution.* Unpublished manuscript.

Shaffer, L. A. (1999). Cross-sex friendships in adolescence: Just friends. Unpublished masters thesis. University of Denver, Denver, CO.

Shaver, P., Furman, W., & Buhrmester, D. (1985). Aspects of a life transition: Network changes, social skills, and loneliness. In S. W. Duck & D. Perlman (Eds.), *The Sage Series in Personal Relationships* (Vol. 1, pp. 193–217). London: Sage.

Sherman, L. W. (1975). An ecological study of glee in small groups of preschool children. *Child Development, 46,* 53–61.

Sherman, A. M., De Vries, B., & Lansford, J. E. (2000). Friendship in childhood and adulthood: Lessons across the life span. *International Journal of Aging and Human Development, 51*(1), 31–51.

Sherman, M. D., & Thelen, M. H. (1996). Fear of intimacy scale and validation and extension with adolescents. *Journal of Social and Personal Relationships, 13*(4), 507–521.

Shotland, R. L., & Craig, J. M. (1988). Can men and women differentiate between friendly and sexually interested behavior? *Social Psychology Quarterly, 51,* 66–73.

Shulman, S., Elicker, J., & Stroufe, L. A. (1994). Stages of friendship growth in preadolescence as related to attachment history. *Journal of Social and Personal Relationships, 11,* 341–361.

Shulman, S., Laursen, B., Kalman, Z., & Karpovsky, S. (1997). Adolescent intimacy revisited. *Journal of Youth and Adolescence, 26*(5), 597(21).

Sias, P. M., & Cahill, D. J. (1998). From co-workers to friends: The development of peer friendships in the workplace. *Western Journal of Communications, 62*(3), 273(27).

Simon, C. J. (1997). Can women and men be friends? *The Christian Century, 114*(6), 188(7).

Sims, M., Hutchins, T., Taylor, M. (1998). Gender segregation in young children's conflict behavior in child care settings. *Child Study Journal, 28*(1), 1–16.

Sippola, L. K. (1999). Getting to know the "other": The characteristics and developmental significance of other-sex relationships in adolescence. *Journal of Youth and Adolescence, 28*(4), 407–418.

Sippola, L. K., & Bukowski, W. M. (1999). Self, other, and loneliness from a developmental perspective. In K. J. Rotenberg & S. Hymel (Eds.), *Loneliness in childhood and adolescence* (pp. 280–295). New York: Cambridge University Press.

Sippola, L. K., Bukowski, W. M., & Noll, R. B. (1997). Age differences in children's and early adolescents' liking for same-sex and other-sex peers. *Merrill-Palmer Q. 43*, 547–561.

Smith, A. B., & Inder, P. M. (1993). Social interaction in same and cross-gender pre-school peer groups: A participant observation study. *Educational Psychology, 13*, 29–42.

Smith, A. B., & Inder, P. M. (1990). The relationship of classroom organization to cross-age and cross-sex friendships. *Educational Psychology, 10*, 127–140.

Smith, J., & Baltes, M. M. (1998). The role of gender in very old age: Profiles of functioning and everyday life patterns. *Psychology and Aging, 13*(4), 672(2).

Snell, W. E., Jr. (1989). Willingness to self-disclose to female and male friends as a function of social anxiety and gender. *Personality and Social Psychology Bulletin, 15*, 113–125.

Snodgrass, M.A. (1989). The relationships of differential loneliness, intimacy, and characterlogical attributional style to duration of loneliness. In M. Hojat & R. Crandall (Eds.), *Loneliness: Theory, research, and applications* (pp.173–185). Beverly Hills, CA: Sage.

Solano, C. H. (1986). People without friends: Loneliness and its alternatives. In V. J. Derlega & B. A. Winstead (Eds.), *Friendship and social interaction* (pp. 227–246). New York: Springer-Verlag.

Spencer, T. (1994). Transforming relationships through ordinary talk. In S. W. Duck (Ed.), *Dynamics of relationships: Understanding relationship processes* (Vol.4, pp. 58–85). Thousand Oaks, CA: Sage Publications.

Sroufe, L. A., Bennett, C. Englund, M., Urban, J., & Shulman, S. (1993). The significance of gender boundaries in preadolescence: Contemporary correlates and antecedents of boundary violation and maintenance. *Child Development, 64*, 455–466.

Stack, S. (1998). Marriage, family, and loneliness: A cross–national study. *Sociological Perspectives, 41*(2), 415–428.

Steier, F. (1991). *Research and reflexivity.* New York: Sage Publications.

Stern, D. N. (1985). *The interpersonal world of the infant: A view from psychoanalysis and Developmental Psychology.* New York: Basic Books.

Stewart, S. L., & Rubin, K. H. (1995). The social problem–solving skills of anxious-withdrawn children. *Development and Psychopathology, 7*, 323–336.

Sullivan, H. S. (1953). *The interpersonal theory of psychiatry.* New York: W. W. Norton.

Swain, S. O. (1992). Men's friendships with women: Intimacy, sexual boundaries, and the informant role. In P. M. Nardi (Ed.), *Men's friendships* (pp. 153–171). Newbury Park, CA: Sage.

Tajfel, H. (1981). *Human groups and social categories: Studies in social psychology.* Cambridge: UK: Cambridge University Press.

Talbott, M. M. (1998). Older widow's attitudes towards men and remarriage. *Journal of Aging Studies, 12*(4), 429(1).

Tannen, D. (1990). Gender differences in topical coherence: Creating involvement in best friends talk. *Discourse Processes, 13,* 73–90.

Tannen, D. (1990). *You just don't understand: Women and men in conversation.* New York: William Morrow.

Tannen, D. (1994). *Gender and discourse.* New York: Oxford University Press.

Tannen, D. (1995). *Talking 9 to 5: Women and men in the workplace.* Burnsville, MN: Charthouse International Learning Corporation.

Terrell–Deutsch, B. (1999). The conceptualization and measurement of childhood loneliness. In K. Rotenberg & S. Hymel (Eds.) *Loneliness in childhood and adolescence* (pp. 11–33). Cambridge, UK: Cambridge University Press

Terry, R., & Coie, J. D. (1991). A comparison of methods for defining sociometric status among children. *Developmental Psychology, 27,* 867–880.

Tesch, S. A. (1989). Early-life development and adult friendship. In R. G. Adams & R. Blieszner (Eds.), *Older adult friendships: Structure and process* (pp. 89–107). Newbury Park, CA: Sage.

Thibaut, J. W., & Kelley, H. H. (1959). *The social psychology of groups.* New York: John Wiley & Sons.

Thorne, B. (1986). Girls and boys together … but mostly apart: Gender arrangement in elementary schools. In W. W. Hartup & Z. Rubin (Eds.), *Relationships and development* (pp. 167–184). Hillsdale, NJ: Lawrence Erlbaum Associates.

Thorne, B. (1993). *Gender play: Girls and boys in school.* New Brunswick, NJ: Rutgers University Press.

Thorne, B., & Luria, Z. (1986). Sexuality and gender in children's daily worlds. *Social Problems, 33,* 176–190.

Tice, D. M., & Baumeister, R. F. (2001). The primacy of the interpersonal self. In C. Sedikides and M. B. Brewer (Eds.), *Individual self, relational self, collective self* (pp. 71–88). Philadelphia, PA: Psychology Press.

Trinke, S. J., & Bartholomew, K. (1997). Hierarchies of attachment relationships in young adulthood. *Journal of Social and Personal Relationships, 14*(5), 603–625.

Troll, L. E., & Skaff, M. (1997). Perceived continuity of self in very old age. *Psychology and Aging, 12*(1), 162(8).

Urberg, K. A., Degirmencioglu, S. M., Tolson, J. M., & Halliday–Scher, K. (1995). The structure of adolescent peer networks. *Developmental Psychology, 31,* 540–547.

Usui, W. M. (1984). Homogeneity of friendship networks of elderly blacks and whites. *Journal of Gerontology, 39,* 350–356.

Verschueren, K., Marcoen, A., & Schoefs, V. (1996). The internal working model of the self, attachment, and competence in five-year-olds. *Child Development, 67,* 2493–2511.

Vygotsky, L. S. (1978). *Mind in society: The development of higher psychological processes.* Cambridge, MA: Harvard University Press.

Vygotsky, L. S. (1979). Consciousness as a problem of psychology of behavior. *Societ Psychology, 17,* 29–30.

Vygotsky, L. S. (1981). The genesis of higher mental functions. In J. V. Wertsch (Ed.), *The concept of activity in Soviet psychology.* Armonk, NY: M. E. Sharp.

Vygotsky, L. S. (1986; originally published 1934). *Thought and language.* Cambridge, MA: MIT Press.

Wainrib, B. R. (1992). Introduction: Gender issues in the aging population. In B. R. Wainrib (Ed.), *Gender issues across the life cycle* (pp. 159–162). New York: Springer Publishing Company.

Walen, H. R., & Lachman, M. E. (2000). Social support and strain from partner, family, and friends: Costs and benefits for men and women in adulthood. *Journal of Social and Personal Relationships, 17*(1), 5–30.

Walsh, C. (1997). Perspectives (reflections on platonic friendship) *America, 177*(13), 5(1).

Wegner, D. M., Giuliano, T., & Hertel, P. T. (1985). Cognitive interdependence in close relationships. In W. Ickes (Ed.), *Compatible and incompatible relationships* (pp. 253–276). New York: Springer Verlag.

Weiss, R. S. (1973). *Loneliness: The experience of emotional and social isolation.* Cambridge, MA: MIT Press.

Weiss, R. S. (1974). The provisions of social relationships. In Z. Rubin (Ed.), *Support systems and mutual help* (pp. 17–26). Englewood Cliffs, NJ: Prentice-Hall.

Weiss, R. S. (1982). Attachment in adults. In C. M. Parkes & J. Stevenson-Hinde (Eds.), *The place of attachment in human behavior* (pp. 171–184). New York: Basic Books.

Weiss, R. S. (1989). Reflections on the present state of loneliness research. In M. Hojat & R. Crandall (Eds.), *Loneliness: Theory, research, and applications* (pp.1–16). London: Sage.

Weiss, R. S. (1998). A taxonomy of relationships. *Journal of Social and Personal Relationships, 15*(5), 671–683.

Wellman, B. (1992). Men in networks: Private communities, domestic friendships. In P. M. Nardi (Ed.), *Men's friendships* (Vol. 2, pp. 74–114). Newbury Park, CA: Sage.

Wells, A. J. (1992). Variations in self-esteem in daily life: Methodological and developmental issues. In R. P. Lipka & T. M. Brinthaupt (Eds.), *Self-perspectives across the life span* (pp. 151–185). New York: State University of New York Press.

Wells, T. (1999). Changes in occupational sex segregation during the 1980s and 1990s. *Social Science Quarterly, 80*(2), 370(1).

Werebe, M. J. G. (1987). Friendship and dating relationships among French adolescents. *Journal of Adolescence, 10,* 269–289.

Werking, K. (1992). *The communicative management of cross-sex friendship.* Unpublished dissertation, Purdue University.

Werking, K. (1994). Hidden assumptions: A critique of existing cross-sex friendship research. *Personal Relationship Issues, 2*(1), 8–11.

Werking, K. (1995, October). *Media portrayals of cross-sex friendship.* Paper presented at the Organization for the Study of Culture, Language, and Gender. Minneapolis, MN.

Werking, K. J. (1997a). *We're just good friends: Women and men in nonromantic relationships.* New York: The Guilford Press

Werking, K. J. (1997b). Cross-sex friendship research as ideological practice. In S. W. Duck (Ed.)., *Handbook of personal relationships* (391–410). New York: John Wiley & Sons.

Weston, K. (1991). *Families we choose: Lesbian, gays, kinship.* New York: Columbia University Press.

Whaley, K. L., & Rubenstein, T. S. (1994). How toddlers "do" friendship: A descriptive analysis of naturally occurring friendships in a group child care center. *Journal of Social and Personal Relationships, 11,* 383–400.

Winstead, B., Derlega, V, Lewis, R. J., Sanchez-Hucles, & Clarke, E. (1992). Friendship, social interaction, and coping with stress. *Communication Research, 19*(2), 193(19).

Winstead, B. A., Derlega, V. J., Montgomery, M. J., & Pilkington, C. (1995). The quality of friendships at work and job satisfaction. *Journal of Social and Personal Relationships, 12*(2), 199–215.

Wood, J. T. (1994). *Gendered lives: Communication, gender, and culture.* Belmont, CA: Wadsworth.

Wood, J. T. (1995). *Relational communication: Continuity and change in personal relationships.* New York: Wadsworth Publishing Company.

Wood, J., & Dindia, K. (1998). What's the difference? A dialogue about differences and similarities between women and men. In J. Canary & K. Dindia (Eds.), *Sex differences and similarities in communication: Critical essays and empirical investigations of sex and gender in interaction* (pp. 19–39). Mahwah, NJ: Lawrence Erlbaum Associates.

Wood, V., & Robertson, J. (1978). Friendship and kinship interaction: Differential effects on the morale of the elderly. *Journal of Marriage and the Family, 40,* 367–375.

Wright, P. H. (1982). Men's friendships, women's friendships & the alleged inferiority of the latter. *Sex Roles, 8,* 1–20.

Wright, P. H. (1984). Self-referent motivation and the intrinsic quality of friendship. *Journal of Social and Personal Relationships, 1,* 115–130.

Wright, P. H. (1988). Interpreting research on gender differences in friendship: A case for moderation and a plea for caution. *Journal of Social and Personal Relationships, 5,* 367–373.

Wright, P. H. (1989). Gender differences in adults' same- and cross-gender friendships. In R. G. Adams & R. Blieszner (Eds.), *Older adult friendships* (pp. 197–221). Newbury Park, CA: Sage.

Wright, P. H. (1998). Toward an expanded orientation to the study of sex differences in friendship. In D. J. Canary & K. Dindia (Eds.), *Sex differences and similarities in communication: Critical essays and empirical investigations of sex and gender in interaction* (pp. 41–63). Mahwah, NJ: Lawrence Erlbaum Associates

Wright, P. H., & Keple, T. W. (1981). Friends and parents of a sample of high school juniors: An exploratory study of relationship intensity and interpersonal rewards. *Journal of Marriage and the Family, 43,* 59–570.

Wright, P. H., & Scanlon, M. B. (1991). Gender role orientations and friendship: Some attenuation, but gender differences abound. *Sex Roles: A Journal of Research, 24*(9/10), 551(16).

Yager, J. (1997). *Friendshifts: The power of friendship and how it shapes our lives.* Stamford, CT: Hannacroix Creek Books.

Yee, M., & Brown, R. (1994). The development of gender differentiation in young childen. *British Journal of Social Psychology, 33,* 183–196.

Yerby, J. (1995). Family systems theory reconsidered: Integrating social construction theory and dialectical process. *Communication Theory, 4/5,* 339–365.

Yingling, J. (1994). Constituting friendship in talk and metatalk. *Journal of Social and Personal Relationships, 11,* 411–426.

Young, A. M., & Acitelli, L. (1998). The role of attachment style and relationship status of the perceiver in the perceptions of romantic partner. *Journal of Social and Personal Relationships, 15*(2), 161–173.

Youngblade, L. M., & Belsky, J. (1992). Parent-child antecedents of 5-year-olds' close friendships: A longitudinal analysis. *Developmental Psychology, 28,* 700–713.

Youngblade, L. M., Park, K. A., & Belsky, J. (1993). Measurement of young children's close friendships: A comparison of 2 independent assessment systems and their associations with attachment security. *International Journal of Behavioral Development, 16,* 563–587.

Youniss, J. (1980). *Parents and peers in social development.* Chicago, IL: The University of Chicago Press.

Youniss, J., McLellan, J. A., & Strouse, D. (1994). "We're popular, but we're not snobs": Adolescents describe their crowds. In R. Montemayor, G. Adams, & T. Gullotta (Eds.), *Personal relationships during adolescence* (Vol. 6, pp. 101–122). Thousand Oaks, CA: Sage.

Zeifman, D., & Hazan, C. (1997). A process model of adult attachment formation. In S. W. Duck (Ed.), *Handbook of personal relationships* (pp. 179–195). New York: John Wiley & Sons.

Zera, D. (1992). Coming of age in a heterosexist world: The development of gay and lesbian adolescents. *Adolescence, 27,* 849–854.

Author Index

Subject Index